LADY KILLERS

LADY KILLERS

Deadly Women Throughout History

TORI TELFER

JOHN BLAKE

Published by John Blake Publishing Ltd,
3 Bramber Court, 2 Bramber Road,
London W14 9PB, England

www.johnblakebooks.com

www.facebook.com/johnblakebooks
twitter.com/jblakebooks

This edition published in 2017

ISBN: 978 1 78606 121 8

British Library Cataloguing-in-Publication Data:

A catalogue record for this book is available from the British Library.

Printed and bound in Great Britain by Clays Ltd, Elcograf S.p.A.

3 5 7 9 10 8 6 4 2

Papers used by John Blake Publishing are natural, recyclable products made from wood grown in sustainable forests. The manufacturing processes conform to the environmental regulations of the country of origin.

Every attempt has been made to contact the relevant copyright-holders, but some were unobtainable. We would be grateful if the appropriate people could contact us.

John Blake Publishing is an imprint of Bonnier Publishing
www.bonnierpublishing.com

To Charlie

"This hatred of what is human; still more, of what is animal; still more, of what is material; this horror of the senses, of reason itself; this fear of happiness and beauty; this longing away from all appearance, change, becoming, death, desire, longing itself – all this implies (let us dare to comprehend it!) a *will to the Nothing,* a horror of life, an insurrection against the most fundamental presuppositions of life; nevertheless, it is and remains a *will!*"

– NIETZSCHE, *A Genealogy of Morals*

"Let no one think me a weak one."

– EURIPIDES, *Medea*

CONTENTS

The Elusive Population

When we think about serial killers, we think about men. Well, "man," actually – some vicious, twisted sociopath, working alone. He probably has a dreadful nickname, given to him by the media with loving precision: the Ripper, the Vampire Rapist, the Son of Sam, the Shadow Killer, the Berlin Butcher. His nickname is his brand, a nightmare name for a nightmare man whose victims are, more often than not, innocent women.

It's true: men spill most of the blood in history books. And serial killers, specifically, are overwhelmingly male. During the past hundred years, less than 10 percent of serial murderers were women – or so we think. (The records are far from immaculate. In 2007, an exhaustively researched book listed 140 known female serial killers. A blog for the men's rights movement lists almost 1,000. We do know that the number, whatever it is, has increased in the US since the 1970s.) Society tends to sink into "collective amnesia" about female violence, so much so that when Aileen Wuornos was charged with seven violent murders in 1992, the press pronounced her "America's first female serial killer" and continued to do so for decades following.

Aileen wasn't America's first female serial killer – not by a long shot. But female serial killers are master masqueraders: they walk among us looking for all the world like our wives, mothers, and grandmothers. Even after they've been apprehended and punished, most of them eventually sink back into the mists of history in a way that male killers do not. Historians are *still* wondering who Jack the Ripper was, but almost never concern themselves with his creepy countrywoman, Mary Ann Cotton, who claimed three or four times as many victims, most of them children.

It's not that society doesn't recognize the existence of evil in women, because women have been portrayed as conniving and malevolent and the bringers of the apocalypse since Eve ate the apple. But we seem to prefer evil women ensconced in our fiction. They might lead men onto the rocks (the Sirens), frame them for murder (*Gone Girl*), or suck out their breath in a poem ("La Belle Dame sans Merci"); it's when they enter real life and start slaying real people that our imaginations balk. We can't imagine that they did it, you know, *on purpose.* Typically, women are seen as solely capable of reactive homicide – murder done in self-defense, a burst of passion, an imbalance of hormones, a wave of hysteria – and not instrumental homicide, which can be plotted, calculated, and performed in cold blood.

Thus the infamous 1998 quote from Roy Hazelwood of the FBI: "There are no female serial killers."

What happens when people are confronted with a female serial killer? When ideas of the "weaker sex" break down and we're staring into the unnerving eyes of a woman with dried blood under her fingernails? First, we'll probably check to see if she's hot or not. (A 2015 study took pains to determine which of the sixty-four female serial killers they profiled were of "above-average attractiveness.")

This helps their crimes go down easier – a spoonful of sugar, etc. Today, we remember the killer Erzsébet Báthory as a sexy vampire who bathed in virgin blood, which isn't at all true, but it makes her less human, more myth – and in turn excuses us from asking uncomfortable questions like: if men are supposed to be the aggressors, why do Erzsébets exist? In general, people take pains to link female serial killers to lust at every possible turn, even if their crimes have nothing to do with it. A clickbaity 1890 essay titled "Truth About Female Criminals" lays it out well, caps lock and all: "Native or foreign, young or old, handsome or hideous, she plants herself confidently upon the vantage-ground of SEX."

If the woman in question isn't hot? Burn her at the stake! And give her a silly nickname while you're at it, like Giggling Grandma, Hell's Belle, or Arsenic Annie. In 2015, an elderly Russian woman was caught on camera carrying a pot alleged to contain the head of her best friend, and the media promptly christened her Grannyball Lecter. These are not names calculated to keep us up at night; they're punch lines to the great overarching joke that is female aggression. (There goes Arsenic Annie. She's never fully dressed without a restraining order!)

Like nicknames, archetypes can be useful organizational tools, but they, too, often end up suppressing more nuanced ideas of evil and darkness in femininity. For example, the image of woman as nurturer is lovely, conjuring up shades of Mother Earth herself, but Mother Earth is also a merciless destroyer whose wrath obliterates guilty and innocent alike. That side of her, however, is rarely invoked when talking about women. Or what about the archetype of the mannish, violent female? That one really confuses the critics. Due to the "myth of female passivity," a woman who doesn't internalize her anger is often seen not just as masculine but as, almost literally, a man. It's seemingly the only way to understand her. When seventeenth-century Paris was suffering from a spate of female poisoners, one journalist mused, "One must not suppose them like others, and they are sooner compared to the most evil men."

Listen, I do understand that it's easier to swallow serial killing when it's diminished by a nickname or sweetened by sex or organized by archetype. People have endless tricks up their sleeves for softening the violence of the female: dehumanizing female serial killers by comparing them to monsters, vampires, witches, and animals; eroticizing them until they feel safe (*Bad Girls Do It!: An Encyclopedia of Female Murderers*, "Hot Female Murderers That You'd Probably Go Home With"); even shrieking the tired Kipling quote, "The female of the species is deadlier than the male!" and then walking away, satisfied that the situation has been sufficiently analyzed. I get it. Murder is scary; who wants to claim it? Who wants to understand it? But at the end of the day, I believe there's something to be gained from acknowledging female aggression, even when it's sick and twisted. Otherwise, we're living in denial. And just for the record, this denial is exactly why so many charming grandmothers managed to kill for decades without being suspected of a thing.

If there's one word I would use to describe the women in this book (other than "yikes"), it would be "hustle." Time and again I found myself gasping in grudging admiration at the number of jobs these ladies worked, the number of husbands they conned, the number of times they fooled the authorities. I disagree with their stoic and deranged belief that the best way to rid themselves of their problems and to move forward in the world was to murder. But I acknowledge their sick drive to improve their circumstances. (This is not really applicable to the ultrarich killers, like Erzsébet, who were basically just flailing about in the darkness, choking on their own power.) Nietzsche touched on this drive back in 1887, when he wrote, "Man will desire *oblivion* rather than not desire *at all*."

We could ask ourselves, "Why do women kill?" But I think we might as well ask, "Why does anyone kill?" And that's a subject for a longer and more sobering book than this one. People kill for all sorts of reasons: anger, greed, malignant narcissism, petty irritation. Murder is such a horrible conundrum, because it's so unnatural (snuffing out a human life – it's like playing God), and yet it's still so predictable. From the beginning of time, we've been sleeping, eating, having sex, and murdering each other (sometimes in that order, *female praying mantises!*). It's Humanity 101. You'll see a lot of pearl clutching in the historical records presented in this book, and I find that kind of amusing. Oh, we're surprised that people are "still" killing each other? We're shocked that women, too, are both the inheritors and the performers of all this horror?

In the introduction to *War and Peace*, Leo Tolstoy brings up the case of Darya Nikolayevna Saltykova, a Russian serial killer from the 1700s who appears in this book. "On studying letters, diaries, and traditions [of Darya's time], I did not find the horrors of such savagery to a greater extent than I find them now, or at any other period," he writes. "In those days also people loved, envied, sought truth and virtue, and were carried away by passion."

While every woman in this book was molded by her era, it's a fallacy to think their crimes, "the horrors of such savagery," happened in some primordial sociocultural soup that we, in our flawless present, have evolved out of. Sure, one day I fully expect we'll live in a utopian pod culture where all the stories of our past transgressions as a human race will be gloriously burned down, like the library of Alexandria, and we'll brainwash ourselves into believing in our own perfection. But until then, we have to face the facts: there are, indeed, female serial killers.

These lady killers were clever, bad tempered, conniving, seductive, reckless, self-serving, delusional, and willing to do whatever it took to claw their way into what they saw as a better life. They were ruthless and inflexible. They were lost and confused. They were psychopaths and child slayers. But they were not wolves. They were not vampires. They were not men. Time and again, the record shows: they were horrifyingly, quintessentially, inescapably human.

LADY KILLERS

THE BLOOD COUNTESS

Erzsébet Báthory

Here's something so seductive about the word "murderess." It's mostly that serpentine double *s* at the end that gives the term its poisonous charm. And then there are the stories: Lilith, Lady Macbeth, Medusa, Medea. We can't get enough of them. They make great literary antagonists, but it's even more electrifying – for the morbidly curious, at least – when they turn out to be real.

One of the earliest female serial killers in history was the type of girl to really put the double *s* into murderess – a woman who has been memorialized, sexualized, and vampirized since records of her trial were discovered in the 1720s. She was the grande dame of serial killers; the OG female sadomasochist; the woman who inspired not one, not two, but eight black metal band names; the dreadful Hungarian countess herself: Erzsébet Báthory.

Today, Erzsébet is a symbol of the demented, sadistic decadence of the aristocracy – or else she's an example of just how dangerous it is to be a powerful woman, depending on which academic paper you're reading. We don't quite have everything we need to charge her with her crimes. There are rumors of an incriminating diary lost somewhere in Hungary, and there are scholars who want to clear her name. With so many vanished centuries between her life and ours, we may never get definitive, forensic proof of her guilt.

And yet she certainly seemed to find herself around a lot of blood.

A Girl and Her Castle

Erzsébet Báthory was given the trappings of an enviable life. She was born on August 7, 1560, into one of the most powerful clans in Central Europe, and she had the ridiculous wealth and impeccable scholastic pedigree to prove it. Her Protestant parents spared no expense when it came to giving their precocious daughter a classical education. She spoke not only Hungarian and Slovak – the language many of her servants would have spoken – but Greek, Latin, and German, too.

But all was not well in the world of little Erzsébet. Rumors abound that she suffered from terrible epileptic seizures as a child. Also, her parents happened to be cousins. Like many formidable clans back then, the Báthory family had a penchant for inbreeding, which, historically, has led to more than one noble with a weak constitution and a propensity toward madness.

Legend has it that Erzsébet witnessed some terrible things during her childhood, like the ghastly sight of a man getting sewn into the stomach of a horse. His crime? Theft. As the story goes, little Erzsébet cackled at the sight of the peasant's head sticking out of the horse's body. Many of the folkloric anecdotes about her childhood are attempts to explain her later crimes, but regardless of the particulars, Erzsébet probably did see a good deal of violence as a child. In those days, it was more than acceptable to beat your servants – according to Hungarian law, peasants were the "property" of the nobles – and it's also likely that Erzsébet would have attended the occasional public execution.

Now, she wasn't just smart and freakishly unbothered by violence. Erzsébet was also really, really pretty. A portrait from 1585 depicts a haunted, delicate beauty with a high white forehead – women of the time plucked their hairline so as to look more aristocratic, a la Queen Elizabeth I – staring out of the frame with huge, mournful eyes.

When she was ten, Erzsébet became engaged to fifteen-year-old Count Ferenc Nádasdy, the son of another powerful Hungarian family. As was common back then, Erzsébet moved to the Nádasdy palace during the engagement and began learning to run her in-laws' massive estates. Rumor says she had an affair with a peasant boy during this time, became pregnant, and was forced to give the child away in a very hush-hush manner, while her fiancé castrated the unfortunate lad and threw him to a pack of wild dogs. Whether or not this is true, Erzsébet would eventually develop a reputation as a woman with a ravenous libido, and young Nádasdy would soon become famous for his mad and creative violence.

Erzsébet, at fourteen, married her intense fiancé on May 8, 1574, in front of forty-five hundred guests. The lavish celebration raged on for three days, and Nádasdy topped off the event by giving his bride the craggiest, loneliest castle in Hungary, called Castle Csejthe, as a home of her own. It was done up in the Gothic architectural style and perched on top of a foreboding hill. Nádasdy had no idea of the crimes Erzsébet would later commit in Csejthe's dark, isolated halls.

The Nádasdy-Báthorys were now an incredibly wealthy couple with plenty of social cachet, but they barely saw each other. It took ten years for them to have their first child, which was unusual for married couples at the time. If Erzsébet were infertile, that would have been considered an acceptable reason for Nádasdy to divorce her. But it wasn't biology that kept them childless for so long. It was battle. Three years into their marriage, Nádasdy left for the Hungarian border to fight off the Ottomans, while Erzsébet moved between their many castles to oversee their lands and keep their numerous household accounts in order. Her letters to him are polite and respectful, with only the occasional flash of the strong-willed personality she was keeping at bay, like when she reprimanded him for waltzing off to Transylvania without informing her.

The Ottomans invaded in a more serious way in 1591 – the start of what has been called the Long War – and Nádasdy went off again to a fiercer and bloodier conflict. The man loved war. He was great at war. This time around, he earned the nickname Black Knight of Hungary because of his reputation for ever-more-inhuman cruelty. He made sure to learn all the best Turkish punishments from his enemies before he killed them, and if he was feeling sporty, he might even play catch with their severed heads. Then he'd return to his wife, riding high off the bloodlust, the screams of his enemies still ricocheting deep inside his brain.

The Long War was draining Hungary's wealth so steadily that the ruling Hapsburg family found themselves short on cash, but Erzsébet never felt the pinch of wartime because Nádasdy was sending her a steady stream of Ottoman treasures. The Nádasdy-Báthorys grew so rich, in fact, that they ended up loaning money to the Hapsburgs so Hungary could continue to fight. Now the king himself was in their debt. The two of them must have felt invincible.

Star Kicking

While Erzsébet and Nádasdy didn't see much of each other in those days, they carved out time to bond over a very specific mutual interest: torturing young servant girls.

Nádasdy, of course, was more than familiar with violence. You don't get to be the Black Knight of Hungary without skewering a few enemies on your way to the top! And Erzsébet already had her fair share of experience with punishment, given that she was in charge of hundreds of peasants on a daily basis. The couple witnessed and even encouraged cruelty in each other, resulting in a long-distance relationship characterized by bloody reciprocity: a little less "staring longingly at the same moon" and a little more "stabbing people at the same time."

Nádasdy taught his bride how to roll up a piece of oiled paper, place it between the toes of a disobedient servant, and then set the paper on fire – a fun game he called star kicking. He also reportedly bought Erzsébet a sort of clawed glove that she used to slash her servants' flesh. Once, he allegedly covered a young girl with honey and forced her to stand outside so she would be incessantly stung by insects. In short, the Black Knight was a fount of inspiration for an impressionable young sociopath like Erzsébet.

Nádasdy wasn't Erzsébet's only sparring partner, either. In 1601, a mysterious woman named Anna Darvolya joined their household as Erzsébet's companion. Locals described her as a "wild beast in female form," and she was rumored to be a witch. Once she arrived at the castle, Erzsébet's personality started to change. "The Lady became more cruel," her servants said. If Nádasdy taught Erzsébet to torture, Darvolya taught Erzsébet to kill.

"No Butcher Under Heaven Was More Cruel"

Now and then, servant girls died at the Nádasdy-Báthory household, but it was nothing worth raising a royal eyebrow over. In the eyes of the ruling classes, these young peasants were utterly disposable.

After an antifeudalist uprising was squelched in 1514, a new Hungarian legal code called the Tripartitum reduced the rights of peasants and serfs to almost nothing, while protecting the nobles who abused them.

Erzsébet wasn't just sheltered by the law; she was above the law. By this point, the king of Hungary had been forced to borrow money from the Báthory-Nádasdys so many times that Erzsébet was basically untouchable. (At the time of Nádasdy's death, the king owed him almost eighteen thousand gulden, a practically unpayable debt.) Tucked away in her craggy castle on a hill, Erzsébet could do whatever she wanted.

This isn't to say nobody noticed anything unpleasant happening to Erzsébet's servants. Local pastors grew suspicious when Erzsébet kept asking them to perform funeral rites for servant girls who'd died of "cholera" or "unknown and mysterious causes." At one point, she asked them to bless an oversize coffin, but the pastors balked when they heard a rumor that it contained *three* dead bodies. The speculations grew so outrageous that one of the pastors dared to pull Countess Báthory aside after a sermon and call her a murderer to her face. "Your Grace should not have so acted because it offends the Lord, and we will be punished if we do not complain to and criticize Your Grace," he said. "And in order to confirm that my words are true, we need only exhume the body [of the latest dead girl], and you will find that the marks identify the way in which death occurred."

The countess hissed that she had relatives who wouldn't tolerate these shameful accusations, and the pastor responded, "If Your Grace has relatives, then I also have a relative: the Lord God. . . . Let us dig up the bodies, and then we will see what you have done." Erzsébet stormed out of the church, and eventually Nádasdy managed to appease the pastor. But Nádasdy couldn't cover for Erzsébet forever.

The Black Knight died of illness in 1604, when Erzsébet was

forty-four years old. Again, servants noticed a change in her. She was growing more and more violent, insatiably so. Maybe it was stress: she was now managing extensive properties without the quick income from the spoils of the Long War. Maybe she was recoiling in horror at the aging process: legend has it she was incredibly vain. Or maybe some sort of latent psychosis, from that infamous Báthory inbreeding, began to rear its head. Either way, what had started as a shared hobby with Nádasdy and Darvolya quickly turned into a full-blown obsession, and Erzsébet became fanatical about torturing and killing young girls. She reaped them from the towns surrounding her various castles – nubile peasant children with strong, expendable bodies – and when she was finished with them, she flung them back over the castle walls to be eaten by wolves.

As before, Erzsébet didn't work alone. Along with Anna Darvolya, she gathered a gruesome torture squad: her children's nurse, Ilona Jó; an old friend of Ilona Jó's, who went by Dorka; a washerwoman named Katalin; and a disfigured young boy known as Ficzkó. Darvolya, Dorka, and Ilona Jó were the cruelest of the bunch and took pride in their macabre creativity. Ficzkó helped, but he was awfully young. Katalin was the most softhearted; she'd try to sneak food to the broken-down girls, and once she herself was beaten when she refused to participate in the torture.

It usually started with a servant girl's mistake. Maybe the girl would miss a stitch, causing the countess to turn on her with a snarl. Erzsébet would begin by slapping, kicking, or punching the servant, but eventually she'd dig deeper, producing some imaginative punishment to satisfy her craving for blood. Those who made sewing mistakes were tortured with needles, while a girl who stole a coin was branded with that same coin. Erzsébet played mind games, pricking the girls' fingers with pins and saying:, "If it hurts the whore, then she can pull it out." Then, when the girls pulled out the pins, Erzsébet would cut off their fingers. She'd often strip her servants naked before she beat them, and once bit a chunk out of a girl's face when she herself was too sick to get out of bed.

If the torture stopped there, it was a pretty good day for the servant girls, but Erzsébet was rarely satisfied with pinpricks and severed fingers. No matter which castle the countess was staying at, she had a specific torture chamber to play around in, and the brutalities that occurred in them were absolutely appalling. The torture squad would burn the girls with irons or beat them "until their bodies burst." Once, Erzsébet put her fingers inside a girl's mouth and tore her face apart. There were also reports of pincers used to rip out the girls' flesh, and rumors of forced cannibalism. "What outrageous cruelty! No butcher under heaven was, in my opinion, more cruel," wrote the horrified Csejthe pastor to a friend after learning what happened deep inside Erzsébet's dungeons. Some members of the torture squad had specialties: Dorka liked to cut the girls' fingers with shears. Darvolya liked to give them five hundred lashes. And Erzsébet liked it all.

"Anywhere she went," confessed Ilona Jó, "she looked immediately for a place where [we] could torture the girls." A townsman heard from several servant girls that "their mistress could neither eat nor drink if she had not previously seen one of the virgins from amongst her maids killed in a bloody way." Without death, it seemed, Erzsébet felt incomplete.

Bloodbath

Let's stop here for a moment. Is this all seeming a little too gory to be true? A beautiful countess ripping apart young faces? Murdering virgins? Feeding their flesh to each other? After a certain point, the cataloguing of Erzsébet's crimes begins to feel farcical. Thanks to the graphic nature of the trial transcripts, the Báthory legend ballooned to ludicrous proportions in the centuries after Erzsébet's death, and many of the rumors that sprang up involved a potent mix of sex, narcissism, and blood.

One of the most enduring rumors claims that the countess bathed in the fresh blood of her victims to preserve her beauty forever and ever. The story goes like this: When a servant girl ruined some aspect of Erzsébet's toilette, Erzsébet slapped the girl so hard that peasant blood spattered across her noble face. After washing off the blood, Erzsébet noticed that her skin looked younger than it had before – perfectly smooth, with that elusive, almost translucent quality she thought she'd never achieve again. She thus became maniacal about soaking in tubs of virginal blood during top-secret 4:00 a.m. baths.

Unfortunately for the vampire obsessives among us, this is almost certainly not true. None of the servants who testified against Erzsébet mention anything about the countess bathing in blood. In fact, what they do mention is that so much blood was spilled during torture sessions that you could scoop it off the floor, meaning Erzsébet didn't seem too concerned with saving – much less bathing in – the precious blood that poured from her victims. It turns out the first mention of her blood baths appeared over a century after her death, in a 1729 book called *Tragica Historia* that was written by a Jesuit scholar after he discovered the Báthory trial transcripts.

It's easy to see why the blood bath rumor has persisted, though. Not only is it a compellingly creepy image, but it also solves the distressing idea of a murderess who kills just because she's a killer. It means we don't have to worry about the question of evil in the Báthory case. Vanity is a much more palatable explanation for her crimes, because then all that bloodshed simply comes down to a misguided desire to look good for the boys. (Or the girls. Because Erzsébet only killed women – a rarity in the realm of female serial killers – rumors abound that she was doing it out of repressed lesbianism.)

But be not disappointed at the lack of blood baths. Plenty of blood was shed at chez Erzsébet, so much that the walls were spattered with it. Erzsébet would get so drenched with gore that she occasionally had to stop midtorture and change her shirt. While her affinity for stripping her maids naked may hint at some sort of fetish, and her dealings with Darvolya and the occult may have occasionally focused on preserving her youth, it seemed that what the countess truly liked was pretty straightforward: to absolutely destroy the body.

The Gynaeceum

Rumors of Erzsébet's violence were now flying everywhere, but nobody could do anything about it, because she was still killing peasants, and peasants couldn't press charges against nobles. Parents would sell their child to Erzsébet for a lump sum, and if the child died of "cholera," well, that was just too bad. Sure, Erzsébet was now killing so many girls she couldn't even bury them properly – the shallow graves in her courtyards were sometimes disturbed by dogs – but the countess remained unassailable.

Then, like many a serial killer after her, she grew reckless, she got messy, and she killed the wrong people.

By 1609, her cruel collaborator Darvolya was dead of a stroke, and Erzsébet was running out of money. She was now taking advice from her lady steward, Erzsi Majorova, rumored to be a "forest witch" – a local peasant woman familiar with herbalism and the occult.

Surely by now Erzsébet was half mad with loneliness. Nádasdy and Darvolya were dead. Her children were married and gone. Her confidants were washerwomen, forest witches, and a young boy who barely knew what he was doing. None of these people could understand what it meant to be Erzsébet Báthory: to be powerful and rich and beautiful and aging and cruel, to be the only one in charge of holding her own dark world together. Did Erzsébet have close friends in her social circles? Probably not, given her heavy reliance on peasant women and the fact that she panicked after most social obligations, taking out her anxious energy on the bodies of her servants. Even her violence seems tinged with a terrible isolation. You can't beat a girl to death in a gloomy torture chamber without flailing your arms in the darkness.

Anyway, by 1609, Erzsébet decided she needed more money and, supposedly, a source of better, richer blood. The folkloric version of this story says that peasant blood was no longer staving off the countess's aging, so the forest witch Majorova suggested that the blood of noble girls might be more effective. Really, though, Erzsébet was just running out of people to kill. Parents were beginning to actively hide their daughters from her when she came through town looking for "workers." Maybe she was also feeling a little bit rash. A little vengeful. There was just one problem: peasants were easy to deal with, but nobles would definitely notice if their daughters went missing.

So Erzsébet hit on the brilliant idea of pretending to open a finishing school for young women, called a *gynaeceum*. The fees for this counterfeit *gynaeceum* would provide Erzsébet with some much-needed liquidity, and the daughters of nobles would provide exactly what she needed them to provide. She didn't bother thinking this plan through to its logical conclusion – tens of dead girls, powerful parents crazed with worry. She just ushered in a gaggle of aristocratic youngsters and, well, finished them.

When wealthy parents began inquiring about the state of their offspring, Erzsébet's bizarre excuse put everyone on edge.

She claimed that there were no girls left on the premises because one of the girls had been so jealous of her classmates' jewelry that she'd murdered every single one of them and then, um, committed suicide.

Needless to say, the countess wasn't convincing anyone at this point. In fact, people were beginning to see horrifying evidence of her crimes right in front of them: girls with bruised bodies running errands in town, girls with burned hands scrambling into Erzsébet's carriage, girls with disfigured faces walking dejectedly in the countess's entourage, and even a girl who escaped from the castle and ran into town with a knife still quivering in her foot.

And now noble blood had been shed and noble families were crying out. This was enough for the king, Mátyás, to move against Erzsébet.

"Send, Oh Send Forth, You Clouds, 90 Cats!"

In February 1610, the king ordered his palatine, György Thurzó, to begin an investigation against Countess Báthory.

Awkwardly for both Thurzó and Erzsébet, Thurzó had been one of Ferenc Nádasdy's best friends. The two were so close, in fact, that when Nádasdy was on his deathbed, he asked Thurzó to protect his wife. And now Thurzó was being asked to shake all the skeletons from her closet. But he was a loyal subject of the king, so he forged ahead with the investigation, determined to uncover the truth while still treating Erzsébet as fairly as possible.

Hundreds of people affirmed the rumors of Erzsébet's terrible violence, placing the number of dead girls around 175 or 200. They spoke of seeing bloodstains on the walls, of hearing screams and the sound of beatings. None of the people Thurzó spoke to were actual eyewitnesses, but many of them had seen the high number of burials taking place around the castle and had noticed that certain parts of Erzsébet's estates were always guarded carefully.

Convinced that Erzsébet was guilty, but torn about his promise to her dead husband, Thurzó wrote to Erzsébet's son and sons-in-law, asking for their advice. The men reached a secret decision: Thurzó could investigate the crimes, as long as he promised Erzsébet would never be brought to trial. She could be locked up, and her servants could be interrogated, but her family wanted to avoid the spectacle of having their mad countess take the stand. It's telling that Erzsébet's children didn't bother to insist she was innocent. "Public punishment would shame us all," wrote her son-in-law.

By December, Thurzó was almost ready to act, but before he could arrest such a powerful woman, he had to be completely certain she was guilty. So he invited himself and the king over to her castle for a Christmas Eve dinner. Erzsébet acted like a gracious hostess, but she was barely holding it together, and ended the night by serving the men a mysterious gray cake she'd cooked up with her forest witch, Majorova. The cake was shaped like a pretzel and had a communion wafer in the center. Once the men tasted it, they became sick – and, convinced she was trying to poison them, left right away.

On New Year's Eve 1610, an increasingly paranoid Erzsébet met Majorova outside the manor house of Castle Csejthe to watch the movements of the stars and clouds. They were planning to cast a spell for protection and asked a scribe to write it down. When Majorova was satisfied that the conditions were right, the women began to chant.

"Help, oh help, you clouds!" they cried. "Help, clouds, give health, give Erzsébet Báthory health! Send, oh send forth, you clouds, 90 cats!" The cats were instructed to destroy Thurzó and the king and anyone else trying to bring the countess grief. Unbeknownst to the countess, however, Thurzó was hiding in the darkness around

Castle Csejthe at that very moment, determined to catch her in the bloody act.

Once Erzsébet went back inside, Thurzó crept toward the manor, accompanied by a party of armed guards. Right away, they stumbled across the body of a mutilated girl near the entryway, and found two more girls dying right inside the doors. The sound of screaming led the men to one of the torture chambers, where they caught the torture squad at work.

It's unclear if Thurzó actually caught the countess herself in the act, or simply discovered her henchpeople, but he was finally satisfied as to her guilt. Erzsébet was dragged to the castle proper and forced to watch the rest of the search, which revealed even more girls "hidden away where this damned woman prepared these future martyrs." As the men moved through the dark halls, Erzsébet cried that she was innocent, and that all this violence was the fault of her servants. The next day, she was formally imprisoned in the dungeons of her own castle – dungeons that had held her victims' bodies only hours before.

A Wild Animal

A grand total of 306 people testified against the Blood Countess, including the members of her torture squad, who were now being tortured themselves. Their testimonies were beyond incriminating.

"The Lady beat and tortured the girls so much that she was covered in blood," said Ilona Jó.

"They were taken to be tortured even ten times in a day, like sheep," said Ficzkó.

No one knows for sure how many girls Erzsébet Báthory killed. Her four accomplices claimed the number of dead girls fell between 30 and 50 – and they'd know best, for obvious reasons – while the staff at another one of Erzsébet's castles said she'd killed 175 to 200 girls. The king heard through the grapevine that she'd killed 300, and one young witness claimed the countess had murdered as many as 650 girls and kept their names written in a little ledger.

Ilona Jó, Dorka, and Ficzkó all received the death sentence. Since Ilona Jó and Dorka had been personally responsible for so many "serious, ongoing atrocities perpetuated against Christian blood," their fingers were torn out by heated iron tongs before they were executed and thrown into a huge bonfire. Because of his youth, Ficzkó was given a slightly more merciful sentence: beheaded and then burned. Katalin, the most unwilling of the accomplices, was thrown into jail.

As promised, Erzsébet was never taken to trial, but instead condemned to lifelong imprisonment in her own blood-drenched castle. Several pastors visited her there and found her furious and unrepentant. When they asked her to think about how much suffering she had inflicted on others, Erzsébet merely snarled that her powerful relatives would soon come and save her. She maintained that Ilona Jó, Dorka, Ficzkó, and Katalin were the guilty ones – and when the pastors asked her why she hadn't commanded her servants to simply *stop torturing*, Erzsébet responded that she herself was afraid of them. At another point, she hissed that she wouldn't confess a thing, even if they tortured her with fire.

Erzsébet hated Thurzó most of all, and as she tried to convince her relatives to release her, she continually lashed out at the palatine for imprisoning her. At one point, Thurzó lost his temper and screamed, "You, Erzsébet, are like a wild animal. You are in the last months of your life. You do not deserve to breathe the air on earth or see the light of the Lord. You shall disappear from this world and shall never reappear in it again. As the shadows envelop you, may you find time to repent your bestial life."

But was Erzsébet such a beast?

In the centuries since her imprisonment, several scholars and biographers have insisted that Erzsébet was innocent and/or that the trial of the accomplices was a show trial that shouldn't have resulted in Erzsébet's rather under-the-table conviction. They argue that the whole thing was a setup, masterminded by Thurzó and the king, designed to imprison a political rival, to incapacitate a powerful widow, and to seize all those delicious Nádasdy-Báthory lands. They say Erzsébet's lack of trial was unfair, and that the confessions of her accomplices, achieved through torture, cannot be taken as fact.

But many of the cries about Erzsébet's innocence don't take into account certain cultural and historical factors, like the agreement between Thurzó and the Báthory children to *avoid* trial, or the fact that torture was a common part of inquisitional trials like this one and would not have been considered strange or suspicious in this case. (These were violent times all around, as is made pretty obvious by the fact that Ilona Jó and Dorka had their fingers torn off as part of their official sentence.) The argument that the king wanted to seize Erzsébet's wealth and cancel his debt to the Nádasdy-Báthorys doesn't hold water either, because when Nádasdy died his six-year-old son would have become the owner of the estates in name and, when the boy turned fourteen, in practice. By the time Erzsébet was arrested, she no longer owned those vast swathes of Báthory-Nádasdy land, and the king would have had to imprison the whole family in order to claim their fortune and cancel his debt. Plus, under the rules of the Tripartitum, Thurzó was not allowed to gain any material wealth from prosecuting Erzsébet, so he couldn't have been framing her just to get rich.

Another sticking point for those who believe in Erzsébet's

innocence is the fact that Thurzó began investigating Erzsébet when there was no hard evidence against her, only rumors of her violence, and she was never informed of the inquest that was starting. But all this was perfectly legal under the Tripartitum. Thurzó was simply enacting something called a common inquest, intended to determine whether or not a crime had been committed. It was a standard way to gather evidence against nobles before informing them that they were about to be dragged into court – or imprisoned in their own dungeons, as the case may be.

All this is not to say Erzsébet was absolutely the flesh-eating, blood-bathing ogre the court believed her to be. Much of the testimony against her was hearsay, and confessions achieved through torture will always be rather suspect. There was obviously a lot of misinformation swirling around the whole affair, like the part about the 650 dead girls. There are many more theories about why the king would have wanted to frame her – she was Protestant, he was Catholic; she was a powerful woman, he didn't like that – too many to get into here. Maybe someday someone will uncover a ledger of victims written in her spidery handwriting. Until then, we'll always be a little bit in the dark.

With Erzsébet imprisoned, all legal documentation about the trials was sealed. The countess was put under house arrest in her own castle. Parliament decreed that her name would no longer be spoken in society. And the towns around Csejthe grew quiet for the next hundred years.

Murderess

Despite the court's best efforts to act as though Erzsébet Báthory had never existed, her story spread and spread, especially once the trial transcripts were rediscovered in the 1720s. Today, the Blood Countess is a hugely popular figure in the world of horror, gore, and sexy vampires, featured in everything from a Venom single (notable lyric: "Counteeeess BAAAATHORY") to poetry, novels, and films. Historian Raymond McNally has even argued it was Erzsébet who inspired Bram Stoker's *Dracula*. Run a search on Google Images for "Erzsébet Báthory" and you'll see just how sexualized her legend has become: you'll find everything from manga of the countess sporting bloody nipple clamps to fan art featuring a nude Erzsébet reclining seductively in a bathtub full of – well, you know.

Out of the 306 testimonies collected by Thurzó, sex is mentioned once, maybe twice. The trial was not an investigation into sexual deviance; it was an investigation into rumors of torture and death. But in the centuries since, plenty of sex-drenched tales have popped up, like the rumor about her peasant lover and subsequent pregnancy, or whispers that she slept around when Nádasdy was off fighting Ottomans. One persistent tale concerns her aunt Klara, reputedly a bisexual and a sadist. As the story goes, during Nádasdy's long absences, Erzsébet liked to visit Klara's castle, where Klara would teach her niece all about witchcraft, torture, and making love to a woman. Another rumor says that Erzsébet and Anna Darvolya were lovers.

Her story has a sick glamour, sure. Who isn't drawn to the idea of a vampiric countess with long black hair and a penchant for ripping apart lithe nudes? She makes a seductive antagonist, worthy of the serpentine sound of *murderess*. But these stories of lovers and sadism are simply ways of making her monstrousness appealing. They're a distraction, a bizarre attempt to mitigate her crimes: "She beat up girls . . . because it was a fetish for her!" "She was a psychopath . . . but also a lesbian!"

Really, Erzsébet may simply have been the most frightening and least pretty thing of all: a heartless killer. The fan art that features a voluptuous Erzsébet with blood-splattered cleavage isn't scary – what's scary is that portrait of Erzsébet from 1585. What's scary is staring down the otherworldly blankness in those big, four-hundred-year-old eyes.

Countess Erzsébet Báthory died on August 22, 1614, after complaining that her hands were cold. The last thing she did was lay down in her bed and sing, beautifully. She was buried in holy ground, but her body was later removed, after residents complained, and taken to the Báthory crypt. That crypt was opened in 1995. No trace of Erzsébet was found.

THE GIGGLING GRANDMA

Nannie Doss

Nannie Doss was her own PR agent. She overpowered the news in the mid-1950s by flirting on camera, cracking morbid jokes, and framing her horrible crimes as nothing more than a fluke on the path to finding Mr. Right. After all, she was just a silly, love-struck grandma who would never intentionally harm a fly, much less murder four husbands in cold blood. Everything she did was done in the name of love. And love could justify anything. Right?

One of the many virtuous, refined, and, yes, straight-up *housewifely* skills the forty-nine-year-old Nannie possessed was her ability to bake a mean cake. She could whip up the type of cake that would make a lonely farmer marry her on the spot. One day, she sent a buttery homemade confection all the way from her home in Tulsa, Oklahoma, to Goldsboro, North Carolina, intending to woo a sixty-year-old dairy farmer named John Keel. The man was smitten with her humorous letters and her obvious skill in the kitchen and hoped that Nannie would soon head east to be his bride. Nannie was stuck in Tulsa for the time being, caring for a "sick, aged aunt," but Keel felt sure they'd be together shortly.

But before Keel could get his hands on a ring, he learned something horrifying about his lady love: she had just been arrested. There was no aged aunt. There had never been an aged aunt. The person she had been "caring" for was her husband, and now he was dead.

"I'm sure mighty proud, mighty proud that she didn't come to my part of the country," Keel said later.

Thinking Crooked

The Nannie that Keel thought he knew was born Nancy Hazle in 1906. Her family owned a farm in Calhoun County, Alabama, and her parents were strict: Nannie had to work in the fields from a very young age, and she was by no means allowed to run around with boys. Today, rumors abound that her father was abusive and that Nannie rebelled by sleeping around as much as she could. We don't know this for a fact, but we do know that he was controlling and that she liked boys – a lot. In fact, the austerity of her boyfriend-less upbringing was something Nannie would rebel against for the rest of her life.

Long before she thought of boys, though, she suffered a terrible accident. When Nannie was seven, she was riding along in a train when the whole thing crunched to a sudden stop and she split her head wide open against the metal bar of the seat in front of her. She felt the repercussions of this injury forever: awful headaches and a sense that sometimes she was "thinking crooked."

The Hazles were perpetually poor, and by the time Nannie was fifteen – a gap-toothed, rosy-cheeked cutie – she had dropped out of school to work on the farm full-time. That same year, she got married. It wasn't exactly a Romeo and Juliet type of situation; the man, Charlie Braggs, was someone her strict father had already approved of for her. But Braggs himself was thrilled with the match at first. Nannie presented herself to him as a "church woman," and Braggs found her "a pretty girl, good build and lots of fun."

Nannie, however, found it difficult to stay put. "She was quick tempered," said Braggs. "Her whole family is like that. Sometimes she would get mad for a reason and sometimes it seemed not. She'd pout and then go off for days or weeks, often with other men." He found out she was "no more Christian than if she had never heard the Bible preached."

They had five children, but three of them died young, and Braggs harbored a few unspeakable suspicions about that fact. He'd noticed that two of the babies had showed symptoms of severe stomach troubles just before they died, and had "turned black so quick." His misgivings left a horrible taste in his mouth. But what could he do? Motherhood was a woman's world, and a mystery to him.

Something else went wrong during their marriage: Nannie's father left her mother. Nannie despised him for it, and refused to let him see his grandkids. Perhaps in her mind, her father had failed to hold up his end of the bargain, which was to fully inhabit the role of husband. The breakup only increased her adoration of her mom, though. "I'd get down on my knees and crawl anywhere for my mother," she said, years later. This love would eventually come under severe questioning, but Nannie was always adamant about this one thing: she loved her mother, and she would never hurt someone who she loved so purely.

Motherhood didn't suit Nannie herself, though, and neither did marriage – at least, not the imperfect marriage she had with Braggs. After eight years of fighting and suspicion, Braggs grew tired of chasing Nannie around Alabama and filed for divorce. Sensing that Nannie was either unfit or unwilling to take care of their two remaining girls, he kept their oldest daughter and sent the other to live with Nannie's dad.

Years later, Nannie told a reporter that she didn't hate men, despite what her actions implied, because some men were good. She certainly enjoyed male company. She was always pursuing men: writing to them, flirting with them, marrying them. And the men she met *were* good – at least, that's what their friends, neighbors, and family members said. Nannie told a different story. In her version of events, she was forever the innocent princess, disappointed again and again by a long line of unsatisfactory suitors.

Lonely Hearts

On the night of Friday, November 26, 1954, the police of Tulsa, Oklahoma, were surprised to see a plump, jovial, quintessentially grandmotherly figure brought into the police station on suspicion of murdering her fifth husband. The woman, Nannie Doss, was coquettish and hilarious, and the police were taken aback by her cheerful disposition. "She talks a lot," said detective Harry Stege, "but not about the case." She laughingly brushed off questions about arsenic and autopsies and unhappy marriages. She smoked a cigarette. Her eyes sparkled.

It took twenty-four hours of on-and-off interrogation before Nannie admitted that okay, fine, *yes*, she had poisoned her husband Sam Doss by spiking his coffee with rat poison. Around midnight, she signed a formal statement admitting that she was a murderer.

Meanwhile, reports were trickling into the police station of more dead husbands, a dead step-grandson, and other long-held suspicions people had about the "smiling, talkative widow." After a weekend of continued interrogation, Nannie giggled at the police officers and told them she was finally ready to clear her conscience. Sam Doss wasn't her only victim, she declared. She'd had five husbands, and she'd killed four of them.

After Charlie Braggs divorced her, Nannie had married an older man named Frank Harrelson from Jacksonville, Alabama, who had children from a previous marriage. According to Nannie, Harrelson was a mean, abusive drunk. She tolerated his weekend benders for fifteen years, until the day he came home plastered and snarled, "If you don't come to bed with me now, I ain't going to be here next week."

"I decided I'll teach him," said Nannie. "And I did." Harrelson was in the habit of drinking cheap "rotgut" whiskey from an old fruit jar hidden in a flour bin, so Nannie found the jar and stirred in a healthy portion of liquid arsenic. The next time Harrelson ducked out for a secretive nip of the hard stuff, he died.

Nannie's next spouse was Harley Lanning of Lexington, North Carolina. He was also a drinker and, on top of that, a massive flirt. Nannie couldn't stand how popular Lanning was with the ladies, and she snapped when Lanning threw a raging party while she was out of town. The party was so wild that police had to come by and, according to Nannie, haul the partygoers "out of bed." In a blind fury, Nannie poisoned a plate of Lanning's food in 1952. He was dead before the weekend.

With three husbands out of the way, Nannie was ready to change her approach. Her search for Mr. Right had failed miserably so far, since she kept getting stuck with flirts, drinkers, or men like Braggs who didn't accept the fact that sometimes a girl just wanted to run away from home for a week or two. So she took matters into her own hands and signed up for a mail-order husband. For five dollars, she became a card-carrying member of a "lonely hearts club" called the Diamond Circle, based out of St. Louis. Each month for an entire year the fine curators of the Diamond Circle would send her a list of "lonely men," and Nannie could contact whomever she liked.

She struck up a correspondence with a darkly handsome Kansan named Richard Morton, and things moved quickly from there. On January 21, 1953, the operator of the Diamond Circle received a letter from Morton:

Will you please take our names off your list – R. L. Morton Sr., Emporia, Kas., and Mrs. Nannie Lanning, Jacksonville, Ala., for we have met and are very happily married. She is a sweet and wonderful woman. I would not have met her had it not been for your club.

It didn't take long for things to fall apart, though. Morton worked nights at a pool hall, but during the day he liked to put on his best suit and head out on mysterious business. This disturbed Nannie. Why would he go to town all dressed up when his "sweet and wonderful" wife was right there at home? Even worse, when she was away on a trip to North Carolina, she somehow heard that Morton had purchased a set of rings during her absence. Rings could only mean one thing, she theorized: he was seeing someone else.

"I lost my head and blew up when I found out he had been running around with another woman," she said. She decided that if Morton could make secretive purchases, so could she – so she came back from North Carolina with a bottle of liquid poison stashed in her suitcase. Later, police would speculate that Morton had initially bought the rings as a gift for Nannie but then pawned them to follow her to North Carolina, perhaps realizing that she was furious at him. If that was the case, here was the grand, romantic gesture she'd always wanted – she just didn't know it. Instead, she stirred poison into his coffee, convinced he was cheating on her.

If her first four marriages had been tinged with vice – alcohol and violence and lust – her final marriage was so prosaic that it threatened to drive Nannie insane with boredom. Sam Doss was a real dud, a parsimonious highway worker and part-time Free Will Baptist minister living in Tulsa, Oklahoma. He wouldn't let her buy a TV set, even though she really wanted one. He wouldn't let her dance.

"He got on my nerves," said Nannie, when asked to explain why she tried to kill Doss two separate times. At first, she stewed up a huge kettle of boxed prunes and doused them with poison. (Prunes were a major hit in the 1950s. President Eisenhower declared that his favorite food in the world was a dessert comprised partially of whipped egg whites, prune pulp, and unflavored gelatin called Prune Whip.) It turned out Doss's appetite was the only generous thing about him. "He sure did like prunes," said Nannie. "I fixed him a whole box and he ate them all."

The dish sent Doss to the hospital for twenty-three days, but didn't quite finish him off, so the day after he returned, Nannie fixed him the Richard Morton special: piping hot coffee with a dollop of rat poison. It did the trick, as she knew it would.

Fortunately for the remainder of America's lonely gentlemen, prunes and coffee were the last dishes Nannie ever poisoned. The attending physician refused to sign Doss's death certificate without an autopsy to determine the cause of death. Oddly enough, Nannie loved this idea and agreed that they should definitely figure out what killed Doss because "it might kill someone else." Her husband's vital organs were sent to a lab in Oklahoma City, and the pathologist there returned the damning evidence: Doss had enough arsenic inside him to kill eighteen part-time Free Will Baptist ministers.

In a photo taken after her long confession was over, Nannie Doss is leaving the courthouse with the homicide captain. She is smiling broadly and looks perfectly at home.

"Charmed 'Em, Poisoned 'Em"

Though Nannie's flirtatious demeanor corroborated her story somewhat – lonely hearts club member looking for love in all the wrong places – the police weren't convinced she was telling the whole truth. There were too many other mysterious deaths linked to her name, including those of her mother, father, two sisters, two of her children, and a step-grandson. But when they tried to get her to admit to killing her relatives, Nannie's attitude changed abruptly. "You can dig up all the graves in the country," she snapped, "and you won't find any more on me."

Although Nannie acted deeply offended by the insinuations, the evidence was pretty damning. She'd been hanging around both her sisters and her beloved mother right before they died. Then, the day after her mother's funeral, Nannie had pranced off to marry Richard Morton – not exactly the picture of bereaved daughterhood. And the brother of Frank Harrelson (husband number two) called the police to report a chilling anecdote from a decade earlier: he and Harrelson had been walking past a cemetery when Harrelson pointed out the little grave that belonged to his grandson, muttered that the boy had been poisoned, and then said, simply, "I'll be next."

None of this fit with the image Nannie had so carefully crafted: that of a breezy, good-humored grandmother who flirted with police, smiled at the press, and cracked jokes about the whole silly situation. Okay, so maybe she'd killed a husband or two, but it was all tinged with a bit of *Arsenic and Old Lace*-esque humor (a movie that came out when Nannie was thirty-eight, by the way), and anyway, her husbands were cheats, liars, abusers, and prudes. In light of that fact, her murders were, well, *practical*. Just the sort of get-'er-done move you'd expect from a sensible housewife.

But other sources vehemently denied that Morton or Lanning had ever cheated on her. In fact, the salacious story of Lanning's supposed orgy was contradicted by none other than Charlie Braggs, Nannie's first husband. In a peculiar twist, one of Nannie and Braggs's surviving daughters had ended up marrying Lanning's nephew, and the party that the police interrupted was actually just an innocent family visit. "All that happened was that the police heard there were strangers in the house, which is out in the country by itself, and went out to see who it was," said Charlie Braggs. "Nannie wrote us a terrible letter after that, but there was no more calm, steady man in the world than Harley Lanning."

Sam Doss's brother also began poking holes in Nannie's story. He had been suspicious of her from the start: "No woman is going to travel a thousand miles or so to marry some plain working man just because she wants him." He watched Nannie torture the puritanical Sam Doss by smoking openly and wearing scandalous outfits, and he disagreed with the popular perception of Nannie as "simple, candid, open, cheerful." That wasn't the Nannie he knew. "She was a smart one," he said. "She was shrewd, very shrewd. And I seem to remember that she sometimes would tell you one thing and the next time just the opposite."

Despite her detractors, Nannie was enjoying a newfound celebrity. She hammed it up for the press, and they rewarded her with splashy headlines:

**CALM, AFFABLE GRANDMOTHER TELLS OF
POISONING FOUR OF FIVE SPOUSES**

TULSA GRANDMA CHARMED 'EM, POISONED 'EM

NANNIE DOSS ONCE CARRIED A PISTOL; WAS WELL LIKED

Moments before she appeared on TV to be interviewed, the cameraman suggested she remove her glasses and smile for the camera, quipping, "You might get another husband if you look nice." Nannie replied, "Ain't that the dying truth," and then cracked up at her own pun. She was Oklahoma's biggest news story of 1954, and she knew it.

Nannie was certainly not the first or last serial killer to achieve and even enjoy celebrity, but she was a celebrity at an interesting time in America. Think of everything cliché you know about the 1950s: housewives spent their days vacuuming with martinis in hand and a look of existential horror in their eyes, and every home was outfitted with a TV set. Nannie's celebrity fit perfectly into this social landscape. She was the twisted parody of the housewife, a woman seemingly obsessed with marriage and, uh, cooking, but a woman who used her feminine charms to catch and *kill* men instead of catching and keeping them. She wore cat-eye glasses and lipstick; her hair was curled; she was photographed in a double string of pearls. She appeared on TV, giving interviews and flirting with cameramen, creating an intimacy between audience and murderer that would have been unthinkable in the case of previous lady killers, and enabling her reputation to spread farther and farther.

Perhaps the version of femininity that Nannie presented to the world seemed, in a dark way, more appealing – and certainly more accessible – to her female peers than the versions they were receiving from other sources. After all, when the rest of America's housewives changed the channel away from the coverage of Nannie's case, they would have been presented with goddesses like Marilyn Monroe, glimmering in tight white dresses and marrying baseball stars, so perfect as to feel utterly foreign.

"Darling, How We Miss Thee"

Nannie's court-appointed lawyers refused to make a plea for her, insisting she was mentally incompetent, so she was given a default plea of not guilty. Nannie herself continued to flirt with everyone in power. On her way to the courthouse, she told the prosecuting attorney that she'd been cold in her jail cell, and to prove it, she placed one of her freezing hands on the back of his neck. When the police woke her from an evening nap to interrogate her, she laughed, "I don't know why you guys get me up at this hour to talk to me. I've been talking to you for a week." Her lawyers finally had to tell Nannie to stop chatting to the police altogether, for fear that she'd let something slip about all those dead family members.

Meanwhile, bodies were being dug up all over the country. Arsenic was found in every one of Nannie's dead husbands, and the murder charges racked up against her accordingly. None of these findings were a surprise, since Nannie had already admitted to these particular murders, but there was one shocking reveal: despite Nannie's insistence to the contrary, an autopsy revealed that her mother's body was also loaded with arsenic.

Why was Nannie so loath to admit she'd killed her mother? She'd been practically giddy about the murders of her disappointing husbands, as if she were entitled to take their lives. Considering how enthusiastically she agreed to the autopsy of Sam Doss, it almost seems as though she *wanted* her husband killings to come to light. And yet she couldn't bear the suggestion that she harmed her mother. She had constructed a narrative that she only killed those deserving of death, and killing innocent family members didn't fit with this story. *I'd get down on my knees and crawl anywhere for my mother,* she insisted, and the papers printed it, word for word.

Though the image she manufactured was one of harmless, lovelorn femininity – an image reliant on both sexist and ageist assumptions about who could be dangerous, and when – Nannie, the alleged mother killer, actually had a horrific dark side. This might seem obvious, since she murdered, what, eleven people, including a child? But strangely – or perhaps predictably – she didn't really scare people. For the American public, Nannie was forever an affable grandmother, the punch line to a joke.

Many serial killers – Ted Bundy comes to mind – make waves not just for their crimes but for their ability to pass as normal, nonviolent, even charming. (Direct from Bundy: "I was a normal person. I had good friends. I led a normal life, except for this one small but very potent and destructive segment that I kept very secret and close to myself.") When they're not committing their monstrous crimes, they walk among us, looking perfectly innocent and, in Nannie's case, plump, cute, and grandmotherly. Isn't that part of what's so horrifying about serial killers? The idea that Bundy could have been your next-door neighbor, that Nannie could have fixed you a cup of coffee?

Now, Ted Bundy, who was among other things a rapist and a necrophiliac, seems objectively "scarier" than Nannie, who giggled and poisoned prunes. But serial killers aren't scary because they're male; they're scary because they destroy order. Or rather, they reveal that what we perceived as order and normalcy (the all-American boy, the giggling grandma, the housewife vacuuming vacuously) has been a violent lie all along. In the 1950s, Nannie Doss looked far more like the average housewife than Marilyn Monroe did. She embodied the order of things: mothering, marrying, cleaning the kitchen floor. And yet she brought death in her wake.

By December 5, the press learned that this "gentle grandmother" had another morbid hobby: she loved to compose tombstone epitaphs. Her step-grandson's tomb read: "Darling how we miss thee." Lanning's said, simply: "We will meet again."

"The Cleverest Criminal I Ever Interviewed"

At Nannie's preliminary hearing on December 15, the judge decided to turn her over to the state asylum so doctors could determine whether she was insane or not. "Arsenic Nannie" wasn't upset about the compulsory ninety-day stay. In fact, she was relieved. It seemed, to her, like a little luxury.

"Now maybe I will get some rest and won't have to answer so many silly questions," she laughed. She had high hopes for her asylum vacation, telling a jail matron, "Maybe those docs at the hospital will teach me to think straight."

True to form, Nannie thoroughly enjoyed herself at the asylum, where she celebrated her fiftieth birthday. She was getting plenty of attention due to her continued celebrity status, and she made sure to primp every time the staff psychiatrists came around to examine her. One of the doctors raved about her behavior to the press, noting that she still suffered from headaches – a holdover from her childhood accident – but that otherwise, her health was perfect. In fact, *she* was nearly perfect. "If you had small children," he said, "you'd be delighted to have her as a babysitter."

His supervisors disagreed. On March 14, a group of medical examiners declared Nannie "mentally defective with a marked impairment of judgment and will power" and recommended she be recommitted to the asylum. But the prosecution pressed on, demanding she at least be tried for murder, so Nannie was tossed back into jail while her attorneys entered a plea of "not guilty by reason of insanity." A sanity hearing was set for April, with everyone rolling their eyes about it as the dueling sides gathered their experts. "The hearing shapes up as a battle of contradictory testimony by psychiatrists," snarked a little paper from South Carolina.

Nannie disliked the confining setup of jail and wanted to go back to her tiny slice of asylum paradise, where everyone knew her name.

"You can't see people [in jail], and I like people," she complained. Perhaps what she meant was that in jail, people couldn't see *her*. Still, she managed to charm another man or two from behind bars. One "elderly suitor" went so far as to mail her a marriage proposal – but Nannie tore his letter up. "I've had enough husbands," she told the press, who were, as usual, hanging on her every wisecrack.

Her sanity hearing turned out to be a jumble of he-said/she-said analysis, with Nannie's sanity or lack thereof batted back and forth like a badminton shuttlecock. "Mrs. Doss is mentally defective and is now insane in the legal sense. She also has been crazy for a long time," thundered a doctor for the defense. The prosecutor hissed that he had five psychiatrists on hand who were all ready and willing to declare her sane, and then quoted from a doctor's report: "She is a shrewd, clever, sharp, calculating, selfish, self-aggrandizing female whose aggressive behavior under frustration releases her hostility toward men, particularly her husbands." A superintendent from the state asylum noted that Nannie would giggle "extensively at nothing" for ages and then fall into long, dark depressions. If that wasn't insanity, what was? The prosecution's experts scoffed. Nannie was a sociopath, one of them said, and a "shrewd, calculating female who feigned insanity to escape the electric chair . . . the cleverest criminal I ever interviewed." At that final statement, Nannie laughed out loud.

After three days of this, it took the jury a mere fifteen minutes to decide that Nannie Doss was sane. The killer herself heartily concurred. "I'm as sane as anybody," she chuckled. "I guess I ought to know better than anybody if I'm crazy. I've never felt more sane in my whole life." She chewed gum while the verdict was declared, and grinned at the photographer as he took her portrait.

Nannie's official trial was set for early June, and so everyone was shocked when, on May 17, she suddenly pled guilty. She was hoping for a lighter sentence and thought maybe an unexpected plea of guilty would earn her some clemency. It's also possible she misunderstood the implications of pleading guilty. She wanted to be sent back to the asylum – where she'd felt so free and so popular – and perhaps she didn't realize it was too late for that. She'd been officially declared sane, and with this plea of guilty, she was now officially a murderer.

Her sentencing took place on June 2, where the prosecution urged the judge to consider the death penalty. Nannie sat between her attorneys, chewed more gum, and "wore an attractive blue party dress." The hearing was brief, but the sentence was long: life in prison. It would have been the electric chair, but the judge couldn't bear the thought of killing a woman. "This court has never heard of a woman being put to death for any crime in Oklahoma," he said. "It may happen some day . . . and the people of this state would very reluctantly see such come to pass."

After the sentencing, Nannie remarked, "I have no hard feelings."

Out of the Headlines

Nannie entered prison on June 4 and dropped out of the news until a reporter interviewed her in September. "I thought everybody had forgotten me," said Nannie. "I thought I was just out of the headlines." She mentioned she'd lost eight pounds in jail because she did the laundry "the hard way," but complained that her headaches were getting worse.

Nannie also told the reporter she was "tricked" into signing the statement about Doss's poisoning. This wasn't the first time she hinted at a conspiracy; months before, she told a reporter from the *Tulsa World* that she had been duped into confessing the murders of her four husbands, and that she got the idea for her confession from a magazine story. Perhaps Nannie realized her status as a celebrity murderer would not last forever, and so she no longer wanted to claim that identity for herself. She was dreaming up a better angle on her own story: innocent "lonely hearts" lady hoodwinked by the police.

Otherwise, Nannie seemed happy enough, with no desire to go back to her old routine of marriage and housework. "I am a funny person," she said. "If they'd turn me out right now I'd go straight to the hospital at Vinita and be content to spend the rest of my life there. That sounds sort of crazy, doesn't it."

Though the asylum may have been her ultimate ideal, Nannie still adored prison. She got to do everything she didn't get to do with Sam Doss: she saw movies, she watched TV, and she participated in the occasional dance ("strictly for the 50 women prisoners"). She loved the jail matron, Mrs. N. F. Whitaker, who was "just like a mother" to her. Nannie had a small heart attack in September and took a month of bed rest, but other than that, she was having a wonderful time. Her surviving family members didn't visit her – but perhaps she expected that. Prison, she said, was "just like being at home."

But what did home even mean for Nannie Doss? She resented her father for leaving her mother and breaking up their nuclear family, but then she went on to destroy five separate portraits of the American marriage herself. She framed her husband killings as the act of someone who was disappointed in love – silly Nannie, always a little too intense in her search for Prince Charming! – but she wouldn't claim responsibility for the deaths of her family members. Nannie seemed to have very specific ideas about the roles husbands and family should play, and she reacted furiously when people disappointed her by not fulfilling those roles. (From the prosecution, remember: her "aggressive behavior under frustration releases her hostility toward men.") It seems likely that her issues originated from, or were exacerbated by, her early childhood head injury, since numerous studies in recent decades have linked frontal lobe injuries to increased incidents of violent, uncontrollable social behavior. Perhaps her wounded, extreme reactions also stemmed from her earliest and greatest disappointment in another human: her father, who stifled her girlish longings for romance, who practically arranged her marriage, and who put the final nail in the coffin that held her ideals of love when he abandoned her mother.

But none of this was explored in much depth in the press, nor in the decades following. These days, Nannie is still remembered as the hilariously murderous grandma who read romance novels in jail and was obsessed with trading in her husbands for newer models.

This attitude continues today toward older women who kill. The disparity between the grandma archetype (smiles at us from under a halo of white hair, bakes great pies, contains a fount of cozy knowledge about the good old days) and the murderer archetype (physically strong, usually male, follows his victims down dark alleyways, crawls through bedroom windows) is just too much to reconcile. People tend to collapse back onto humor to deal with and/or to diminish it. As an editorial about Nannie Doss once chirped, "Grandma, you rat!"

In 2015, a sixty-eight-year-old Russian woman named Tamara Samsonova was arrested on suspicion of not just serial murder but cannibalism, and she pulled a total Nannie during an interview when she blew a kiss to court reporters. Her headlines are tinged with macabre hilarity: she's the "GRANNY RIPPER," "GRANNY FROM HELL," and "GRANNYBALL LECTER." These are funny names, to be sure, but the crimes she's accused of are as horrendous as those of Jack the Ripper himself. Yet somehow when she does it, it's kind of a joke? (In the grand tradition of female serial killers being forever linked to the kitchen, security cameras captured footage of Samsonova carrying a pot that was thought to contain the head of her last victim.) Or consider Melissa Ann Shepard, an eighty-one-year-old alleged serial killer from Canada, who was given the Nannie press treatment in 2016. One article about her crimes began: "She looks like a sweet old lady, but . . ." while another called her a "rosy-cheeked killer." Aw! In a way, this is a narrative we've been *trained* to laugh at; for example, the entire film *Arsenic and Old Lace* is predicated on the situational irony of old women who kill. But we're talking about taking a human life here, and when it happens in the real world, it's horrible. Canada's "rosy-cheeked killer" drugged a man with benzodiazepine and ran over him twice with a car. Nannie killed the mother she claimed to love. These are tragedies, not comedies, at the end of the day.

We've got to hand it to her, though: Nannie was smart. She knew how to work her best angles. She was clever enough to realize that as a husband killer, she could hide behind this dopey, lovesick persona and possibly escape with her life. If she'd appeared in the press as a matricidal maniac, she would never have gotten the attention she did – the chuckles from cameramen, the jibes from police officers, the doctor who genuinely believed she'd make a *great* babysitter. (And Nannie adored that attention, Nannie who always felt so constricted by the men in her life, from her controlling father to puritanical Sam Doss.) She was like a reality TV star emphasizing only the most marketable aspects of her shady past. Slowly, her story turned into a twisted fairy tale: the fickle princess who couldn't find what she wanted, the doomed suitors who couldn't give her what she needed.

In prison, Nannie retained her signature humor. In May 1957 she quipped, "When they get short in the kitchen I always offer to help out, but they never let me work there." The press, still charmed by her, reported this widely. But after two years of being locked up, she told a journalist from the *Daily Oklahoman* that she'd lost the will to live. She wanted to be tried again in Kansas or North Carolina, where she had also been charged with murder. "Maybe they would give me the electric chair," she said.

Alas, life stretched on uneventfully for the murderess whom nobody took seriously. Seven years into her sentence, she faked another heart attack, which got her out of the prison, at least momentarily. (Doctors couldn't find anything wrong with her. Grandma, you rat!) Ten years into her sentence, on June 2 – the same day she'd been sentenced to life in prison – Nannie Doss died of leukemia.

Her notoriety was all used up by then. People had stopped paying attention years before. Headlines called her "Husband-Killer" and "Mate-Poisoner" and "Admitted Slayer" when they announced her death, because her name alone was no longer enough to remind the world why they should care.

THE WORST WOMAN
ON EARTH

Lizzie Halliday

At the tail end of the 1800s, a woman named Lizzie was serving time for arson in Pennsylvania's Eastern State Penitentiary. She had been a model prisoner for the first one and a half years of her sentence, but two months before her release date, she began acting strange, a bit unhinged. So she was transferred to an asylum, where the physicians confirmed her insanity and looked after her until it was time for her to walk free.

Lizzie then made her way to the state of New York to hunt for work. In a little town called Newburgh, she met old Paul Halliday, who was looking for domestic help. He'd been married before and fathered six children, one of whom was mentally handicapped and still lived at home on the Halliday farm. Lizzie informed Halliday that she had just arrived from Ireland six weeks ago. They agreed on a salary of forty dollars a month.

Before long, Halliday realized it would be cheaper to marry Lizzie and get her work for free than to pay for her services. Plus, there was something oddly charming about her – he didn't mind the thought of having her as a wife. So he proposed, and the two began a relationship that Halliday's children described as one of "peculiar influence."

See, Lizzie brought trouble in her wake like an avenging angel, but no matter how many horrors she inflicted on her husband, he never left her. During the spring of 1891, Halliday came home to find a heap of smoking ashes where his house once stood. Lizzie, who was standing by the ruins, nonchalantly informed him that his handicapped son had just been burned to a crisp. She claimed that the boy died trying to save her from the flames. This story, however, was belied by the fact that when they identified the son's bedroom door in the rubble, it was clearly locked, and Lizzie herself was carrying the key.

And yet Halliday stayed with her. Less than a month later, Lizzie burned down his barn and mill, declaring that he needed a new one anyway, and then ran off with another man, determined to become a horse thief. She was quickly apprehended and thrown back in jail, where she immediately began tearing out her hair and screaming at anyone who would listen. This pandemonium got her acquitted on grounds of insanity, and she was sent across the Hudson River to the Matteawan State Hospital for the Criminally Insane.

Halliday scoffed at this development. Lizzie was "perfectly sane," he insisted, and "hoped by her present actions to obtain immunity for her crimes." But the doctors at the asylum disagreed with him. They kept her for a year and then released her into Halliday's custody, saying that she was cured.

The couple muscled through another year of marriage, and then Paul Halliday disappeared.

Lizzie told the neighbors her husband was away on business, but some of them had noticed suspicious activity around the Halliday farm during the past couple of days – eerie sounds, figures creeping about at night. Besides, there was just something *weird* about Lizzie Halliday, and the neighbors didn't particularly trust her. So one day, when Lizzie was out, they decided to search the Halliday farm. They wondered, nervously, if they'd find a body.

They found two.

Naturally Ugly

In 1860, Lizzie Halliday was born Elizabeth Margaret McNally in County Antrim, Ireland, and came over to New York State with her parents and nine siblings when she was still a child. On American soil, she grew into a tempestuous adolescent. "She was inclined so much to quarreling that the family all disowned her for years," said her brother John. "She could not stay in a place any time when working out on account of her violent temper."

She was a highly physical, unpredictable girl. At one point, she attacked her father; another time she sprang violently at her sister Jane. If she showed love, it was with equally mad conviction. When she returned home after a long absence to find that her father had passed away, she flung herself on his grave and began tearing away the earth with her bare hands.

Lizzie was short but incredibly strong, and people always noticed her muscular limbs, as well as her lovely, translucent Irish skin. But her large nose and larger forehead drew mockery and even disgust from observers. One neighbor hissed that Lizzie had a "repulsive face, and the most peculiar nose I ever saw." A landlord called her "naturally ugly."

She wasn't educated, but she was cunning, and she was always on the hunt for money. Unfortunately, she left poor impressions on many of her employers: she wore unusual clothes, she was subject to mood swings, and, quite frankly, she scared them. Once she threw a knife at a young man who was teasing her; another time, she spat in the face of a little girl. When an employer tried to correct her baking methods, Lizzie went screaming to the nearest courthouse, claiming the employer had assaulted her. In fact, she was *always* popping up in court; she even tried to arrest two young boys who pointed their toy pistols at her. But when her mood lifted, she could be found attending a Methodist church or staring in fascination at a nearby religious revival.

Between jobs, she got married, and between marriages, she took more jobs. At the age of fifteen, she married an old army deserter who went by the fake name Ketspool Brown. The two spent their relationship locked in fear; Lizzie told her family that Brown wanted to murder her, while Brown informed his doctor: "I am afraid of her; she has threatened my life." They had a son, and childbirth sent Lizzie into a spiral of depression. She visited her sister and complained that she heard nonstop singing and saw lights flashing around the room. At one point, while she sat mending a dress, she cried, "What's the use of living?" and tore up the garment.

After three years of marriage, Ketspool Brown died of typhoid fever, and Lizzie worked her way steadily through three more husbands, all of whom were significantly older than her. None of the marriages were happy. She tried to kill one husband with a cup of poisoned tea, and tore up his featherbed in the streets for no apparent reason. Her fifth husband was young and handsome, unlike the rest, but things fell apart when he confessed to Lizzie that he had "pounded his first wife to death." Terrified, she took her son and ran off to Philadelphia, where she opened a shop, insured it, and then burnt it down for the insurance money, destroying several neighboring houses in the process.

After doing two years in the Eastern Penitentiary and, subsequently, the asylum, Lizzie was released, only to find that her son had disappeared. "My boy is now about twelve years old," she told a reporter years later. "I've never been able to find him since."

Heart's Blood

A few miles from the Halliday farm, there lived a sweet, harmless family called the McQuillans: seventy-four-year-old Tom, his wife, Margaret, and their nineteen-year-old daughter, Sarah. It was the summer of 1893, and Sarah was on vacation and thoroughly enjoying it. On August 26, a woman showed up at their house in a wagon and introduced herself as Mrs. Smith, saying she was looking to hire a cleaning lady. Sarah would have normally taken the job, but she was preoccupied with her lounging, so Margaret volunteered. A neighbor thought Mrs. Smith seemed odd, and urged Margaret not to take the position. But Margaret brushed her off and drove away with Mrs. Smith, calling out, teasingly, "Goodbye, if I shouldn't see you again!"

A few days later, the so-called Mrs. Smith returned to the McQuillan house in a panic, saying Margaret had fallen from a ladder and desperately wanted to see her daughter. Tom McQuillan wanted to go himself, but Mrs. Smith was adamant: Margaret insisted on seeing Sarah. So the girl got in the wagon and the two drove away.

When two days passed with no word from his wife or daughter, Tom McQuillan grew suspicious and set out to find Mrs. Smith's house. He soon realized the woman had given him a fake address and a false name; no one knew who he was talking about when he inquired about the mysterious Mrs. Smith who needed her house cleaned.

Meanwhile, one of Halliday's sons was also starting to suspect foul play. His father had been absent for too long, now, and Lizzie's excuses weren't adding up. After keeping an eye on Lizzie for a few days to see if he could figure out what was going on, the son went to the police and procured a search warrant.

When the local constable and his crew arrived to search the house, they found Lizzie preoccupied with cleaning blood from a carpet. Upon spotting the men in her doorway, she sprang up, outraged, and threatened to kill them if they tried to enter her home. The constable ignored her, and Lizzie snatched up a board and smacked him on the hand, screaming that she would "cut his heart's blood out."

Undeterred, the men investigated the premises. The house seemed empty, but the barn soon gave up its terrible secret. Under a layer of garbage, covered by a pile of hay, they found the bodies of Margaret and Sarah McQuillan. Their feet and hands were tied, and their heads were wrapped in cloth. Both woman had taken multiple bullet wounds to the chest.

At first, Lizzie shrugged off the awful evidence, saying that if something bad had been done, she had nothing to do with it. But soon enough she began acting peculiar. She picked at her clothes, claiming there were potato bugs crawling across her. Later, when a curious neighbor asked her about the discovery of the bodies, she refused to look at him, but had a "sneak look" in her eyes as she turned away. Slowly, a question began forming in the minds of everyone around her. It was a question people would ask of Lizzie Halliday for the rest of her life: was she insane, or was she faking it?

Successful Women Adventuresses

Lizzie was arrested and hauled off to jail in Burlingham, while back at the Halliday farm, the search for bodies continued. Paul Halliday's surviving children were now sick with worry about the fate of their father, so one of his sons brought a friend and snuck into the farmhouse early one morning to see if the police had missed anything. When the two men reached the kitchen, they noticed some of the floorboards didn't match the others and pried them up.

Beneath the floorboards, the earth looked loose and fresh. The men brought over a crowbar and sank it into the ground until it met with resistance – but the object they hit wasn't firm, like a rock or a brick. There was something soft down there. Thoroughly spooked, they ran for backup.

Soon enough, the son's worst fears were confirmed: Lizzie Halliday had buried his father under her own kitchen floorboards. The "badly decomposed" corpse of old Paul Halliday had multiple bullet wounds in the chest and had been struck hard on the head – so hard that the left eye was knocked out of its socket.

On September 8, 1893, Lizzie was shipped off to a second jail in Monticello, New York. News of her crimes had now spread throughout the entire region, and her old house back near Newburgh was stripped to the bones by morbid artifact hunters. In Monticello, hundreds of people lined the streets to watch her arrival. The jailers hurried her into her cell without any problem, but every now and then she'd let out a "deafening shriek," as though to "appraise the public on the outside that she was in confinement."

Lizzie was a performative prisoner, which didn't help her public image. People thought her alleged insanity was a bit too much, what with all the incoherent monologues and earsplitting screams.

She tore at her clothes, ripped her blankets to pieces, refused food, and answered questions with deranged nonsequiturs. Plus, most of this wild behavior happened when someone was watching. If you managed to catch a glimpse of Lizzie when she thought she was alone, you might find her sitting "moodily and lost in thought" on her bed, the apparent picture of sanity. The public waffled: was she or wasn't she? On September 12, the *New York Times* declared definitively: MRS. HALLIDAY NOT INSANE. By November 7, the headline cried: MRS. HALLIDAY WAS INSANE. No one could make up their mind.

In those days, the public instinctively distrusted any plea of insanity. People called it the insanity dodge, convinced that certain prisoners falsified madness to go free. The common misconception was that there was "widespread abuse" of this plea, used by shady lawyers as "a last resort for cheating justice." In reality, the public's suspicions were unfounded. "Public delusion . . . is that the insanity dodge is a thing which succeeds very frequently," said Dr. Carlos F. MacDonald in 1895, discussing Lizzie's case at a meeting of the Medical Society of the State of New York. "It is wrongfully put forth in a certain number of cases, but it is a well-known fact that it seldom succeeds where it is wrongfully offered."

One woman wanted to decide for herself if Lizzie was using the insanity dodge. Nellie Bly was an intrepid girl reporter who was already famous for her sharp investigations into the Women's Lunatic Asylum on Blackwell's Island and the lurid baby-buying trade in New York City. She used her considerable celebrity to score an exclusive two-part interview with Lizzie, and in October, Bly faced the triple murderess in her cell. The cell was decorated, Bly noticed, with photos of lingerie models and political figures that had been torn out of magazines. A spread titled SUCCESSFUL WOMEN ADVENTURESSES was displayed on the windowsill, along with a little tin can full of flowers.

It took a while to get Lizzie talking about the McQuillan murders – at first, she only wanted to discuss the state of her finances back in Newburgh – but Bly finally got Lizzie to open up. Sort of. Lizzie concocted a crazy tale about the night of the murders, claiming she had been drinking moonshine and eating bread and butter with Paul Halliday and the three McQuillans when, out of nowhere, someone chloroformed her. While Lizzie was out cold, that same mysterious person managed to kill both Paul Halliday and the McQuillan women, and Lizzie woke up with no idea that anything bad had happened.

Bly was understandably skeptical about this wild recounting, and asked Lizzie why she hadn't noticed the bloodstains and bullet holes in the house, or the fact that something had clearly been buried under the kitchen floor. "I didn't see anything," Lizzie responded, coolly.

Lizzie had used this bizarre rhetoric before, actually – acknowledging that she was there at the scene of the crime, but totally denying any responsibility. When she was jailed for arson back in Pennsylvania, her alibi had been similarly passive and self-victimizing: "Oil was poured out of a lamp over the floor and a match set to it. I saw it all, but I didn't do it. I didn't speak because I was afraid I would be killed, but I lay in bed with my eyes open watching the whole thing done."

During the interview with Bly, Lizzie mentioned a mysterious "gang" that liked to shoot their victims "where it would do the most good" – that is, directly in the heart. In a second interview with Bly, she took out the bit about the chloroform but brought back the gang, claiming she had been outside when the murders happened, watching everything through the window. "The McQuillan women were sitting on the sofa and [a man] shot them," she said. "I heard the one moan when she was hit and then she opened her eyes and said: 'My God! Did you bring me here to murder me?'"

Bly knew she was getting nothing but lies from Lizzie. Eventually, she grew annoyed and decided to push the issue. "I believe that you alone and unaided killed your husband and the McQuillan women and buried them," she snapped at Lizzie. "I don't believe you were ever insane one moment in your life, and that you are the shrewdest and most wonderful woman criminal the world has ever known."

Lizzie just smiled at her.

Determined to get a confession, Bly pushed harder. "Did you or did you not kill those people?" she asked. It was almost midnight in the jail cell. "Some other time. My head feels bad now," said Lizzie. "Some other time."

Bly got up to leave, but stopped in the doorway of the cell to ask one last question: did Lizzie repent of her crimes?

Lizzie smiled again. "God will send you back to me," she said in response. And Bly, with a "little chill" running through her body, left the prison.

"She Deserved No Friends, No More Than a Cat"

Lizzie grew increasingly violent as she waited for her trial. She attacked the sheriff's tiny wife, she removed the steel shanks from the soles of her heavy boots and tucked them away to be used as weapons, and she tried to set her jail cell on fire. She also went on a hunger strike. When none of that got her released, Lizzie tore a strip of cloth from the bottom of her dress and tried to hang herself from the door of her cell. By the time the sheriff cut her down, her eyes were bulging and her features were distorted, but she was still breathing. Five days after her attempted hanging, Lizzie smashed the window of her cell and lacerated her throat and elbows with a shard of glass. The sheriff found her sitting on her bed, covered in blood. "I thought I would cut myself to see if I would bleed," she told the doctor. After this, she was chained to an iron ring that jutted from the middle of the cell floor.

Skeptics continued to insist this was all an act. Why else would she have hung herself by the door, moments before she knew the sheriff would be passing by? Others thought her suicide attempts were all too real, because Lizzie believed her trial was imminent. It had actually been postponed until the spring – it was now almost Christmas – but nobody had bothered to tell Lizzie.

Her trial finally began in Monticello on June 18. A thin, subdued Lizzie entered the courtroom, and people lined the street outside, hoping to catch a glimpse of the murderess. Her lawyer, George H. Carpenter, was gunning for the insanity defense, while the prosecution attempted to establish that money was her motive for killing the two women. Thomas McQuillan sobbed as he identified a set of rings that had belonged to his murdered daughter. Lizzie pinched her nose so tightly it became raw.

The defense admitted pretty much everything: Yes, the bullets matched the gun. Yes, the rings belonged to Sarah McQuillan. They tried to explain away the blood on the carpet by saying that Lizzie wasn't very clean and "did not take the usual precautions taken by women." In other words, the stains were period blood, not "heart's blood." The fact that this argument was even ventured reveals the public's impression of Lizzie: that she was uncivilized, unhygienic, practically feral.

George H. Carpenter knew he couldn't prove Lizzie was innocent, but he thought he might be able to prove she didn't know right from wrong. His argument was twofold: (1) Lizzie Halliday was clearly insane, and (2) there was no motive for the crime – which further proved she was insane. Carpenter brought in an asylum superintendent and three doctors to confirm her insanity, as well as the jailer from Lizzie's days as an aspiring horse thief. The jailer told the court that Lizzie used to yell "Ma! Pa! Nancy!" from her cell. "Wild as a hawk," he said. "She was insane then . . . and is insane now."

During the trial, multiple physicians stopped by Lizzie's cell to examine her for signs of madness. They often found Lizzie chatting to the Holy Ghost. Once, she lunged at them with the lid of her toilet held aloft, ready to crack some skulls. She gave nonsensical answers to the most basic questions. Her age? "Nineteen skunks." Her address? "I washed your shirt." Her father's name? "You took my property."

"She is shamming," said one doctor, "and is overdoing the art."

George H. Carpenter argued passionately for his pitiful client, noting that Lizzie never spoke a word in her own defense; instead, she sat silently without a single relative or friend in the room while the crowd stared at her "as if she were a wild beast or a monster." He begged the jury to take the randomness of the McQuillan murders as proof this woman knew not what she did. But the prosecuting attorney urged the jury to instead consider "exterminating the prisoner as an enemy to society." She was not at all insane, he said, noting that in her day-to-day life Lizzie Halliday was perfectly able to keep appointments, feed her horse, and otherwise function in polite society. And as a counter to Carpenter's plea that Lizzie had no friends, the prosecutor sniped, "She deserved no friends, no more than a cat."

The jury only took a few hours to come to their conclusion: Lizzie Halliday was not insane in the slightest, and was guilty of murder in the first degree. Lizzie covered her face with her handkerchief and kept silent. George H. Carpenter wept.

The Insanity Commission

MRS. HALLIDAY TO DIE, ran the headlines the next day. Lizzie had been brought, shuffling, into the court that morning, and stood with no sign of comprehension in her eyes while the judge read the verdict: death by electric chair. It was the first time a woman had ever received this sentence.

Now that the idea of Lizzie's death had become tangible, the public suddenly began to question the fairness of the decision. They hadn't expected the electric chair. It struck many as too harsh, especially since they'd never seen a woman die that way before. Within days, people began to discuss petitioning the governor of New York, Roswell Pettibone Flower, to appoint a commission that would look more closely into the question of Lizzie's sanity.

By July, Governor Flower agreed to do so, and appointed three doctors to take a long, hard look into Lizzie Halliday's psyche. Papers applauded this decision as a humane act, while still vacillating on the question of sanity/insanity themselves. Her insanity would explain so much, since her crime against the McQuillans felt so senseless. She didn't benefit from it, and she barely knew the women. On the other hand, she'd just been declared officially sane in the court. "Country folks" had one explanation for her mental state: simple "cussedness." "The lack of motive was evident to them," wrote one journalist, "and thus they went back to the theory of depravity."

Governor Flower's doctors observed Lizzie during the month of July, while she waited to die. They noted her rapid pulse, her "extreme emaciation." She was beginning to show symptoms of diabetes and suffered from an "excessive menstrual flow." She'd stuffed bits of her dress into her nose and ears. She seemed to be numb all over: flies crawled across her face and she didn't brush them away; the doctors pricked her with a knife and she didn't flinch. She drooled constantly, her nose dripped, she cursed everyone without being provoked, she kept repeating the number thirteen, and she seemed to think there was a river running outside her cell door. The doctors transcribed some of her ramblings:

> He broke a spine of my ribs. You've got that bear sewed up in me. It's you that done it. You sewed them up in me. You broke three of my legs. You pitched me down from the garret. You put a coat of shingle nails over me. They don't want you in their house. They're going to saw off my nose. Take them snakes off me. You brought them in a basket. You tied them around me.

The doctors acknowledged her intelligence – the intelligence necessary to plan and execute multiple murders – but also noted her inability to resist impulse. She didn't have the "power to choose," they said. The violence burst from her without her being aware of it. "Conscious-impulsive insanity," one doctor termed it. He was deeply offended that the previous testimony of a doctor named Mann – a "so-called expert" who had given in to "the demand of an excited and clamorous public" – had almost led to Lizzie's execution. There was no doubt in his mind that Lizzie was unable to control her deeply violent nature.

The other doctors agreed. They couldn't say for sure if Lizzie recognized the "nature and consequences" of her crimes, but they were positive she lacked the "power to choose between committing and not committing them." Because of this, they declared her insane.

This was the first time anyone had taken a nuanced view of

Lizzie's mental state, and it saved her. She was sent to the state criminal asylum at Matteawan and locked up for life.

Matteawan State Hospital for the Criminally Insane

Lizzie thrived at the asylum. Upon her arrival, she raved about bugs and muttered incoherently, but the superintendent sat her down and told her that if she wanted to be treated well at the hospital, she needed to act as politely as possible. Surprisingly, Lizzie listened. She began to clean herself, she stopped cursing at the doctors, and she even started doing little chores. Because she was still a celebrity, journalists would occasionally trek out to the hospital to report that the country's bloodiest murderess was now engrossed in her sewing.

But at the end of August 1895, mere days after one journalist wrote that Lizzie had "lost that fierce look which characterized her insanity" and was "quiet, industrious, and contented," Lizzie began plotting again.

She'd become pals with one Jane Shannon, who was also homicidal, and the two developed a grudge against a pretty young attendant named Kate Ward. Lizzie insisted that she had "become sane" and should be sent back to regular jail, and was sure all the asylum workers in general – and Ward in particular – were conspiring to keep her at Matteawan. So one day, Lizzie and Shannon snuck up behind Ward in the bathroom, ready to shed some blood.

Lizzie, strong as ever, threw Ward to the floor and stuffed a towel into her mouth. While Shannon held the girl down, Lizzie began to tear out her hair, scratch at her face, and pummel her with brutal force. By the time the other attendants realized what was happening in the bathroom, Ward was unconscious. Had they arrived any later, Ward would likely have died.

Lizzie did her time in solitary confinement for the attack, but eventually the superintendent allowed her back into the regular life of the asylum. She'd calmed down, she was behaving again, and the years began to pass uneventfully for her. She gained sixty pounds after months of having starved herself in jail. She got a bad case of the measles in 1896, and the press reported it dutifully.

In 1897, Lizzie became fixated on the idea of false teeth. She wanted every single one of her teeth replaced, convinced that a fresh set would make her look more attractive. So she began to fake toothaches, and told the doctors that the only cure for her would be the removal of every tooth in her head. The doctors inspected her and found all her teeth perfectly healthy, but Lizzie kept complaining, and about six months later, she finally got her way. She was taken on a little outing to a town called Fishkill Landing, where some brave dentist gave her a shiny new set of teeth.

A crowd gathered around the dentist's office to wait for her, and when Lizzie emerged she grinned widely, looking very pleased with herself. Perhaps she felt like she had officially moved up in the world. She would never have been able to afford false teeth years ago, when she was working as a housekeeper and running from husband to husband with her little boy on her arm.

The next autumn, a group of inmates wrote and starred in a "thrilling war drama" at the asylum. Lizzie Halliday watched from a row close to the stage. She hadn't cried or spoken a word during her own thrilling drama, but now, in the audience, she sobbed every time the hero was in danger. The press repeated this fact with relish. The moment looked like a poignant end to Lizzie's story – a redemption, even.

The Last Killing

Nellie Wicks was one of the best attendants at Matteawan. She was only twenty-four and had already been promoted to head attendant of the women's department. Wicks had dreams of leaving the asylum to study nursing, but she mostly kept those dreams to herself.

One of her star patients was Lizzie Halliday, who was now in her midforties. Lizzie had become so calm and reliable that she was given sewing privileges, which meant she had access to a whole basket of materials: fabric, thread, scissors. Sometimes she muttered a vague death threat, but the entire asylum had learned to ignore those. Lizzie never acted on them anymore.

By the autumn of 1906, Wicks announced that she had big news: she was going to leave the asylum and study to be a trained nurse. Lizzie was heartbroken and begged Wicks to stay, but Wicks assured her everything would be fine. As the date of departure grew nearer, Lizzie stopped begging and began to threaten her, saying she would rather kill Wicks than let her go. As usual, no one paid any attention to Lizzie's threats, especially not Wicks. She knew the two of them had a special bond, and she genuinely believed Lizzie would never harm her.

But deep in Lizzie's psyche, the old murderous impulses were beginning to wake. One morning, as Wicks walked into the bathroom, Lizzie crept in behind her, clutching a pair of scissors that she'd taken from the sewing basket. Wicks didn't notice that anyone else was in the room until Lizzie struck her hard on the head. When Wicks crumpled to the floor, Lizzie snatched her keys and locked the bathroom door from the inside. She then proceeded to stab Wicks over two hundred times: in the face, in the neck, and "where it would do the most good" – the heart.

Attendants heard Wicks screaming, but by the time they managed to break the door down, it was too late. Wicks was unconscious and bleeding heavily. She died on a cot twenty minutes later. Instead of becoming a nurse, she earned a dubious fame: she was now the first known United States female law enforcement officer to be killed in the line of duty.

When the coroner asked Lizzie why she'd done it, Lizzie responded, "She tried to leave me."

The Worst

Back to the old question of whether Lizzie was faking it. Over a century later, the insanity commission's report still rings true: Lizzie was intelligent, cunning, and at times self-aware, but unable to resist her own surges of violence. (And let's be honest – even if she *was* stone-cold sane, the very act of pretending to be insane for decades does seem, in itself, like a type of madness.)

But it's also likely Lizzie was faking certain things. She seemed aware of what "insanity" looked like in the public's opinion, and she performed it: the hysterical shrieks from the jail cell, the way she calmed down when she thought no one was looking. None of this negates the overall diagnosis of the insanity commission – none of this makes her sane! – but it does explain why spectators and the press were so torn about her. They were picking up on an underlying shrewdness, and this made it hard for them to fully accept that she had no idea what she was doing when she nicked the scissors to kill Wicks or lured the McQuillan women home with her or bashed Paul Halliday so hard on the head that his left eye fell out. She may have been "wild as a hawk," but she knew how to premeditate murder, which is what made her such a terrifying cipher.

Some people tried to explain away her crimes in far more sexist and, quite frankly, ridiculous terms – perhaps because "madness" was such a vague, threatening, and ultimately unsatisfactory explanation for murder. There were those who speculated that Lizzie's "wild mental condition" happened every time she was pregnant, but that all her children were born dead. Some were convinced she had a secret lover who helped her drag the heavy bodies of the McQuillan women out to the barn – because, they said, Lizzie wasn't strong enough to drag the bodies herself. Others claimed Lizzie had been a "young and comely member of a roving band of gipsies" in her youth, and somehow the seed of that freedom bloomed to violence in her heart. There were even those who believed Lizzie was actually Jack the Ripper, come over to America to wreak havoc on more female bodies. When someone finally asked her if she was the Ripper, Lizzie snapped, "Do they think I am an elephant? That was done by a man."

Perhaps the vaguest explanation for Lizzie's crimes – beyond simple "cussedness" – came from the newspaper headlines that followed her every move. In print, she was talked about in a language of excess, of superlatives: "Multimurderess," "Arch Murderess," "The Worst Woman on Earth." She became a symbol of the unimaginably awful, the greatest female horror that turn-of-the-century New York had ever seen. There was a glee to the term, with its echo of freak show terminology: "Come see the Worst Woman on Earth, appearing after the Two-Headed Lady! Fifty cents for a peek!"

A century later, multimurderess Aileen Wuornos would earn another major superlative – the *first* female serial killer – that demonstrated, as it did with Lizzie, the potent combination of media frenzy and "collective amnesia" that makes lady killers so intensely scrutinized during their lifetime and so eminently forgettable afterward. Wuornos was not the first, just like Lizzie was probably not the worst. But it sounded really good to phrase it that way. And it made people look.

Perhaps because she seemed so steeped in violence, so intrinsically homicidal, Lizzie triggered greater disgust in the courtroom and in the media than other female serial killers who claimed more victims than she did. Lizzie murdered – well, she murdered like a man. Most female serial killers use poison, not physical violence, and go after the people closest to them. Not Lizzie Halliday. Lizzie stabbed, shot, bludgeoned, and hunted down strangers. (No wonder she drew comparisons to Jack the Ripper.) Even her appearance confirmed this idea that she was somehow unfemale. There was nothing about Lizzie that charmed the public, no appealing detail to latch onto the way that people latched onto other, prettier killers. Lizzie was seen as squalid and savage: wild as a hawk, friendless as a cat, bleeding openly onto the carpet, letting flies crawl all over her face. Not simply nonfemale, in fact, but nonhuman.

And though she "only" killed five people (as far as we know), the fact that she kept murdering even after she was sentenced contributed to the idea of her as an unredeemable killer, someone who would *always* be bad – the worst, the very worst. Even the apparatus of law and medicine couldn't quell the ceaseless violence within her. They tried to contain her, but they couldn't stop her and they couldn't save her, because what she needed to escape – what she could never escape – was herself.

On June 28, 1918, poor, mad, shrewd Lizzie Halliday died of Bright's disease (a perpetual inflammation of the kidneys). She was fifty-eight years old and had been in the asylum for almost half her life. None of her relatives claimed her body, so she was buried in the asylum cemetery, where the graves are marked only by numbers. Decades later, the asylum closed down. After years of receiving superlatives in the papers, Lizzie lies beneath a nameless gravestone, overrun with grass and flowers.

DEVIL IN THE SHAPE
OF A SAINT

Elizabeth Ridgeway

Elizabeth Ridgeway was raised in a good Christian home but met the devil somewhere along her path. At the end of her life, she'd chalk up her wrongdoings to a "familiar spirit" – a witch's demon, so to speak – who laid with her throughout the night and whispered evil in her ear. Elizabeth didn't care one way or another about the church, preferring to stay home and stir her cauldron. She was a woman who took offense easily and lied effortlessly, all while fretting about the impossibility of love. And even though she lived in the seventeenth century and appears in only two surviving sources from the era, she feels surprisingly knowable, familiar spirit and all.

Elizabeth was born in a tiny British town named Ibstock during the second half of the 1600s. Her father was a farmer with the last name Husbands. Though Ibstock was a sleepy little town, it wasn't immune to the type of frightening country violence that seemed to flare up out of nowhere. When Ralph Josselin, a vicar from a village to the south, stayed overnight in Ibstock, he was shocked to learn that a man had been murdered right outside his lodgings while he slept. "I have cause for ever to praise God for the mercyes of this day," he wrote in his journal, shaken.

Violence, God, and men – these were the elements that made up Elizabeth's life.

Flirting in Seventeenth-Century England

Elizabeth lived at home until she was about twenty-nine, a spinsterhood long enough to make her little town assume she was a "Religious Maid, and a follower of the Presbyterians." But this was a façade; Elizabeth informed a preacher she was "indifferently inclined to the Church and Private Meetings." She had a bad temper and a very low tolerance for those who disagreed with her. When she and her mother had a spat – either "some falling out about their Household Affairs," or a lecture from her mother about "some other thing she disliked in [Elizabeth]" – the daughter immediately dispatched the mother with poison.

With Mother dead, Elizabeth kept house for her father, who was oblivious to the real cause of his dear wife's sudden demise. After another year at home, though, Elizabeth decided it was time to move on. She craved stimulation and might even have found her father kind of annoying, since he – like her deceased mother – surely made a habit of telling her what to do. So she left her father's farm and took a job in town, working and living as a servant in a wealthier household.

Her master was rarely home, so Elizabeth had the freedom to entertain all the male visitors her wild young heart desired. And entertain she did. Her favorite way to flirt was to talk about love and marriage, heavily implying that she thought this particular man might be the one, and making plenty of promises she never intended to keep. She did have a couple of favorites among her scores of paramours: she liked John King, and she *really* liked Thomas Ridgeway. King was a servant at another household in Ibstock, hovering at about the same social level as Elizabeth. But Ridgeway was a tailor with two apprentices, and his name carried a certain degree of cachet in the town.

While Elizabeth was flirting with her suitors, she was also harboring a major grudge against one of her male coworkers. It started over some minor disagreement, perhaps about household chores, but instead of confronting the other servant, Elizabeth bottled up her rage until she couldn't take it anymore. This was typical of her; she had always been characterized by a "dogged, sullen Humour." After all, she'd killed her mother under similarly petty circumstances. The servant who irritated her was a perfectly healthy young man in the morning, but after Elizabeth mixed white mercury into his broth, he began complaining that he didn't feel well, and died in agony a few hours later.

By the time summer was winding down, Elizabeth realized she'd let the John King/Thomas Ridgeway situation go on for too long. Both men clearly expected that she would marry them – she had been "so free" with them that their expectations were understandable, given the social mores of the time, and there was no easy way to extricate herself from this love triangle without breaking hearts and scandalizing society matrons – unless somebody died.

At this point, Elizabeth knew for sure that she preferred the richer and more influential Ridgeway. But she couldn't let King find out until she was ready to dispose of him, or else he might fly into a rage and, if he so desired, ruin her reputation. So she continued to lead King on with whispers and kisses, till she found the opportunity to "season him some Draught which sent him into the other World."

Poor John King, expecting a wife, found that his lover was a killer instead. His death was not pleasant. Not only was it sudden, but it was bizarre and highly memorable: his blood "turned black," his insides burned, his stomach was consumed by a violent, gnawing sensation. Elizabeth was relieved when he was finally in the ground.

With John King dead, Elizabeth spent the winter in coy servitude, knowing it would look suspicious if she immediately ran off with her other paramour. Finally, on Friday, February 1, 1683, she married Thomas Ridgeway. Her father had explicitly forbidden her to marry this man, but Elizabeth didn't listen or care.

Ashby-de-la-Zouch

The first three weeks of marriage passed in a blur of "seeming mutual Love," at least to outsiders. You could have caught the newlyweds strolling through the market at Ashby-de-la-Zouch and shopping for household goods, lost in a fog of wedded bliss. Of course, if you took the time to follow the couple through the market, you would have seen Elizabeth slip off to make a covert purchase from an old widow – two pennyworth of a mysterious white powder. But who was paying attention to those sorts of details at the time? The town flirt was married, the bachelor was happy, and it looked like all was well in the Ridgeway home.

Elizabeth, though, was not happy. After a year of hinting at marriage, she found that it wasn't what she wanted after all. Secretly, she was "frustrated of her expectations in her marriage: for she could not love her Husband as she ought." Now, being unhappy in marriage is no small matter, but Elizabeth did have a history of turning on people for the smallest inconveniences. Maybe Ridgeway chewed with his mouth open. Maybe he disagreed with her – Elizabeth couldn't stand that. Or maybe, without the scintillating foil of John King, Elizabeth realized that Ridgeway was actually a total bore.

To add insult to injury, Ridgeway wasn't exactly the wealthy, prestigious tailor she'd originally thought. Shortly after their marriage, his sister demanded that he pay her back a debt of twenty pounds – a sum that would have completely bankrupted him and his new bride. So instead of comfort and prestige, Elizabeth was suddenly faced with the prospect of poverty and embarrassment. Her unhappiness with the whole situation tortured her so much that she thought about poisoning herself to escape from the relationship. But she couldn't breathe a word of this to anyone. She'd just gotten married to a man she'd been pursuing for months, and to express dissatisfaction would have made her seem ungrateful, irresponsible, crazy.

If nothing else, Elizabeth was certainly solution-oriented. Before too many days had passed, she put aside thoughts of suicide and "converted her despair into revenge." There was an easy way to rid herself of her doomed marriage, and she'd played this game before. She waited until a peaceful Sunday morning, three weeks and two days after their wedding, when Ridgeway left for church without her. As Ridgeway worshiped, Elizabeth boiled a pot of broth and stirred in some of the white powder she'd purchased in Ashby-de-la-Zouch. When Ridgeway came home, Elizabeth smiled and served him dinner.

Ridgeway ate most of his meal, though he complained to his young apprentices that there was something a little gritty in the dish. Thirty minutes later, he began to throw up. He tossed and turned in "great torment" for hours, and finally died in anguish after midnight.

He was buried without suspicion. Elizabeth was widowed – and free.

The Body Bleeds

A few days later, Ridgeway's teenage apprentices ruined everything for Elizabeth. They, too, had noticed the gritty substance lurking at the bottom of Ridgeway's bowl. The boys suspected poisoning; Elizabeth, in turn, suspected the boys of suspecting her. So she attempted to shut them up with a bit of arsenic-laced porridge, and when they refused to eat it, she changed tactics, promising she would make it worth their while if they kept their mouths shut. It didn't work: one of the terrified boys ran to Thomas Ridgeway's relatives, saying he was pretty sure Elizabeth had just murdered her brand-new husband.

News of the poisoning soon reached the justice of the peace, a "Gentleman of great Judgment and Prudence" named Sir Beamont Dixey, who ordered an inquest by the coroner. The coroner gamely dug up Ridgeway, who had been dead for eight days, and took a peek inside his decomposing corpse. It was clear that Ridgeway had been poisoned, and Elizabeth was whisked away to the jail in Leicester.

During this time, some courts still practiced "cruentation," a medieval method of proving guilt. The accused murderer would be required to touch the victim's corpse, and if the accused was guilty, the theory ran, then the corpse would begin to bleed. Allegedly, Thomas Ridgeway's father forced Elizabeth to touch her husband's moldering body, an act that – shockingly! – "she was very averse to." A source claims that when she finally touched it, the corpse "burst out at Nose and Mouth bleeding, as fresh as if new Stabbed."

On Friday, March 14, Elizabeth pleaded not guilty before a jury of twelve, all of whom quickly agreed that she'd poisoned Ridgeway. She was sentenced to death by burning. There was some backlash against the harsh verdict, since certain "tender people" argued that the testimony of a sixteen-year-old apprentice shouldn't be enough to convict her, but the judge stood firm. Instead of granting her a retrial, he asked a clergyman named John Newton to counsel her during the last days of her life.

Now, this John Newton – not to be confused with the famous preacher and abolitionist of the same name in the 1700s – was a mild, self-deprecating man with the best of intentions. He was horrified by Elizabeth's crime, but he approached her with a certain grace. He wanted to provide her with the counsel she so desperately needed, to help her understand the gravity of her crimes, and to ease her transition from this life into the next.

Unfortunately, Elizabeth was still "indifferently inclined" to men of the cloth and had no interest in making John Newton's job easy. This was just so Elizabeth: unmoved by matters of life and death, uninterested even in the fate of her soul.

False Creature

Newton visited Elizabeth in jail every day for a week and a half, determined to extract a full confession. He was shocked to find that Elizabeth – this weepy woman who had been protesting in court that she'd never killed a soul – was actually quite difficult to work with. She took obvious pleasure in fabricating confessions, weaving elaborate stories to confuse him, and generally laughing in his face.

The first lie she told Newton concerned the death of John King: she claimed that her husband, Thomas Ridgeway, had murdered King without her knowledge. According to Elizabeth, she had no idea *why* Ridgeway would have wanted King dead, but just before Ridgeway died, he cried out in horror that "God's hand was just upon him, for the wrong he had done to that person so deceased." She even insisted, coy and ironic, that in a way she blamed *herself* for King's death. His ghost, she said, often appeared to her!

Elizabeth had several siblings, and when Newton talked to them, they quickly informed him that she was lying. She'd told them a slightly different story about her former lover: she still claimed that Ridgeway had killed him, but in this version, Elizabeth maintained that she knew all about the murder and had in fact condoned it. Since Thomas Ridgeway and John King were rivals for her heart, said Elizabeth, they understandably hated each other, and even after Ridgeway married Elizabeth, he still talked about getting revenge on his hapless opponent. (Her siblings must not have been paying very close attention to Elizabeth's life, because this timeline was impossible. King was already dead by the time Ridgeway and Elizabeth got hitched.) "For a time [I] endeavored to dissuade him," said Elizabeth to her siblings, who relayed all this to Newton, "but at last permitted him by saying these words, 'Do what you will with him.'"

When Newton tried to confront Elizabeth with her lie, she replied sanctimoniously that she "dare not judge" her husband for whatever he might have done, and refused to admit any guilt in the matter.

By now, Newton was irritated at Elizabeth, and probably mad at himself for believing her ghost story. He went home and stewed over the "reserved, stupid, uncertain, yea, and *false Creature* I had to deal with."

A week after Elizabeth was sentenced to death, another witness popped up with evidence against her: this person, her neighbor, had seen her buying poison at the Ashby-de-la-Zouch market. After this incriminating development, Elizabeth finally admitted that she had indeed purchased poison, but wouldn't admit what she had used it for. Newton nipped back into Elizabeth's cell to get the inside scoop, but all he got was an infuriating vagueness: she refused to confirm or deny the purchase of the poison, and she wouldn't even admit that she had *previously* admitted to the purchase. The pastor left in a huff, refusing to visit her again until she entered into a "better mind" and sent for him of her own accord.

Being a clergyman, Newton would have had plenty of people to visit during the week, but he couldn't shake the thought of Elizabeth, because he couldn't figure her out. He knew she wasn't actually stupid, "because she otherwise appeared sufficiently Apprehensive and Knowing." Maybe, he theorized, her silence stemmed from a desire to keep her own reputation as clean as possible; she didn't want to "imprint the mark of her Infamy upon her the deeper by her own Confession." What's more likely is that Elizabeth was hoping for a reprieve. She knew there were still certain "tender people" who thought her trial had been unfair; maybe she thought she'd be handed some sort of last-minute pardon if she kept her mouth shut.

That being said, she couldn't stop toying with John Newton. She pretended at least three times that she was ready to give a full confession, and each time Newton raced over to her cell, only to be disappointed. Ironically, if she was really hoping to save her own life,

Newton could have been a useful ally. She could have fed him a sob story, convinced him of her innocence, and begged him to talk to the judge on her behalf. Instead, she went out of her way to torment him.

During one of these fake-outs, Elizabeth began by telling Newton she was ready to reveal the whole truth and nothing but the truth, and ended up constructing her craziest tale yet. It went like this: There was a man from a town called Hinckly who was completely obsessed with her, and his obsession didn't stop when she married Ridgeway. Instead, the man from Hinckly turned into something of a stalker and decided that the only way he could have Elizabeth for himself was by killing her new husband. So one Sunday, when Ridgeway was away at church, the man snuck into Elizabeth's house and slipped poison into a bowl of broth. Elizabeth saw this happen and didn't stop it, nor did she hesitate in feeding the poisoned bowl of broth to Ridgeway.

Elizabeth informed Newton that she was under oath not to reveal the name of man from Hinckly, but if Newton watched very closely at her execution, he would spot the man in the crowd, "for his Countenance would betray his Guilt." Newton, bless his innocence, believed this bizarre tale, and was appalled that Elizabeth had sworn not to reveal the identity of her husband's murderer. "I discovered to her the wickedness of such an Oath," he wrote, "and that it could no ways bind her to such an Hellish Concealment." But Elizabeth still refused to name him, and Newton left, frustrated once again.

Clearly, Elizabeth liked to manipulate people. The drama with John King and Thomas Ridgeway was a perfect example of this: she skillfully navigated the social mores of her time to bring the men so deep into her web that (a) they both thought they were going to win her hand in marriage and (b) they both ended up dead.

The gleeful element to her manipulation – laughing in Newton's face, blowing air kisses (or whatever the seventeenth-century equivalent was) at Ridgeway and King – seems at odds with her suicidal thoughts and tendency toward gloominess. But she seemed to revel in the power she had over people, and perhaps it was the only thing she truly enjoyed. The agency she felt when she toyed with others must have helped her claw her way out of the "dogged, sullen Humour" and, yes, the "despair" to which she was so susceptible. Centuries later, researchers would divide female psychopaths into two broad categories, and the first – women who seek sensation, who are prone to boredom, who lack empathy, and who love interpersonal deception – describes Elizabeth to a fault. She often felt jaded, frustrated, and claustrophobic, and in those moods, she murdered the people who were encroaching on her life. Her mother told her what to do, criticized her character. Her coworker disagreed with her, invaded her professional space. John King *really* inconvenienced her by his annoying habit of believing what she said. And Thomas Ridgeway may have been the biggest headache of all: a man who was suddenly taking up space in her home, waiting in her bed, telling her what to do, expecting her to have the soup ready when he came home from church.

In another era, Elizabeth might have channeled her boredom and sensation seeking into some sort of high-powered career. Here, in her tiny town, with her reputation as first a "Religious Maid" and then an incorrigible flirt, there weren't many cures for ennui. Elizabeth certainly found one. It just wasn't very pretty.

The next day was a Sunday, and Elizabeth was taken to church along with an assortment of other criminals. Newton preached, and he flattered himself that his sermon on obedience had finally convinced Elizabeth to make an honest confession. Alas, Elizabeth still had no interest in telling the truth, even though she was scheduled to die the next day. She also refused to see Newton that night. Instead, she chatted with her father, cackling about how the man from Hinckly was nothing but a lie. Her father must have been appalled at his heartless daughter, wondering by now if she'd murdered her own mother, wondering why she was so comfortable laughing about death.

It wasn't until the morning of her execution – Monday, March 24, 1684 – that Elizabeth confessed. Perhaps it finally sank in that "she must die, and that her Denials would avail her nothing."

Newton, gratified that his tricky confessee was coming around at last, found her tearful and "in contemplation of approaching Death and Judgment." She admitted that she had killed her husband because of her inability to love him and because of the shock of his debt. She spoke of her suicidal tendencies: three years ago, around the time of her mother's death, she had purchased poison with the intention to kill herself, and she had again planned to poison herself with the arsenic from Ashby-de-la-Zouch before she ended up using it on her husband.

A pamphlet from London about the "most Barbarous and Cruel Murders" of Elizabeth Ridgeway gives us a far spicier recounting of her final confession. In it, she supposedly admits to another confessor that for the past eight years she had "lain with a Familiar Spirit." This demon first tempted her to poison herself, and, subsequently, "anyone that offended her." Elizabeth confessed that she was always carrying poison hidden in her hair, and would renew her stash whenever she went to market. She admitted to the murder of her mother, her coworker, and John King, and acknowledged that she had been planning to kill both of her husband's apprentices, too.

Despite the poison-in-the-hair detail and the demonic overtones, this wasn't the dramatic unburdening people had hoped for, as Elizabeth "did not seem very free in her Confession, mentioning only those with whose Death she had been charged." Many people were suspicious that during her eight years with the familiar spirit, she'd killed others. But Elizabeth had never seemed particularly concerned with the act of confession, and if any other crimes were burdening her soul, we'll never know them.

Lamentable Girl

Newton finally realized he'd never get an immaculate conversion narrative from Elizabeth. She simply wasn't going to fall on her knees and tear out her hair in guilt. And so, when he told the story of Elizabeth Ridgeway to his congregation, he apologized to his readers for the "Lamentable Form, as well as Matter" of his tale. The topic was unsavory – "horrid Poysoning" – and he wished desperately that he could present his parishioners with some sort of final atonement. He tried as hard as possible to make Elizabeth seem truly repentant, saying that she cried during her last confession and "did earnestly entreat me to make known [her confession] as the real Truth," but that's about as cathartic as it gets.

Unfortunately, Newton's portrait of a somewhat-penitent Elizabeth is contradicted by Elizabeth's final actions. The authorities kept her in prison for most of the day, hoping she'd confess to additional murders, but she said nothing. She may have been afraid to die, but fear didn't silence her; when Newton and another clergyman offered to assist her to the stake, she snapped that she didn't need them to make any sort of divine intercession for her, as she could "Read and Pray as well as they could." A hungry crowd came out to see her burn, yearning for last-minute revelations, but Elizabeth disappointed them by declaring that she'd already confessed in prison and wouldn't repeat or add anything to it.

Before the time came for her execution, Elizabeth was forced to witness the execution of two brothers – a last-ditch effort to terrify her into admitting more crimes. One of the brothers was offered an awful clemency: he could go free if he would act as an executioner for both Elizabeth and his own brother. The man refused, and the siblings were hanged together, with Elizabeth watching.

The accounts of Elizabeth's day insisted that she was the worst, the most evil. (Sound familiar?) Centuries later, her crimes seem practically quaint. It's a perfect example of the obliterating nature of history: after a while, as we grow overwhelmed with the horrors of our present day, the past loses its bite, becomes almost picturesque.

But if we try to categorize evil, we can say that Elizabeth probably wasn't "the most" of anything at all. She was angry, yes, and sullen and callous and suicidal. She was quick to jump into relationships and quick to end them. But she certainly wasn't the most "barbarous Example" of violence and death that the century had ever seen, despite what people claimed. She doesn't even seem particularly bloodthirsty. Rather, she comes across as numb – insensitive to death and willing, at least twice, to end her own life. We see this in the extraordinary indifference she had toward John Newton, who was probably kind of annoying in the way he kept popping into her cell and pressing her for a confession, but who also wanted desperately to bring her some measure of peace. A woman who can laugh about lying to a pastor the night before her execution does not seem like the type of woman who fears death very much. Maybe she did carry poison in her hair, after all.

Just before the end, Elizabeth raised her voice. She begged the authorities to let her be hanged first and then thrown on the fire, but they refused. Instead, they tied her to the stake and lit the kindling around her feet. When the flames touched her, she let out a piercing scream and tried to leap away from the fire. This meant – somewhat mercifully – that she choked, because a rope was tied around her neck and the smoke was beginning to crowd her lungs. Then, unconscious, she burned.

VIPERS

Raya and Sakina

In the poorest district of Egypt's Alexandria, there once lived a woman known for burning too much incense. It didn't matter if it was day or night; the house of this woman, Raya, was always wreathed in thick, sweet smoke. Her neighbors thought it was odd, but they had their own lives to contend with. There were cafés to run, neighborhood toughs to appease, authorities to avoid.

Though the city of Alexandria was praised for its beauty and sophistication, if you crossed paths with Raya and her younger sister, Sakina, you were probably looking for vice. Theirs was the criminal underworld: streets of runaways and prostitutes, rooms smelling like resinous hashish. Their district, al-Labbān, was full of shady businesses designed to service the occupying British troops, and the Alexandrian elite mostly ignored whatever unsavory trouble was brewing there. The police usually ignored it, too. After all, it was 1919, and there was a revolution to take care of.

See, the Egyptian people had been led to believe that their country would become a self-governing nation after World War I ended, and when that didn't happen, nationalists rose up against the British occupation. Strikes, riots, and demonstrations exploded across the country, and for quite some time the police were more preoccupied with politics and rebels than with brothel madams and drug dealers. "Where are the police?" bemoaned the journalist Fikri Abaza. "The government has been too intent upon training the hordes of its secret political police to concern itself with training forces necessary to safeguard our internal security or personal safety."

It was pretty obvious – at least to those who could read the coded and illicit activities simmering under the authorities' noses – that Raya and Sakina were mixed up in something sketchy. But people were just too busy to care. Even if the incense *did* seem a little peculiar. Even if *occasionally*, from one of the sisters' apartments, they heard someone scream.

Pearl of the Mediterranean

Raya was born around 1875, and little Sakina came along a decade later. Their family lived in an isolated village in Upper Egypt, and their childhood was both unregulated and full of overwhelming adult responsibilities, the way childhoods often are when parents are abusive or absent. Their folks were both: their father was gone, and their mother was a narcissist who failed to show them much, if any, love. They had an older brother, but he couldn't hold down a job. Money was always tight, so Raya and Sakina took on the burdens of their family together, scraping together an income in whatever ways they could. Needless to say, they were forced to grow up fast.

As the family moved aimlessly around Upper Egypt, the girls found work selling roasted vegetables or waitressing in cafés. Eventually, Sakina turned to prostitution, sleeping with clients in exchange for food. When their self-absorbed mother occasionally deigned to contribute to the family's income, she'd pull off a robbery or two. Raya and Sakina would often join her.

This transient life spooled on for them until Sakina grew tired of living hand-to-mouth. First she got married, then she got divorced, then she took a lover and ran away with him. They landed in the city of Tanta, broke up, and Sakina began working as a prostitute again. By 1913, she was in the hospital being treated for venereal disease, where she met her second husband, Aḥmad Rageb. When she recovered, the two of them ran off to Alexandria.

Soon enough the entire globe was rocked by World War I, and Rageb left to join the Labor Corps. He returned home a couple of times, but his visits were never pleasant: on the first, he found his wife working as a prostitute; on the second, he discovered that she'd moved in with another man and wanted a divorce. Rageb gave in. By 1916, Sakina was married a third time to a man named Muhammad 'Abd al-'Āl who worked at a number of cotton factories.

Clearly Sakina was a bold one, unafraid of social and marital repercussions. (Rageb could have taken legal action against her for adultery, but he didn't – maybe because he was just too mild-mannered, maybe because he was afraid of her.) She was always willing to talk openly about her sex life, and this fact, coupled with her long history of divorces, affairs, and remarriages – not to mention her various stints as a prostitute – would later contribute to the general idea that she was way too sexual for her own good. Libidinous, if you will. Concupiscent. She also picked up a nasty alcoholism habit at some point, which only contributed to her image as, well, totally out of control. The owner of her favorite bar noted that she could drink ten to fifteen glasses of wine in one hour without passing out.

While Sakina moved around in the world, Raya stayed home. She too got married, and when her husband died, she married his brother Hasab Allah – a not uncommon practice in those days. Hasab Allah wasn't such a catch. He had a reputation for thievery and hashish smuggling, and he'd already been banished from at least one city. But Raya was familiar with the life of petty crime, and the two stayed together and had a daughter. Sakina's city- and husband-hopping were apparently not for her older sister, as it wasn't until 1916 that Raya and Hasab Allah decided to join Sakina in Alexandria. He would work at the port as a day laborer. She would find her own sort of employment – as she always did.

Alexandria, the Pearl of the Mediterranean, was chaotic and cosmopolitan and cerebral, forever haunted by the ghost of its famous burned library. But for Raya and Sakina, its beaches, parks, hotels, and museums may as well have been in another city altogether. People like them, who hailed from Upper Egypt (the Ṣa'īd, in Arabic), were known as Ṣa'īdīs, and Ṣa'īdīs were at a distinct disadvantage in the city: they tended to make less money than Alexandrian natives, they had trouble assimilating completely due to their darker skin and distinct accents, and they were accused of all sorts of moral failings, viciously stereotyped as "feeble-minded, lustful, hot-tempered, and vengeful."

But if Raya and Sakina were easily placed as outsiders, at least they weren't alone. Alexandria was a land of opportunity for thousands just like them: almost one-third of its population originated from somewhere else. The city was "porous," writes scholar Nefertiti Takla; there were boundaries, yes, but one could move through them. The railway station brought in workers from all over Egypt, while European sailors poured in through the port. And from the port, a main street ran like an artery straight into the dense heart of al-Labbān, where outsiders and locals alike could find all the debauchery their hearts desired.

Gold Bracelets

The sisters settled in al-Labbān, took a long hard look at the social and economic climate, and decided that the best thing to do would be to open a brothel. After all, World War I was still raging, there was a military camp full of occupying British soldiers nearby, and those soldiers wanted a few things badly: booze, drugs, and girls. The sisters' most successful brothel was located next to said camp, and it was known as – wait for it – the Camp. Money poured in from the lusty, eager soldiers. The sisters thrived. Raya would say later that during the war, she always had money in her pocket. Sakina made extra cash by selling gold on the black market and attempting to open a café. At one point, she even hawked rotten horse meat to unsuspecting home cooks, for which she did a short stint in prison.

Like many a good lady killer before them, the sisters had hustle. They saw a demand; they created supply. Business boomed during their first three years together in Alexandria, and it was all thanks to them, since both of their husbands were off working as manual laborers for the British army.

We don't know much about the characters of these husbands, but consider this: during the war, one of their jobs was to carry dead soldiers off of the battlefield, picking their way through the carnage and the screams and the blood. When they returned to their wives, surely they brought some of that trauma back with them. Raya certainly preferred the years when her husband was away, though she framed it in financial terms: when he returned, she no longer had money in her pocket, because he took it from her.

The Camp, though popular, was technically a covert operation. Though prostitution had been regulated in Egypt since 1882, running a legal brothel was a bit of a headache. It required paperwork, taxes, and weekly medical exams for the workers. Plus, it meant you had to openly admit you were running a brothel, which meant you were more or less giving up on any chance of joining bourgeoisie society. Because of this, most owners and sex workers preferred to work underground. By keeping their business secret, the sisters were able to fill the brothel with sex workers of a slightly higher class, who prostituted themselves covertly because it let them appear respectable in public. These women were basically contractors: when they used the rooms owned by the sisters, they'd pay Raya and Sakina half of what the clients gave them.

Although we often think of prostitution as coercive, being a sex worker was a well-paid gig at the time – one of the best-paying jobs a woman could get, actually – and even lower-middle-class women dabbled in it. The occupation's profitability was advertised by the large amount of gold that sex workers wore in public. As they made more and more money, workers would invest in thicker and thicker bracelets, ostensibly guarding their money by keeping it close to their bodies, but also showcasing the very value of said bodies. If you were a john, you wanted to sleep with a girl who had so many bracelets that she jangled.

The world may have rejoiced when World War I ended in late 1918, but the sisters did not. Fewer British troops meant fewer clients, and fewer clients meant that their prostitutes started looking for better-paying gigs. The husbands returned and took over the running of the business, which was probably frustrating for the sisters, who had thrived on controlling the means of production in their own clandestine way. Then the police shut down the Camp, and so the sisters teamed up with their landlord, Amīna bint Mansūr: she ran a hashish café on the first floor of a building while Raya and Sakina plied their trade on the second, luring the café's customers upstairs. When this, too, was eventually shut down by police, the sisters moved their business to their own homes, which created spatial difficulties. Surely people were starting to get annoyed at each other after long weeks of scheduling the use of the rooms and stepping on various toes.

During the war, the sisters' workers were often able to pay for their *own* gold jewelry, because business was going so well. After the war, though, money was tighter for everyone, and so the sisters started buying jewelry *for* their workers. The girls were now in their debt, and Raya and Sakina began to treat them less like contractors and more like servants, occasionally forcing them to perform manual labor along with sex work. Worse, the sisters and their landlord would sometimes sell their girls to other brothels – wrenching them away from families and lovers – in order to make a little extra cash.

Needless to say, the environment in the brothel was growing increasingly hostile, and this wasn't helped by the presence of a number of neighborhood toughs, known as *fitiwwa*, who were more or less a cross between mobster and Robin Hood. They would protect residents and settle disputes – Raya and Sakina used them to guard their clients and keep their neighbors quiet, ensuring that no one called the police on the brothel – but the fitiwwa would also abuse the neighborhood's most vulnerable members. These men were known to rape the girls, and they weren't afraid to hurt Raya if she disagreed with them. For Raya, who'd gotten a taste of independence during the war, this new male-dominated business model may have been highly offensive, even unbearable.

In short, everything was changing, everyone was on edge. Alexandria itself was rocked by the revolution of 1919, and laborers from street cleaners to postal workers went on strike, temporarily paralyzing the entire country's economy. The old underground order of World War I – the brothels near the camp, the black market for rotting horse meat, the absent husbands – was being replaced by a new order, and bringing along all the inevitable friction that results from a changing of the guard. But whatever their personal disappointment with this new order, Raya and Sakina were scrappy, and they recognized a shifting economic climate as well as anyone. They needed a new plan.

Seventeen Dead Girls

Toward the end of 1920, the police began receiving complaints about a terrible smell emanating from Raya's home. Neighbors had always thought it was a little unusual that Raya was constantly wreathing her home in such heavy clouds of incense, but she quickly explained to them that since her customers drank and smoked in her house, she used incense to mask the scent of their revelry. At first the neighbors believed her. But eventually they smelled something not even incense could disguise – a cloying, heavy, rotten odor.

Seemingly unrelated was the fact that in early November, a house on nearby Makoris Street needed a new water and sewage system, and so the family that owned the house asked their nephew Ahmad to start construction. Ahmad had terrible vision, but he began the job gamely, digging beneath the floor of one of the rooms. Before long, his shovel hit something hard, and a disgusting smell seeped into the air. Since Ahmad's eyesight was so bad, he reached over to pluck the offending object from the dirt – and realized to his horror that he was holding a human arm.

The police tore over. (Well, knowing what we now know about these police, perhaps "ambled" is a better verb.) Ahmad informed them that the last person to live in the room was a woman named Sakina, who had been evicted about a month earlier. Meanwhile, other police officers were investigating the stench coming from Raya's home, and when they found the source of the smell – multiple corpses buried under Raya's floorboards – the sisters were suddenly people of interest.

This wasn't the first time Raya and Sakina had been hauled off to the police station for questioning. Over the past year, there had been numerous cases of missing women who were reportedly last seen with the sisters, but every time Raya and Sakina were brought into the station, they managed to convince the police that they had nothing to do with the case. Sakina had always been especially persuasive, and now, being interrogated about the body beneath her old apartment floor, she maintained her innocence. However, when the police informed Raya that corpses had been found in her room, too, the older sister broke down, and the two were arrested.

All in all, seventeen female corpses were linked to the sisters, including corpses found in the room of their former landlady. Newspapers even published photos of the bodies, which leer from the dirt, nearly mummified but still visibly human. In some of the pictures, you can make out hair. Again, journalists bemoaned the lack of police attention: "Where was the police when these crimes were committed? Some of these bodies have turned into skeletons, showing that the victims were murdered a long time ago." The decomposed state of the corpses was a slap in the face to people who believed the police had been looking out for them. If these women had been dead long enough for their bodies to turn into *this*, wasn't that visible evidence that the authorities didn't care who lived and who died in the streets of al-Labbān?

Suffocation

Two years earlier, one of the girls who worked for the sisters showed up wearing a new set of gold bracelets. The girl may not have noticed Raya staring at her jewelry, but Raya certainly noticed the gold – and grew paranoid, certain that this particular prostitute was keeping more than her fair share of the profits. A month later, the girl was dead.

Today, the sisters' crimes are retold as crimes done in pursuit of gold and gold alone. Raya and Sakina are remembered for the creepy way they haunted nearby marketplaces, looking for women who jangled with costly jewelry, luring them back to their apartments, and plying them with drugged wine before killing them and stripping their bodies of every gemstone, every anklet, every delicate filigree.

The truth was, not all the victims were killed for gold, and plenty of them weren't strangers, either. Many, if not most, were slain because they had crossed Raya, who may have been the decision maker of the group – the one who determined who to kill, and when. Raya was frequently plagued by suspicion, convinced she was being cheated left and right. For example, one of the squad's few nonprostitute victims was a woman named Zannūba, a poultry saleswoman and friend of the sisters, who stopped by Raya's house to collect a debt and was killed that same day. Raya was also merciless to sex workers who broke their agreements with her; at least twice, when one of her contractors disappeared for a while without properly excusing herself, she was murdered immediately upon her return.

When they were ready to claim a life, the sisters would offer the unfortunate victim a glass of wine laced with drugs. As their prey grew dizzy and disoriented, the sisters and their husbands (and/or the fitiwwa) would go to work. They allegedly developed an efficient four-person killing system that took place with minimal noise and very little blood: someone crammed a wet cloth into the victim's mouth; two others pinned her hands and feet; the fourth strangled her to death. (Who, exactly, was in the room when the murders happened? Though many within the sisters' circles were interrogated, including their former landlady and numerous fitiwwa, eventually the court determined that the squad consisted of six people: the sisters, their husbands, and two fitiwwa named 'Urābī Hassan and 'Abd al-Rāziq Yūsuf.)

The autopsies of the victims support this narrative, more or less. The pathologist determined that the victims were (a) all female, (b) between twenty and fifty years old, and (c) had all died of asphyxiation. He found no evidence of cutting or beating or bludgeoning, and guessed the women had all been plied with alcohol before being suffocated. The testimony of Raya's daughter also supported this; the girl claimed she'd seen her father, Hasab Allah, spike glasses of alcohol with white powder before giving them to the victims, who would clutch their stomachs in agony before finally passing out. Even Hasab Allah himself eventually admitted that this was true.

But Hasab Allah and the other accused men quickly faded into the background as a shocked, horrified nation zeroed in on Raya and Sakina, the deadliest sisters they had ever seen. In the eyes of middle-class Egypt, these sisters were so much more than criminals: they were a glaring symbol of everything that was wrong with a society where women walked, unveiled, through the streets.

"Their Evil Was Transported Everywhere"

It wasn't long before the entire country had heard about Raya and Sakina. Until that point, the Egyptian press almost never focused on crimes committed by and within the lower class, but editors recognized just how titillating this story could be, and they pulled out all the stops reporting it. Murderous sisters who dealt in sex and violence? The headlines wrote themselves.

Even Egyptians who couldn't read knew about Raya and Sakina, not just because newspaper articles were often read aloud at coffee shops, but because the papers printed the sisters' mug shots – quite possibly the first time the Egyptian press had *ever* published photos of criminals. "Newspaper boys on every street cry out 'Raya and Sakina, Raya and Sakina for a piaster,'" ran the Cairo weekly *al-Haqā'iq*. "And thus their evil was transported everywhere, to the houses and to the kids in the schools and to the factory workers and in every neighborhood they took notice of this crime. And the hearts in people's chests sensed it and its echo has reached even the dead in their tomb."

The fact that this case was scandalous, horrifying, and thus extremely exciting wasn't the only reason it spread. The arrests of Raya and Sakina – and the realization that their victims were also women, many of whom were prostitutes – tapped into existing anxiety about the erosion of Egypt's moral values, especially when it came to the changing role of women. See, by 1920, women were starting to patronize traditionally male spaces like markets, bars, and coffeehouses – and the fact that they were now getting murdered seemed, to some people, to be exactly what they deserved. The press blamed the victims for their own deaths, saying that if they hadn't been walking about so shamelessly and/or working as prostitutes, they never would have encountered the deadly sisters. "What is the force that compelled these women to enter these whorehouses and bring about their own destruction at the hands of the murderers?" ran one editorial. "The answer is easily comprehensible . . . it is the loss of decency on the part of men and women." Another editorial insisted on the moral failings of the victims: "Raya . . . found those with weak souls."

"Loss of decency" is an awfully weak hook on which to hang serial murder. The fact was that these victims were moving about in a newly "porous" society where women had to work to survive, prostitution was often the most lucrative offer on the table, and the police weren't paying very much attention. It was partially this attempt to stay flexible in an unstable society that led to their downfall. Raya and Sakina themselves had marinated in a similar cultural broth for a long time: trained in petty crime from childhood onward, they learned how to slip under the radar of the police and were forced to make alliances with very abusive, very dangerous men in order to live. This was the world they knew, and it led them to crimes so dreadful they were said to have "blackened the forehead of the twentieth century."

Given this anxiety about the dark potential of women's increasing liberation, the media focused less on the sisters' actual roles as murderers and more on their vice-ridden behavior, reasoning that their "greed and pursuit of pleasure were uniquely female traits that had grown out of control in the absence of male supervision." The courtroom was shocked by Raya's constant cursing and Sakina's brash descriptions of her sex life, and there was a pervasive fear that, if released, Raya and Sakina would somehow manage to pervert other women. The specter of the sisters as hugely corrupting forces even spread its tentacles overseas. Papers in Arkansas and Wisconsin reported that some of the victims had been tourists who were "lured in on sightseeing trips," implying that the sisters had managed to reach across the Atlantic and prey on innocent Americans. It was as if being murdered was contagious – something girls could catch from their peers, like a cold, or the desire to wear a miniskirt.

When they weren't being portrayed as "uniquely female" deviants, the press compared the sisters to animals: vipers, tigers, snakes, and wolves. The paper *al-Rashid* published an illustration of Raya as a beast with claws, towering over a trembling girl and hissing, "There is no escape for you from my talons." One editorial screamed, "Raya, you are not human . . . you are a beast in the desert, a fox that embraces deception, a treacherous wolf."

This rhetoric was surprisingly effective. At one point, a rumor spread around Alexandria that Raya and Sakina were being displayed at the zoo. People dashed over to catch a glimpse of the infamous duo, but found only animals in the cages.

"Women's Crimes Generally Demand an Element of Mercy"

The criminals went on trial in May 1921. People crowded around the Alexandria courthouse for a glimpse of the ticketed event, and the newspaper *al-Ahram* published the full trial transcripts every day to a captive readership. Police monitored the crowds in fear of a riot, but the audience was of one mind that week. "There is not one person asking for a drop of mercy for Raya and Sakina and the rest of the individuals in the gang," ran the paper *al-Muqattam*.

There was, however, some controversy over the appropriate punishment for the sisters' crimes. No woman had ever been given a death sentence, but the prosecutor, Suleiman Bek Ezzat, was willing to fight for it. He sketched out a brief history of female criminals to demonstrate that Raya and Sakina were different: "Firstly, women's crimes generally demand an element of mercy and compassion, such as crimes in which women are driven to kill their husbands' second wives or in which they poison someone who has brought them harm. Secondly, the death penalty [used to be] executed publicly." That is, the awful sight of a woman being executed publicly was reason enough to avoid it. Nobody felt Raya and Sakina had earned the right to mercy or compassion – opportunism was a much less sympathetic motive than jealousy or self-defense – and death sentences were no longer performed outside the prison, so Ezzat argued that any social hesitation to execute a woman was no longer relevant.

The trial was spotted with vague statements, inconsistencies, and sketchy behavior. During Sakina's testimony, she wolfed down a large meal that had been set in front of her, implying that perhaps she'd been starved in jail as a means of extracting a confession. The two fitiwwa declared outright that they were starved and verbally abused. The criminals' statements were all over the place: Raya and Sakina insisted they hadn't been present at the times of the murders; the fitiwwa expressed their innocence; Raya and Sakina pointed at the fitiwwa; their husbands declared that the fitiwwa hadn't done a thing. The defense had little to go on, and mostly just tried to shift the blame around from defendant to defendant – not Raya, but Sakina; not Sakina, but Hasab Allah; and so on and so forth.

Witnesses came forward to give chilling testimonies. One neighbor said she'd seen the husbands deliver Zannūba, the unfortunate poultry saleswoman, to Sakina's house. For hours, the neighbor overheard the group drinking and carousing, but at dawn she was stopped cold by a terrible scream. "When I asked

Sakina about it in the morning she said it was nothing," said the neighbor. Another witness explained that Zannūba "knew too much about their activities . . . they killed her to silence her once and for all."

Though the judges ultimately decided that Raya and Sakina were accomplices, not perpetrators, it didn't lessen their sentences. Supposedly Ezzat overheard Sakina saying that she planned to be released in fifteen to twenty years, at which time she'd start working as a prostitute again. Upon relaying this information to the court, Ezzat demanded that the judge "sever these two corrupt members from the nation."

The court did just that. When the magistrate handed down six death sentences for Raya, Sakina, their husbands, and the fitiwwa, fifteen minutes of sheer pandemonium broke out in the courtroom. A new precedent had been established: women without mercy would receive no mercy.

Things Even Men Can't Do

The guards brought Sakina out of her cell on the morning of December 21, 1921. Her hands were shackled.

"Toughen up," said one of the guards. "Be strong."

Upon hearing this, Sakina turned on him. "I am a strong woman," she snarled. "If I can take on a hundred, I can take on a thousand."

Say what you will about Sakina, but she certainly knew herself. "Be strong"? What was Sakina if not strong? She worked horrible jobs as a child. She moved away from home years before her sister could work up the courage to do so. She demanded a divorce. She sold rotting horse meat in order to survive. She held her tongue at the police station while her older sister cracked and confessed everything.

Something in Sakina must have been loosened after hearing the guard lecture her, because she spoke again and again during her final moments. "I murdered," she cried when her death sentence was read aloud. "I murdered, but it's okay because I fooled the government of al-Labbān." (In another account, she says, "I fooled the police.") As she was being handed off to the executioner, she thundered, "This is the place where strong people stand. I'm a strong woman, and I've done things that even men can't do."

It's an epic final monologue on her part, full of fire and defiance, and when her words were published in the papers, Sakina – the slut, the alcoholic, the corrupter of respectable women – suddenly looked like an antiestablishment hero. After all, fooling the absentee police was exactly what she'd done; she'd been dragged into the station for questioning numerous times, and every time she convinced the police to let her go. She may have even gotten away with it one last time if it weren't for her sister. Now, the media was giving Sakina grudging glances of admiration. The paper *al-Ahrām* lauded her as "one of the craziest and most courageous people to stand at the scaffold."

After the sisters were hanged, they entered into public mythology almost immediately. Six months after their death, a traveling troupe of actors debuted a play about the sisters, declaring that one of its core themes was the "rage of women." More art followed: commentary from famous contemporary writers, books, films, a 2005 TV show. The 1953 film *Raya and Sakina* portrays a battle between the heroic police and the evil sisters, who – in the film – are captured right before they kill again. This was nothing like the real case, which shed a harsh and unflattering light on

Alexandria's police force. "Where were the police? How could this happen in the twentieth century?" mourned one journalist – continuing the mournful refrain that had played alongside the case from start to finish.

(It happened again in the twentieth century, actually, a mere twelve years after Raya and Sakina swung from the gallows. In 1933, another pair of killer sisters rose out of the lower classes in France. The two Papins also had a rough childhood and an abusive mother. When they brutally claimed two victims from the middle class, they too turned into bizarre symbols of a revolution against the bourgeoisie. Alas, poor journalist – the twentieth century was only going to get worse.)

Today, separated from Raya and Sakina by a century of violence, it's tempting to pore over their mug shots and look for glimmers of their personalities, their innermost thoughts, or even their merciless hearts. After their death, the poet and literary critic Abbās Mahmūd al-Aqqād warned observers against this tendency. There was nothing intrinsically barbaric in the faces of Raya and Sakina, he said, nothing that screamed "murderer." If you saw evil in their faces, it was merely a projection.

But even the poet himself fell victim to the fallacy he was trying to warn the public against, admitting that there was a degree of "insensitivity" apparent in their faces, though "insensitivity, by its very nature, does not catch the eye." See? It's impossible not to look, and we see what we seek there. In the photos, the sisters stare back at us forever: upset, afraid, defiant.

The sisters' faces – and everything we project onto those faces – still terrify people today. Their very names have fallen out of favor with young Egyptian parents. *Raya, Sakina*: these are now the phonetics of evil. Tourists trudge around al-Labbān to gape at a house that may or may not have belonged to them. And so their myth lives on, clinging to the streets where they used to hustle, hovering behind people's shoulders, and beckoning to the respectable women who head outside, who can't help peering into the shadows. Even in death, the sisters wield power. Now and then a mother, irritated at her young daughter, will tell the girl that if she doesn't start to behave, Raya and Sakina will find her.

THE WRETCHED WOMAN

Mary Ann Cotton

Some say Jack the Ripper was England's first serial killer, but that's only because the others have been forgotten.

About forty years before Jack came along, England suffered through a terrible spate of murderers. This crew, however, lacked the Ripper's slick, gory charisma – slaying prostitutes and then mocking the police by mailing them a kidney or two – and so they never achieved his level of immortalization. They were poor, migratory, and desperate. They did it for the life insurance, or to have one less mouth to feed. They got caught. They were women.

When nineteenth-century England experienced a decade known as the Hungry '40s, a brief national spotlight fell upon female criminality. The silk, cotton, and wool industries had declined in 1839, leading to widespread economic depression, and a handful of reckless ladies began to kill as a means of harsh survival. At least nine were convicted of serial murder. There was Sarah Dazely, the "female Bluebeard" who killed multiple husbands. There was Mary Milner, who poisoned her in-laws. Even as the economy creakily improved, women continued to murder, like Catherine Wilson, a nurse who dosed her patients with sulfuric acid instead of medicine. And by the time the 1860s rolled around, the deadly sisterhood was joined by a pretty young woman named Mary Ann Cotton who couldn't bear to have anyone standing in her way.

The fact that it had happened before didn't make it any less shocking. Besides, this girl was worse.

Fine Dark Eyes

Mary Ann Cotton, née Robson, was born in 1832 to poor teenage parents who moved frequently so that her father, a miner, could find work. She was an exceptionally pretty kid, and almost a century later, an old neighbor still remembered her "fine dark eyes." Although her father fell down a mining shaft to his death when she was nine, and her little sister died young, Mary Ann would later characterize her early childhood as "days of joy." They were free of the obligations that would haunt her for the rest of her life: marriage, motherhood, and money.

The days of joy ended for Mary Ann after her father died, when she had to help support the family. She was a hard, skilled worker; as a teenager, she took jobs as a Sunday school teacher, a dressmaker, and a maid for a wealthy family. This last gig gave Mary Ann a glimpse into the luxuries that money could buy, and it changed her forever. She was never rich as an adult, but she always splurged on cleaning women. In a world characterized by crushing poverty, unsanitary conditions, and rampant sickness, she took great comfort in the knowledge that every so often, a maid would stop by the house, get down on her knees, and scrub the floor.

When Mary Ann was nineteen, she married a man named William Mowbray. The ceremony took place twenty miles from her home, possibly because Mary Ann was already pregnant and wanted to avoid a scandal. No family or friends were present. This would be the first of many times Mary Ann stood at the altar pregnant and, except for her lover, entirely alone.

Marriage seemed like a way out of poverty, but marriage to William Mowbray turned out to be just another form of destitution. Mowbray took his teenage bride to a shantytown in the southwest of England, where Mary Ann gave birth to four or five children, all of whom died without being registered. (At the end of her life, she couldn't remember the exact number of babies she'd had during this time.) When the Mowbrays finally moved back to the north, it was with one living daughter, Margaret Jane, who died soon after the move from "scarletina anginosa and exhaustion."

It's not hard to imagine the psychological toll that the rough landscape, the seemingly inescapable poverty, and the infant deaths took on Mary Ann. Her first foray into motherhood had ended almost as soon as it begun – she had taken a lover and ended up with five or six tiny graves. Perhaps this gave her the feeling that her children were disposable: ill suited to the world and barely worth remembering.

The couple continued to move so that Mowbray could work one rough, poorly paid job after another. He eventually found a position on a steamer ship, so the two of them settled in a town near the coast, where they had three more children: Isabella, a second Margaret Jane, and baby John Robert, who died one year later of "diarrhoea." The reuse of the baby names implies a certain dispensability of the babies themselves. The first Margaret Jane died in 1860; the second was born in 1861. It was an odd rebirth.

Mowbray was away at sea for months at a time now, and soon

enough Mary Ann took up with a red-haired miner named Joseph Nattrass who lived in a neighboring town. Nattrass may have been the love of her twisted life, or just the closest thing to luxury she could find in that little town. Either way, she fell hard for him, and they would stay in touch for years. His arrival also coincided with a curious change in her personality. Before Nattrass, Mary Ann had followed her husband from shantytown to shantytown; after him, she began to take matters into her own hands.

How, exactly, did Mary Ann change from someone who watched those around her die to someone who *caused* those around her to die? Perhaps her venture into murder was a way to move closer to Nattrass by shucking off her previous identity as someone else's wife. Or maybe she couldn't take Mowbray's long ocean absences anymore and eventually snapped under the pressure of single motherhood. Maybe she just truly hated those around her, and one day she simply thought to herself: *enough*.

Whatever spurred the sea change in her, it stuck. Mary Ann quickly learned what arsenic could do to the human body, and how easily it dissolved into hot tea.

Fevers

Mowbray died in 1865 – maybe innocently, maybe not. His cause of death was listed as "typhus fever and diarrhea," which doesn't *quite* fit the symptoms of arsenic poisoning unless the doctor who filled out the death certificate confused "typhus" with "typhoid." Typhoid fever did in fact look a lot like arsenic poisoning, and doctors of the time often used the terms "typhus" and "typhoid" interchangeably. Regardless, his death was exceptionally convenient for Mary Ann. She collected a large sum of insurance money, scooped up her two young daughters, and moved to the town where Nattrass lived. Before long, the second Margaret Jane was dead of "typhus fever," just like her father, and Mary Ann shipped Isabella off to live with her grandmother. Isabella would live to be nine – the oldest of Mary Ann's murdered children.

But just as Mary Ann found herself child-free and living in the same town as her red-haired crush, she discovered a truth far more unpleasant to her than death: Nattrass was already married. This put a wrench in her plans, but Mary Ann approached it in her usual prosaic fashion. Instead of pursuing Nattrass further, she immediately moved back to her former town and took up nursing. She turned out to be a wonderful nurse, with a knack for making her male patients feel extraordinarily comfortable.

One of her patients was a "well proportioned and muscular" man named George Ward, and he was totally smitten by the arrival of this pretty new worker. One minute he was groaning in his sickbed, and the next he was being nursed to health by an angel. He proposed almost immediately. Again, no one from Mary Ann's family attended the service, which was quick and kind of depressing. The "witness" on the marriage certificate was the groom from the wedding right before theirs.

During her brief marriage to Ward, Mary Ann never got pregnant. This was unusual for her, and some biographers wonder if it meant Ward was disappointing in bed. This sort of speculation is often flung at female serial killers, implying that their dark need to kill is linked to a ravenous sexual appetite and that one can be exchanged for the other (i.e., when Mary Ann didn't get her kicks from Ward in the bedroom, she got her kicks from poisoning him). But Ward was certainly disappointing in some way or another, because he died after a mere fifteen months of marriage, suffering from the classic symptoms of arsenic poisoning: diarrhea, stomach pains, and a tingling in his hands and feet.

With her second husband out of the way and the majority of her children dead, Mary Ann continued this new, fatal hustle. She moved again and applied to work as the housekeeper for a wealthy father of five. His name was James Robinson, his young wife had recently died, and he was everything Mary Ann was looking for in a man. She moved into the Robinson home before the Christmas of 1866, and a week after her arrival, the youngest Robinson child was dead, with only twenty-four hours between the first sign of sickness and the fatal convulsion. Mary Ann already had her eye on Robinson, and now she was clearing the playing field of all other distractions.

The death of his child didn't dampen James Robinson's passions, though, and Mary Ann was pregnant by early March. But then her mother got sick, and Mary Ann was called away to nurse her. Perhaps she resented the interruption, because nine days later – despite Mary Ann's supposed skill as a nurse – her mother lay six feet underground. The neighbors were suspicious. Mary Ann had not only loudly predicted the death of her mother a few days before her passing, but had then proceeded to rummage through her dead mother's possessions in a way that the neighbors found tactless and overeager. Still, Mary Ann ignored their whispering, grabbed her daughter, Isabella, and ran back to Robinson.

April 1867 was a bad month for the Robinson household. Within the span of ten days, three of the children were rolling about in bed, foaming at the mouth, and vomiting compulsively. Nine-year-old Isabella, the last Mowbray, died of "gastric fever"; six-year-old James Robinson died of "continued fever"; his eight-year-old sister, Elizabeth, died of "gastric fever." All of these "natural causes" were easy cover-ups for arsenic poisoning. The fact that the deaths came in such quick succession shows us how heavy-handed Mary Ann could be with the poison and how impatient she was with the requirements of quasi step-motherhood – but it also shows us just how frequently children died back in those days. Even this triple death didn't make anyone particularly suspicious. Life limped on.

James Robinson married his children's murderer in another solitary ceremony sometime during August 1867. Their first daughter was born that November, and she was dead of "convulsions" within months. (Mary Ann used pregnancy as a way to secure marriage, but she wasn't especially interested in raising the children.) Robinson was solidly in denial by this point. Later, he would admit that "at the time, he would not let his mind dwell on some thoughts: that he dare not."

By 1869, Robinson and Mary Ann had another child together, baby George – and they were also beginning to argue fiercely about money. Robinson was learning that Mary Ann made a habit of minor financial deceptions: she ran up little debts, she kept money she claimed to have spent, and she enlisted his last surviving son to pawn clothes for her. They fought about the latter incident furiously, and Mary Ann grew so upset that she ran away, taking baby George with her. While she was gone, Robinson boarded up the house and moved in with his sister. Later, in a plaintive letter, Mary Ann would spin this action as betrayal on his part: "I left the house fore a few days I did not wish to part from him . . . When I returned ther wos no home for me."

After a few months away, Mary Ann sashayed back into town with baby George and dropped him off at a friend's house in order to "mail a letter." She never returned for the child. Eventually,

George was reunited with his father. Mary Ann must have realized she was never going to get back together with Robinson – who certainly should have suspected by this point that he was married to an insatiable killer – and so she was freeing her hands for her next project.

"It Is No Fever I Have"

Now, at thirty-seven, Mary Ann worked and wandered. She was free of husband and children for the third time in her life, and rumor has it she moved in with a lusty sailor and then stole all his wealth when he was away at sea. But it wasn't long before she jumped back into the domestic fray. The home was, after all, her battleground, her wrestling mat – the place where she did her best and bloodiest work. She was the dark underbelly of the Victorian era's feminine ideal: the idea that nothing was sweeter, nothing was purer, than a good woman at home.

Mary Ann began to correspond with an acquaintance from her younger days – a wealthy spinster named Margaret Cotton. Margaret had a brother, Frederick Cotton, who was a widower with two sons and, like Robinson before him, desperately needed a housekeeper. Poor Margaret probably thought she was doing her brother a favor by sending over the qualified and charming Mary Ann, but she had no idea what horrors Mary Ann was about to bring down on the entire Cotton family.

Mary Ann became Frederick Cotton's housekeeper at the beginning of 1870, and four weeks later, his loving sister Margaret was dead. Margaret's money went straight to her brother and her brother went straight to Mary Ann, who was soon pregnant. She married Cotton in the fall, despite the fact that she was still technically married to her previous husband. Later, this would be the only crime she'd confess to: bigamy. A few weeks after the wedding, she took out life insurance on his sons.

In 1871, the new fivesome moved to West Auckland: Mary Ann, Frederick Cotton, his sons Frederick Jr. and Charles Edward, and the new baby, Robert Robson. In West Auckland, Cotton found work as a hewer at a coal mine, but the move also profited Mary Ann – because, conveniently enough, they moved onto the same street as a certain redheaded miner from her past. Joseph Nattrass was no longer married, and Mary Ann had no compunctions about getting rid of her latest husband. She'd buried men before.

Mary Ann had always been a quick killer, relying on the realities of poor hygiene, the misdiagnoses of doctors, and the high rate of infant mortality in Britain's tiny towns to explain the fact that death followed her wherever she went. But now she was getting even more reckless. She no longer had time to stay married for a few years or to let her children celebrate one last birthday before she snuffed them out. Frederick Cotton died quickly, and just as quickly Nattrass moved in with her and the children as a "lodger."

Now, Mary Ann surely intended to marry Nattrass when she killed Cotton. Murder and remarriage had been her modus operandi up to this point, and for a while marrying Nattrass must have seemed like the final step to achieving the life she wanted. Nattrass excited her. He represented love and rash adventure, and he may have unknowingly inspired her to become a killer. But Mary Ann wanted more than just love. She craved money, too, and before she could marry Nattrass, she met a new man. He was richer than Nattrass, and at this point in Mary Ann's life, that was everything.

The new man, a tax collector, went by the name of Quick-Manning. He'd been suffering from smallpox when he met Mary

Ann, who was still taking on nursing jobs, and she charmed him the way she charmed all her patients. Meanwhile, the town's sympathy for Mary Ann was beginning to drain away. They had felt terrible for her when she arrived in town and almost immediately became a widow with three tiny children to care for, but when Nattrass moved in with her, people started growing suspicious. And her seduction of Quick-Manning really put everyone on edge.

Worse, it was pretty obvious to neighbors that Mary Ann was mistreating the Cotton children. The poor kids looked like they were starving. When a neighbor gently brought it to Mary Ann's attention, she responded that the Cotton kids were "weak-stomached" and didn't have much of an appetite. The reality was that Mary Ann had always had a low tolerance for children of any sort, whether they were hers or not, and she needed to clear the way to Quick-Manning. So she killed Frederick Cotton Jr. ("gastric fever"), poisoned her baby Robert Robson ("convulsions and teething"), and began to poison Nattrass himself ("typhoid fever") – all within twenty days of each other. A neighbor girl came by to help nurse the sick children, and noticed that the baby was barely breathing, staring off into space with glazed, unmoving eyes. "He's dying," said the girl. "Who shall I fetch?" Mary Ann responded, "Nobody."

Joseph Nattrass knew his lover was poisoning him, but by that point there was nothing he could do. He was too close to death. Every so often, his body would shake with a paroxysm that caused him to clench his hands, grit his teeth, and draw his legs up, while his eyes rolled back in his head until only the whites were showing. Another neighbor who stopped by to help noticed that there was something unnatural about his illness. "I saw him have fits, he was very twisted up and seemed in great agony," she reported. "He said,

'It is no fever I have.'"

As Nattrass convulsed, the tiny corpse of Robert Robson lay stiffly nearby. The baby had died four days earlier, but Mary Ann was waiting for Nattrass to perish so she could bury them at the same time. She wanted to save a little on funeral expenses.

One Last Child

Once all that messy business was over, Mary Ann got pregnant. Quick-Manning was the father, and she was all primed to marry him, but there was just one final problem standing in the way: her stepson, Charles Edward, the last Cotton boy. She resented everything about him, and must have cursed herself for leaving one kid alive for this long. Neighbors noticed how cruelly she treated little Charles: beating his ears, pulling at his hair, and, on Easter, throwing his one tiny treat – an orange – into the fire.

One afternoon, a local grocer and druggist named Thomas Riley stopped by Mary Ann's house to ask if she could nurse another smallpox patient. As they chatted, Mary Ann kept bringing the conversation back to Charles Edward: how much of a burden he was, how the responsibility *weighed* on her. Charles Edward cowered in the corner of the room, listening. Mary Ann batted her eyes and asked Riley if he could possibly put the child into the workhouse. Riley said no.

Unfazed, Mary Ann replied, "Perhaps it won't matter, as I won't be troubled long. He'll go like all the rest of the Cotton family."

Six days later, Riley was walking past Mary Ann's house and caught sight of her in the doorway, openly distraught. She told him that Charles Edward was dead, and begged him to come inside and look at the body.

Inviting people in to witness her victims had always been one of Mary Ann's tricks. She was unperturbed by doctors and encouraged them stop by and recommend cures for the "typhoid fever" and "convulsions" her patients always seemed to be suffering. This was one of the ways she avoided detection – playing the bereaved nurse, mother, and wife. By inviting Riley to come inside and witness the corpse, she was placing a bet on herself: that Riley would read the death of the sickly, starving child as natural – inevitable, even – and wouldn't dream of accusing his weeping stepmother.

But with this death, and her casual remark about the "rest of the Cotton family," Mary Ann had gone too far. Riley was certain that she'd murdered her tiny stepson. He refused to look at the body, and instead went straight to the police.

An inquest was held, and Charles Edward's poor little body was laid out on a table. The postmortem was a sloppy one, because the boy's death was ruled "natural." Still, the doctor must have had his suspicions, because he was careful to preserve some of Charles Edward's viscera, which he buried in jars in his own yard.

Mary Ann went on her way, but her days of freedom were numbered. The town gossips and local papers had already picked up on Riley's suspicions, and people eventually convinced the doctor to investigate Charles Edward's body again. So the doctor dug up the jars, analyzed their contents using a more systematic technique, and found arsenic in everything. He ran to the police station at midnight, and Mary Ann was arrested the next day.

The Short Drop

Initially, Mary Ann was only accused of the murder of Charles Edward, but soon enough the charges expanded to include the murder of Joseph Nattrass, Frederick Cotton Jr., and the baby Robert Robson. Their bodies were exhumed and tested, and huge amounts of arsenic were found in all three. Police tried to exhume Frederick Cotton Sr., but in a bizarre twist, they couldn't find his body anywhere, despite digging up several graves in the process.

Mary Ann gave birth to Quick-Manning's child in prison, and during her trial she would breast-feed the baby in front of the court, refusing to talk. It was a savvy move, working the jury's sympathies by tapping into Victorian ideals of femininity. (The era's perfect woman was captivated in all her stifling glory in the 1854 narrative poem "The Angel in the House," which gushed, "For she's so simply, subtly sweet/My deepest rapture does her wrong.") How could this silent, breast-feeding mother be capable of *murder*? Reporters watched her in the courtroom, noting her "delicate and prepossessing" beauty, which was deliberately obscured in the portraits of her that ran next to their articles.

Her defense latched onto the fact that no arsenic had actually been discovered in her house at the time of Charles Edward's death. They argued that the boy had been accidentally poisoned by arsenic fumes rising off the green wallpaper in his bedroom and by flakes of the arsenic-and-soft-soap mixture Mary Ann used to clean house. The prosecution brought in a prestigious doctor to discount this theory. There was simply too much poison in the corpses, the doctor said. Joseph Nattrass's body, for example, contained four times the amount of arsenic necessary to kill a man.

The only time Mary Ann broke down was when the defense gave a melodramatic speech about the implausibility of a mother killing her own child. "A mother nursing [her baby] . . . seeing its pretty smiles, while she knew she had given it arsenic!" they wailed. "Making its limbs writhe as it looked into her face, wanting support and protection!" How could any "simply, subtly sweet" Victorian mother possibly be accused of such horrors? At this point in the proceedings, Mary Ann started to cry. Sympathetic onlookers may have interpreted her crying as agreement with the defense: *Yes, exactly, I could never do that to a baby*. Really, though, the defense was describing exactly what Mary Ann had done numerous times, to numerous babies. She knew all about the ways that "pretty smiles" could turn into writhing and vomit and foaming at the mouth.

Ultimately, Mary Ann was convicted of "the awful crime of murder" for the death of Charles Edward. "You seem to have given way to that most awful of all delusions," said the judge, ". . . that you could carry out your wicked designs without detection." She blanched as she heard her sentence read aloud: death by hanging.

The hangman chosen to execute Mary Ann Cotton was a controversial figure with several botched executions under his belt. He preferred to use a "short drop" from the platform, which occasionally had the unpleasant side effect of *not* breaking the prisoner's neck. When this happened, the hangman would have to press down on the shoulders of the dying as they strangled slowly, spinning at the end of the rope.

During her final days, Mary Ann wrote frantic letters to family and friends, asking them to petition for a reprieve. She had no idea what was going on with her trial; at one point, she wrote that the lawyer for the prosecution would be "thare to defende mee."

She continued to insist she was innocent, and her letters took on a martyred, incredulous tone as she complained about the "lyies that has been told A Bout me." She also begged her one surviving husband, James Robinson, to visit her and to bring baby George. Naturally, he refused.

She did make one final maternal gesture, though, when she arranged for her last child to be adopted. But even this was tinged with malice. Apparently, days earlier, she had been caught "rubbing its gums with soap," thinking that if her baby grew ill, "her life might be spared until its recovery."

Mary Ann had been a mother, now, for exactly half of her life. Whether she liked it or not, her existence up to this point had been largely defined by being secretly pregnant, or publicly pregnant, or recently pregnant, or pregnant with another man's child. Seduction and, by extension, pregnancy, had been one of her most faithful weapons (the other was a nefarious white powder available at any pharmacy). Mary Ann used her fertility to control the rise and fall of her life. Giving away this last baby was a powerful sign that everything – the seduction, the marriage, the birthing, the poisoning – was very much over.

Was Mary Ann a sociopath, addicted to the rush of killing the innocent? Was she a capitalist, climbing the social ladder of husbands in a desperate attempt to gain some autonomy? She was clearly striving for something, but it's unclear what she wanted most. Money? Freedom? Other people's pain? She saw marriage and motherhood as a form of imprisonment – one that she desperately wanted to break free from – but also as a form of salvation, and so her methods were cyclical to the point of madness. She killed one husband only to marry the next; she poisoned one child and soon became pregnant with another. What did she think would happen with that next husband, that next baby? Was she expecting something to kick in deep inside her: a final sense of satisfaction, comfort, maternal instinct, love? No matter how many horrors she inflicted on other people, nothing ever *really* changed for her. And so she never escaped her hall of mirrors, forced to relive her own sordid history time after time.

Frightfully Wicked

Mary Ann walked the four minutes from her cell to the scaffold on March 24, 1873. She was forty years old, wearing a black-and-white-checked shawl that disguised the fact that her arms were bound to her sides with a belt. Those types of shawls were considered fashionable in surrounding towns, but after Mary Ann was photographed in hers, the trend quickly died off. A crowd of people gathered outside the jail to catch a glimpse of her. The journalists inside wrote that she looked like "a doomed wretch," sobbing hysterically as she shuffled forward. On the scaffold, she shuddered when the rope went around her neck. Her last words were "Lord, have mercy on my soul" – and then the ground dropped from under her feet.

It took her three minutes to die, and the executioner had to steady her twitching body with his own hands.

"The announcement of her execution may dispel a popular idea, long too prevalent, to the effect that a female assassin, however frightful her wickedness, may generally hope for a reprieve in consideration of her sex," ran the *Burnley Advertiser* a few days later. "But the atrocities of Mary Ann Cotton put her beyond the pale of human mercy, for, unless she was fearfully maligned, no more hideous monster ever breathed on earth." Of course, England had no idea that in fifteen years their most famous serial killer would start disemboweling prostitutes in the poorest areas of London. *He* would then be the most hideous monster to ever breathe on earth, and would capture the attention of the press in a way that Mary Ann Cotton never did.

About a week after she died, a moralizing play called "The Life and Death of Mary Ann Cotton" opened. For a while, children sang about her on the street: "Mary Ann Cotton, she's dead and she's rotten/lying in bed with her eyes wide open." But soon enough she was forgotten, and the cycle of birth and death went on as before in the little towns of England.

Dame Darcy

THE TORMENTOR

Darya Nikolayevna Saltykova

Darya Nikolayevna Saltykova liked the ritual of church: the liturgy, the tithing, the regular pilgrimages. She was, in a way, a creature of habit. Predictable. Ticking through life like a clock. Once a year, for example, she'd head out of town to visit the sacred reliquaries and cathedrals of the Russian Orthodox Church. At home, she maintained an almost meditative torture practice, beating her servants for hours and killing the ones who bothered her most. Even her torture was predictable: she beat the ones who failed to clean her house properly. Tick. Tock.

Some might look at her behavior and see the worst sort of religious hypocrisy: paying lip service to good while worshiping evil. But Darya saw nothing duplicitous about her behavior. She was merely acting out of a message she'd internalized: that she was legitimately better than others, and as such could act as she pleased. Why should she wring her bloody hands and pray for forgiveness? *She* was the one who chose to forgive – or not. She felt as untouchable as a god.

The Young Widow

Darya's world was a privileged one. She was a wealthy Russian noblewoman, she was related to statesmen and princes, she had an army of servants at her disposal, and the law was firmly on her side. She could expect to be treated with dignity and given the benefit of the doubt no matter what she did – because even if the law didn't technically support all of her actions, her fellow Russian nobles certainly would. These aristocrats didn't like to set precedents they couldn't take back – like, say, the risky precedent of holding nobles accountable. No. They liked life as it was: safe for them, and dangerous for everyone else.

Darya was born in March 1730, the third of five daughters. She married well: her husband, Gleb Alexandrovich Saltykov, was the captain of the Cavalry Regiment of the Russian Imperial Guard. The Saltykov family was famous and well connected, related to a veritable who's who of other noble families: Stroganovs, Tolstoys, Tatishchevs, Shakhovskies, Musin-Pushkins, Golitsyns, and Naryshkins. Surely this marriage brought with it a considerable amount of social pressure and even stress for Darya, as she mingled with future statesmen and the grandchildren of ancient tsaritsas. And Darya wasn't an educated woman. She never learned how to read.

Darya and Saltykov had two sons – Theodore and Nicholas – but their marriage didn't last long, as Saltykov died in 1756. Darya was suddenly a widow at the age of twenty-five. We can imagine that she felt, at some level, both overwhelmed and abandoned. She had her young boys to take care of, and she was suddenly in charge of two very sizable estates. Her dead husband had owned a mansion in Moscow on Kuznetskaya Street and a summer estate that presided over the village of Troitskoye. Immediately, unexpectedly, both of them were Darya's.

When she wasn't running her new estates, Darya was taking her annual pilgrimage to one Orthodox shrine or another. She liked the city of Kiev, famous for its religious architecture, and she sometimes traveled to see the beloved icon Our Lady of Kazan, one of the most sacred relics in the entire country. The gilded portrait featured a pensive close-up of the Virgin Mary with a tiny Christ standing solemnly on her lap.

Perhaps Darya enjoyed the grave, almost foreboding look in their eyes. Maybe she liked the thought of a Christ who never smiled. At the very least, she probably relished being away from home, because as soon as she returned, her responsibilities came closing in on her. Both the Moscow and the Troitskoye estates came with souls. Hundreds of souls. And Darya owned them all.

Souls

Darya lived during a time when a nobleman's wealth and influence weren't measured by how much land he owned, or how much money he possessed, but how many serfs worked for him. Serfs were Russian peasants who lived and labored on their proprietors' land. They owed the proprietor toil, money, or a combination of both, but they weren't *technically* slaves because they could hypothetically save up to buy their freedom. You know, the way Sisyphus could hypothetically rig some sort of structure to keep his boulder from rolling back down the hill for all eternity. Serfs had existed in Russia for centuries, but by the mid-1700s, Russia was approaching what you might call peak serfdom. Serf owning had turned into a form of conspicuous consumption, and it was totally out of control. For example, during Catherine the Great's reign, the richest noblemen prided themselves on their serf orchestras and serf ballets.

But this was an awkward time for Russia to be conspicuously consuming millions of peasants. Catherine the Great was about to take over the throne, and she wanted to show the world that Russia was an enlightened country and that she was a humane and modern ruler. And yet – the serfs! Somehow the issue of serfs' rights never quite caught up with Catherine's vision for a shiny new Westernized country. Even in the most liberal circles, the sight of serfs working in the gardens and plowing the fields would have been a constant visual reminder that it was never possible to leave human cruelty entirely behind, no matter how modern your world had become.

These serfs were referred to as "souls," and a nobleman's power over his souls was practically unlimited. A few years before Darya's birth, one imperial decree noted that nobles were under no obligation to treat their souls like humans, but that "the proprietors sell their peasants and domestic servants not even in families, but one by one, like cattle."

Nobles would physically punish their serfs all the time, often using a thick Russian leather whip called the knout. This was considered more than acceptable, although the nobles weren't allowed to actually kill the serfs. Catherine the Great noted in her memoirs that many households in Moscow kept a selection of "iron collars, chains and other instruments of torture for those who commit the slightest infraction." She'd been struck by one particularly bizarre case: an aging noblewoman kept her hairdresser locked in a cage in her bedroom, because the noblewoman didn't want society to know she wore fake hair – and the serf was the only one who could have exposed her.

To add insult to injury, serfs had no way to defend themselves under the law. The authorities, forever paranoid about a murderous uprising, were convinced that legal protection for serfs would lead to feelings of safety, and feelings of safety would lead to insubordination. So not only could their masters send them off to Siberia without a trial, or force them to work in the mines for the rest of their lives, but if any serf dared complain about this to the authorities, that in and of itself was reason for punishment. Even Catherine the Great, who prided herself on her humanity, published an imperial degree saying that if a serf tried to present a petition against his master, he would be whipped and transported to the mines of Nerchinsk for life.

Therefore, as a serf, your quality of life was entirely dependent on the whims of your master or mistress in all their odd, distrustful, spoiled glory. Granted, there were plenty of benevolent landowners in Russia during those days, and their serfs enjoyed peace, prosperity, support, and copious free time in which to cultivate their own land. But Darya wasn't one of them. There was blood on the walls and the stairs of her estates.

"I Am My Own Mistress"

Darya was obsessed with cleanliness, and liked her floors the way she liked her Orthodox icons: immaculate. She also had a hair-trigger temper, and the resulting combination was bad news for the female servants who cleaned her house. The sight of an improperly washed floor or an imperfect batch of laundry would send Darya flying into a vicious rage. She'd grab the nearest stick, rolling pin, or whip, and begin to beat whatever quivering girl was responsible for the botched job.

All around the country, nobles were whipping their serfs for similarly trite infractions – but Darya didn't know when to stop. It wasn't long before her neighbors in Moscow began to hear horrible rumors about the Saltykova serfs: Darya locked her maidservants in an empty hut and starved them for days, Darya's girls had bloodstains on their clothes. The villagers of Troitskoye were whispering, too. Something was wrong at Darya's summer home, they said. Once, they heard that a cart coming out of the estate was carrying the body of a servant girl. When they peered inside, they saw that the girl's skin was flayed, her hair ripped out.

The fatal beatings, or at least the bulk of them, started in 1756, the same year Darya became a widow. The first official complaint against Darya was registered in 1757, and it concerned the murder of a pregnant woman named Anisya Grigorieva. It was a double murder, really: first, Darya beat Grigorieva with a rolling pin until Grigorieva suffered a miscarriage. Then, religious Darya called a nearby priest to come and give the dying woman her last rites, but Grigorieva passed away before the priest showed up. Once the priest appeared, he took one horrified look at the body and refused to bury it without a police inspection.

The police arrived, took the abused corpse to the hospital for an autopsy, and – didn't do a thing about it. The dead woman had a deep wound by her heart, and her entire back was blue and swollen. Clearly she hadn't died of natural causes. But what were they going to do, arrest a noblewoman? Absurd!

When Grigorieva's frantic husband went ahead and filed a complaint with the police, Darya found out right away. She filed a counterpetition asking the police not to believe the husband's testimony, but instead to punish him and then send him back to her. Perhaps money exchanged hands at that point. Either way, the police listened to Darya and did nothing about the husband's complaint. When they returned him to the estate, Darya sent him into exile, where he soon died.

This could have been the moment Darya was brought to justice.

She had just killed a pregnant woman, and there were multiple witnesses to both the crime and the aftermath: the husband, a serf who'd been forced to beat Grigorieva too, another serf who buried the baby, the priest, the police, and the doctor(s) who performed the autopsy. If this complaint had been properly investigated, tens – or possibly hundreds – of lives would have been saved. But no one bothered. These were serfs, after all. Nobles were already selling them "like cattle."

So Darya killed and killed again, confident in her impregnability and furious at her serfs for each petty mistake, for getting in her way, for being her responsibility, for existing. If she was a god, then her serfs were her pitiful playthings. She could make them clean; she could make them cook; she could make them scream and bleed and beg. Typically, she would force another servant to begin the beating, and then she'd take over until the victim died. Sometimes she commanded her male serfs to beat their wives or relatives in front of her. In Troitskoye, she threw boiling water onto a peasant girl and then beat her to death. Villagers remembered seeing the body: the scalded skin had actually begun to peel off the bones.

Mostly, Darya killed women, but occasionally she'd turn on a man. One of her male serfs, Chrisanthos Andreev, was in charge of overseeing the unfortunate housemaids, and when Darya became convinced he was doing an inadequate job, she beat him and threw him outdoors to stand in the cold for the entire night. The next morning, Andreev was brought back inside, nearly frozen, where Darya clamped a pair of red-hot tongs over his ears. She then proceeded to pour boiling water over his body and, when he fell to the floor, she kicked and punched him. When she'd finally had enough, she asked another manservant to drag the bleeding man away from her. As soon as the poor peasant was out of Darya's sight, he died.

It went on and on, a litany of horrors. Darya lit one woman's hair on fire and pushed an eleven-year-old girl down a stone staircase. She fed her servants once a day so they were perpetually weak. She would grab logs of wood – tucked in every room, meant for fireplaces – and use them as makeshift clubs. Neighbors heard her screaming, "Beat more!" When one of her male serfs dared to insult her, Darya grabbed his hair and began smashing his head against a nearby wall.

Though her stablemen and housemaids repeatedly escaped and cried murder to the local authorities, they were captured and brought right back to Darya, where they would be beaten and shackled, or even sent into exile. "You will not do anything to me!" Darya scoffed at one stableman who attempted to report her. "No matter how much you report or complain about me, the authorities will not do anything to me. They would not trade me for you."

Her fearlessness wasn't irrational bravado. As Grigorieva's death proved, the system supported Darya, and by this point Darya had been falsifying evidence and bribing key authority figures for years. If the priests refused to bury one of her victims, then her superintendent, Martian, would file counterfeit papers about the death, saying the girl died suddenly of sickness and didn't have a chance to make her confession, or the priest was late, or the girl was so sick she couldn't speak, making a final confession impossible. Sometimes the papers would claim that the victim had run away, when in truth she was buried right there in the graveyard. The paper describing the death of the eleven-year-old girl that Darya pushed down the staircase said that the girl had simply . . . stumbled.

If the complaints reached the officials, Darya bribed the officials. She kept a ledger of the gifts she sent to these powerful men: food, money, even serfs themselves. In fact, one official was so accommodating that he would actually visit Darya and teach her how to deal with the denunciations that kept popping up against her. "Had Saltykova not been sheltered and helped by her protectors, there would have been fewer beatings and deaths," raged one of her stablemen, who had seen the atrocities go on, unchecked, for years.

At one point, while watching yet another girl get beaten to death, Darya started to scream. "I am my own mistress," she cried. "I am not afraid of anyone." This belief that she was superior, unassailable, and even *consecrated* by the law was integral to her sense of self. Perhaps she killed to prove one simple point: that she could.

Love and Gunpowder

Today, in the dark corners of the Internet, you can find people attempting to pin Darya's many crimes onto something kind of melodramatic, palatable, and easy to understand: a broken heart.

After her husband's death, Darya took up with her handsome young neighbor, Captain Nikolai Andreyevich Tyutchev, whose Troitskoye estate brushed right up against hers. All their serfs knew they were having an affair. But their love didn't last, and the couple broke up just before the Lent of 1762, when Darya was about to turn thirty-two.

The captain didn't stay single for long, and Darya took great offense to this fact. Then she learned that not only was the new woman younger than her, but the captain was planning to *marry* this beautiful upstart. Darya couldn't take it. She paced around, determined to enact some sort of horrible revenge on them both, and finally hit upon a deranged plan: she was simply going to have to blow them up.

Blinded by vengeance, Darya sent one of her men to purchase five pounds of gunpowder, which she then mixed with sulfur and wrapped in hemp cloth. She commanded her serf to hide the flammable mixture around the new woman's house, and then to lie in wait until the captain arrived. Once the lovers were ensconced inside, the servant was instructed to set the house on fire, blowing them up in flagrante delicto.

This scheme was too crazy, even for Darya's hardened male servants. The first servant she sent over simply refused to burn the house down, so Darya beat him to a pulp when he returned. She then sent him back, along with another servant, but they claimed that their attempts to start the fire had failed. Frustrated, Darya changed her approach. If bombing wasn't going to work, maybe assault was the ticket. She commanded a new crew of serfs to lay in wait along the roadside until the couple drove by in their carriage, and then to leap out and beat them both to death.

At this point, the serfs decided that their only way out of this unhinged revenge fantasy was to secretly inform the captain that Darya was plotting against him. So they did, and the captain immediately strode to the police and filed an accusation against his ex.

Darya was unflappable when the police questioned her about it. "I did not send the peasants Roman Ivanov and Leontiev to set fire to the house of Ms. Panyutina, nor did I commanded others to beat them," she responded coldly. She claimed that during the time of the alleged assassination attempts, she'd been sick, holed up in her Moscow estate with a priest nearby. In other words, she was a good religious woman who would never dream of revenging herself on a single soul, no matter how horribly he'd betrayed her.

Clearly, Darya was a bit *upset* with the captain. But this broken heart was in no way the wound that turned her into a vicious serial killer. She had been murdering serfs long before any of this happened. The event simply serves as a neat hook on which to hang the hat of our speculation: that in order for Darya to be able to commit such atrocities, she must have been driven half mad by something else.

"Madness," in fact, is a common explanation for Darya's crimes.

When the people of Moscow found out about them, they thought she was insane, and people today still wonder the same thing. (Surely every serial killer in history has been thought insane at one point or another. How else to explain the repetitive, horrible, practiced violence?) But rather than insane, Darya comes across as horribly logical. The drama with the captain demonstrates her terrible ability to plot and outline and rationalize: she purchased the correct materials, revised her plan as necessary, and smoothly denied her guilt. Even the logic behind her serf killings was pretty consistent. If a servant did not clean properly, she deserved to die. If a servant complained to the authorities, he deserved to die. The serfs were her property, and she was allowed to give them performance reviews. It was all perfectly reasonable to Darya.

Anyway, madness and logic have always been cousins. The writer G. K. Chesterton once spoke of the "exhaustive and logical theory of the lunatic," saying that the madman "is not hampered by a sense of humor or by charity." Darya certainly wasn't hampered by charity, or by anything at all. If she occasionally wanted to blow up an ex-boyfriend, she didn't want to hear that she was being "crazy." She simply wanted to know that the naked bodies of her former lover and her rival were sizzling like pigs on a spit. If she told her serfs to do something, she wanted the act done, no questions asked. God in heaven! Was no one *listening* to her?

The Escape of the Husbands

Nobody knew about Darya's reign of terror better than Yermolai Ilyin, the man who took care of her horses. Ilyin had been married three times, to three hardworking women, each of whom had the terrible misfortune of being "employed" by Darya. They had beautiful names: Katerina, Theodosia, Aksinya. And Darya slaughtered them all.

Darya knew Ilyin loathed her because of what she'd done to his wives, but warned that if he ever attempted to report her, she would whip him to death herself. Ilyin knew her well enough to know she wasn't making empty threats – but there's only so much cruelty that the human psyche can take. Finally, desperate and reckless, Ilyin decided to fling himself on the mercy of a system that didn't care whether he lived or died.

In April 1762, Ilyin and his fellow serf Savely Martynov showed up in the city of St. Petersburg, ready to make their case against Darya. They clutched a letter containing an almost inconceivable accusation: that over the past six years, Darya had killed more than one hundred people. The two were convinced that if only they could get their letter into the hands of the brand-new empress, Catherine the Great, she would do something about it.

It was a suicide mission – but it worked. Their story sounded just outrageous enough to catch the attention of the St. Petersburg authorities, who forwarded it to the Justice Board along with a note asking the board to begin an investigation into the life of Darya Nikolayevna Saltykova – the noblewoman, the mother, the widow of a fine man, the upstanding churchgoer.

"I Do Not Know Anything; I Did Not Do Anything"

If Darya flew into rages over unclean floors and ex-lovers, we can only imagine her wrath when she found out that two of her serfs had managed to turn the authorities against her. But she couldn't make good on her threats to beat them to death, because the great eye of Empress Catherine was slowly turning toward her, and life as she knew it was about to change forever.

In a way, this case surfaced at the perfect time for Catherine the Great. See, Catherine was trying to show the world that this was a new era for Russia – a humane and enlightened era, when having noble blood was no longer an excuse to do whatever you wanted – and so she needed to make an example of someone. Because before the law, everyone was equal!

Well, sort of. The truth was that Catherine was also under a lot of pressure to handle the case diplomatically. Since Darya belonged to a prestigious family, other aristocrats were taking particular interest in this, ahem, unfortunate situation. They wanted to make sure Catherine didn't set any precedents she couldn't take back. (Surely they, too, had blood on their hands: serfs whose beatings had gone a little too far, stories of bribes and hasty burials.) Still, the accusations against Darya were far too serious for Catherine to sweep under the rug with a wink at Moscow's noblest families. By now, the number of deaths attributed to Darya had skyrocketed to 138. Like it or not, the Justice Board was dealing with one of the worst serial killers in history, male or female.

Due to Catherine's personal interest in the case, the investigation against Darya was incredibly methodical. This was no semi-shady Báthory trial: investigators talked to hundreds of witnesses in both Moscow and Troitskoye, carefully confirming and reconfirming each allegation against the noblewoman. These witnesses were as knowledgeable and precise as an investigating officer could wish. They remembered the names of the dead peasants and the dates on which they died; they corroborated each other's stories. If the slightest shadow of a doubt were cast on any witness – contradicting testimonies, qualms about the witness's veracity, or facts that couldn't be proven – the Justice Board interpreted that particular case in Darya's favor. They also threw out multiple cases for lack of evidence. Darya's stance on the 138 deaths was short and sweet: "I do not know anything; I did not do anything," she said, over and over.

Despite all this, the Board *still* found her guilty of thirty-eight murders, and under suspicion of murder in twenty-six more cases. The fact that Darya refused to confess, however, caused Catherine a great deal of anxiety, and her concern is demonstrated in the sheer number of letters she wrote about the case. On principle, Catherine strongly disapproved of torture – writing, famously, "All punishments by which the human body might be maimed are barbarism," – but she wanted Darya to admit to at least *something*. At one point, she wrote to the Board, "Explain to Saltykova that the testimonies and facts of the case mean that official torture will have to be performed if, frankly, she does not confess her involvement in the crimes. Therefore send her a priest and make him accompany and exhort her for a month. And if she does not repent, then prepare her for torture."

Catherine didn't really intend for Darya to be tortured, but she hoped the *idea* of torture would scare her into acknowledging her crimes. "Show her the torture chamber," Catherine wrote, "so that she will know what awaits her. Give her one last chance for admission and repentance." At the same time, Catherine was anxiously re-reminding the authorities that no matter what happened, Darya wasn't to be harmed. Establishing a precedent of torture or executing members of the aristocracy was deeply unpopular and far too risky. "Carefully observe that there be no unnecessary bloodshed," she wrote, "and all those involved in these crimes be properly questioned, and all the facts be collected and recorded. After that give it all to me."

Darya never confessed to a thing.

"A Completely Godless Soul"

"Here is the decree we give to our Senate," ran Catherine's imperial verdict on October 2, 1768. "Having considered the report provided to us by the Senate on the crimes committed by the inhuman widow

Darya, the daughter of Nicholas, we have found that she does not deserve to be called a human being, as she is actually worse than the most famous murderers, extremely hard-hearted and cruel, not able to curb her rage." The decree laid out her punishment: First, Darya would be led to a scaffold in Moscow's central square, where she would hear the Justice Board's sentence, which was to be read without ever mentioning Darya's family name or her husband's name – erasing her identity as a social human, effectively shattering all the familial ties she had in the world. Then, she would be locked underground for the rest of her life.

During the years of the investigation, Darya had become infamous. Now there were crazed rumors circling around Moscow that she was a cannibal, and people were dying to see this notorious killer in person. Catherine encouraged the spectacle by sending invitations to all the noble houses, demanding that they come and watch Darya's punishment. This was also a veiled threat: she was warning the nobles that their abuses of power had real consequences. There was an Enlightenment coming, after all. They couldn't get away with everything anymore.

October 18 was a Sunday, and the season's first snow fell on Moscow, but that didn't stop the crowds of people who came to Red Square to gape at the "inhuman widow." At noon, Darya was brought outside and bound to a pole. A sign hung around her neck: THE TORMENTOR AND THE MURDERER. A guard stood next to her as her sentence was read aloud. One fascinated viewer allegedly reported that Darya's eyes were "not of this world." After an hour, she was taken away in shackles.

Darya's punishment wasn't bloody, but it was long and horribly isolated. She was put in an underground prison cell called a repentance chamber, accessed only by a nun and a custodian. Not a single beam of light was allowed inside, except for a candle during meals. She sat this way, in total darkness, for eleven years. Aside from eating and drinking, she had only one activity: every Sunday, she was allowed to stand under a ventilation tunnel that led up to a local church, so that she could hear the liturgy.

What did Darya think, Sunday after Sunday, as she heard the priest pray, "Oh holy God, who out of nothing has brought all things into being, who has created man after Thine own image and likeness, and hast adorned him with Thine every gift"? Did Darya feel anything for the bodies she'd broken, created in that "image and likeness"? When the liturgy touched on sin and evil and the need for sanctification, did she think about herself? Or did she simply stand there in the darkness, under the ventilation tunnel, with her mind far away and her otherworldly pupils dilated from lack of light?

Horrible Darya. She had internalized the conditions of serfdom so deeply that perhaps she truly believed she was virtuous in the eyes of God for disposing of these monstrous, unworthy, subhuman souls. Her entire world told her she was superior: she watched the serf orchestras, gasped at the serf ballets; she saw that serfs were punished for even *attempting* to criticize their masters. Even in her beloved church, she was probably never taught that serfdom was wrong. A pastoral guide published in 1776 "virtually ignored the existence of serfdom." The historian Richard Pipes spelled it out even more forcefully when speaking of the Russian church: "No branch of Christianity has shown such callous indifference to social and political injustice." The silence of the priests would have said it all: These serfs are nothing to us. Nothing to God. Nothing.

And so Darya simply carried this mindset to the logical extreme: if the serfs were nothing, if they were lesser life forms than she, if *she* were the valuable one – upheld by the law, coddled by the church – then she could do whatever she wanted to them. She felt entitled to their work, their blood, and perhaps even their very souls.

But she didn't kill them all, of course. She wasn't actually a god. And so, as she wasted away underground, the peasants who survived her took to calling her Saltychikha – a nickname with no real meaning, but a tiny sociolinguistic rebellion nonetheless. Aristocrats never referred to each other with diminutives like that, so the very existence of this nickname indicates that it was given to her by the serfs. "Saltychikha" suggested a simple village woman, someone who was a bit rough around the edges. It would have appalled Darya to hear her noble name so altered. The fact that the nickname stuck – even appearing a century later in the introduction to *War and Peace* – was a small victory for the souls.

In 1779, Darya was transferred to a chamber carved out of rock with a small barred window. Rumor has it she slept with one of the guards and gave birth to a child, but she would have been almost fifty by that point. Moscow hadn't forgotten about her – the "monster of humankind," they called her, the "completely godless soul" – and curious kids would sometimes peek through the window to catch a glimpse of the abominable Saltychikha. When they did, she would growl and spit at them – confirming rumors of her brutality, and convincing everyone that she still hadn't repented of her crimes. As far as we know, she never did.

She remained imprisoned for a total of thirty-three years, until her death on November 27, 1801. The state councilor visited her once in her old age – curious, perhaps, if nobility could stay noble after decades underground. He noted that Darya had grown stout, and that "all her movements now betrayed that she went mad." She was her own mistress no longer, after years of stumbling about in the darkness.

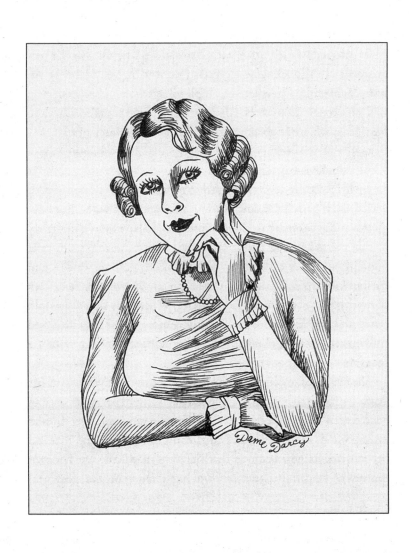

ICEBERG ANNA

Anna Marie Hahn

ne summer day in 1937, three generations boarded a train heading west to Colorado Springs: a pretty thirty-one-year-old blonde, an adolescent boy with the face of a cherub, and a very sick old man. The boy ran up and down the aisle of the train, bringing glasses of cold water to the old man, who was parched and querulous and slept fitfully. Then, to amuse himself, the boy slumped down in his seat and began to draw. He sketched for a while and eventually presented his work to the man: a picture of a skull.

The sick old man looked at the drawing with terror in his eyes. "Witches!" he screamed, snatching the paper and holding it aloft. "Witches!" The little boy snickered at his dismay, and soon the whole train car was laughing, too. When he realized no one was going to help him, the old man folded up the paper and tucked it into his pocket, and then continued to sleep and wake and sleep again, as if he were struggling to fight through a nightmare.

Love at First Sight

Anna Marie Hahn had a tranquil, storybook childhood that was destroyed when adulthood descended on her too fast, like a lightning bolt, and a dark lover broke her heart. At least, that was what she wanted people to believe. She was born in 1906 in the idyllic Bavarian town of Füssen, which was perched on the edge of the Alps and known for its violin makers. Her father, George Filser, was a furniture manufacturer, and their family was religious, well-off, and respected. Anna was the youngest of twelve, though five of her siblings were dead. She was probably adored and spoiled by her entire family. Her mother, Katie, always admitted that Anna was her favorite.

Into this whimsical German town crept a man named Dr. Max Matscheki. He was a famous Viennese physician working on a cure for cancer – "one of the greatest doctors in the world" – and as handsome as a movie star. He wooed nineteen-year-old Anna sweetly; they swayed together on the dance floor as he whispered romantic promises into her ear. "It was the kind of love that every young girl thinks about, this love at first sight," said Anna. "I was happy then." Matscheki swore he would marry her, and eventually, borne along on this idealistic narrative, Anna tumbled into bed with him. Why not? She was secure in his love and excited for their future together. But when Dr. Max Matscheki found out that Anna was pregnant, he balked. There was someone else, he said. A wife in Vienna. "It was just like a mountain falling on me," said Anna. "Not killing me but just smothering me and crushing me."

The story was raw and poetic. There was just one problem: no Max Matscheki ever practiced medicine in Vienna. The doctor was a figment, a shadow lover, a stand-in for some ordinary man. But the child was very real, and when Anna's conservative family found out she was expecting, they were mortified. There was no hiding a teenage pregnancy in their small, pious town. As soon as Anna's son, Oscar, was born, the family decided she should get out of their sight altogether – and leave for America.

Anna was actually happy to go after enduring the town's gossip for nine long months. "I could no longer stand those things that people were saying about my misfortune," she recalled. It took her two years to get a visa, and she left at age twenty-two, leaving her son behind until she could establish herself overseas. The trip across the ocean, away from Oscar, must have been excruciating. "The little pleasure that I have gotten out of life has been from my boy," she said.

Until the end of her life, Anna spoke fondly of Dr. Max Matscheki. Perhaps she liked the way the story made her sound: a dreamy, innocent, sexually appealing girl, tossed madly about on the waves of a foreign love affair. A victim. The tale about Oscar's parentage was one of her most cinematic lies – sex *and* a cure for cancer! – but it was also her most innocent. Nobody died because of it.

America!

To fund her trip, Anna wrote to her uncle Max Doeschel, who lived in Cincinnati, and asked him for a loan. The two weren't close – in fact, Doeschel had never heard from his niece before. Still, he sent her $236 and waited, unsure what sort of person to expect. Later, Anna would boast that he sent her a mind-boggling $16,000. But she was always lying about money.

Anna arrived in Cincinnati in February 1929, a "pretty blonde" who spoke English well. She contracted scarlet fever almost immediately and was sick for several months, but by April she was healthy enough to find employment at a hotel. As soon as she began making money, she started behaving like a different person. Doeschel and his wife were confused by her generous income – she "was more than able to take care of her own financial needs" – especially since she hadn't offered to repay their loan yet. She had a habit of making extravagant purchases and then acting secretive about them, as though to disguise the fact that they were "too expensive for a housework girl." She even told them she was building a house, which didn't make any sense. How in the world would she be able to afford *that*? But logic be damned: Anna wanted to be seen as the sort of person who *could* build herself a house if she wanted to.

At the hotel where Anna worked, she met a mild, mousy figure named Philip Hahn. He was no romantic Viennese doctor, but she liked that he promised some sort of safe harbor. "He was nice to me and said he loved me and wanted to marry me," she said. Then again: "I was afraid at first when he talked about marriage." When Hahn agreed to act as Oscar's father, Anna finally relented, and the two married a year later. By July 1930, Anna was ready to go back to Germany and get her son.

Her aunt and uncle were blindsided when Anna returned to Cincinnati with a tiny blond boy in tow, since she'd never mentioned him before. Fed up with her lies and weirded out by her behavior, the two eventually decided to cut all ties with her, just as her nuclear family had done back in Germany.

The United States had already begun its sickening economic collapse into the Great Depression, and Anna's thoughts turned ever more toward money. She was addicted to betting on horse races, and often signed bad checks when she lost wagers. She opened a restaurant with her husband and then tried to burn it down for insurance money. She tried to burn down her own house for the same reason. Perhaps money fed into some huge romantic delusion she had, the same delusion that led her to insist that her uncle had sent her $16,000 for her trip to America – a fairy-tale amount, implying wealthy, indulgent relatives and a luxurious trip across the Atlantic. Regardless, gambling and arson soon stopped satisfying her, and she began to look for bigger game.

Today, some evolutionary psychologists have theorized that male serial killers are "hunters" while females are merely "gatherers," sensibly collecting resources from their victims instead of doing it out of a deep and unslakable thirst for violence. Anna may have technically collected money from her crimes, but she was a hunter to the core. She set her sights on her victims like she was looking through a rifle scope and stalked them with heartless, single-minded purpose. And like a true predator, she preyed on the weak. She was actually kind of a sloppy criminal, but her victims were lonely and innocent and easy to fool. They thought the rest of the world had forgotten about them, and wanted desperately to believe that the blonde woman bending over them was something like an angel.

"My Girl"

One of her earliest paramours was a man named Ernest Kohler, her sixty-two-year-old landlord. Kohler was the owner of a large, lovely house, and in 1932 he was renting two of the rooms to the Hahns and another to a doctor who never locked his office. Sometimes Anna would sneak in and forge prescriptions for narcotics on the doctor's blank prescription pads. But mostly she flirted with Kohler.

Kohler died suddenly on May 6, 1933. His death was a windfall for Anna. He left her his beautiful old house, valued at $12,000, plus a car, $1,167 in a savings account, and heaps of expensive antiques. Sure, it was a bit awkward when the coroner's office received several anonymous phone calls insisting that Kohler had been poisoned, but

Anna carefully explained that no, he'd died of esophageal cancer. The coroner gamely checked his esophagus, found no poison, and sent Kohler to the crematorium in peace.

For Anna, this was the perfect relationship. She liked her men elderly and lonely and preferably German, so they could bond over their shared heritage. These men were usually retired (which meant they were potentially sitting on healthy piles of cash) and neglected by society (which meant they were especially vulnerable to her charms). She offered herself up to them as a sort of attendant-cum-girlfriend, willing to nurse, cook, or flirt at the drop of a hat.

These men must have pinched themselves: there they were, sitting around in their lonely bachelor apartments, and suddenly this golden creature appeared at their doors, willing to laugh at their jokes and cook them decadent, nostalgia-inducing meals. Sometimes she would even let them kiss her, and soon enough the men found themselves throwing around words like "engagement" and "honeymoon." She was a miracle, really. A second lease on life. And such a treat to look at: vivacious, with big hazel eyes and a delicate beauty that was hard to capture on film.

Anna's next male friend was a sixty-three-year-old coal dealer named George E. Heis, who called her "my girl" and devoured her *Hügelsheimer Pfannkuchen,* the Bavarian pancakes she whipped up for him. When Anna coyly informed Heis she had divorced her husband (lies!), the smitten man began to drop hints about marriage.

What *was* Philip Hahn doing all this time, anyway? He had become a very minor character in the play of Anna Hahn's life. He disapproved of her friendships with elderly men, but Anna ignored his protests. She poisoned one of his meals once, but her attempt was so halfhearted we can only surmise that Hahn meant nothing to her; he wasn't even important (or rich) enough to kill. Hahn, who became violently ill after the meal, suspected that she'd tried to murder him, and, understandably, their marriage began to cool. But he stuck around, perhaps for Oscar's sake.

Back at Heis's apartment, Anna often sidled up to her aging paramour with innocent little requests for money, and he lent to her willingly – sometimes the cash out of his pocket, sometimes money from his business, the Consolidated Coal Company. By the time her "loans" reached two thousand dollars, the company's credit manager popped up, demanding an explanation. Heis was forced to admit that he had a pretty new girlfriend and couldn't say no to her. The credit manager, impervious to the madness of love, began pressuring Anna to repay her loans.

This was something of a reality check for Heis. He began looking at Anna with colder, more dispassionate eyes, and he realized that not only did Anna ask him for money all the time, but her cooking often made him feel sick. In fact, some days he could barely get out of bed. Heis ran his suspicions past the credit manager. Was his girl trying to poison him? The next time Anna showed up with her signature dish – spinach sprinkled with white granules that *seemed* to be salt – Heis told her that he wanted his two thousand dollars back, and that he never wanted to see her again.

Heis had no idea he was effectively signing death warrants for Cincinnati's other aging bachelors, but his demands forced Anna to speed up her hunt. At the end of 1936, she met Albert Palmer, seventy-two, and they bonded over their mutual love of betting on horse races. Like Heis, Palmer called Anna his girl and devoured her cooking. They planned a trip to Florida together. She left him cloying little notes that probably drove him wild: "My Dear Sweet Daddy," ran one note, "I'll see you tomorrow then with all my love and a lot of kisses. Your Anna." She sweet-talked him out of two thousand dollars, which she used in part to pay Heis.

But eventually Palmer, too, grew wise. He began to ask Anna if there was any way she could start repaying her loan to *him*, and she responded by serving him dinners that wrecked his health. He may have also overheard neighborhood gossip about Anna's recent affair with Heis. Hurt and furious, Palmer gave Anna an ultimatum: she could either repay the two thousand dollars right away, or she could become his girlfriend – permanently and exclusively. Anna never had to make that choice, because on March 26, 1937, Palmer died of what appeared to be a heart attack.

Anna unearthed her next benefactor by showing up at a random apartment building and boldly asking a woman if "any old men lived here." When she found out that a German immigrant named Jacob Wagner was renting one of the apartments, she told the suspicious tenant that oh, yes, that's right, Wagner was her uncle – even though she hadn't known his name minutes before. She then slipped a note under his door, organized a meeting, and hit it off with Wagner immediately. "I have a new girl," Wagner boasted to a pal. His new girl often asked him for loans and assured him she was good for it by showing him a forged bankbook that indicated she had over fifteen thousand dollars in the bank. Was the number any connection to the imaginary sixteen thousand from her uncle? Maybe that was her dream amount: a number she associated with stability and fairy-tale happiness.

Anna was getting sloppy. She was juggling multiple men, some of whom moved in the same circles as others. Her requests for money were becoming bizarre – if she really did have fifteen thousand dollars in the bank, why would she have needed a loan? – and she was now baldly hunting for victims by asking strangers where she could find "old men." But that was Anna's genius: targeting the isolated. She certainly made some people suspicious – the woman at Wagner's apartment remembered her weird question forever – but for the most part, there simply wasn't anyone around to care.

While Anna pursued Wagner, she killed again for the low, low price of eighty dollars and a rabbit fur coat. She befriended an elderly widow by dressing up in a fake nurse's uniform and offering her services, and then stole the valuables that the widow kept under her bed. ("I just loved to make old people comfy," Anna said later.) She bought herself a beautiful coat with the profits and offered to find the "culprit" if the unsuspecting widow paid her eighty dollars. Afterward, she finished off the poor woman with a dish of poisoned ice cream.

Back at Wagner's apartment, things were getting creepy. Wagner began to look askance at Anna when his bankbook went missing, but Anna assured him she'd done nothing wrong and placated him with well-seasoned food and drink. Soon enough he was in the hospital, "semi-conscious, retching with pain, and in a state of shock and dying." It was a horrifying sight. Arsenic can make its victims crazed with thirst; shortly before he died, Wagner begged a nurse for something to drink, whispering: "Ich könnte ein Fass voll Wasser trinken!" ("I could drink a barrel of water!")

Anna showed up at the nearest probate court like a classically trained actress ready to play Lady Macbeth. After she'd cried a sufficient number of demure yet heartrending tears, she suggested that perhaps one of the deputies should search Wagner's apartment, just in case there were any, say, important papers lying about? Sure enough, the deputy found a handwritten will on Wagner's mantel:

> I hereby make my last will and testament and I am under no influence. I have my money in the Fifth Third Bank. After my funeral expenses and all bills are paid, I want the rest to go to my relative, Anna Hahn. I want Mrs. Hahn to be my executor. I don't want any flowers, and I don't want to be laid out.

The will – surprise, surprise – was written by Anna herself, and the level of cold-blooded confidence Ms. Hahn displayed in directing authorities straight to her forgery is pretty impressive. She was a careless criminal, and part of her carelessness was due to her utter lack of empathy. Last will and testament? An old lady's eighty dollars? Nothing was sacred to her; nothing got under her skin. And just like so many of her other con jobs, this one worked. At the time, authorities had no reason to suspect this charming, distraught blonde, and apparently nobody cared enough about Wagner to prove or disprove Anna's place in his family tree.

Her rampage continued: a few weeks later, she befriended sixty-seven-year-old George Gsellman, a German-speaking Hungarian immigrant who considered himself to be a bit of a ladies' man. After meeting Anna, he boasted to one of his exes, "You wouldn't marry me, and now I went and got a young blonde German schoolteacher." Anna only managed to charm him out of a hundred dollars, but that was a lot of money for Gsellman. In fact, Gsellman's banker noted that it was the largest sum his client had ever withdrawn.

One night, an ecstatic Gsellman told two of his neighbors that he was getting married the next day! By morning, the bridegroom's body was stiffening on his bed. There was a half-eaten meal on the stove, laced with eighteen grains of arsenic. This was far more than was necessary to kill a man, but who cared? Not Anna.

Witches

Poison is for weaklings, they say. The English poet Phineas Fletcher (1582–1650) may have been the first to coin the term "coward's weapon," but the opinion has not dissipated in the centuries since; even a character in George R. R. Martin's *Game of Thrones* recently sniped that poison was a gutless way to kill. Poison is sneaky, it's slow, and you can poison someone without spilling a drop of their blood or awkwardly making eye contact with them midimpalement. As such, it doesn't get a lot of cred for being scary. Poisoners simply don't terrify people the way, say, disembowlers do.

But that's unfair, because poisoning requires advance planning and the stomach for a drawn-out death scene. You need to look into your victim's trusting eyes day after day as you slowly snuff out their life. You have to play the role of nurse or parent or lover while you sustain your murderous intent at a pitch that would be unbearable for many of those who've shot a gun or swung a sword. You've got to mop up your victim's vomit and act sympathetic when they beg for water. While they scream that their insides are on fire, you must steel yourself against the dreadful sight of encroaching death and give them another sip of the fatal drink. A coward's weapon? Not so much. Poison is the weapon of the emotionless, the sociopathic, the truly cruel.

Anna Hahn was not a coward. She knew how to draw death out, to make it hurt like hell. Her final victim was a lot like the others, but for some reason, Anna was exceptionally nasty to this man. She poisoned him until he was writhing in his own feces. His last days were a nightmare sequence of pain and hallucination, and she killed him hundreds of miles from his home.

Johan Georg Obendoerfer was a semiretired cobbler, a widower, and the proud grandpa of eleven grandchildren. One day, he was surprised at his shop by a charming, blonde, German-speaking lady who dropped by to see if he could fix one of her high-heeled shoes. Perhaps Anna – who was still seeing Gsellman at the time – already knew what sort of man worked there, and the broken heel was just a ruse. Regardless, Obendoerfer fell hard for her.

After a few weeks of dating, Obendoerfer seemed like a changed man. He shaved off his mustache to appear younger, and he began dropping hints about getting engaged. Anna told him, coquettishly, that they should take a vacation together before she really committed. She claimed to own a beautiful home on a cattle ranch in Colorado, and she told Obendoerfer that they should bring Oscar, check it out – and if they liked it, maybe the three of them could move there for good. Obendoerfer loved the idea, so Anna quickly murdered Gsellman and began to plan the trip.

Obendoerfer had never been happier. A second life was opening before him like some sweet-throated flower: a bride, a marriage, acres of wild American land to call his own, and even a kid. On July 20, 1937, he packed his satchel and strode over to Anna's house, grabbing a celebratory beer on the way. Anna had prepared a delicious dinner to kick off their journey – a dinner seasoned with those white granules with which she so loved to cook. By morning, Obendoerfer was so sick that Anna and Oscar had to help him into the cab.

The three of them pressed on anyway, taking the train from Cincinnati to Chicago – where Anna checked herself into a fancy hotel with Oscar and tossed Obendoerfer into a cheap motel room nearby – and then on to Denver, where they disembarked for a few days. On their first morning there, Anna and Oscar went to check on Obendoerfer and found him writhing in bed, splattered with feces and vomit. Anna pretended to soothe him by feeding him cool chunks of watermelon as Oscar watched, but Obendoerfer couldn't keep anything down. So she left the man in his misery and busied herself with the tricky business of stealing his life savings.

Anna wrote a letter to his banker in Cincinnati, claiming that Obendoerfer was planning to move to Denver, wanted to transfer his money to the Denver National Bank, and needed one thousand dollars to tide him over in the meantime. For the next week, she haunted the Denver National Bank to see if the money had arrived, growing more and more frustrated as the days went by.

Meanwhile, Obendoerfer's hotel room had gotten so disgusting that the housekeeping staff refused to go inside. After the hotel owner peeked in and saw Obendoerfer curled in a fetal position, moaning and surrounded by his own filth, he urged Anna to take him to the hospital. Anna scoffed that she barely knew the man. Then she bundled Obendoerfer onto a train to Colorado Springs.

At this point, Obendoerfer surely suspected he was being poisoned, but he was lost in a fog of agony. All he could do was beg for water and stare blankly out the train window. When Oscar showed him the skull drawing, Obendoerfer seemed to muster the strength to accuse the two of them – *witches, witches!* – but everyone simply laughed at his terror. He must have curled against the glass then, with the skull drawing folded next to his heart, wondering blearily how he had mistaken these witches for angels.

The fact that Oscar was right there next to the dying man is one of the creepiest parts of Anna's story. Oscar probably didn't understand the full extent of what was happening, but still, he saw it all. He smelled the vomit, he witnessed the old man's agony, he watched his mother feed Obendoerfer chunks of poisoned watermelon. (Anna carried a salt shaker of arsenic with her, and would liberally "salt" Obendoerfer's food.) With his soft curls, perfect features, and attentive, intelligent face, Oscar certainly helped Anna seem nonthreatening, even Madonna-like. So some people who knew him said he was a "mean little kid" who killed animals for fun and once shot a BB gun at his friend. So what? Maybe his mother kept him around because he made her look good.

In Colorado Springs, Anna and Oscar left Obendoerfer to fend for himself while they went sightseeing. When the two arrived back at the hotel, Anna noticed that the door to the owner's private rooms was slightly ajar. Peeking inside, she saw two diamond rings sparkling on the dresser. She pocketed them, but as she was leaving the room, she ran smack into the hotel owner's wife, who was naturally suspicious. Anna explained that she was simply curious how the rooms looked. The theft of those rings in broad daylight was a stupid, careless, greedy mistake on her part – and a fatal one.

With the rings rattling around in her pocket, she finally checked Obendoerfer into the hospital, registering him as a homeless person. He died there, without ever reaching the paradise he had been promised.

Cincinnati's Number One Female Criminal

At the beginning of August 1937, police in Cincinnati opened a secret investigation into the death of Jacob Wagner after receiving a tip from one of his friends, who'd noticed a strange woman hanging around Wagner's house in the days before he died. Meanwhile, detectives were heading over to Anna Marie Hahn's place on a seemingly unrelated charge: the theft of two diamond rings, which Anna had pawned for $7.50 on her way back to Cincinnati.

When the police showed up at Anna's doorstep, she protested her arrest loudly. At first, they took her in on charges of grand larceny, but arresting Anna was like tugging on a loose string – suddenly, everything seemed to be unraveling. They discovered that she had nursed Jacob Wagner right before he died, that she'd been in Colorado Springs around the time a Cincinnati resident named Obendoerfer died suspiciously, that she had poison hidden in the rafters of her house, and so on, and so on. This pretty jewelry thief was starting to seem like the biggest criminal Cincinnati had ever produced.

The day after her arrest, warrants of "fugitive murder and larceny" were signed against her by one Detective Walter Hart. In reaction, Anna combed her hair, smiled, and told the press they were welcome to take her photo. "Here I am, boys," she said – blonde, hazel eyed, and icily calm. "Make this a good picture of me." Was she afraid of all this accumulating evidence? She was not. "How can they make such a charge?" she asked. "I can face anything there is to come."

Mother's Prayers

Something in Anna's case appealed to the women of Cincinnati. It wasn't that they empathized with her, per se, but they were desperately curious to see how she acted in court, and the fact that she was a mother touched their hearts. On the day of Anna's arraignment, the courtroom was crowded with fifteen women to every man, women that had waited long hours outside the door to make sure they were the first ones inside. Anna showed zero emotion in the courtroom, but it didn't matter. When Oscar ran up to whisper something in her ear, several of the women wiped their eyes and one juror sobbed openly.

The jury skewed as female as the audience. It consisted of eleven women and one very good-looking man, and the press quickly nicknamed the lot of them "the Petticoat Jury." Journalists were understandably excited about this case, which was already shaping up to be fiery, sensational, and rife with opportunity for long editorials.

In fact, the only people who *didn't* seem to care about the case were Anna's siblings back in Germany. Upon being notified that their sister was arrested, they responded that they were "uninterested" in the case's outcome and were going to hide the news from their aging mother so as not to upset her. Still, Anna convinced herself that one of her sisters would show up once the trial had officially started. "It would be a comfort to me to have some member of my family with me," she mused.

Anna was thinking about her family a lot in jail, especially her mother. She sent her a telegram that read, "Just pray for me." (Her siblings never bothered showing it to their mother.) During one of the prison's Sunday services, she requested a hymn called "Mother's Prayers Have Followed Me," unaware of the irony: her mother had no idea where Anna was or what she'd been doing.

Other than Oscar and Philip Hahn, none of Anna's family ever showed up to support her. They'd written her out of their lives a long time ago. They were officially "uninterested." Not shocked, appalled, heartbroken, or righteously indignant – uninterested. Did that mean, perhaps, they were also *unsurprised*? Had they always detected a darkness in Anna? Even in her youth, did they sense her cruelness, her lack of empathy, and pull away from her as soon as they could drum up an excuse?

"That Woman Tortured Me with Tortures of the Damned!"

Anna's trial was set for October 11. She would be tried for the murder of Jacob Wagner, because the prosecution thought his would be the easiest one to prove. They had the handwritten will and an expert who could prove it was forged. And they had the exhumation results, which showed that there was enough arsenic in Wagner's body to have killed him twice over.

The prosecutor, Dudley Miller Outcalt, was the best in the biz, a brilliant orator with a flair for courtroom drama. The press adored his fiery opening statement, during which he declared that he would prove Anna Hahn "killed so many men that there is not another person like her on the face of the earth." On the other side of the aisle, Anna's defense team quaked; they had never handled a serious criminal case of any sort, much less a major murder case. Plus, one of their members, Joseph Hoodin, was suffering from a bad cold. Hoodin ended up being a rather pitiful figure; at one point, he declared that he was planning to bring out fifty-three witnesses to prove Anna's innocence, but he was only able to deliver two. He eventually called the gig "a job nobody can handle."

In contrast to these intense, emotional lawyers, Anna was developing a reputation as an ice queen. Every time she appeared in court, she was impeccably turned out – her fellow prisoners, obsessed with their celebrity cell mate, would do her hair – with a gold cross around her neck and flat, emotionless eyes. In prison, she read the newspaper articles that tried to analyze the "phlegmatic enigma" of her personality, amused. Her denial was calm, consistent, and relentless. "They'll never get a confession out of me, because I can't confess to something I never did," she told a reporter. "But I supposed the death of anyone past sixty anywhere in the country now will be laid to me."

Her calm seemed to mask a certain delusion, because things were not looking good for Anna Hahn. Arsenic had been found in the bodies of not just Wagner, but Palmer, Gsellman, *and* Obendoerfer, and on October 22, the judge declared that the prosecution could now admit the other poisonings into evidence, instead of just discussing Wagner's murder. Witness after witness took the stand to skewer her. There was the tenant who remembered Anna inquiring if "any old men lived here," the neighbors who talked about her abnormally unflustered attitude toward death, and bank employees with records of her suspicious financial behavior – bringing in checks that didn't quite look right, and so on. Handwriting experts determined that Wagner's will had been forged by Anna herself. A toxicologist studied Anna's favorite summer purse and found grains of arsenic all over the lining. Doctors presented the horrified jury with the brains, livers, and kidneys of the murdered men, floating gruesomely in jars of preservative.

The prosecution's star witness was George Heis, he of the

poisoned spinach and the unpaid debt to the Consolidated Coal Company. He became known as their "living witness," and his presence in the courtroom was ghastly and damning. Really, the prosecution could not have asked for a more incriminating visual: George Heis, skeletally thin, confined to a wheelchair, pointing at Anna with shaking hands and telling the jury that *this* was the woman who had tried to murder him in cold blood.

Finally, both Oscar and Anna took the stand. Oscar had been coached to give certain answers, and he spoke carefully: yes, he brought Obendoerfer water; no, he didn't realize that the old man was dying. The boy only slipped up once, when he admitted that his mother had initially asked him to lie about meeting Obendoerfer on the train. Anna was even calmer than her son. The prosecution tried their best to crack her, but Anna wouldn't crack. If she had a conscience, it remained buried deep inside her, invulnerable to remorse, rhetorical pressure, and the looming threat of a guilty verdict.

Outcalt's closing remarks brought down the house. "Anna Hahn is the only one in God's world that had the heart for such murders!" he cried to the jury. "She sits there with her Madonna face and her soft voice, but they hide a ruthless, passionate purpose the likes of which this state has never known!" Hoodin's response was lackluster: sure, Anna wasn't perfect, but then again, who was? He went on to claim that the prosecution couldn't prove precisely how the arsenic got into Wagner's body. No one bought the argument. Hoodin's only stroke of genius occurred when he reminded the jury that Anna was a mother. As everyone in the courtroom wept, Hoodin urged them to spare her so she could return to her boy. Even Anna managed to drum up a tear or two.

But it was too late to humanize her. Outcalt stood up again to finish his speech, calling Anna sly, avaricious, cold-blooded, and heartless. And then he pulled out his grand finale. "In the four corners of this courtroom there stand four dead men," he cried, and pointed at each corner as he bellowed their names: "Jacob Wagner! George Gsellman! Georg Obendoerfer! Albert Palmer!"

The jurors were breathless. Outcalt continued in a thunderous voice. "From the four corners of this room, bony fingers point at her and they say to you, 'That woman poisoned me! That woman made my last moment an agony! That woman tortured me with tortures of the damned!'"

It was a brilliant rhetorical flourish: bringing the dead men to life in horrifying contrast with the accused, who sat there, pale and motionless, looking for all the world like she was carved out of wax.

The stunned petticoat jury returned the harshest verdict possible: guilty – without a recommendation of mercy. This meant that the death penalty was mandatory. As the ruling was read aloud, many of the jurors had tears standing in their eyes. Anna did not.

The True Anna

In December 1937, while her lawyers scrambled to find a way around the death penalty, Anna was moved to the Ohio Penitentiary in Columbus, where a special cell was built to isolate her from the rest of the inmates. She was the only female prisoner there. At first, the matrons in charge of her were impressed by the tiny blonde woman. "She is the bravest woman I ever saw," said the wife of the warden. Obsessive strangers wrote to Anna, offering to take her place in jail or asking if they could have her clothes after her execution.

It was there that Anna decided to write her "confessions," and they are full of deluded excuses. A psychiatrist might spot a couple of classic psychopathic traits in the document, including "blame externalization": she tried to pin her crimes onto various childhood sicknesses, accidents, and surgeries, and expressed a lot of confusion about why she did them, as though she were utterly nonresponsible for her actions. "I was sitting there hearing a story like out of a book all about another person," she wrote. "I couldn't in my mind believe that it was me, Anna Marie Hahn, who loved people so well and wanted friends all the time. God above will tell me what made me do these terrible things. I couldn't have been in my right mind when I did them. I loved all people so much."

Her lawyers kept up the desperate battle for Anna's life, claiming that she was "tried as a hunted animal," because the introduction of the other murders as evidence had biased the jury beyond all hope. As Anna's execution date loomed nearer and nearer, they took their protestations to the governor of Ohio to see if he would reduce Anna's sentence to life in prison. Anna was convinced he would. On December 1, Oscar testified in front of the governor's executive secretary, asking for his mother's life as a Christmas present.

The sentimental display didn't work. When Anna learned her final bid for life had failed, she collapsed, screaming, "Oh my God! I didn't think he could do that to me! He should let me live for my boy!"

Anna had always been a shape-shifter. She had a psychopath's charm: it could be directed with laser-like precision, and if she focused it on someone, they became convinced that she was warm, loving, vivacious. If she didn't bother to charm someone – like her relatives, and various suspicious neighbors – she appeared secretive and devious, a "strange woman" who wore fake nurse's uniforms and seemed weirdly unmoved when her elderly friends died. And now, with all hope gone, a new Anna emerged – wild, hopeless, completely undone. She would pace around her cell in the middle of the night, sobbing and chain-smoking cigarettes. At points, she would cry out, "My God! What about Oscar?"

"In her last twenty-four hours," reported one of the matrons who guarded her, "Anna Hahn changed from the poised, confident, proud, and even vain woman she had been continuously since she was first arrested into a little witch – a demon with a wild look in her eyes. When she knew the jig was up, she became the true Anna."

Beneath the Mask

The day before her execution, Anna and Oscar spent hours together. Anna couldn't touch her lunch. When visiting hours ended, and the matrons began to hint it was time for Oscar to leave, Anna started kissing Oscar's face repeatedly.

The matrons told her again that Oscar had to go. She ignored them and continued to kiss him. Finally, one matron had to physically tear Oscar away from her. "Don't take him from me!" Anna screamed. Oscar wept as he was led from his mother's cell, and Anna leapt at her matrons with such violence that she had to be injected with a sedative.

For years, Oscar had been her little blond sidekick, accompanying her on the most gruesome of adventures. He was the only family member who never left her. (Hahn, ever passive and forgettable, had slowly drifted out of the papers during the trial.) They say psychopaths don't feel love, but her last moments with her son imply – if not love, then dependence, even obsession. Anna may have seen Oscar as an extension of herself, a tiny mirror she'd created with her shadow lover, an escape hatch. But at the end, she lost the willing little actor who kept begging and begging for her innocence, and then she was truly alone. He was adopted by another family, and they changed his name.

On December 7, 1938, Anna walked down death row, as

condemned men wished her "good luck" and "God bless you" from their cells on either side of the corridor. "Goodbye, boys," she responded. Her hair was disheveled, her face was grey, and she wasn't wearing the gold cross that she'd worn throughout her trial.

The moment the door to the execution chamber opened, Anna collapsed at the sight of Old Sparky, the electric chair. It had never held a woman before. "Please don't. Oh, my boy. Think of my boy. Won't someone, won't anyone, come and do something for me?" she cried, looking around the room at people who had no ability whatsoever to save her – the attending priest, the three physicians, the horror-struck journalists. "Isn't there anybody to help me? Anyone, anyone. Is nobody going to help me?"

Throughout her life, Anna Hahn had been utterly callous in the face of death. She could stare at a weakened old man, covered in his own vomit and poisoned by her own hand, and say that she barely knew him. She dealt in death as though it were just another one of her con jobs, like the forgery and the bad checks and the stolen rings. But now that death was staring back at her, Anna couldn't take it. She had to be carried, thrashing and screaming, to the electric chair.

A guard attached one electrode to a shaved place on her head and a second electrode to her bare calf. As Anna locked eyes with the priest, the guard fitted a black leather mask over her face. The priest asked her to repeat the Lord's Prayer after him, and she did so, crying behind the mask. Some of the journalists in the room repeated the prayer along with her. As she stumbled over the line "Lead us not into temptation but deliver – " three guards pressed three buttons, and an electric current surged through her body. The sound was "like a Fourth of July sparkler," according to one of the journalists. Her body rose slightly out of the chair and her thumbs turned upward.

Afterward, the physicians checked for a heartbeat and found

none. "I am surprised she broke," said the warden, who had tears in his eyes. "I had expected her to remain cool." She'd been cool for years, but Death, of course, would always be more cold-blooded. The warden noted that no convict in the prison's history had ever been as terrified as Anna Hahn was when she faced the electric chair.

THE NIGHTINGALE

Oum-El-Hassen

Oum-El-Hassen was a Moroccan dancing girl gone bad. Not "bad," you know – impudent and bewitching and unrestricted – but *bad*: evil, heartless, and inscrutable. She began her public life as a gorgeous cabaret girl and ended it with public humiliation, her once-beautiful face veiled in white. Her story trickled down from her trial in Fez to the tiniest American newspapers, like the *San Antonio Light* and the *Oshkosh Daily Northwestern*, which reported breathlessly that this famous North African beauty was now the cruelest of them all, but never really stopped to fact-check her story. She was the beauty *and* the beast, a total enigma, forever doomed to be portrayed through someone else's eyes.

Oum-El-Hassen, who went professionally by the name Moulay, was born in 1890 in the "white and dazzling" city of Algiers, the coastline capital of Algeria. She grew into an ethereal beauty and a wonderful dancer, and began working as a prostitute at the age of twelve. Before long, she was being lauded as "the most beautiful cabaret girl in Northern Africa."

Though her role in society was an inherently vulnerable one, Moulay was smart about it. She noted those who were in power, and she chased their loyalty. At the turn of the century, Algeria was part of French North Africa, and so Moulay chose to adore the French – especially French soldiers. Later, a journalist would write that there was a "savage friendship [between] French blood and her own," and Moulay apparently vowed that she would never sleep with a man who wasn't a member of the French army. Her loyalty to the soldiers was certainly appreciated, but it was also uninvited. A woman can be loyal to an army, but an army is rarely loyal to a woman.

Years later, the French writer Colette would observe bleakly that if Moulay hadn't been so shrewd, her life would have followed a sad and familiar arc: beautiful prostitute found dead in a ditch. But Moulay was never fated to be one of that "uncertain and miserable number" of young dead girls. She knew violence was inevitable in her line of work, and so she chose the side of the violent.

One Thousand Frenchmen

Young Moulay was a clever businesswoman, and by the time she reached her twenties, she was running a popular brothel in Fez. Here, she entertained French officers and all sorts of important city officials with "gaiety, luxury, young dancers, fine firm Berber women, inscrutable Chleuhs, passive daughters of the South." (This description was written by a French journalist, and is perhaps representational of how these French officers interacted with Moulay's dancers: plucking their favorites from an impersonal and dehumanizing lineup.) Though much of Moulay's private life is a mystery, we do know that she was in love once. For five years, she lived with a French colonel, and at one point she gave birth to a baby girl, whom she sent back to her sister in Algeria. In general, her life was going well. She was wealthy and respected. And things were about to get better.

On March 30, 1912, Sultan Abdelhafid of Morocco signed the Treaty of Fez without *really* letting the people of Fez know what was going on. This treaty turned Morocco into a French protectorate, and Moroccan nationalists took the signing as a huge betrayal. They stewed in silence for a week or two – days that were "heavy with menace," according to an eyewitness – and then, on April 17, Moroccan troops rose up against their French commanders and subsequently "spread to the streets of Fez in search of any European they could find."

It was a bloodbath. As the rioters streamed through the streets, Moulay turned her back on her countrymen and hid thirty French officers in her brothel instead. When protestors pounded at her door, expecting to search the place, they were shocked to be greeted by Moulay, who was brandishing a gun. She took a bullet in the hand for her pains, but ended up shooting one of the rebels in retaliation. That day, as the officers quivered in her back rooms, over seven hundred people were slaughtered in the streets – mostly Moroccans.

An ocean away, the histrionic American press reported a more colorful version of the story. They claimed that Moulay disguised the officers as prostitutes: shaving their moustaches, dyeing their skin darker, plastering their faces with makeup, cloaking them in wigs and turbans and silk robes, and handing them fans with which to hide their masculine features. She then arranged them into a seductive tableau, carefully positioning her regular girls in front of the soldiers.

And so, the story goes, when the furious rioters broke down the door, they were first distracted by this alluring scene, and then taken aback by Moulay, who was holding a pistol at eye level and daring them to come closer. She demanded they leave her business alone, and then, in a kinder tone, suggested they come back to enjoy her girls another day, when everyone was a bit calmer. Most of the rioters agreed to this idea, but when one showed signs of recognizing a French officer, Moulay shot the Moroccan through the heart.

Drag or no drag, the French were endlessly grateful to Moulay for services rendered. "She is rich, she is loved, she is adulated," crowed their newspapers. The officers rewarded her with eleven thousand francs, and people started to murmur that she should be appointed to the prestigious Legion of Honor. Moulay herself was incredibly proud of what she'd done, and later changed the number of officers she'd saved from thirty to sixty. But respectable France couldn't stomach the idea of bequeathing their highest award to a prostitute who ran a cabaret, and so she was ultimately passed over. The rejection "broke her heart," reported the *San Antonio Light*, "because it permitted respectable women to snub her." That was the thing about Moulay: she wanted to be adored, but she chose people who wouldn't, or couldn't, openly love her.

Despite this rebuff, Moulay's passionate loyalty to the visiting army did not abate, and in 1925 she saved French lives again. A high-ranking Moroccan official was planning to kill a garrison of French soldiers by orchestrating a religious uprising during an annual festival, and Moulay caught wind of the plot. She went straight to a French general to warn him, and the general in turn managed to shut down the revolt. Numerically speaking, she'd just done the French an even bigger favor than she had during the 1912 Fez riots. Later, when she had fallen from her "adulated" position, she liked to remind people that she'd saved the lives of "one thousand Frenchmen."

But for now, she was still famous, beloved by the French army, and queen of the Fez underground. She may have been the madam of a brothel, but she was as respectable and respected as a woman in her position could hope to be.

Then she vanished.

The Body in the Basket

No one really knows why Moulay went deep underground, or what she did there. Maybe she lost a lot of money. Maybe the colonel finally broke her heart. Darker rumors abound: she got mixed up with drug traffickers; she became involved in the "white slavery" trade; she started smoking hashish and sank slowly into the haze of addiction. Eventually, she lost her brothel license and at some point moved out of Fez and relocated to the seedy part of Meknès, a city about fifty miles southwest. She ran her new brothel with the help of a "sordid, fetid" old servant named Mohammed Ben Ali, who quickly became her right-hand man.

This brothel was not the swanky cabaret where Moulay had amused France's highest-ranking officers with "gaiety, luxury, young dancers." Instead, her new business was frequented by crueler men who didn't expect things to be fancy – or even clean. Moulay, for her part, just didn't seem to care about much anymore.

"The men she receives are demanding, the women she offers them languish," reported *Paris-Soir*. Her business was notable for its "grime and beatings" and the "odious practices" of its orgies, and the results showed on the starving, bruised bodies of the girls who worked there. Moulay was paranoid that her girls would secretly beg for help during their "amorous conversations" with patrons, and so she sometimes hid behind a curtain to spy on them.

Perhaps Moulay grew irrationally angry every time she looked at these girls, who were no longer the "fine firm" specimens she'd paraded before the French army years before. These new prostitutes, skinny and damaged, were a visual reminder of her fall from grace. And so she began to abuse them, helped along by Mohammed Ben Ali. The girls were starved and locked up so that they couldn't escape, and beaten at the slightest provocation. At least seven of them were struck so fiercely and so often they were eventually crippled.

By autumn 1936, Moulay was about forty-six years old. She was no longer supple and young; her looks had "dissolved in the fat of middle age." Her days of luxury and adulation were far behind her, and her life was filled instead with violence – and one particularly horrible secret.

Children sometimes frolicked in the streets outside Moulay's brothel, and one day a group of kids stumbled across something that piqued their interest: a heavy basket tied shut with string. They scrambled over each other to open it. Nothing could have prepared them for the contents inside. "Feet, hands, a head and its hair, a torso and young breasts" loomed out of the basket – a sick shadow box, a body in pieces. The broken flesh was surrounded by mint, fennel, and thyme, all stuffed inside the basket to disguise the smell of decay.

Soon the police were knocking on Moulay's door, demanding an explanation. Moulay received them, haughty and dismissive. Yes, she said, the dead girl was Cherifa, one of her former "boarders" – a euphemism if there ever was one – but she had no idea how Cherifa had ended up in the basket. She then reminded the police that she'd saved the lives of a thousand Frenchman, in case anyone had forgotten to keep track.

Mohammed Ben Ali wasn't so cool under pressure, and as soon

as the police turned to him, he began to babble about revenge and beatings and strangulation. But Moulay silenced him immediately. "Mohammed is a fool," she said. "He doesn't know what he's talking about."

The skeptical police investigated Moulay's house anyway. They discovered weapons in Mohammed Ben Ali's room and a couple of suspicious bloodstains. As they continued to search, they heard strange noises coming from behind one of the walls – a faint scratching, and then a mewling that sounded a lot like a cat.

Moulay told them that it was indeed a cat. She'd been having repairs done on one of the walls, she said, and the feral animal was accidentally plastered up in the process. The police made as if to knock down the walls, and Moulay calmly dissuaded them, saying that she'd already hired a professional to come and free the cat. He would be able to do a cleaner job, she cooed. She was so convincing that the police were about to leave, when from behind the wall, they heard the voice of a child: "Help! There are four of us here and we are dying."

Colette Attends the Trial

Word of the sensational crime spread quickly across the city, and Moulay became a celebrity once again. This time, it was an unpleasant fame. Hustlers began selling jewels to the morbidly curious, swearing that they were "snatched from the throat" of Moulay herself. In anticipation of drama, gory details, and general human tragedy, the French papers sent their best journalists to Fez to cover the trial.

The celebrated French writer Colette showed up in Morocco less interested in the back-and-forth legalities of the trial and more interested in knowing the unknowable Oum-El-Hassen. In the courtroom, Colette sat very near to Moulay – so close she could have touched her – and eyed the now forty-eight-year-old woman like a hawk. Moulay was dressed entirely in spotless white robes. She held a white handkerchief over her mouth, so that the only visible parts of her face were her curved nose and her "very dark green-brown eyes, lavishly treated with blue kohl." But when she lifted away the handkerchief to speak, all traces of elegance were lost: she was missing teeth, and her mouth was "flat, ungracious, made for gossiping, invective and – perhaps – cruelty."

There was a horrific spread of evidence at the front of the courtroom: a little shrine of household items allegedly used to kill and dismember poor Cherifa. There was the infamous basket that held Cherifa's hacked-up body, a pot in which Cherifa was supposed to have been boiled, a knife, a revolver, a garrote, and a "pestle for grinding scalps rather than almonds." Saddest of all were the pink and white pieces of cotton that had been wrapped around the mutilated limbs. There was no sign of blood on any of this fabric because, according to Mohammed Ben Ali, Cherifa had been too thin to bleed.

The murder of this dancing girl appeared to be merely a synecdoche for Moulay's "chamber of horrors" as a whole. Everybody was pretty certain that Moulay had killed again and again during her time in Meknès. After all, only about half of her "boarders" were accounted for. The prosecutor, M. Julin, announced, "Of 14 girls known to have been inmates of this house in a year, three have disappeared, four are dead, and seven have been tortured so badly that they will be invalids for life. Once a girl entered this haunt she was never seen again outside."

Another of the dead girls was finally identified: her name was Aicha, and she was a dancer at Moulay's house of horrors long before Cherifa arrived, but "lost her health and looks under the abuse until she was no longer of interest to the guests." With no use for Aicha anymore, Moulay allegedly murdered her with a loaf of bread stuffed full of strychnine.

Aicha and Cherifa were, at the very least, named in the press, but Moulay's other victims were fated to remain nameless forever. Her business was a place of utter darkness, a fetid drain where the poorest and youngest beauties of society seemed to catch, spin, and disappear. The details of the other two deaths – as well as those three missing girls – never surfaced, and no one came forward to mourn them.

The Hot Tea Dance

Neither Colette nor the French reporter Paul Boué – on location for *Paris-Soir* and calling in his reporting by phone – provided a detailed narrative of the night Cherifa died. (We do, however, have a date: November 21, 1936.) Somehow, though, a dramatic retelling of that fateful night wended its way into the American press. The account is more interesting for its speculative detail than for its accuracy – the American journalist seems to be trying to cram every exotic cliché he can into the story – and so it ends up telling us more about the Western press's opinion of Moulay than about Moulay herself. This is both intriguing and torturous. We want to know what happened, but instead, we get a flattened, exoticized, eroticized story of a girl who dances like a trapped princess and a woman with the cruelty and heartlessness of a witch.

Cherifa was a such a talented dancer, the story goes, that she was often forced to perform an elaborate ritual for clients called the Hot Tea Dance, which was invented by Moulay herself. During this performance, Cherifa was stripped naked, and Moulay placed a tray loaded with cups of boiling mint tea on the girl's head. Thus burdened, Cherifa was required to dance and perform acrobatic tricks without scalding herself. She managed to complete the routine about once every four times, but she was usually burned.

One evening, Moulay was entertaining some particularly important guest who was high on hashish and feeling exceptionally cruel. The tense spectacle of the Hot Tea Dance wasn't doing it for him that night, so he topped it off with a little entertainment of his own invention: sticking pins into Cherifa's naked back, heating them with a cigarette lighter, and watching her squirm.

Cherifa snapped. As the man busied himself with one of the pins, she spun around and, with an acrobat's strength, punched him right in the stomach. When he crumpled, she kicked him so hard in the chin that she almost broke his neck. Before she could finish him off, Moulay and Mohammed sprang on the rebellious girl – and that was the beginning of the end.

Though this story may well be fictionalized, it alludes to a surprising number of truths hidden between the accounts of mint tea and sinuous nude dancing. We know that Cherifa *was* brutalized, starved, and forced to sleep with horrible men. We know that Moulay *was* a wicked mastermind who used her creativity and intellect to please her clients. The tea tray and the cigarette lighter add color, but they're not the real point of the story. What's important here is that Moulay, once again, aligned herself with the victimizer, not the victim.

Speaking of reportage, though: what of the Moroccan press? Where are the accounts written in Arabic about Cherifa's murder, about Moulay's ghastly brothel? As a matter of fact, there was almost no large-scale Arabic-language Moroccan press extant in Moulay's day. Since Morocco was a French protectorate, there were French papers published *in* Morocco, but those mainly targeted, well, the

French. Attempts by nationalists to run Arabic-language papers were frequently squelched by French colonial authorities in order to ensure that the idea of protectorate as ideal state wasn't challenged. So what we know of Moulay, we know in French or English. Colette's account (written in French) is the best we have, but even though her reportage is at times quite empathetic, and though she takes the devastating effects of colonialism into account, she is not Moulay's countrywoman. What we're left with is an imperfect portrait of a strange, cruel woman who never did manage to break free from the tentacles of the country she loved – or pretended to love, or was forced to love – not even in print.

In the courtroom, Mohammed Ben Ali – who had tried to admit everything to the police earlier – was more than willing to keep talking. He even stood at the front of the room and acted out the murder for the benefit of his disgusted and fascinated audience. According to Ben Ali, once he and Moulay grew tired of kicking and beating Cherifa, they each picked up one end of a garrote and wrapped it around the girl's neck. Slowly, patiently, they pulled the cord in opposite directions. Later, the two dismembered her, "boiled the remains for twenty-four hours to make them unrecognizable," and then packed her away in the basket full of herbs. But they were remarkably careless with the body: not only did they fail at rendering the remains "unrecognizable," but they barely bothered to hide the basket. Cherifa's broken body could no longer bring in money, and so it meant nothing to them.

"The Proper Fashion"

There were plenty of witnesses against Moulay, but the most pitiful ones were the emaciated children who had been pulled from behind her wall. In court, people were astounded by their thinness, their raw animal terror – one of the girls burst out screaming when she saw Moulay in the courtroom – but what nobody expected was that these children, who had seen it all happen through a crack in the plaster, had nothing to say. They had been so starved and abused that they hardly had the capacity to form memories, much less recall and process them on command. "They barely murmur, wail quietly, prostrated," Colette wrote. When asked why they didn't try to run away, they responded, "We didn't think about it," or, "Impossible, we were too weak." Colette rather callously saw them as "graceful cattle, but cattle whose impenetrable crushing stupidity is utterly loathsome."

You get the sense, reading over the trial, that these children were something like blank slates, wiped bare by months of torture. When they were rescued, the heaviest of them weighed no more than seventy pounds. "Victim? Certainly," wrote Colette of the only boy, a thirteen-year-old named Driss, who tottered and gasped at the witness stand. "But a victim without memory; he has forgotten the dungeon, the lice, the itching, the hunger, the torture."

Moulay was visibly disdainful of these child witnesses, her old employees. Watching her, Colette noted that Moulay had no sense of guilt about the way she'd treated them. For Moulay, abuse was simply a natural part of the world she knew. It was the way one ran a brothel. "What words or images can we use to make Oum-El-Hassen understand what we mean by cruelty, and how could the accused murderer and torturer communicate to us her conviction that she is innocent?" asked Colette. Moulay seemed to believe that prostitutes should know their place in public, and she was appalled by the trembling and wailing of her former boarders. "Let them entrust this shrieking girl to Oum-El-Hassen and they'll see how to educate them in the proper fashion," wrote Colette, speculating about Moulay's thought process. "A touch of torture, starvation, some shutting away."

Moulay's actions imply that she cared desperately about following the rules – and not just any rules, but the French rules. She informed on the uprising, as dutiful as a telltale child. She eavesdropped on her girls to make sure they followed her instructions, which were simple: pleasure the clients and don't try to escape. But her reliance on the rules was a doomed one, for the game she was playing was rigged. The scholar Marnia Lazreg writes that "the colonial view of prostitution was marked not only by a deliberate neglect of the ways in which colonialism contributes to a flourishing, if not encouraging, of this activity, but also by a constant desire to define prostitution as a sign of deficient moral standards among native people." French soldiers may have paid her rent for a while, but they would never truly claim her as one of their own. She was too contaminated.

Was Moulay so careful about rules because she genuinely bought into this system of colonialism? Or was her loyalty given coldly and calculatingly – you know, betting on the side of the victor? It seems she chose the side of the French as a careful gamble: she would be good to them now, and they would be good to her later. But what a gamble to make, counting on the loyalty of a colonizing nation.

For her entire life, Moulay's position was marked by abuse from above and below. She was colonized; she was colonizer. In 1933, a few years after Moulay warned her Frenchmen about the religious uprising, one journalist lamented over the state of the average Moroccan woman, who was "stuck in a medieval routine" and could "neither read nor write, stays imprisoned in her house." Contrast this with Moulay, who was not the imprisoned woman, but the jail keeper herself. She was liberated from the home, but bought – too fully – into another system of oppression. Though she avoided being one of that "uncertain and miserable number" of dead girls, she contributed to the miserable number. In these economies of flesh, where everyone is feeding off everyone else, a dreadful question starts to emerge: is a life of comparative freedom (Moulay) only able to be purchased with the life of another (Cherifa)? The violence begins to feel inevitable, even mathematical – a horrible equation of power.

In court, a few folks testified about Moulay's character – or rather, her properness, which was her real defense. If she was a proper woman and ran a proper house, how could she be criticized? Proper women can't be executed, can they? But the searing disappointment of the trial, for Moulay, was the fact that none of her beloved officers showed up to defend her. Several of them were summoned, but not one of her clients or lovers appeared in court to explain how *valuable* she was to them, and how *good*. It was quite possibly the great betrayal of her life, and when she realized it, she wept into her white silk handkerchief.

White Silks

Moulay was skewered in the press throughout the trial. Everyone focused on the cruel corrosion of her looks, emphasizing that she used to be beautiful and talented and popular but that now she was evil both inside and out: the "once-glamorous" courtesan gone really, really bad. People even linked the loss of her looks to the increase in her cruelty. "After she lost her beauty she opened a house of prostitution," ran the *Oshkosh Daily Northwestern,* a bit smugly.

The most compelling insight into Moulay's interiority comes from Colette's cold but beautifully written reportage – and even though Colette sat next to the murderess for hours, watching the intricate play of emotions in her eyes, it's still only speculation. In her coverage of the case, Colette puts forth a sort of theory of Moulay's cruelty, saying that Moulay considered brutality to be a rite of passage for young, beautiful women who put themselves in the way of men. "What we call cruelty was the ordinary, bloody, and joyous currency of her life from infancy: the blows, the cord tying the slender limbs, the harsh male embrace, the passion she had for following . . . our first French contingents," wrote Colette. "All that kills, wounds, withers was her first lot as an adventurous girl." Moulay's world taught her that women were "creatures who strictly speaking have no value," and she internalized this message and passed it on to her boarders. "Where could she have learned that punishment exercised on women . . . has any limits?" Colette wondered. What she learned of violence, she probably learned from the French contingents, who were marching through her streets and paying her to spend the night with her North African girls.

Her devotion to the French was finally rewarded, however: she escaped the guillotine and was only sentenced to fifteen years in prison. (Mohammed got away with ten years.) Once her story reached the United States, it ballooned to mythical proportions: the number of victims attributed to her hovered around one hundred, and at least one paper ran a piece claiming that she had been guillotined. The same article reported that, at her execution, her beloved colonel was "seen to dabble his eyes."

The misinformation about Moulay only contributed to the sense of enigma and exoticism that hovered around her. Even Colette couldn't help comparing the trial to something out of the *Thousand and One Nights*. To this day, Morocco still appears sinuous and strange in the Western imagination; descriptions of Fez have hardly changed since Colette wandered, a wide-eyed product of her colonizing motherland, through its streets. (In 2007, the *New York Times* described Fez with breathless amazement, writing that the city's "shrouded figures and forgotten passages can seem impossible to decipher – yet tinged with a deep enchantment.") When Western sources retold Moulay's story, the details about smoky hashish, supple dancing girls, and scalding mint tea all fit nicely into the perennially popular fetish of the exotic woman, playing out against the backdrop of a very strong, very manly, very European army. At the end of the day, what was Moulay to the *Oshkosh Daily Northwestern* but a "shrouded figure" from a fairy tale?

But the true mystery of Moulay isn't her exoticism. It's her motives, which will always be closed to us. Who did she kill to please? Her clients? Her own dark urges? The French? And why? We can only guess at the forces that made her so willing to take a bullet in the hand for the officers of an invading army. We don't know what happened between Moulay and her love, the colonel. We can speculate that she felt broken, abandoned, and haunted by the memories of her glory days, when she was beautiful and when all the soldiers wanted her. But all we can really rely on is the image of her in the courtroom, surrounded by her own instruments of torture, weeping into her white silks.

So Moulay went to prison, and the world wondered why she didn't get the death penalty. Some suspected that she knew more than she was letting on – perhaps she was privy to some "political dynamite"? – or that she still had friends in high places who would have retaliated if the French executed her. But no one reached down from on high to hand Moulay a pardon, so off to jail she went, and she was never heard from again, at least not in "proper" society.

Perhaps her colonel finally appeared to her, tore down the walls of her prison, and stole her away into the warm night air. But if not, Moulay stumbled out of her cell at the end of her sentence and vanished, a second time, into the underbelly of the world that raised and destroyed her.

HIGH PRIESTESS OF THE BLUEBEARD CLIQUE

Tillie Klimek

If you were a woman who wanted to kill her husband, Chicago in the 1920s was the place to be. All you had to do was shoot the cheating bastard in the back of the head and then show up in court, fragrant with perfume and biting your lip in remorse. Your lawyers might ask you to marcel your hair, taking inspiration from the lovely murderesses that walked free before you, like "Stylish Belva" Gaertner and "Beautiful Beulah" Annan – the women who inspired the play *Chicago*. The all-male jury would glance approvingly at your silken ankles as you crossed them, visibly trembling. Go on, let a single tear roll down the side of your perfect nose. You'll go free – but only if you are very, very beautiful.

Tillie Klimek was not beautiful. At forty-five, she was worn down by childbearing, housekeeping, and four suspiciously troubled marriages. She was cursed with a "lumpy figure" and a "greasy complexion." She held petty grudges. She seemed like someone who knew a thing or two about the occult. And she had the audacity to play the husband-killing game without knowing the rules.

Coffin, For Sale, $30

Tillie came to the United States when she was about a year old as part of the first wave of Polish immigration to Chicago. This initial movement, which occurred from the 1850s to the early 1920s, was known as *za chlebem* – "for bread" – and it was largely an immigration of the lower classes. Tillie never learned to speak English perfectly, and later in life, people would accuse her and her family of having the "air of peasants."

As an adult, Tillie's life seemed unremarkable, especially against the breakneck backdrop of Chicago. Bootlegging raged, Al Capone ruled, rival newspapermen shot each other on the bus, and murders by women jumped four hundred percent in forty years. So when Tillie's first husband died in 1914, nobody panicked. When she remarried in a month and lost her second husband ninety days later, nobody said a thing. Violence ran like an artery through the city; there was nothing terribly shocking about the Polish woman who'd just pocketed about three thousand dollars in insurance money and dead men's savings.

Tillie didn't mind flying under the radar, especially since she never had trouble attracting the people she was most interested in: unmarried men. Even though people would later tear into her looks, she certainly possessed her own brand of allure, as she was never lacking for husbands and lovers. Her eyes, especially, were hauntingly pretty (though that might be simple hindsight bias – or, to use an even better term, "creeping determinism" – since now, when we stare into her eyes, we recognize her as a killer). She took her widow's money and spent some of it on a romantic trip to Milwaukee with her latest lover, Joseph Guskowski, hoping he'd soon become husband number three.

Alas, the charms of Milwaukee failed to work their magic on Guskowski, because he didn't propose, and didn't propose, and didn't propose. Tillie started to get irritated. She'd spent all this money on a vacation, and no ring? So as they made their way back to Chicago, she tried to terrify Guskowski into submission by informing him that her first two husbands hadn't died naturally. They'd been poisoned, she told him. Repeatedly. By her.

Guskowski panicked. If he was reluctant about proposing earlier, he was certainly not going to marry her now. When Tillie realized her mistake, she threatened him with prosecution under the Mann Act, which was supposed to save women from prostitution but was actually used to prosecute many forms of "immorality," including consensual adult sexual behavior. *Oh yeah?* Guskowski replied. If she dared to prosecute him, he'd take her straight to the police and expose her for the murderess that she wa –

Apparently Guskowski never stopped to think that angering Tillie might be a horrible idea, because a few days later, their argument ended for good when he dropped dead.

By 1919, Tillie was a newlywed again. She and her third husband, Frank Kupezyk, moved to Chicago's 924 North Winchester Avenue, a building known to this day as Old Lady Tillie Klimek's Haunted House. Their marriage wasn't altogether happy, and Tillie soon took a lover named John, who would stop by to smooch Tillie on the porch after Kupezyk had gone to work. (Neighbors noticed.) Life went on – normally, if not ideally – until two years into their marriage, when Kupezyk fell desperately ill.

One afternoon, as her husband lay sick in bed, Tillie came bounding out of her apartment, waving the newspaper. She showed it to her landlady, who was shocked to see Tillie pointing to an ad for a thirty-dollar coffin. The coffin was a steal, and Tillie declared that she was going to buy it. "My man, he's got only two inches to live," she informed the horrified woman. She also bought a few yards of expensive black fabric and sat by Kupezyk's sickbed, humming as she sewed herself a lovely funeral hat.

Kupezyk died on April 25, 1921, and while he lay stiffly in the living room, dressed in his funereal finest, Tillie blasted dance music from her Victrola. At one point, she even reached into her husband's coffin, grabbed his ear, and shouted, "You devil, you won't get up anymore!" As soon as he was in the ground, she collected $675 in life insurance and went searching for her next man.

But rumors began to circulate around Tillie's neighborhood. How had she known her husband was so close to death? People started whispering that she was psychic, that she could see death coming down the pipeline just in time to buy a cheap coffin. Of course, Tillie only knew that Kupezyk was "two inches" from death because she'd been poisoning him like clockwork. But to her credulous neighbors, the woman appeared omniscient.

Rough on Rats

One of the attendees at Kupezyk's funeral was a gentle, hardworking, fifty-year-old widower named Joseph Klimek. Some called him an alcoholic, but he stridently denied those charges. Klimek didn't really care about paying his respects to Kupezyk; he'd come to the funeral to set eyes on the newly single Tillie. His friends were nudging him in Tillie's direction, and after years of bachelorhood, the idea of a wife was comforting to Klimek.

After the service, Tillie didn't stay to flirt. "She felt too bad to see people," Klimek explained later. But after a few weeks of gentle pursuit, Tillie agreed to marry him. Klimek was overjoyed; his days of loneliness were over forever. "I married Tillie for a home," he said.

And what a cozy home it was! He appreciated her skill with the crochet hook, and he *loved* her cooking.

Sure, Tillie had a past, but Klimek didn't care about her former lovers. She was reformed. He was sure of it. "As soon as we were married, she burned up all the photographs of her husbands and her man friends," he said. "And she tore up all her letters. She had my picture over the mantel; that was all."

Unbeknownst to the romantic Klimek, Tillie wasn't so happy with her little slice of domestic bliss. She began complaining to her cousin, Nellie Koulik, who had a dead husband of her own under her belt. When Nellie suggested a divorce, Tillie responded, "No, I will get rid of him some other way." Nellie knew exactly what she meant, and before Tillie left, Nellie slipped her a little tin of powder marked ROUGH ON RATS. It was a household poison made up of arsenic tinted black with coal, easy to purchase at any friendly neighborhood drugstore, and it had an eye-catching logo: a rat, dead on its back, overlaid with the slogan: DON'T DIE IN THE HOUSE. Nellie always kept some on hand. UNBEATABLE EXTERMINATOR, ran the text beneath the logo. THE OLD RELIABLE THAT NEVER FAILS.

Tillie went home and began to whip up a series of wonderful, home-cooked meals for Klimek, each one seasoned with a healthy dash of Rough on Rats. Klimek ate and ate, growing sicker and sicker. His legs stiffened and his breath began to smell like garlic – two of the more innocuous signs of arsenic poisoning. Around that time, two of his pet dogs died suddenly.

Klimek's insurance money was practically glimmering on the horizon when his brother John ruined everything by getting suspicious. Despite Tillie's loud objections that she could nurse Klimek herself, thank you very much, John insisted on bringing in his own doctor to take a look at his brother. The doctor immediately recognized the symptoms of arsenic poisoning and whisked Joseph away to the hospital, notifying the police in the process.

On October 26, 1922, Tillie was arrested for the attempted murder of Joseph Klimek. The following day, her cousin Nellie was arrested for providing her with the arsenic. While Tillie was carted away in the squad car, she turned to the officer next to her. "The next one I want to cook a dinner for is you," she said. "You made all my trouble."

Exhumations

It soon became apparent that Joseph Klimek's poisoning wasn't an isolated incident. Anonymous letters begged the police to dig up the bodies of Tillie's third husband, old Frank Kupezyk, and Nellie's first. Lo and behold, their corpses were marbled with arsenic. Clearly, Tillie had enemies who had long suspected that her "psychic" qualities were rooted in murder. ("Don't die in the house!") Newspaper headlines began to take on a Frankensteinian quality: BODIES OF MATES OF PAIR ORDERED DUG UP; 3 MORE BODIES TO BE EXHUMED IN KLIMEK CASE; BODIES OF OTHER RELATIVES WILL BE EXHUMED.

Meanwhile, Tillie was taken to the hospital to see her last living spouse. Did she feel bad for trying to murder him? She did not. As he plied her with furious questions, she replied, "I don't know. Don't bother me anymore." When she overheard him asking a nurse for a glass of water, Tillie shouted at the nurse, "If he makes any trouble for you, take a two-by-four board and hit him over the head with it!" Still, she kissed him before she left, baffling onlookers.

It soon became clear that Tillie had killed more than just her husbands. As the police were busily exhuming bodies, two of Tillie's cousins showed up at the station and told them to dig deeper. They claimed that Tillie had killed four of their siblings, all of whom died after a creepy dinner party at Tillie's place. Tillie had been in an argument with their mother, and took her rage out on the children by serving them poisoned food.

A common thread was emerging among many of Tillie's crimes: petty revenge. She killed Joseph Guskowski because she felt snubbed by his lack of engagement ring, and she grew so furious over minor slights and disagreements that it was dangerous to be around her when she was in a bad mood. Two of her neighbors came forward to tell the police that they fell deathly ill after Tillie fed them poisoned candy. One woman said it was because she and Tillie had gotten into an argument, and the other claimed that Tillie had spotted her talking to Klimek and hadn't liked it.

As Tillie and Nellie were formally charged with murder – Tillie for the murder of Frank Kupezyk and Nellie for the murder of her first husband – the exhumations took an even more disturbing turn. "Poison mystery trails" led detectives to three tiny graves: those of Nellie's twin infants and granddaughter. Nellie had given birth to the twins while she was still married to her first husband, but he refused to acknowledge them as his. (At the time, Nellie was already embroiled in a tempestuous affair with the man who would become her second husband, Albert Koulik.) One of the twins died at eight months; the other died a month later. The third dead baby, the grandchild, was allegedly poisoned after Nellie's daughter criticized Nellie for "her manner of living." Just like her murderous cousin, Nellie had a quick trigger finger and a low tolerance for disagreement.

The police could barely keep up with the accusations that were now pouring in. It was like a dam had broken in Tillie's community, and people finally felt free to confess their deepest, darkest suspicions about their allegedly psychic neighbor and her child-killing cousin. Everyone was sure they were being poisoned. One of Nellie's sons suspected that his mother had been slowly poisoning him. One of Nellie's daughters suspected Tillie of poisoning *her*. Even Nellie's sister, Cornelia, was brought into jail because her son-in-law was convinced she'd been giving him poisoned moonshine. Poison, poison everywhere, and not a drop to drink! The total alleged victim count hovered at twenty: twelve dead, seven alive but in poor health, and one missing (a mystery man known only as "Meyers," suspected to be another husband or lover of Tillie's). And that's just counting humans. One neighbor claimed that their dog had died suddenly after Tillie "voiced objections" to its obnoxious barking.

The community had gone poison mad – and to the police, the situation felt almost unstoppable. They began to talk of a witchy "poison belt" that stretched throughout Chicago's Little Poland, with Tillie ruling over it as the "high priestess of the Bluebeard clique." The cousins were now facing the gallows.

"They Just Died Same as Other People"

In jail, the accused women exhibited very different personalities. Nellie smiled more, spoke less English, and was prone to hysterics. She allowed photographers to take her picture, but not until she'd slicked back her hair. When asked about the case, she insisted that her accusing son had simply made a "joke" that the "big men" were taking too seriously. In contrast, Tillie was silent, controlled, and defiant, an "automaton of emotions." The only time she showed any real feeling was when she burst out in her own defense: "I didn't rob nobody! I didn't shoot nobody; I didn't poison nobody; I didn't kill nobody. I didn't! Everybody pick on me. Everybody make eyes at me like they going to eat me. Why do they make eyes at me? I tell the truth. Anything I did I did to myself. Nobody else."

The prosecutor assigned to the case – William McLaughlin, assistant state's attorney – was out for Tillie's blood. McLaughlin had a knack for hyperbole and seemed determined to secure his own immortalization through this trial. He fed journalists the melodramatic quotes they wanted to hear, calling it "the most astounding wholesale poisoning plot ever uncovered" and "the most amazing death plot in recent criminal history." He claimed that the cousins threw "poison parties" at which they fed arsenic-drenched entrees to large swathes of relatives. In fact, he was convinced that Little Poland was haunted by an entire *network* of female Bluebeards, and that Tillie and Nellie were simply the (crude, unattractive) tip of the iceberg. He wouldn't be satisfied with a life sentence for Tillie, either. He wanted her to hang.

Outside of the courtroom, several of Chicago's feisty "girl reporters" were hot on the case, including the amazing Genevieve Forbes, who worked the crime beat in an era when women simply were not on the crime beat. Forbes scored a series of intimate interviews: she talked to Joseph Klimek in the hospital, she tracked down Tillie's distraught parents, and, finally, she got an audience with Tillie herself.

With her merciless journalist's eye, Forbes recognized nuances in Tillie that no one else bothered to understand. She saw Tillie as a dangerous, vengeful woman who used poison as a means of assuaging her wounded pride and who held her secrets close to her chest. She tore into Tillie's looks – "a fat, squat, Polish peasant woman, 45 years old but looking 55, with a lumpy figure, capacious hands and feet, and dull brown hair skinned back into a knot at the back of her head" – but grudgingly acknowledged her secretive intelligence. "Tillie Klimek is a spectator at her own drama," she wrote.

The court never gave Tillie that sort of credit, and the trial took a distasteful turn when the judge asked for a "psychopathic lab report" on the two accused women. According to the examining doctor, both women were "sub-normal mentally and sufferers from dementia praecox," with intellects no higher than those of an eleven-year-old child. The judge took the whole thing a step further by bringing up one of the era's pet subject: eugenics. He was irritated because one of Nellie's sons had already been declared "of feeble mind" years before, and he was convinced that criminality ran in this family's DNA. "If we had a fieldworker, a eugenics expert, to check up on the history of this whole family at the time one moron was discovered, then the police might have been warned to watch this woman," he said. "When we find one case we can seek out and locate the nest."

Note that neither of these women spoke perfect English. If their examination had been conducted in English, it's quite possible they would have simply been unable to complete it properly. It does seem like Nellie was significantly more naïve than her cousin, but Tillie was no fool, and the lab report especially underestimated her. "She has brains," Forbes had noted, "and they are the yardsticks for her emotions." But she wasn't fluent, and she didn't want to explain herself anyway, so the court insisted that her crimes were the result of a childlike intellect – or the sloppy, disagreeable work of a peasant.

Since Chicago was so thoroughly out of control in the 1920s, it's not surprising that Tillie's trial turned into something of a circus. On numerous occasions, the judge was forced to yell, "This is not a theater!" Oh, but it was. The witnesses against Tillie included gossipy neighbors, three grave diggers, and a "lady undertaker," and the audience was obsessed with them. One of the grave diggers scandalized the court with his tale of Tillie's lover John, who often visited Tillie after Frank Kupezyk left for work. "Once I seen him kiss her," said the grave digger. When the prosecutor asked what happened next, the grave digger replied, "Why then, Tillie put up some newspapers in front of the window, so I couldn't see in." Everybody cracked up at that – even Tillie.

But by the end of the trial, nobody was laughing, and even Tillie's impassive demeanor was starting to splinter. When the coroner's chemist swore he'd found arsenic in the bodies of all three of her husbands, she finally began to exhibit signs of anxiety. Still, she gave her own solid defense, wearing the fateful black hat that she'd sewn next to Kupezyk's deathbed. She insisted that Kupezyk died of alcohol poisoning and denied culpability in each one of her other husbands' deaths. "I loved them; they loved me. They just died same as other people," she said. "I not responsible for that. I could no [sic] help if they wanted to die."

McLaughlin was practically begging the jury for the death penalty. He was sick and tired of women getting away with murder. "Gentlemen, the death penalty has never been inflicted upon a woman in this state," he cried. "This defendant is like a good many other women in this town. She thinks she can get away with it. There are a lot of women, gentlemen, who are awaiting your verdict in this case. I feel that the death penalty should be inflicted, and I mean it."

He was right: Tillie was exactly like "a good many other women in this town," in that she was a husband killer. Four hundred percent, remember? But unlike many of the other women, who wept and flirted from the witness stand, Tillie did not, in fact, "get away with it." She received a guilty verdict for the murder of Frank Kupezyk and was sentenced to life in prison – the harshest sentence ever given to a woman in Cook County at the time.

No Beauty

Nellie's trial was something of a mess. Maybe the court never took her as seriously as Tillie, the ice queen, because despite the fact that her own kids testified against her, Nellie walked free. Once she was acquitted of the charge of giving Tillie poison, McLaughlin wearily dropped the other charge against her. Her first husband's body was undeniably full of arsenic, but nobody felt like delving into this supposed "Bluebeard clique" any further now that its high priestess was in jail.

Other murderesses were filing into the courthouse now, and they were much easier on the eyes. In two short years, "Stylish Belva" Gaertner and "Beautiful Beulah" Annan would be preening behind the bars of the same jail, posing for reporters in their slips and using every feminine wile in the book (including, but not limited to: tears, fashionable hats, and great tailoring) to walk free.

This was the ugly truth behind the verdict: Tillie may never have been locked up for life if she had been more attractive. Yes, she was clearly guilty, but Chicago had dealt with guilty husband killers before, and the pretty ones consistently walked free. Twenty-eight women had been acquitted of murder in Cook County alone in recent years, and they were all good-looking. The latest woman to be released was Cora Orthwein, a "dashing, well dressed north side beauty." Only four had been found guilty before Tillie came along: Hilda Axlund ("not a beauty"), Vera Trepannier ("more than middle aged"), Emma Simpson ("judged insane"), and Dora Waterman ("no beauty").

Of course, though Tillie was only technically on trial for the murder of Frank Kupezyk, it was pretty clear to most observers that she was a serial killer – and not just a serial killer, people thought, but the mastermind behind an entire "poison ring." Even so, both the press and the courtroom loved the passionate violence of women who killed husbands and lovers, which is exactly what Tillie did. Orthwein, for example, shot her lover after a night of boozing and ferocious fighting. Who's to say that if Tillie had been young and blushing, her story wouldn't have been framed differently, despite its higher rate of violence? They might have portrayed her as a delicate husband seeker, continually offended by her coarse peasant lovers. A serial lover who just happened to kill.

The courts and the press were well aware of their bias, but they also seemed to revel in it. There was something so *sexy* about a bad woman going free. Society's moral outrage was reserved for women like Tillie, who didn't look good doing evil things. A *Tribune* column called "A Line o' Type or Two" published a vicious telegram mocking Chicago for the ugliness of its latest murderess: "Chicago's bid for fame in boosting Tillie Klimek will fall flat," it ran. "Suggest you have eligibility classes as to beauty, social standing, and so forth before allowing any more murders."

After one especially ridiculous trial, where two gorgeous blonde sisters were acquitted of murder, the irritated prosecutor remarked that "blonde curls or dark eyes seem to have a faculty of making juries forget the most clinching evidence." Genevieve Forbes put it the most bluntly: "Tillie Klimek went to the penitentiary because she had never gone to a beauty parlor."

The Devil Won't Get Up

One point that apparently never came up at the trial was the question of abuse. Most of the evidence pointed to money as

Tillie's motive, since she collected tidy little sums after each husband's death. Because of this, perhaps the court didn't feel the need to delve further into her psyche. But concurrent juries were extraordinarily sympathetic to any whiff of spousal abuse in these husband-killing cases, so one wonders why it wasn't ever mentioned by Tillie's defense. After all, both Tillie and her parents insisted that Klimek and Kupezyk were no-good alcoholics, and then there was that whole business of Tillie yelling in Kupezyk's dead ear, "You devil, you won't get up anymore." Did she kill solely for money and revenge, or was she running from a devil or two?

Money certainly wasn't her only motivation, as there were plenty of times when Tillie killed with no hope of a life insurance payout. She held overblown grudges and used poison to silence anyone who irritated her, whether it was a neighbor who dared to flirt with her husband or a dog that wouldn't stop barking. Genevieve Forbes, at least, certainly seemed to think Tillie was an enigma that hadn't been solved yet. But the city at large was ready to move on to prettier criminals. For a while, they'd focused on Tillie's crimes and her looks, but no one was terribly concerned with her demons. So they labeled her "squat" and "ugly" and locked her up for life.

Tillie led a peaceful life in prison; she told Forbes a few years later that she was all caught up on her spring sewing and enjoyed the prison food. She spent thirteen years in jail while the public zeroed in on bigger, sexier murder cases, and then died in prison on November 20, 1936. The newspapers listed her age as four years older than she actually was. In death, as in life, nobody cared much about making Tillie look good.

Despite whatever mild domesticity Tillie displayed in jail, she still harbored a secret or two. After all, her alleged lover

"Meyers" was never found. And a few years after the trial, when her last husband finally passed away, the doctors reported that he had succumbed to tonsillitis. But when they cut him open and examined his insides, they found that Joseph Klimek's weakened body was still absolutely full of arsenic.

SORCERESS OF KILKENNY

Alice Kyteler

Are you hoping to destroy a woman in pre-Enlightenment Europe? You've got a few convenient options. You could accuse her of sexual misconduct – always an effective tactic. You could claim that she killed her baby. Or you could bundle all your allegations into one dramatic package, dripping with sex and superstition, and call her a witch – then dust off your hands and let the mob take over as you settle down to enjoy a warm bowl of sheep's head broth.

The woman at the heart of Europe's first real witch trial may have actually been Europe's first documented female serial killer, but the theatrical accusations thrown at her – sleeping with demons! Cooking with the brains of unbaptized children! – quickly obscured her real crimes. Dame Alice Kyteler was a quadruple husband-charmer, a fearless social climber, and a dangerous enemy. She was charming, powerful, enterprising, and good with cash. If you look closely at her life, you'll start to notice patterns, like the fact that she left a number of dead husbands in her wake, but these patterns have faded from the annals of history. What people remember about

Alice, when they think of her at all, is that she may or may not have ridden on a greased broomstick.

Centuries after Dame Alice was accused of being the "mother and mistress" of a witch's coven, it's easy to read the documentation of her case and feel smugly confident that no, the woman did *not* offer up nine raw peacock eyes to some dark demonic force nicknamed Robin, Son of Art. She was falsely accused because she had too much money, because society found powerful women dangerous and/or annoying, and because people wanted to steal her land. Her society's reaction to her was nothing new, either. A thousand years before Alice came along, the Roman poet Juvenal was already muttering that "there is nothing more intolerable than a wealthy woman."

Outrageous, right? Then again, there were all those dead husbands to consider.

Maleficia

It was nearing the end of the thirteenth century, and the Irish city of Kilkenny was a wonderful place to live. The surrounding countryside was lush and green. An attractive castle loomed nearby, radiating protection, power, and order. And the city was overrun with marriageable men.

Through the streets of this fair city strode Alice Kyteler, sometimes called Dame, sometimes called Lady, proud descendent of Flemish merchants. As a young lady, Alice had plenty of social clout already, due to the fact that she owned land, was related to the Kilkenny sheriff, and boasted a smattering of friends in high places. Her stock continued to rise when she married a rich banker named William Outlawe around 1280; *his* relatives included people like the lord chancellor of Ireland. The two had a son, William Jr., and Alice lavished her attention and resources on the boy. He would always be her favorite.

After about twenty years of marriage, Outlawe died. Conveniently, William Jr. was now old enough to take over his father's lands and the family banking business, and Outlawe's generous will meant that both Alice and her son would be just fine in a pinch. More than fine, actually – they were suddenly richer and more influential than they'd been before his death. It was almost as though losing dear old Dad was a good thing.

Alice rapidly moved on to a new man: Adam le Blond, who came from a powerful landowning family. The newlyweds made a formidable pair, with connections in the very highest social circles; at one point, they even loaned the king, Edward I, five hundred pounds to help finance the Scottish wars. Le Blond was apparently enamored of his stepson, because he had no problem lending William Jr. three thousand pounds, which the young man promptly buried in the ground for safekeeping. This was a massive amount of money in those days. To put it into perspective, a man might earn one penny (240 of which went into a single pound) for a day's hard labor. A woman would earn half of that.

All of this favoritism began to breed resentment in Kilkenny. William Jr. looked spoiled, and people didn't exactly love the fact that Alice had profited from both her marriages. Even the sheriff, Alice's relative, envied her privileged position. So one night in 1302, he crept over to William Jr.'s house with a group of townspeople and shamelessly dug up those three thousand pounds. The group claimed that since the money was discovered in the ground it counted as "treasure trove" – hidden valuables that had no owner – and, as such, belonged to the king. Alice and le Blond protested, but instead of returning the money, the sheriff accused them of homicide and threw them in jail.

Homicide? Seemed like a charge pulled from the ether – and in some ways it was, designed to keep the sheriff from getting in trouble for stealing the money in the first place. But people had been whispering about Alice for a while now. They suspected that she was up to something.

The couple was soon released, since they were rich and powerful and nobody had any real evidence against them, but the animosity toward Alice and William Jr. continued to grow. Out of thin air, it seemed, le Blond abruptly revised his will, making William Jr. his sole heir and simultaneously canceling all of the young man's debts, which included the loan of the three thousand pounds. This was especially shocking because le Blond already had biological children, who surely met the news of their vanished birthright with horror.

Then, with his affairs in order, Adam le Blond died. It was another convenient death, happening exactly when Alice and William Jr. stood to profit most.

By 1309, Alice had found herself a very appealing third husband: the wealthy knight Richard de Valle. Like the husbands before him, de Valle must have been extraordinarily smitten with his bride, because even though he, too, already had biological children from a previous marriage, he decided that William Jr. was his favorite. De Valle began showering his stepson with money and various important business responsibilities; for example, William Jr. was granted powers of attorney to collect debts owed to the de Valle family.

When de Valle died, Alice was owed one-third of his considerable lands – her widow's dower – but one of de Valle's sons tried to claim it for himself, possibly out of resentment at his stepmother, who was already a landowner many times over. Clearly, he failed to realize that his stepmother was not someone to be trifled with. Alice had an iron backbone (and an impressive Rolodex, so to speak), and instead of giving in to her stepson, she marched him straight to court – and won. Now, not only was she wealthier than ever, but she was officially a wicked stepmother in the eyes of de Valle's newly orphaned children.

Behind closed doors, Alice had clearly been encouraging her husbands to sign over their wealth to her and her beloved son. Maybe it wasn't intentional, malevolent manipulation; maybe she was just so charming that they did it voluntarily. We don't know exactly what she did to make all of her husbands change their wills, or whether she was stirring something noxious into their broth as they did so. All we can do here is recognize a pattern: Alice consistently turned a profit after each husband's death, and then quickly moved on to another wealthy man.

Now, patterns often point to something: a truth, a source, a secret. And this particular pattern would live a very long half-life; people will probably be killing their loved ones for profit until the end of time. When a woman does this, she's termed a "black widow," based on the largely-incorrect premise that all female black widow spiders devour their mates after sex. If there was ever any forensic evidence implicating Alice in her husbands' deaths, it crumbled to dust ages ago along with their bodies. But her next batch of stepchildren certainly suspected that she was a black widow, though they didn't have a name for it yet. Instead, they called it like they saw it: magic.

Alice's fourth husband lived, but it wasn't pleasant. His name was Sir John le Poer, and over the course of their marriage, his health began to deteriorate in odd ways. He grew extremely thin. He lost all the hair on his body. His fingernails and toenails began to drop off. To those familiar with the apothecarial arts, le Poer's health problems would have seemed consistent with slow, gradual arsenic poisoning. But to everyone else, his sickness looked like the work of a witch.

Le Poer apparently held no suspicions against his bride, because soon enough he was happily making revisions to his last will and testament. This shiny new version provided generously for Alice and William Jr., ensuring that they would be comfortable long after le Poer's spirit left his emaciated, hairless body.

The revised will infuriated the le Poer kids – Alice's new stepchildren. First they had to witness their father marry this wealthy, arrogant widow, and now they had to watch him sign away their birthright? In 1324, they marched over to the nearest bishop and told him that Alice had bewitched their father, muddled his mind, and poisoned her previous three husbands. They were basing their claims on a prevalent belief in *maleficia* – spiteful acts performed by witches against the community – which was often used to explain things like sickness, death, and natural disasters.

Do something, said the stepchildren. Arrest the witch.

The le Poer children could not have brought their fears to a more sympathetic listener. His name was Richard de Ledrede. He was an Englishman and the bishop of Ossory. When he heard "witch," he thought "heretic," and he hated nothing more than heretics.

Heresy

Richard de Ledrede was a foreigner from England and a moral legalist and not very good at the interpersonal aspect of his job. He was probably a brilliant scholar; he had no political connections – and certainly no social ones – that would have helped him score the bishopric of Ossory in 1317. When appointed bishop, he was praised for the rather dry virtues of "respectability" and "clean living." What this description failed to mention was his religious zeal, his single-minded passion for rules, and his knack for making enemies.

Ledrede's education took place right as a wave of witch-hunting hysteria swept across France, a hysteria that was encapsulated in the sensational trials of the Knights Templar. The Catholic Church was just beginning to articulate its changing stance on the issues – and intersections – of sorcery, witchcraft, and sacrilege. Witchcraft was no longer just characterized by magic and acts of maleficia. It was now seen as something in direct opposition to the church itself: heresy.

The pope at the time, John XXII, was a paranoid man. He had convinced himself that his enemies were constantly trying to assassinate him through dark, sorcerous means: by sending him a devil trapped inside a ring, by melting tiny wax effigies of his body, and so forth. On February 27, 1318, he launched the first important papal bull against witchcraft. It didn't officially state that witches were heretics, but by the time it was written, the correlation between the two was fully formed in the mind of the church. This bull, and the pope's paranoia, effectively paved the way for what was to come: inquisitions, persecutions, and burnings all across Europe.

Ledrede's attitude toward witches and heretics was nourished in this frenetic broth, and he began his career "armed with a religious zeal which made [him] rapidly unpopular" with his Irish parishioners. They wanted to sing bawdy songs; he wanted them to sing Latin hymns. They were proud of their land of saints and scholars; he saw evil all across Ireland. These parishioners were accustomed to obeying both the rules of their Irish king and the rules of the church, and the best bishops were able to tactfully walk this line, but Ledrede couldn't do it. He was "totally lacking in any practical diplomatic sense" and would have thrown out the king's rules in a heartbeat if the church demanded it. He also built himself a "lavish palace" in Kilkenny, which did nothing to endear him to the populace.

His diocese quickly grew to hate him and did everything they could to make his life miserable. By 1320, the pope was forced to compensate Ledrede for all sorts of grievances: he'd been locked up by his own parishioners, he'd been falsely accused of various crimes, his servants were abused, he was denied tithes, and someone stole a hundred shillings from him in a violent fashion.

Though they grew to loathe each other, Dame Alice and Ledrede actually had a lot in common. They were both ambitious, tough, and absolutely unwilling to back down. They were despised by many of their contemporaries, but this hatred never stopped them from doing whatever they wanted. Both seemed possessed of a certain slightly psychotic, single-minded purpose: Ledrede lived to enforce the law of the church; Alice lived to accumulate wealth for herself and her son. In another life, they could have been co-conspirators, but here they were separated by too many unalterable dichotomies: woman vs. man, king vs. church, Ireland vs. England, the fluidity of social connections vs. the intransigence of the law.

Fi, Fi, Fi, Amen

When Ledrede heard that a rich older woman was terrorizing Kilkenny, killing husbands left and right, the case seemed like the perfect outlet for his religious zeal. Plus, it would be a great way to please the pope. So despite the fact that the le Poer children were simply bringing a good old-fashioned charge of witchcraft against their evil stepmother, Ledrede decided that he was dealing with a "diabolical nest" of heretics. He dashed over to Kilkenny to investigate, and soon enough he had "uncovered" a veritable cult of eleven witches, led by the dreadful Dame Alice Kyteler herself.

With Ledrede on board, the charges against Alice suddenly swelled. The original charge, made by the le Poer stepchildren, declared that Alice had bewitched and killed her first three husbands and was currently murdering her fourth. But the new charges had far more heretical implications: Alice was said to have denied the Christian faith, sacrificed animals, sought advice from demons, and twisted church ceremonies into demonic parodies of themselves (i.e., lighting candles and excommunicating her husbands, all while shrieking, "Fi! fi! fi! Amen!"). She was also charged with boiling a ghastly stew in the skull of a beheaded robber that was comprised of ingredients like rooster intestines, "certain horrible worms," the brains of unbaptized children, and the nails of dead men. Finally, she was accused of sleeping with a demon named Robin Artisson, or Robin, Son of Art, who was supposedly the source of all her wealth. He would appear to her as a cat, a black dog, or a dark-skinned man with two companions – and lest anyone think sleeping with a spirit was an incorporeal act, their lovemaking was so stickily tangible that Alice's maid Petronilla had to clean up after them.

These charges, melodramatic as they are, have all sorts of interesting implications. They indicate not just a subversion of the Catholic Church, but a subversion of wifehood and motherhood, what with all the excommunicating of husbands and the boiling babies' brains. Romping around with Robin was probably the most glaring of Dame Alice's alleged subversions: in the first place, she was having sex (out of wedlock) with a shape-shifting demon (not exactly husband material); in the second place, the fact that Petronilla had to clean up after them implied the "spilling of seed," which according to the Catholic Church was a sin, since it meant sex without the possibility of pregnancy.

Ironically, these colorful accusations provided a nice big smoke screen that distracted everyone from the initial accusations against Alice. If she *had* killed her previous husbands and was currently poisoning Sir John le Poer, as her stepchildren swore she was, then she had been subverting her roles as a wife and mother (or at least stepmother) all along – like, *really* subverting those roles, by intentionally widowing herself and ruining her stepchildren's futures. But other than the stepchildren, nobody was paying much attention to that far more realistic possibility. There were demons to discuss and women to burn!

Though Ledrede's anti-Alice zeal stemmed from his hatred of heresy, the local sentiment against Alice was informed by more prosaic irritations. Alice was, quite simply, a thorn in their side. She had been for quite some time. Everything about her was a menace to the Kilkenny patriarchy: she was an heiress, she was strong willed, she was independent (even though she was still technically married, it's hard to imagine she felt tied down by the ailing le Poer), and she'd been at this game for at least forty years. Nothing was more intolerable than a wealthy woman!

It's not that she was just a threat to the male *egos* of Kilkenny. It was a far more literal threat than that. Alice was an economic threat to her stepchildren and to anyone else who had a vested interest in any of that sweet Outlawe/le Blond/de Valle/le Poer wealth. She was a living example of the dangers of female inheritance, a subject that weighed heavily on the minds of the Irish at the time. And the witchcraft charges against her reflected this fear and resentment of her affluence. They were designed, wrote the historian Norman Cohn, "to show that Lady Alice had no right to her wealth, that it had been wrested from its rightful owners by truly diabolic means, that it was tainted at the source."

But though wealth was what got her into trouble, wealth was also what got her out of it. Ledrede could accuse her of defying the Catholic Church all he wanted, because Alice was backed by the secular gods: money and power.

The Passion of Ledrede

As Ledrede attempted to weave a net of accusations around Alice, the dame was pulling a few strings of her own. Her old friend, the lord chancellor of Ireland, learned about the scuffle in Kilkenny and tried to convince Ledrede to drop the charges. When Ledrede kept trying to arrest Alice, the lord chancellor gently informed him that Alice simply *couldn't* be arrested yet, because she hadn't even been properly accused of a crime. To this, Ledrede "indignantly" responded that "the service of the church was above the forms of the law of the land."

This was just so Ledrede. The laws of the land were hindering him, so he decided to strike off on his own. He commanded Alice to appear in court, but instead, she ran off to Dublin. Fuming, Ledrede went ahead and excommunicated her, and then demanded that her son, William Jr., show up in her place.

One of the Kilkenny authorities, Arnald le Poer – possibly related to Alice by marriage – decided to try his hand at appeasing Ledrede. He went to visit the raging bishop in person and attempted to talk him out of his plan, but Ledrede was so difficult and persistent that Arnald ended up walking out in a blind fury himself. The next day, Arnald had Ledrede thrown into prison until William Jr.'s court date had safely passed. This wasn't entirely legal, but there was nothing the bishop could do about it. As much as Ledrede may have thundered on about the rules of the church being superior to the laws of the land, both church and law usually ended up bowing to men like Arnald, who had money and soldiers at their disposal.

In prison, Ledrede screamed that sorcerers and heretics were protected in godforsaken Ireland while religious men like him were locked up. This would have only encouraged the antiforeigner sentiment Arnald was fostering against this "alien from England." When a few sympathetic parishioners stopped by the prison to bring Ledrede food, Arnald declared that the bishop wasn't allowed to have visitors at all. The bishop retaliated by placing the entire diocese under an interdict – meaning that everyone was temporarily banned from participating in the sacraments and other church rituals – even though he was not technically allowed to do this. Their struggle devolved into a series of delicious ad hominem attacks: as Ledrede raged from prison, Arnald invited everyone in the community to come forward and complain about him. Parishioners stepped up eagerly, embarrassing the bishop by accusing him of "grievous crimes."

When Ledrede was finally released from prison, he made a huge show of it, marching out "in triumph, full-dressed in his pontifical robes." He had doubled down on his decision to trap Alice, and immediately set a new court date for William Jr., since Alice was still hiding out in Dublin. But before he could drag William Jr. into court, Ledrede was served a court date of his own. The king himself had gotten wind of the chaos in Kilkenny and wanted an explanation for that illegal interdict. Ledrede tried to get out of it by arguing that the journey to court was too dangerous, since it took him through the lands of "his enemy" – Arnald – but no one listened to this excuse.

Even now, with the king involved, Ledrede didn't seem to realize he was fighting a losing battle. In fact, he was absurdly overconfident. During one of Arnald's customary meetings in court, Ledrede marched in wearing full bishop regalia, accompanied by a squad of religious men and holding the bread of the Lord's Supper in a golden vessel – the transubstantiated body of Christ himself, according to the teachings of the Catholic Church! He hoped to intimidate Arnald into helping him arrest Alice, but all the golden vessels in the world couldn't protect Ledrede from mockery. Arnald exploded, calling him a "vile, rustic, interloping monk carrying dirt in his hands," and forced him into one of the seats reserved for criminals. Humiliated and offended, Ledrede cried out that "Christ had never been treated so before since he stood at the bar before Pontius Pilate."

Although Ledrede's conflict with Alice had been waylaid by his ridiculous skirmish with Arnald, Alice had been paying close attention to all of these proceedings, and decided it was time for a little power play of her own. She managed to get Ledrede indicted in a secular court for defaming her character and excommunicating her "uncited, unadmonished, and unconvinced of the crime of sorcery." The fact that Alice managed to turn the law on her accuser in the face of her own looming witchcraft trial demonstrates once again how savvy and well connected she was – not to mention how bold.

By the time Ledrede fought his way through this latest legal obstacle and *finally* managed to get permission to try Alice for witchcraft, it was too late. Alice, who was always so astute when it came to maneuvering through society, decided that a trial wasn't in her best interest, and fled to England.

Humans

Alice's supposed accomplices, with their tales of demons and peacock eyes and dead men's nails, did not have the wealth or the connections to skip town. After Alice left, several of them were arrested and thrown into jail. Under torture, they confessed to all of their purported crimes and claimed that Alice was their dreadful leader, "the mother and mistress of them all."

Petronilla of Meath, the woman who'd allegedly cleaned up after Robin and Alice, was unlucky enough to become the scapegoat for all of Alice's offenses, both real and imagined. After being flogged six times, Petronilla confessed that she had been the medium between Alice and her demon lover. She also said that Alice had a magical broomstick that helped her fly, and that she herself had bewitched local women so that it looked like goats' horns were growing out of their heads. When it came to black magic, said Petronilla, nobody in the world was as powerful as Dame Alice.

Poor Petronilla was burned alive on November 3, 1324 – the first time anyone was given this sentence for heresy in Ireland. But her memory lived on as a symbol of injured and innocent womanhood. (In 1979, the artist Judy Chicago re-reminded the world of Petronilla by including her in a feminist art installation called *The Dinner Party*). Other abuses followed for members of the "pestilential society of Robin, son of Art" – whippings, banishments, excommunications, and more burnings – but Alice was never touched.

It's hard to say which of the major players had the last laugh here. Alice left Ledrede in the dust, but she had to spend the rest of her life in exile. Ledrede eventually succeeded in dragging William Jr. to court, but when William Jr. finally showed up, he was irascible and "armed to the teeth." The two managed to hit upon a testy agreement: the bishop would forgive William Jr.'s offenses if

William Jr. promised to demonstrate he was repentant by going to church, feeding the poor, and paying for a beautiful new cathedral roof made of lead.

Ledrede also managed to get revenge on his nemesis Arnald by accusing him of heresy, excommunicating him, and flinging him into jail, where Arnald eventually died. But revenge was not sweet. Ledrede was now convinced that his diocese was swarming with witches and apostates, and for the next few years, anyone who crossed him risked being painted as a heretic. He grew even more unpopular, if you can believe it, and managed to alienate everyone from his parishioners to the king himself. In 1329, he was driven out of Ireland and, like Alice, forced into exile. A few years later, the beautiful lead roof – his one concrete symbol of victory – was destroyed when the cathedral's bell tower collapsed.

Today, Ledrede has been mostly forgotten, along with the original allegations against Alice: serial murder. Though too many centuries have passed to declare Alice a murderer beyond a shadow of a doubt, later cases of husband killing would end up being chillingly similar to this one: infatuated husbands who start wasting away, wives who gain something material from each death, methodical remarriage. The black widow archetype has become so prominent that it even appears on the FBI's website. Many of its characteristics describe Alice well: the black widow is intelligent, manipulative, usually older, and very organized; she profits from each murder, works patiently over a long period of time, and doesn't hesitate to kill those who trust her.

Perhaps the most compelling piece of evidence against Alice was the fact that her surviving husband, Sir John le Poer, never disputed the accusations against her. In fact, he finally grew suspicious of his beloved and rifled through her belongings until he found a "sackful of horrible and detestable things," which he handed over to Ledrede. That summer, Ledrede built a huge bonfire in the middle of Kilkenny and burned the sack, telling onlookers it contained the powders that were used to poison Sir John le Poer as well as "human nails, hair, herbs, worms, and other abominations."

It's funny how much human imperfection is evident in this case, even though its characters have been dead for centuries. Ledrede wanted to prove that Alice, in all her cruelty and greed, wasn't just *guilty*, but that she was *unhuman:* a demon-loving sorceress who preyed upon men. So he accused her of spectral crimes instead of staring her mortality in the face. And really, who can blame him? For centuries, people have done the same, pinning crimes on magic and hysteria and midnight visitations and madness in an attempt to believe that actions like Alice's are foreign to us, that they're totally outside the bounds of normal human behavior. But they're not. At the end of the day, this ancient case simply highlights the humanity of *everyone* who raged and lied and manipulated their way around Kilkenny: the stubborn, hypocritical, self-righteous Ledrede; the shameless, materialistic, expertly self-preserving Alice; the spoiled brat, William Jr.; and even Arnald, with his petty need to get involved in other people's drama.

Alice entered the annals of history as the dark center of what became known as the Kilkenny witchcraft case, and was remembered ever after as a witch, not a killer. Six centuries later, W. B. Yeats ended one of his bitterest poems with the image of a desperate Alice offering up peacock feathers and cockscombs to her "insolent fiend." Seven centuries later, Kyteler's Inn in Kilkenny lures in tourists with live music, ghost sightings – and a bronze statue of Alice, looking exhausted, holding a toad in one hand and a broomstick in the other.

BEAUTIFUL THROAT CUTTER

Kate Bender

In late 1870, a mysterious quartet crept into the southeastern corner of Kansas. Both men were named John. Both women were named Kate. The older John and Kate were married; the younger John and Kate were siblings. Their last name was Bender, and nobody knew anything else about them.

Back then, Kansas was a place to reinvent yourself. It had only been a state for nine years, and plenty of its residents were still rough around the edges – outlaws who'd moved in from the North and the East to lose themselves in the wild expanses of the prairie. Sure, there were plenty of decent, God-fearing folk clinging to their scraps of farmland, but they lived miles from each other, surrounded by nothing more than the plains and the keening wind.

The Benders were from German stock, as evidenced by their accents, but everything else about them turned out to be questionable, including their names and even their relationships to one another. Some said the younger Benders were actually husband and wife masquerading as brother and sister, or brother and sister who were secretly lovers. One legend claimed that the four were driven out of a German settlement in Pennsylvania because the women turned out to be witches: they frolicked naked in a graveyard at midnight, slept with a "Dark Stranger," hung their clothing on an "infidel's tombstone," and recited the Lord's Prayer backward. Still, since nobody out West knew anything definitive about *anyone's* past, no one blinked an eye when the Bender family materialized on the Great Plains, the nightmare of the American frontier made flesh.

In Kansas, the Benders eventually settled down on a little farm seven miles northeast of a town called Cherryvale, right beside a road that connected the larger cities of Fort Scott and Independence. It was a prime location, and the Benders knew just how to take advantage of it: they threw up a few curtains, they hung a sign, and they opened an inn.

On the frontier, proper Americans placed a high premium on "neighborliness," which they saw as being next to godliness. Being on good terms with your neighbor was more than just a way to score social points; it was necessary for survival, especially in a desolate land dotted with strangers. And opening an inn – with its vague reference to Jesus's birth, its implications of a crackling fire and warm beds – was the most neighborly of gestures.

But this was a one-star inn at best. Really, it was just a tiny cabin divided in half by a heavy canvas curtain. The Benders turned the front "room" into a miniature store and dining area, where passing travelers could snap up tobacco, crackers, sardines, candies, gunpowder, and bullets, along with a home-cooked meal. If you pushed past the dirty curtain, you'd see the back room, which was used for sleeping – overnight guests had to snuggle up next to the Benders. You'd also notice a trapdoor in the floor, which led to a little cellar. Behind the house, there was a small garden, an orchard, and a stable with a few scrawny animals inside. Aside from that, the land was empty.

A careful observer might notice something curious about the Bender homestead: the orchard was always freshly plowed. This seemed like an unnecessary expenditure of farming energy, but the neighbors chalked it up to German idiosyncrasy, and thought no more about it for the next two years.

John Jr. decided that they needed a sign to advertise their wares, and so he found a plank of wood on which he wrote, arduously: GROCRY. Kate, who was always the brains of the family, corrected his spelling. They hung it above the front door, and they were open for business.

A Beautiful Wild Beast

Neighbors thought the two older Benders were weird and kind of unpleasant. Pa Bender, who was about sixty years old, was short, a bit stooped, and "never looked a feller in the eye," according to a neighbor. He said he was born in the Netherlands and ran a bakery in Germany before coming to America, and he spoke nothing but German (with the exception of a few choice English curses). Ma spoke broken English and seemed about fifty years old. She was short and stout, with blue eyes and brown hair, and she was once described as the very picture of Lady Macbeth: in other words, ruthless and unfeminine.

John Bender Jr. was in his midtwenties, fluent in English, and a good deal more handsome than his parents. He wore a tidy little mustache and cut a dashing figure, though he was given to smiling at nothing in particular, and some neighbors thought he was weak-minded. But really, nobody spent much time talking about John Jr. or his parents, because the youngest Bender was Kate, and why would you talk about anyone else when you could talk about Kate?

A lot of ink gets spilled over the physical descriptions of most wicked women, and Kate is no exception. She was a beauty, especially when standing next to her creepy-looking clan, and everyone who wrote about her in the late 1800s stumbled over themselves to describe her allure. She was in her early twenties. She was tall. She had a face "like a young eagle," her eyes flashed, her hair glinted red. Her body? "Well-formed, voluptuous mold, fair skin, white as milk, rose complexion." She lured you in with her "tigerish grace" and "animal attraction" – a "beautiful wild beast." Her beauty was marred only by a small burn or scar under her left eye. (Okay, not everyone gushed about her. The *New York Times* called her a "red-faced, unprepossessing young woman," but they also claimed that John Jr. and Pa were brothers named Thomas and William.)

Kate was bold, intelligent, and a hypnotic flirt. She longed for notoriety, and approached life with a voracious and amoral hunger. Unlike her supposed parents, she was an easy conversationalist and had no problem integrating herself into society. She attended dances (she danced well), rode horses (she rode well), and went to Sunday school and town meetings (she flirted well). She even waitressed at the dining room in the Cherryvale Hotel for a while in 1871, where we can only assume she was tipped well.

Her charms always tended toward the lucrative. One of her quirkier traits was her belief in Spiritualism – a loose, melodramatic system of beliefs that was popular in the United States during the last half of the 1800s and involved mediums, séances, and a lot of fraud. Kate parlayed her Spiritualist tendencies into a side hustle and peddled her petty magic around the area, giving mystical lectures, offering to locate lost objects, curing various diseases with herbs and roots, and selling verbal charms for fifty cents. She even circulated a handbill in 1872 that advertised her services:

PROF. MISS KATIE BENDER
Can heal all sorts of Diseases; can cure Blindness, Fits,
Deafness, and all such diseases, also Deaf and Dumbness.
Residence, 14 miles East of Independence, on the road
from Independence to Osage Mission one and one
half miles South East of Norahead Station.

Much that was written about the Benders at the time goes for a sort of "brute" rhetoric when describing the rest of the clan (i.e., *Look at these insensitive, unrefined Germans who can't speak our language and don't come to our dances and know nothing but toil and violence*). But everyone agreed that Kate was special. And the fact that the youngest and the prettiest ended up being the most evil – the center of the whole Bender operation – was just so deliciously ironic. "A perfect devil," the neighbors called her.

Strange Nights

There were so many travelers in those days, and the land was still so violent, that when stories of missing men began to circulate around Cherryvale, nobody was terribly concerned. Men disappeared all the time back then. It was the price they paid for trying to settle a wild country.

Anyway, business at the Bender Inn was bustling by 1872. Many of the travelers who passed that way were more than ready for a hot meal and a good night's sleep, and Kate was a wonderful saleswoman. Not only would she sell groceries and convince travelers to stay for dinner, but she'd make sure her clothing was artfully disheveled and "accidentally" brush against her visitors as she moved about the tiny room. She always gave her guests the best seat in the house – the one right up against the canvas curtain – so they could watch her work.

A couple of travelers reported dodgy experiences at the Bender Inn, but people didn't take their tales very seriously. One man, who went by the nickname "Happy Jack" Reed, caught sight of Kate in a state of calculated undress when he was riding by. He pulled up short to say hello, and Kate charmed him into the house and seated him at the table, right in front of the canvas curtain. As they chatted, he heard a peculiar sound from outside – a sort of high-pitched cough – and felt something slither away behind the hanging canvas. Moments later, two new travelers walked through the front door. The rest of his meal proceeded without incident.

When Happy Jack stopped by on his return journey, Kate was overjoyed to see him. They began to chat, but were again interrupted by a set of travelers, and these ones happened to be headed right back to Happy Jack's hometown. They were pressing on home that night, so Happy Jack asked them to carry a message back to his family: he was sleeping at the Bender Inn and would be home the next day. At this development, Kate's mood shifted. She tried to convince him not to send the message, but he insisted, and soon Kate grew so irritated that she refused to talk to him anymore. With no one left to flirt with, Happy Jack went to bed.

A piercing scream woke him in the middle of the night. He listened, terrified, and heard several heavy blows, at which point the screaming stopped. Suddenly, he noticed that Kate Bender was standing over his bed, watching to make sure he was asleep. He squeezed his eyes shut and tried to breathe evenly.

Happy Jack wasn't the only lodger who noticed dubious sounds after nightfall. A man named Corlew heard moaning and rustling coming from the Bender's cellar, but Kate, ever the glib talker, assured him it was just a hog that had gotten under the house. Some people's experiences were even worse: a passing saleswoman agreed to spend the night, but got spooked and ran off when John Jr. began to sharpen a nasty-looking knife.

It's worth noting that many of these travelers didn't think much of their experiences at the inn until *after* the Benders left town in a cloud of suspicion and blood. At the time, the family just seemed a little crusty, a little odd. Once the Benders' crimes were discovered, though, these incidents were elevated to the status of myth. The story of spending a night next to Kate Bender was now the story of spending a night next to Death herself, and living to tell the tale.

Innkeepers from Hell

All the signifiers of "business" – the beds, the home-cooked meals, the tobacco, crackers, sardines, candies, gunpowder, and bullets – were obviously a front, because the Benders were actually operating an efficient killing farm.

Kate was the bait, of course. As she flirted, she'd make sure the guest was sitting with his back against the canvas curtain, which was greasy and spotted with mysterious stains. On the other side of the curtain, Pa or John Jr. would wait silently, clutching a hammer. Outside, Ma kept watch. If she saw another traveler pulling into the yard, she'd let out a high-pitched cough – the sound that Happy Jack heard – and the seated guest would then escape with his life. But if Ma was silent, the game was afoot. As soon as the guest laughed or shifted or leaned back, letting his head brush against the canvas, one of the men would bring the hammer down, crushing his skull through the cloth. That's when Kate would leap forward, pull out a knife, and slit his throat.

The trapdoor would be opened, the body pushed into the cellar.

If the victim wasn't fully dead, he'd die there (thus the moaning that Corlew noticed), or else they'd finish him off later. In the middle of the night, the Benders would drag the body out to the orchard and bury it in a shallow grave. The next morning, Pa would plow the ground over and over again to hide that coffin-shaped square of fresh earth.

Their system was abominably genius. They only murdered travelers, and these travelers were almost always alone. None of the Cherryvale locals suspected anything, because no one in the area knew or cared who these travelers were, and by the time word of the missing people reached their families back home, it was impossible to say which of the road's many dangers had killed them. Amid the era's bright hope in American exploration, the Benders soldiered on – a lurid manifestation of the perils that awaited travelers.

Like any good American entrepreneur, they saw an opportunity, and they went for it, mercilessly. The Benders targeted their richest guests: the ones with fine horses, well-made wagons, or fat saddlebags. Since many of these men were headed west to stake claims of their own, they were often carrying large amounts of cash – in some cases, their entire life's savings. One man, John Greary, was sick when he stopped by the Bender Inn, hoping for a rejuvenating night's sleep. He somehow gave them the impression that he was wealthy – maybe he was trying to impress Kate? – and so the Benders were furious when they discovered, after murdering him, that he was carrying only forty cents. Usually, though, the Benders came away with hundreds or even thousands of dollars per victim, not to mention their horses and wagons (which they sold to neighbors who presumably didn't ask questions), and even their clothes. Most of the victims were buried without their shirts.

While the choice of an inn as a front was practical – they owned property next to a main road, after all – the Bender's business played into a classic trope of terror: the idea that the inn, which is supposed to provide refuge from demons on the road, turns out to have the demons inside. (Of course, the Benders weren't trying to make a literary statement with their killing farm, but this trope helps explain why their story catapulted so quickly into myth and misinformation.) Today, we recognize this "hell hotel"/"inn of no return" conceit from books and movies like *The Shining* and *Psycho*, but the idea was already circulating by the time the Benders emerged in the 1870s, appearing in short stories like "The Red Inn" (1831, Honoré de Balzac) and "A Terribly Strange Bed" (1852, Wilkie Collins, published in a magazine edited by Charles Dickens). More broadly, the fear of comfort turned evil is an ancient one. Why do you think the "evil stepmother" appears in so many fairy tales, a maternal figure gone terribly wrong? Why else is the witch's house in "Hansel and Gretel" made so reassuringly out of gingerbread?

The humble, dirty inn, with its crackling fire suggesting "home" and its beautiful Kate Bender standing in for "wife," would have seemed like a glimmering mirage for these exhausted travelers, a respite where they could briefly feel safe. For them, the road was the thing they feared – the road curving into the great, unknown expanses of the West. The last thing they would have expected was that Kate, who'd been smiling at them all night, would whip out a filthy-looking knife and spring at them. They had been longing for her to touch them, but not like that.

Perhaps the saddest thing that happened at the Bender Inn was the murder of a father and his little girl. The man was a German widower named G. W. Longcohr – a former neighbor of Charles Ingalls, the father in *Little House on the Prairie* – and he was taking his daughter to Iowa to live with her grandparents. When Longcohr stopped in the city of Independence, he purchased a wagon and a team of horses from a man named Dr. William York. As Longcohr and his daughter set off in their new wagon, perhaps he gently explained to her that she wasn't going to live with him anymore, at least not for a while. When the sky grew dark, and it was time to think about bed, a tiny country inn appeared on the horizon, its windows all aglow.

I See Graves

The Benders could have continued their killing farm for years if they hadn't murdered the wrong person. It was a classic mistake, really: they wanted to see how much they could get away with, and they overestimated.

Dr. William York was an influential man with a compassionate heart and two very powerful brothers: Alexander M. York, a Kansas senator, and Colonel Ed York, a Civil War veteran. In 1873, when Dr. York learned that Longcohr and his young daughter had gone missing shortly after they purchased his wagon, he decided to investigate. So he set off around March 9 or 10, riding a beautiful red roan pacing mare and carrying almost one thousand dollars in cash. Then he vanished.

Unlike the Benders' other victims, Dr. York was missed immediately. After all, he'd disappeared fairly close to home, and he had a lot of important people looking out for him. Word of the incident was published in papers all over the nation, and search parties began to comb the surrounding countryside. This was a real scandal, a mystery everyone could get behind. The doctor's brothers began painstakingly retracing his final steps and spared no expense when it came to the investigation. They even dragged the nearby rivers. Soon enough, they learned that Dr. York had stopped at a little store just off the road to buy cigars and had mentioned to the shopkeeper that he was planning to spend the night at the Bender Inn.

In early April, Colonel York and his men rode over to ask the Benders a few questions. John Jr. translated Pa's German answers: Yes, Dr. York had stopped by around noon one day to eat lunch, but then he'd gone on his merry way. Kate hung around, charming and cooperative, and told the colonel she'd be happy to help locate Dr. York using her Spiritualist powers – as long as the colonel returned alone, the next day, so she could have a little time to prepare her mind for the clairvoyant trance. "I'll find your brother, even if he is in hell," she insisted. The colonel never returned. Perhaps he thought she was crazy.

Around that time, Cherryvale residents held a public meeting, noting with dismay that they had become the subject of national suspicion. Dr. York's disappearance had thrown a harsh light on the fact that many other people had gone missing around Cherryvale during the past two years. Some of the farmers immediately volunteered to have their lands searched, and others spoke of burning the guilty parties to death when they were discovered. Pa and John Jr., both in attendance, made sure to act casually disinterested. But they knew exactly what was at stake. Soon after the meeting, the four Benders bundled up their victims' cash, loaded their wagon, and – with only their little dog accompanying them – slipped away like ghosts.

Around April 9, sixteen miles away, someone discovered a deserted wagon in the woods near the town of Thayer, where a train station was located. The wagon was riddled with bullet holes, and the horses, still tied up, were famished. There was a little dog milling about. The wagon itself was shoddily constructed out of random pieces of wood, one of which was printed with the word GROCERY.

A few weeks later, several neighbors were passing the Bender property when they heard a calf crying from its pen. Upon closer inspection, they found that the calf was starving and that its mother, tied nearby, was trying desperately to reach it, her udders swollen with milk. After the men released the animals, they peered into the house. It was in total disarray: dishes and food strewn everywhere, a stove full of burned papers, a German Bible discarded in one corner. The Benders had clearly skipped town.

Word of the family's suspicious disappearance soon reached Colonel York, who set off with his posse to inspect the Bender property. Farmers from nearby settlements joined the inspection, curious about the fate of their missing neighbors. The men didn't find any hard evidence at first, but they allegedly stumbled across a series of eerie clues: three hammers, all different sizes; a nasty-looking knife; curious drawings scratched into the floor, symbolizing the twelve signs of the zodiac; little voodoo dolls, or "spite dolls," half-burned in the fireplace.

Soon enough, the men found the trapdoor in the floor of the Benders' bedroom. Upon opening it, they reeled back from the stench. When a few brave ones managed to crawl through the dark portal, they quickly realized that their hands were sticky: the entire cellar was soaked with two years' worth of thick, fetid blood.

But there were no bodies in the cellar and no bodies hidden in the house. The men even rolled the inn away from its foundation – and still, nothing. Eventually Colonel York sat on his wagon to rest and fight off an encroaching sense of despair. Had they been wrong about the Benders this whole time? Just because they were standoffish and surly didn't mean they were killers.

From his seat, the colonel had a clear view of the entire Bender property. As he gazed around, dejected, something in the orchard caught his eye: a series of long, narrow depressions in the ground. He stood up on his wagon.

"Boys," he called, "I see *graves* out there!"

The men rushed to the orchard and began to probe the ground with a slender iron rod, which plunged easily into the depressions. Several accounts say that after the rod was pulled from the first grave, there was human hair clinging to the end. And so they began to dig. The first body they uncovered was buried facedown, with the base of his skull smashed in and his throat cut. When they flipped him over, the colonel's worst fears were confirmed: it was his brother.

In reports, the number of bodies unearthed from the Bender property usually ranges from eight to eleven – though some accounts cite numbers as high as thirty-five. Most of the victims had died of blunt head wounds and slit throats. Two of the bodies were stabbed multiple times, including the sick man who was only carrying forty cents – maybe Kate had mutilated his body in anger upon discovering that he wasn't rich. One of the corpses was a young woman no one could identify. Beneath George Longcohr's body, they found his little girl, a piece of silk cloth tied around her throat. None of the men could figure out how she died. She may have been strangled, but they worried that she was buried alive beneath her dead father.

Disappearing Act

The Benders were primed for escape: they had a serious head start, and they carried thick stacks of dead men's cash – possibly as much as fifty thousand dollars. Four people matching the family's description boarded a northbound train at Thayer, where the bullet-riddled wagon was found. They carried a dog-hide trunk and a sheet stuffed full of their mysterious possessions. Once they got on the train, they effectively vanished.

The people of southeastern Kansas were deeply shaken by the thought that such horrible crimes had happened right under their noses. The murders were especially disturbing because of several factors: the whiff of the occult, the death of the child, and the fact that they had all known the Benders for two years. It turned out the Benders had been making a bloody mockery of "neighborliness" all along. Now, newspapers printed hysterical accounts of the "Human Hyenas in Spiritualist Circles," and amateur detectives set off in groups, hell-bent on lynching the family, with more enthusiasm and bloodlust than investigative skill.

Many were convinced that the Benders had been working with nearby camps of Romani and African American settlers, and so those sites were eagerly raided – perhaps by men who'd been looking for an excuse to do it anyway. Meanwhile, rumors sprouted like wildflowers: the Benders had gone south; the Benders had gone north; the Benders had been killed in a bloody shootout and buried in the deepest of graves. The state of Kansas offered a two-thousand-dollar reward for anyone who brought the fugitives to justice, but no one ever came forth to claim it.

Shades of the Benders were suddenly everywhere. They were infamous now, and they seemed to appear before the hungry eyes of the public like mirages – especially Kate. People swore they saw her in New Orleans, Mexico City, New York, Havana, and even Paris. They said she'd married (or remarried), changed her name, and was continuing her killing spree down South. They claimed that she started cross-dressing in order to work as a cowboy. The paranoia took on a sort of freak-show aesthetic: at one point, a couple supposed to be Ma and Pa were displayed at a theater in Kansas for an afternoon. The owner of the theater charged twenty-five cents to see the pair, and ended up making a "handsome profit."

But none of these unfortunate people were ever proven to be the real Benders. After their disappearance, the family's identity had become as malleable and mercurial as the wind over the Great Plains.

Even the strong arm of the law couldn't prove who the Benders were or where they'd gone. Sixteen years after the discovery of the graves, two women were arrested in Michigan on suspicion of being Ma and Kate and were dragged down to Kansas for a disorganized joke of a trial, where no one could decide whether they were the real deal or not. Public opinion was fiercely divided; for every witness who identified them as Ma and Kate, another insisted that they weren't. Without photos, it was hard to recognize people after many hard-lived years had aged them. Even one of Kate's alleged former lovers couldn't say for sure if the woman in front of him was Kate Bender. Finally, the prosecuting attorney became convinced that they weren't the Bender women after all, and released them back into the wilds of America.

Go West

Part of the reason public opinion was so divided about these two women was that many Kansans fervently believed the Benders had been killed back in 1873, when their bullet-ridden wagon was discovered. It didn't matter that everyone had a different story about *how* they were killed. Some people just felt, in their bones, that the Benders were no longer living. And plenty of men were eager to claim the glory of killing the Benders for themselves.

In 1908, the *New York Times* published a "deathbed confession" from a man who declared that he and his self-made "vigilance committee" had slain the brutal family. In his retelling, the man borrows liberally from the tropes and aesthetics of frontier myth:

The Night was dark, and we feared that they might escape us, but our luck was good. We sighted them racing as fast as they could over the prairie, and shouted to them. The moon had risen, but frequently was obscured by heavy clouds. . . . We set our horses going at breakneck speed, and the bullets flew fast from both sides.

Positioned this way in history, the tale of the Bloody Benders is a quintessentially American one, seasoned liberally with American gothic and American grotesque. It begins with someone settling a wild frontier and ends with someone vanishing into the sunset. It's a classic tale of a stranger coming to town: demonic outsiders who moved in and slew good American people but ultimately came to justice, chased down across the prairie by American horsemen in a hail of gunfire under a ghostly moon.

This deathbed confession probably isn't true – if only because there were so many of these same "confessions" circulating in the years and decades after the Benders disappeared. But it's easy to understand why so many people swore they'd killed the Benders, even beyond the fact that doing so would have been a great claim to fame and a damn good story. Think, for a moment, about how perfectly terrifying the Benders must have seemed to their fellow settlers. This family – which may or may not have actually been a family – was the inverse of everything the frontier wanted to believe about itself. They were so disturbingly suited for their environment that they might feel totally imaginary, like something the collective pioneer mind dreamed up, if it weren't for the fact that we have photos of their orchard, spotted with open graves.

The West, despite all its tangible problems, was marked very heavily by the intangible ideal of, well, idealism. It was a "region of ideals, mistaken or not," according to historian Frederick Jackson Turner (who came up with what we call the frontier thesis): discovery, innovation, democracy, and individualism. The very fact that the West seemed grand and huge and (incorrectly) uninhabited meant "that its resources seemed illimitable and its society seemed able to throw off all its maladies by the very presence of these vast new spaces." Just think of the glorified language we use when talking about all things frontier: the immense sky, the indomitable American spirit, the eternal cry of "Go West, young man!" It's all so beautiful and naïve and idealistic you can practically hear the swelling of the string section in the background: "O beautiful for spacious skies!" (Those words, for what it's worth, were written a mere twenty-two years after the Benders dropped off the face of the earth.)

And in the midst of all this burgeoning optimism came the Benders, literally slashing the throats of American idealists. They were the destroyers of the dream. They snatched the life savings and the shiny new wagons from the men who'd hoped to inherit the earth.

But they were also heirs of the dream, just like all their unfortunate victims. After all, if the West was about a bunch of eager immigrants claiming a land for themselves, plowing it into submission, and being fiercely entrepreneurial about the whole thing – well, that's exactly what the Benders did. They went west to escape their sordid pasts. They opened a business. They raked in the profits. And then, when the tides turned against them, they vanished into a wild land that held promise in one hand and horror in the other.

Of course this deeply offended the sorts of people who would form "vigilance committees." Of *course* plenty of men wanted to claim the outlaw credit for mowing them down on the prairie with horses charging at breakneck speed and clouds obscuring the moon.

"I Tell You, Man, She Was a Bad One"

But these stories of Bender deaths aren't just about reclaiming American idealism. They're also about killing Kate – the main Bender, the worst Bender. And boy, do these stories have it out for Kate. In most of them, she is the one who fights hardest, suffers most, and dies last. "My grief, how she did fight," said the man in the *New York Times*. "She fought tooth and nail like a tiger, and we had to handle her like a bucking bronco." In another account, Kate snarls at her pursuers, "Shoot and be damned!"

Kate's violent, fictional deaths are the price she has to pay for being the wickedest one of all. To the residents of Cherryvale, Ma and Pa were hardened criminals who barely spoke the language, and John Jr. was a simpleminded schmuck, but Kate should have known better. She was young, pretty, seductive – a good *dancer,* for God's sake. She was the one Bender who passed for normal. She went to social events, doled out headache cures, flirted with the husbands, waitressed at the hotel. By tricking her neighbors into thinking she was neighborly, too, she betrayed them the most. And so, in stories, she suffers for it.

In a third account of the Benders' alleged deaths, Ma, Pa, and John Jr. were lynched, but Kate fought so hard that the vigilantes couldn't get the rope around her neck. "I tell you, man, she was a bad one," said one of the men who claimed to be present. "She screamed and bit and cursed and kicked. . . . So someone cracked her skull for her with a stick, and another one put a bullet or two through her brain."

In a fourth account, another group of vigilantes chased the Benders into a cornfield near the Oklahoma-Kansas state line. Pa and John Jr. were killed quickly. The posse tried to capture Ma alive, but she pulled out a little pistol and so they immediately shot her down. Kate, the last one standing, darted behind a cluster of cornstalks, firing steadily at the man who approached her. She hit him in the leg; he staggered but managed to return fire, and Kate collapsed to the ground, wounded but alive. The man limped toward her, shooting steadily. Soon another man joined him, and the two of them riddled her body with bullets. As with other accounts, it took more than one man to kill her.

The violence against Kate in these stories is unsettling, no matter how violent Kate was in real life. At points, these tales feel ominously erotic, as the men describe the ways Kate thrashed about ("like a bucking bronco"), the ways they had to restrain her. You get the sense that these storytellers are deriving pleasure from dreaming about the ways in which Kate might have died; they stretch it out, make it really hurt. It's a socially sanctioned opportunity to indulge in a fantasy of violence against a woman. A man could never talk like this in polite society – in the *New York Times*! – unless the woman in question had been proven really, really bad. Kate, of course, had been proven badder than most.

Thus, scarred by imaginary violence, Kate Bender vanished into myth. And in vanishing, she became stronger, and her legend only grew. She rose from the ashes of her real life to become lovelier and more dangerous than ever, a beautiful throat cutter – forever a symbol of the perils that awaited travelers who dared to flirt with a red-haired girl.

THE ANGEL MAKERS
OF NAGYRÉV

nce upon a time, an anonymous letter appeared in the June 1929 edition of a small Hungarian newspaper called *Szolnoki Újság*, or the *Szolnok Gazette*. The letter declared that something was rotten in the nearby town of Nagyrév: murder. Two decades of slow, deliberate, repetitive murder. "The authorities are doing nothing, and the poisoners are carrying on their work undisturbed," ran the letter. "This is my last attempt. If this also fails then there is no justice."

Police swarmed Nagyrév and a few surrounding villages and quickly arrested dozens of suspects. The once-sleepy town dissolved into chaos. Neighbors began accusing each other of homicide as the police dug up grave after grave in the local cemetery, making sure the residents had a clear view of the decomposing bodies.

Two weeks after the anonymous letter was published, the story spread across Hungary; by the end of the summer, it had gone international. People couldn't believe what they were reading: almost all the suspects were women over the age of fifty-five. What was this wholesale murder plot? Some coven of Hungarian witches, still stuck in the dark ages? Proof, once and for all, that women were intrinsically evil? Nobody could understand how decades of murder could happen, unimpeded, in a little town. Nobody could understand how women could pull this off.

Trapped

Life in Nagyrév was rough and violent. In stereotypical small-town fashion, there was an oppressive sense of inescapability to the place, which was "ringed round as by an iron girdle with huge estates." The residents of Nagyrév had no room to grow: there was no extra land to promise the young, no opportunity for people to move up in the world.

The early twentieth century was a time of enormous worldwide conflict and change, to put it mildly, and Nagyrév felt the strain of the shifting social climate. Village men were returning from the first World War scarred, angry, and suffering from post-traumatic stress disorder. The agricultural crisis of the Great Depression meant peasant farmers could barely sell their goods anymore. Nagyrév had little contact with the outside world due to its poor roads and lack of any train or bus stop. There was no doctor in town. Tensions ran high between the peasants and the town's tiny middle class, and the snobbish behavior of the local pastor, teachers, and other authorities created a climate in which the poor didn't feel like they could share their fears and suspicions with those in power.

Marriage was no escape from any of this. Many of the local men were alcoholics who regularly abused their wives. "Brutish," they were called. Newlyweds often lived with their in-laws, which put everyone on edge, and rigid gender roles meant relationships between men and women were frequently strained. Wives were expected to put up with spousal abuse; men were paranoid that their wives had cheated on them with visiting soldiers while they were away at war. Divorce wasn't unheard of, but it was socially frowned upon, and many women chose to stay in abusive marriages – with the limited benefits of their husbands' meager incomes – rather than striking out on their own.

In this impoverished and isolated world, children were often seen as a burden: another mouth to feed, a baby who would grow up to be just as hopeless as her mother. So peasant women frequently turned to primitive and dangerous forms of contraception like the *facsiga*, a wooden plug meant to be inserted into the cervix. Others might resort to dangerous home-brewed abortions that involved puncturing the womb with a knitting needle, inserting poisonous weeds into the cervix, or trying to stab the fetus itself with a goose feather. If neither wooden plugs nor goose feathers stopped the child from being born, the mother's final option was foolproof: infanticide. The ways to kill an infant were myriad and cruel: starving, poisoning, feeding them to pigs, smothering them with pillows, bathing them in hot water and then letting them catch pneumonia in the cold air. This crime was so common that parents suspected of killing their babies weren't even denounced to authorities. It was simply part of the harsh circle of life.

In 2001, a Hungarian sociologist named Ferenc Moksony studied six hundred rural communities in Hungary and found that suicide rates were higher in isolated, traditional villages. Scholar Bela Bodó took it one step further. "The more marginalized a community and the more frustrated its inhabitants feel about their isolation and poverty, the more likely it is that they will turn to deviant behavior."

This is exactly what happened in Nagyrév.

"They Sent Me into My Grave, They Whom I Loved Most"

For twenty years, the women of Nagyrév killed the men of Nagyrév, and nobody said anything about it.

It was hard to pinpoint the start of the murders. They seemed to spring, fully formed, out of the pastoral Hungarian air. We know that some of the first occurred in the early 1910s, when a woman named Julianna Lipka moved into the house of a sick, elderly, wealthy couple, ostensibly to nurse them. The husband died of old age, but the wife turned out to be a cantankerous burden with a disgusting habit of spitting on the floor. It was far more work than Julianna had signed up for.

When she complained to a group of older women, they told her a secret: if she purchased flypaper and dissolved it in water, a film of poison would rise to the surface. She could then skim off the poison and mix it into food or drink, and the result would be fatal – and totally undetectable. Julianna took their advice and ran with it. First, she killed the elderly woman. Later, she poisoned her own disagreeable stepsister and then her irritating husband. Once she learned how easy it was to improve her life with something as humble as wet flypaper, it was hard to stop.

One of those older women was Zsuzsanna Fazekas, the town midwife, and nobody knew the ins and outs of life and death quite like Zsuzsanna. She could deliver a baby, soothe a farmer's strained muscle, and poison a husband all in a day's work. Since there was no doctor in the village, Zsuzsanna wielded a great deal of power, and the locals were in awe of both her mysterious knowledge and her scandalous exploits. She carried a vial of arsenic in her pocket. She was divorced. She smoked and drank at the local tavern, a place most women would never go. And she was good at her trade: by 1929, she lived in one of the village's finest houses.

Zsuzsanna showed no hesitation when it came to prescribing murder to her desperate female clients, and she passed out poison as though it were a remedy for headaches. Sometimes she'd even commit the murders herself, like when she brought over medicine to "calm down" one woman's difficult husband, a former prisoner of war who struggled with the fact that he had been blinded in battle. There was an unspoken understanding between the two women that the medicine was poisoned, and Zsuzsanna fed it to the husband as his wife stood by. Other times, the midwife suggested different ways of killing. Once, she explained to a very poor mother exactly how to starve her unwanted newborn to death.

Another older woman – Rozália Takács, a masseuse – was also heavily involved in many of the murders. She'd come to homicide in a very personal way, after poisoning her "alcoholic beast" of a husband with arsenic acid. She went on to train a young mother in the fine art of killing her oppressive father-in-law, whispering, "You do not have to torture yourself with him, I'll bring the old man something that will destroy him."

In this way, both the *idea* of murder and the *means* for murder were disseminated through Nagyrév like an evil mist. No woman killed alone. Instead, she'd go to her friends for advice, and they would encourage her, condone her actions, and give her the knowledge – and the supplies – that she needed. It happened an estimated forty-two times in Nagyrév: forty-two murders committed by thirty-four people. This was sisterhood gone bad, and a real feather in the cap of those who believed that if one woman was naturally evil, a group of women were evil compounded.

The intertwined nature of the crimes is clear in the case of Mária

Kardos, one of the town's more colorful citizens. She was richer than the other women, she dressed better, and she had been divorced twice, which was unusual for Nagyrév. After her second divorce, she took a lover – the former village mayor. Meanwhile, her adult son, an ailing twenty-three-year-old from a previous marriage, was proving to be more than she could handle. Mária felt shackled by the constant caregiving and wanted to spend her energy on this new affair. Perhaps she was growing sick of motherhood, too, and thought that the role's requirements would have ended by then. So she purchased arsenic from Zsuzsanna and began to slip it into her son's food. He worsened quickly.

Shortly before her son's death, Mária moved his sickbed outside so he could catch a few final rays of sun. As he lay there, looking up into the sky, Mária remembered something she'd always loved about her boy: he had a beautiful voice.

"I thought I would like to hear him once more," she told the police, later. "So I said: 'Sing, my boy. Sing me my favorite song.' He sang it in his lovely clear voice." She was sad to lose that voice – but once he was dead, she was free, and ready to get married again.

Unfortunately for Mária, the former mayor turned out to be a die-hard womanizer, and he was terribly unenthusiastic about becoming a husband. In 1920, Mária finally convinced him to wed her; local gossips said he "had to be dragged to the city hall like the cattle to the slaughterhouse." Marriage didn't bring romance, though; her new husband still drank and slept around, and before long, the two of them were sleeping in different rooms.

It just so happened Zsuzsanna also hated the former mayor for her own obscure reasons, though she explained away her hatred by saying that he owed her a few sacks of wheat. So once she got wind of Mária's latest situation, the midwife was only too happy to help out. The two women poisoned the man slowly, over the course of a month, and he died in April 1922. Later, editorials would imagine the ghostly rage of the Nagyrév victims like this unfortunate third husband and this ailing son, emphasizing the utter shock, the *betrayal* of these murders: "They killed me, they sent me into my grave, they whom I loved most." But for now, the murderesses were untroubled. As a thank-you gift, Maria gave Zsuzsanna enough money to buy a small calf.

Like many of the Nagyrév killings, these motives seem not just petty, but psychopathically callous: the debt of a few sacks of wheat, the inconveniently sick son. However, these were simply the reasons that the women gave each other for the poisonings: *She spat on the floor. He complained about being blind. I was annoyed. I was overwhelmed.* In truth, these minor inconveniences were only a stand-in for their dark, gaping needs.

This was a generation of women who were given nothing and could expect nothing. This was a generation of women whose husbands had been taken away by the war and returned to them scarred, disillusioned, violent, suspicious, and shell-shocked. Poison wasn't perfect, but at least it brought change. Some of these women murdered out of desperation, like the one whose husband beat her with a double chain. She told the court, defiantly, "I do not feel guilty at all; my husband was a very bad man . . . since he died, I have found my peace." Some killed to be with another man, like the woman who poisoned her husband and married his best friend. Others killed for revenge, such as the woman who poisoned the father-in-law who molested her. Still more used poison to gain material goods, like the woman who murdered her mother for an early inheritance.

The motives varied, but the methods did not. The idea that you could improve your life with poison spread like dark wildfire through the women's circles of Nagyrév. And the fact that the poisoners were so reliant on each other for information and supplies created a dangerous web of guilt in the town. Any one of these women could condemn her friends, but she who opened her mouth would also condemn herself.

Panic in the Village

In the late 1920s, authorities in the nearby city of Szolnok began receiving anonymous letters claiming that something awful was going on in Nagyrév. At first, these rambling, panicked missives were ignored. They were easy to dismiss as village gossip, what with the long-winded name-dropping and the unpleasant subject matter:

> There are many . . . who had fed poison to others . . . Uncle Misi Beke [was killed by] Róza Kiss who [destroyed] her husband and the old Mrs. János Pápai and she also tried [to kill] the aged Sándor Szendi and Mrs. Pista Valki but she did not succeed and who knows how many more.

But as soon as the *Szolnok Gazette* ran one of the letters in 1929 – "the authorities are doing nothing, and the poisoners are carrying on their work undisturbed" – the state bureaucracy was forced to step in, and everything began happening very quickly, as newspapers and tabloids whipped the Hungarian public into a scandalized frenzy. Suddenly, both the media and the government were pressuring local police to get answers, and fast.

So after twenty years of leisurely, undetected murder, Nagyrév was thrown into chaos. Suspects were arrested and interrogated harshly in the house of the local cemetery caretaker. Women were called multiple times during the night for interviews and, when they weren't being cross-examined, forced to face the wall without speaking to each other. Julianna Lipka, by then one of the oldest and frailest suspects, was threatened with flogging. If the police couldn't get a confession, they turned to bizarre scare tactics: one officer hid under a bed in a room where two female suspects were being held and frightened them half to death by grabbing their feet. The terrified, superstitious women – sure some supernatural force was at play – immediately confessed.

The exhumations provided yet another opportunity for intimidation. The bodies needed to be analyzed for poison, yes, but the police made sure to dig up the corpses as publicly as possible. They didn't even bother hiding the nauseating results from the town's children – not even the "glistening brown" brains covered in "short-winged brown corpse-bugs."

As the town descended into hysteria, everyone began pointing fingers at each other. The townspeople distanced themselves from the women who seemed guiltiest, and no one felt this hostility more than Zsuzsanna. Because of her connections to so many of the murders, the midwife was one of the first suspects to be questioned. She must have been terrified; she knew exactly how many villagers could incriminate her.

The police released her on bail for a single day, expecting that she would help them find the other poisoners. Instead, Zsuzsanna wandered around the village in a panic, asking her friends and former clients for enough money to hire a lawyer. But not even a prosperous midwife could afford salvation in Nagyrév. Though she begged and begged, the frightened villagers turned her away. Nobody could risk being connected to Zsuzsanna anymore, no matter how many favors she'd done for them in the past.

The midwife grew more and more unnerved as she stumbled through the town, and by the time she got home, she was swearing loudly that she'd revenge herself on each and every one of her ungrateful clients. She stayed up all night, pacing around her yard. The walls of her life seemed to be closing in around her. In the morning, when she saw the police officers coming down the street to rearrest her, she pulled a vial of poison from her dress and drank the whole thing down.

In some accounts of the Nagyrév poisonings, Zsuzsanna emerges as the driving force behind all the murders, a crazed midwife who thinks she has the power to determine who lives and who dies – a supernatural power, even. A journalist for the *New York Times*, writing from Budapest, compared her to "a figure eminently fit to flit around the bubbling caldron in 'Macbeth,' or to discharge the duties of an African witch doctor." Another called her a "fatuous Eastern deity, perpetually devouring something with her bloody teeth."

Zsuzsanna did play a central role in the killings, but it was less witchy and more business-minded than the papers said. She was an entrepreneur, a kingpin. She distributed poison to women who wanted to kill. She brought over the poison herself, if the women were particularly reluctant. She suggested murder as a solution to tension, unhappiness, abuse, and impatience, subtly legitimizing the action in the minds of her fellow villagers.

Calling Zsuzsanna a witch was an attempt to pin the murders onto a single source, a wellspring of evil. It was easier to do this than to recognize the murders for what they were in Nagyrév: a dreadful phenomenon birthed and encouraged by widespread social issues. The murders were far too communal and decentralized to be pinned to Zsuzsanna, or any other woman, for that matter. The source of these crimes was as imperceptible and pervasive as the poison itself. Economy, culture, and human unhappiness all wove a tangled web in Nagyrév, creating an atmosphere characterized not by one midwife's madness, but by quiet, long-term female desperation.

The police found Zsuzsanna writhing on the ground. They tried to force her to swallow milk and vomit up the poison, but she kept her jaws clenched tight. Realizing their key witness was slipping away, the police searched desperately for a vehicle that could transport Zsuzsanna to the nearest hospital, located in another town. But there were very few ways to get out of Nagyrév, and the neighbors refused to help. They didn't want anything to do with the witch anymore. By the time the police found a ride, Zsuzsanna was dead.

Rural Mystery

The lawyer János Kronberg, who was appointed investigating magistrate of the case, loathed the women of Nagyrév from the start. He arrested as many of them as he could and had them taken en masse to nearby Szolnok, where a crowd waited to gape at them. The tabloid *Kis Újság* noted the sad contrast between the accused – mostly poor, aging women dressed in black who kept their eyes downcast and covered their faces with kerchiefs – and the brightly dressed middle-class mob who hurled insults at them.

The trial was an exciting opportunity for the middle and upper classes to really revel in their social superiority. They were already biased against peasants, and journalists capitalized on this by infusing their coverage with as much prejudice as they could muster. Headlines emphasized the outdated, even primitive nature of the killers: WHERE FOR ONE AND A HALF DECADES NO ONE HAS HEARD THE VOICE OF CONSCIENCE: VISIT NAGYRÉV, THE VILLAGE OF DEATH ON THE TISA SHORE, or WITH MEDIEVAL METHODS CHILDREN DESTROYED THEIR PARENTS TO GET THEIR LAND.

In the prison at Szolnok, the peasant women struggled to adjust to the loneliness, the rat-infested cells, and the nonstop interrogations. It was completely different from the communal village life they used to lead. They were forced to take tests that used the signifiers of middle-class culture to determine their intellectual aptitude by quizzing them on things like taxation, national holidays, and the army. A psychiatrist who examined the women decided that their murders were all inherently linked to sex: they were either frigid or promiscuous, and their supposedly warped sexual drives "had [their] root in rural mystery and an abnormal lifestyle, which had distorted the defendants' psyche and made their behavior unpredictable."

Two of the imprisoned women, humiliated and disoriented, tied their own head scarves to the bars of the prison windows and strangled themselves. The press saw it as an admission of guilt.

Nihilism

The women from Nagyrév never thought it would come to this.

Yes, they had killed people, but many of them didn't even see what they'd done as *murder*. Murder, to them, meant blood and struggle and force. They had simply sent people off to sleep. "We are not murderesses," they told the court. "We neither stabbed nor drowned our husbands. They have simply died from poison. It was an easy death for them and no murder."

Perhaps these women saw poisoning as "easy death" because they were desensitized to dying. They saw just how rough life could be: how people went to war and came back mentally and physically damaged, how food was scarce, how children died like flies whether you killed them or not. (By the 1930s, almost one-third of all peasant children in Hungary died before they were old enough to attend school.) Maybe these women told themselves they were simply speeding along a harsh process that would eventually claim their wounded husbands, belligerent in-laws, and squalling babies anyway.

The paper *Pesti Napló* speculated on the "strange combination of causes" that led to such familiarity with death, and such willingness to cause it. "Yes, it was money; yes, it was hunger for land and yes, it was love and hatred," ran the editorial. "But it was also cultural nihilism, living at the animals' level, the primitive nature of their souls."

Cultural nihilism, yes, certainly. But living at the animals' level? *Primitive souls?* These murders were birthed from very human emotions – uncomfortable, ugly emotions, to be sure, like desperation and lust and anger and irritation, but human ones nonetheless. The women killed to lessen their despair and improve their lot in life. Sometimes that meant gaining something (money, land, a new lover); other times it meant ridding themselves of something (husband, son, parent). "If the men were brutish," wrote the *New York Times*, "the women seem to have been remarkable for the strength and persistence of their passions. The average age of those so far tried is over 55, yet lust played an even greater part than greed in their crimes." That last part wasn't really true, but it made for good copy.

The fact that the women so blatantly – so *humanly* – wanted more than what they were given was uncomfortable for their more prosperous observers, who told themselves that the Nagyrév women were just – outdated. In other words, *their* social circles knew right from wrong, but the message simply hadn't made its way to Nagyrév yet. Really, the climate in Nagyrév was nothing if not a by-product of the world around it – a fact the defense would latch onto soon enough. This fact did not excuse the murderers. But neither did it make them animals.

Funeral Lament

By the end of the year, hundreds of people had been questioned, over fifty graves had been opened, forty exhumed bodies were found to contain arsenic, and the authorities were ready to indict thirty-four women and one man. A rabid public crowded into the courtroom to see these deviants, and when they particularly disliked a defendant, they'd whistle, catcall, or yell demands for harsh sentences.

In the face of all this hatred, it was in the best interest of the women of Nagyrév to appear humble, simple, clean, and grandmotherly. Their only hope for pardon was to seem like good country folk who were either innocent or acted in self-defense.

But the trials splintered the sisterhood of poison apart. Accused women testified against each other; friends and relatives of the deceased men testified against the accused women; some townspeople even gave negative testimonies against their own family members. If the woman on trial had killed an abusive husband, the witnesses from Nagyrév tended to be more lenient, but they turned harshly against those they perceived as having character flaws.

János Kronberg believed every one of the women was guilty, and he wanted them all to hang. His argument was illogically circular but effective: if there was a reason for murder, then a murder happened, and only the accused could have done it. When Kronberg didn't have hard facts, he resorted to smearing the women's characters. He called their testimonies "fairy tales," and believed that poisoning, since it involved cunning, secrecy, and long deliberation, was a quintessentially feminine crime.

The defense didn't have much to go on. They tried to blame the murders entirely on Zsuzsanna, who made a convenient scapegoat now that she was dead. They also tried to argue that the crimes were the result of poverty, saying the Hungarian authorities could have done more to improve the standard of living in Nagyrév. This was certainly true, but it didn't do a lot to prove the women's innocence.

The divorcée Mária Kardos turned out to be one of the most hated figures in the courtroom. She drew great ire from observers by appearing conceited and unrepentant, and she alienated the entire room when she criticized her dead son and deceased third husband. She also wore an expensive head scarf, which irritated the wealthy women of the town, who thought she was trying to rise above her station. During police interrogations, she had confessed her own crimes in excruciating detail, seemingly proud of her actions. Now, she tried to incriminate as many of her townspeople as she could: "We, the women of Nagyrév, all knew what Zsuzsanna Fazekas had been doing. We were as used to her deeds as we were used to seeing the flocks of geese leaving the village for the meadows every morning... No one among the women who have been arrested for the poisonings is innocent."

In an effort to get Mária to show some remorse for her crimes, Kronberg harangued her for her lack of mothering skills, reminding her that birds feed their young, that cows lick their newborn calves, and that a dog will jump into the water to save its puppies, even if it dies in the process. Eventually, Mária broke down. "When one feels desperate, she can do many things," she admitted. Once the interrogation was over, someone in the audience said loudly, "Rope."

Finally, the sentences were handed out. Seven women received the death penalty, including Mária and the masseuse Rozália Takács, who had helped with so many of the murders. Most of the others got life in prison or heavy prison sentences; a few went free because there wasn't enough evidence to convict them.

After the sentencing, the peasant women began a strange, high-pitched wail: "Jaj, Jaj, Istenem, Istenem." This was the lament they used at funerals – "alas, alas, my God" – and it made the wealthy spectators highly uncomfortable. It was too raw, too tangible. They had signed up for a public spectacle, but they didn't want to deal with the unbearable intensity of human despair. Especially not from peasants.

Soon enough, though, the Supreme Court swept in and reduced many of the sentences, embarrassing the local authorities. The court found irregularities in the ways the women had been sentenced, and thought most of the sentences were too harsh, anyway. They eventually took three of the seven women off death row, including Rozália Takács. Mária Kardos received no such leniency; the court reexamined her case and concluded that her premeditated, cold-blooded cruelty meant that she deserved to die. She was hanged early in the morning on January 13, 1931.

"They caused the greatest disappointment," wrote the *Szolnok Gazette* while the trials were taking place. "Instead of witches, demons and crafty murderers we see only kind, poor, old and broken women on the benches . . . Life has brought them little joy. However, they did not deserve anything better."

Dame
Darcy

QUEEN OF POISONERS

Marie-Madeleine,
the Marquise de Brinvilliers

Poison: forever the women's weapon. It fits easily into the home. It's subtle, secretive, tidy. Poison doesn't leave blood on the floor or holes in the wall. Dropping a bit of colorless liquid into broth or wine is the simplest thing in the world. And who, historically, stays at home, boils the broth, and serves the wine? Women, of course.

Paris in the second half of the seventeenth century oozed with poison and the fear of poison and, by extension, the fear of women: the divineresses who dabbled in arsenic, spells, and abortions, and the rich young wives who frequented them. The court of the Sun King grew so paranoid that anyone with a stomachache panicked, sure that someone, somewhere, was trying to do them in. Major advancements in pharmacology, coupled with a very real fear of black magic, created the perfect atmosphere for a witch hunt, known today as the Affair of the Poisons. And many of those accused were female.

"How can . . . those who are so sensitive to the misfortunes of others . . . commit such a great crime?" wrote one bemused commentator, shocked at the number of lady poisoners who were swelling the city's jails. "They are monsters. One must not suppose them like others, and they are sooner compared to the most evil men."

Sure, it was soothing in a weird way to imagine that these poisoners were more like men than girls, but it simply wasn't true. These "monsters" were French noblewomen: they spent hours getting their hair done; they went dancing; they drank the iced champagne that was favored by the king. And the whole fatal affair was kicked off by a reckless little marquise named Marie-Madeleine.

La Brinvilliers

Marie-Madeleine d'Aubray, born in 1630, was the daughter of the civil lieutenant of Paris, a plum job that was both highly influential and very well paid. She had two younger brothers and a little sister who was probably not as cool as she was, given that the sister ended up in a convent and Marie – well, Marie was just one of those bold, lovely, spirited girls, you know? Proud, sensitive, quick-tempered. She had big blue eyes, chestnut hair, and a figure that was "not tall, but exceedingly well formed." She was also smart. One historian who studied her letters reported that her spelling was flawless, "a rare thing with the ladies of her time," and her handwriting was "remarkable – bold, firm, like a man's."

Handwriting wasn't the only precocious thing about Marie. Decades later, she would claim to have lost her virginity at the age of seven to her five-year-old brother – a statement she subsequently denied. But when Parisian gossips caught wind of the rumor, it only increased the atmosphere of taboo eroticism that swirled around Marie for most of her life.

As a young woman, Marie entered the fantastically libertine circles of high Parisian society that centered around Louis XIV's amoral court. It was a dizzying world characterized by "utter heartlessness and a complete lack of moral fibre," filled with scheming, bored nobles who liked to gamble for days without sleeping, spread malicious gossip about each other, engage in very public affairs, toss back glass after glass of iced champagne, and plot the downfall of their enemies.

Despite the corruption that ran through the court like a pulsing vein, there was definitely a sense in Parisian society that being a noble meant you were just *better* than other people. Nobles were convinced that being wealthy and powerful was positively correlated with being good – that being a noble lent their very character a certain nobility. Decades later, Marie's lawyer would argue that she couldn't possibly have committed any crimes because of her "advantages of quality, birth and fortune." A noble could be a little bit naughty – late nights! lovers! too much gambling! – but aristocrats didn't do anything that was actually *criminal*. That was simply unthinkable.

At twenty-one, Marie moved a little deeper into high society when she married the wealthy Antoine Gobelin, whose fortune came from the glamorous field of dye manufacturing. Gobelin's income plus Marie's dowry meant they were now a prosperous couple with considerable social cachet that they could fling around Paris. Even better, Gobelin's land, called Brunvilliers, was eventually elevated to the status of a "marquisate," which, along with a tweak in spelling, turned Marie into the marquise de Brinvilliers – or "La Brinvilliers," if you were writing a gossipy letter about her.

Were they in love? Was anybody in love with their spouse back then? Toward the end of her life, Marie wrote of a deep affection for Gobelin, but shortly after their wedding they were both openly taking lovers. This was scandalous, and yet not at all unusual; in fact, a young, attractive, wealthy married woman was practically expected to have a paramour or two. Taking a lover didn't get you ostracized in seventeenth-century France – it got you talked about. Besides, Gobelin was a weak man who didn't seem to care what Marie did as long as he was free to indulge in his own lackluster affairs. Marie, on the other hand, "possessed superabundant vitality," and it wasn't long before she fell deeply in love with someone who was far better at meeting her needs than her husband was.

Unfortunately, she chose one of the bad guys. Her lover was a devilishly handsome army officer named Godin de Sainte-Croix – a ladies' man with a serious dark side, a brilliant bastard who could wax eloquent on anything from theology to chemistry. For Marie, he was the "demon who brought about the storm and troubled the security of the family." But Marie had always loved the storm. The two were soon the deliciously scandalized talk of the town.

While Marie's husband was busily carrying on affairs of his own and didn't care what she did with Sainte-Croix, her powerful father and brothers weren't so easily distracted. They saw how openly Marie flaunted her affair, and they were absolutely humiliated by it. Other nobles may have tittered in delight at Marie's erotic rampages, but for her male relatives, her behavior was neither aspirational nor a hilarious Parisian joke. It was utter ignominy.

Back then, if you were an important French person and someone was bringing shame on your family, you simply requested a little form for your nemesis's arrest, signed by the king and known as a lettre de cachet. So one afternoon, as the two lovebirds rolled around Paris in their expensive carriage, they were intercepted by guards flashing a lettre de cachet from Marie's father, and Sainte-Croix was promptly dragged off to the Bastille.

You can imagine the anger Marie felt at having her lover wrenched away by her father in public. On her way home, she "raged with the blind fury of a wild animal." This was the beginning of everything for Marie. Later, she would note, chillingly, that "one should never annoy anybody; if Sainte-Croix had not been put in the Bastille perhaps nothing would have happened."

Good People

As Sainte-Croix whiled away six weeks in prison, he may have crossed paths with another prisoner there, a mysterious Italian poisoning expert named Edigio Exili. Serious poisoning hysteria hadn't hit Paris yet, and poison was still thought to be the realm of the sneakier Italians. (A French pamphlet from the time claimed that in Italy, poison was "the surest and most common aid to relieving hatred and vengeance," as though it were simply describing some sort of gastrointestinal medication.)

Marie would eventually claim that Exili taught Sainte-Croix all about the enigmatic art of poisoning. Then she changed her story, saying that Sainte-Croix actually learned about poison from the Swiss chemist Christophe Glaser, celebrated scientist and apothecary to the king. Glaser was famous as much for his scholarship as for his wild recipes that called for ingredients like "the skull of a man dead of a violent death." Of course, poisonous powders were available at any apothecary, so Marie could have picked up a vial of arsenic or antimony anytime she wanted. But these origin stories speak of the lovers' desire to link their crimes to something bigger than themselves. They didn't want to be regular, humble poisoners. They wanted to be co-conspirators with the greats; they wanted their poisoning attempts elevated to the ranks of macabre art.

With Sainte-Croix in the Bastille, Marie had a lot of time to grow angrier and angrier about the temporary loss of her lover. But that wasn't the only stressor on her plate – she also needed money. Her husband was terrible with his finances, there were gambling debts to deal with, and Sainte-Croix was an expensive boyfriend, blowing through her income as though it were his own. Needless to say, her father's wealth was starting to look particularly appealing.

As soon as Sainte-Croix was released on May 2, 1663, he rented a laboratory and began telling people he was an alchemist, or at least really close to becoming one. Ever aware of his bad-boy reputation, he began to hint portentously that he was very, *very* near a big breakthrough. But he also began doing something far more sinister – experimenting with poisons.

Poisoning made sense to the lovers. They needed money, they were furious at Marie's dad, and if they hit upon the right formula, it would look like her father died of gout, stomach troubles, or a really terrible fever. In order to perfect their formula, Marie decided to test it on the patients of Hôtel Dieu, the famous public hospital next to Notre Dame. There, she wandered among the sick, distributing poisoned jams and sweets to her favorites, and weeping inconsolably when they inevitably died.

"Who would have dreamt that a woman brought up in a respectable family . . . would have made an amusement of going to the hospitals to poison the patients?" wrote Nicolas de la Reynie, the chief of police at the time. Marie looked like a good noblewoman, with her big eyes and pretty figure; she acted like a good noblewoman, deigning to stroke the fevered brows of dying beggars. It was hard for authorities like la Reynie to reconcile all this surface-level kindness and nobility with the fact that Marie wasn't actually good at all. (Even when Marie should have been keeping house like a proper wife, she instead brought the evil home. She experimented on one of her servant girls by feeding her a one-two punch of poisoned gooseberries and poisoned ham, which gave the poor servant a terrible burning sensation in her stomach and three years of poor health.)

When the lovers became confident their poisons were undetectable and highly effective, they moved in on Marie's father. Marie planted a servant in his household who began dosing him with arsenic. The year was 1666. It was time for Daddy to die.

"Poisonous Waters"

Over the next eight months, Marie watched her father slip further and further away. After her servant had given him enough poison to destroy his health, Marie joined her ailing dad at his country estate and took over the dreadful process, dropping arsenic into his food and drink. His agonizingly slow death didn't move her; she dosed him with poison almost thirty separate times. When her older brother came to check in on their father, he wrote to his boss in shock: "I have found him in the condition that was told me, almost beyond any hope of recovering his health . . . in such extreme peril." After months of vomiting, tremendous stomach pain, and a burning sensation throughout his insides, Monsieur d'Aubray died on September 10, 1666. The cause of death, according to his doctors? Gout.

The inheritance money was divided among the four d'Aubray siblings, and Marie and Sainte-Croix quickly burned through their share of it. By 1670, they were back where they started: desperate for money, chased by creditors, and resentful of anyone who'd ever opposed their love.

Marie's brothers lived together, conveniently enough, but the older one was married to a woman who hated Marie. This meant that Marie wasn't welcome in the kitchen, and so she was unable to "access" (wink) the tarts, the savory pies, and the wine. So she planted another servant. He went by the name La Chausée, and he was perfect for the job: he'd already worked for Sainte-Croix, he had a criminal record, and, like Marie, he was creepily patient when it came to watching people die. La Chausée went to work right away with a selection of "poisonous waters" (there was a reddish one and a clear one), spiking various drinks and an elaborate meat pie that both brothers ate with gusto. Soon enough, the men were complaining of burning sensations in their stomachs.

The death of Marie's brothers was another excruciatingly drawn-out process. We're talking months of suffering: vomiting, inability to eat, cramps, loss of eyesight, bloody stools, swelling, weight loss, and a constant fire gnawing away at their stomachs. Their bodies grew so "stinking and infected" that it was hard to be in the room with them. It's difficult to imagine the type of sister who could watch her siblings die so slowly, in such agony, but that was the thing about Marie. She was furious. The "violent Passions" that saturated her life included not just lust and greed, but a burning desire for *revenge*. And her brothers, along with her father, made up the patriarchal cage she was constantly rattling against. They sent her off to a weak, boring husband and then punished her when she tried to escape him. They insisted that she behave not just for her own sake, but for the sake of their reputations. She answered them with terrible vengeance.

Her older brother passed away in June, while the younger one lived until September. Autopsies for both brothers revealed the same wrecked insides: the stomach and liver were blackened and gangrenous, and the intestines were literally falling apart. After the younger brother's death, doctors began to suspect the two had been poisoned, but they didn't press the matter. No one had any idea who could have committed the crime, since La Chausée masqueraded so well as a faithful servant and Marie made sure she was miles away when each one died. La Chausée even received a tidy bonus of one hundred crowns for his faithful service.

Now that all her closest male relatives were dead, Marie began plotting the murder of her sister, a devout single gal with a large fortune. She also wanted to poison her sister-in-law, who had just inherited some of the d'Aubray wealth, a fact that irritated Marie. Plus, she'd been toying with the idea of poisoning her husband and marrying Sainte-Croix – though Sainte-Croix didn't seem very excited about that idea. One of the great gossips of the time, Madame de Sévigné, noted that while Marie kept giving her husband poison, Sainte-Croix – "not anxious to have so evil a woman as his wife" – kept slipping the poor man remedies. The result? "Shuttlecocked about like this five or six times, now poisoned, now unpoisoned, he still remained alive."

Needless to say, Sainte-Croix and Marie were no longer in their honeymoon period. A furious Marie even wrote him a letter claiming that she didn't want to live anymore and so had just poisoned herself with his formula, which she'd bought from him at such a high price. In fact, Marie had taken another lover just after her brothers died. This man would be just as destructive to her as Sainte-Croix was, but in a different way; while Sainte-Croix encouraged her crimes, this lover would turn against her because of them. But for now, Marie had no idea that he'd ever betray her. All she knew was that this new man was kind, young, and good.

Sundry Curious Secrets

Jean-Baptiste Briancourt was hired as a tutor for Marie's children in the fall of 1670 and became her lover shortly afterward. Like her husband, Briancourt was a weak, cowardly man, but he must have been an appealing foil for Sainte-Croix, since Marie was feeling especially vulnerable about her relationship with Sainte-Croix at the time (thus the marriage attempts and the threat of suicide). Where Sainte-Croix was unscrupulous and unafraid, Briancourt was moral and wary. He was completely infatuated by the marquise, but also terrified of her; she talked incessantly of poison and told him all about her crimes. He could see how cruel she was to her daughter, and suspected Marie was trying to poison the girl.

Eventually, Briancourt began to wonder if the marquise was plotting to kill him, too. His worst fears were confirmed when Marie asked him to come to her bed at midnight. When Briancourt happened to pass by her room a bit earlier than planned, he saw Marie hiding Sainte-Croix in her closet. The resulting scene was practically vaudevillian: Briancourt showed up at midnight, hurt and silent; Marie tried to tempt him into bed; Briancourt suddenly lunged toward the closet; Marie flung herself onto Briancourt's back, shrieking, to prevent him from opening the door; Briancourt opened it anyway, came face-to-face with a creeping Sainte-Croix, and screamed, "Ah, villain, you have come to stick a knife into me!" At that, Sainte-Croix scrambled out of there as fast as he could, and Marie rolled on the floor screaming and crying and threatening to poison herself. Eventually, Briancourt calmed her down by promising to forgive her, all the while hatching a plan to flee in the morning.

Marie was cracking. She may have been cool about murdering relatives, but the torrid relationship with Sainte-Croix was starting to fray her. She was beginning to realize that this man had, in a way, stolen her entire life. She had given him her wealth and her time and her love; she had bound herself to him with the most horrible secrets. In turn, he had taken and taken from her without remorse and, now that things were getting messy, he seemed to be pulling away. Finally, in his last great betrayal of Marie, Sainte-Croix died before his crimes were ever discovered, leaving her to take the fall for both of them.

Legend says that on July 30, 1672, Sainte-Croix was whipping up poisons in his secret laboratory, wearing a glass mask to avoid breathing the dangerous fumes. As he bent over the fire to stir some devilish pot, his mask shattered, and Sainte-Croix was immediately killed by his own poison. His actual death wasn't nearly so poetically just. He simply died after a long illness, with none of the authorities suspecting him to be a criminal. In fact, he died a good man in the eyes of the church: he was able to perform his final devotions and receive the last rites.

He was, however, disastrously in debt, and so the Paris courts sent over a commissary to put his affairs in order. (Ironically, the commissary came from the same building where Marie's father used to work.) The man initially uncovered a mysterious scroll titled "My Confession," but since Sainte-Croix wasn't accused of anything at the time, he decided that the document was some sort of sacred declaration between a man and his God, not meant for public consumption. As such, he tossed it into the fire.

But the commissary also discovered a little box full of cryptic vials and powders, which turned out to be things like antimony, prepared vitriol, corrosive sublimate powder, and opium. Even stranger, the box came with a note saying that upon the event of Sainte-Croix's death, the contents should be immediately given to the marquise de Brinvilliers. "All that it contains concerns her and belongs to her alone," ran the note. "In case she dies before I do . . . burn it, and all that is in it." There were also multiple papers and envelopes marked "to be burnt in case of death," and one biographer reported that Sainte-Croix actually dared to label an envelope "Sundry Curious Secrets." Unsurprisingly, the commissary turned the box over to the police.

The whole affair only grew more suspicious when Marie rushed over to the authorities late at night, demanding that the box of poiso – uh, "curious secrets" – be handed over to her. She should have played it cool, acting nostalgic for the effects of a deceased lover, but her "very eager and extraordinary manner of demanding it" immediately caused the authorities to become apprehensive. Instead of giving her the box, they decided to test its contents, and fed two of the most enigmatic liquids to a selection of animals, all of which died within hours.

When Marie's sister-in-law heard about the mysterious box full of poisons, she went on a legal rampage, demanding vengeance for her husband's murder. She lodged an accusation against La Chausée, who was dragged off to jail, and she told the authorities to snatch up the marquise de Brinvilliers immediately.

Marie fled the country.

Ordinary and Extraordinary Questions

While French authorities scoured the continent for the marquise, La Chausée went to trial. As a low-ranking member of society with a criminal record and an angry noblewoman on his case, he never stood a chance. He was found guilty before he had confessed a thing, based solely on "conjectures and strong presumptions." On March 24, 1673, the judges sentenced him to be executed after undergoing torture: the "ordinary and extraordinary questions."

The questions were a form of water torture in which the victim's nose was pinched shut, his body stretched backward over a trestle, and copious amounts of water forced down his throat – twice as much water for the extraordinary as for the ordinary. After groaning through the questions, La Chausée was then shoved into a horrific torture device called the *brodequins*: with his legs stuck between planks, wooden wedges were slowly hammered into the space between plank and leg, eventually crushing his calves. La Chausée refused to confess a thing during the torture, but once he was released from the *brodequins,* the truth came pouring out of him. (Apparently this was common with torture – the sheer relief of being free from the pain often brought about a veritable torrent of confession.) He was then tied to a wheel, beaten with iron bars, and left to bleed out in agony. An execution like this was known as being "broken on the wheel," and brings to mind a sort of cross – one where the victim dies facing the sky.

For exactly three years and one day after La Chausée was sentenced to death, Marie avoided capture. She moved around Europe, surviving on small amounts of money sent by her sister – the same sister she had once planned to kill. When her sister died in 1675, Marie was left to survive as best she could and eventually rented a convent room in Liège, which was then an independent city-state full of French troops. This was a huge mistake. Word soon reached the Parisian authorities that the infamous La Brinvilliers was hiding out in a convent, and they descended on her.

As Marie was dragged back to Paris for trial, she tried to kill herself multiple times by attempting to swallow pins and mouthfuls of crushed glass. If she'd been the talk of the town during her halcyon days with Sainte-Croix, she was even more famous now. A rumor began to circulate that she had tried to impale herself by pushing a sharp stick between her legs. As a friend wrote to Madame de Sévigné, "She thrust a stick – guess where! Not in her eye, not in her mouth, not in her ear, not in her nose, and not Turkish fashion [anally]. Guess where!" La Brinvilliers had carried on a public affair for so many years that now even rumors of her suicide attempts framed her in a hypersexual light. But Marie was no longer the wild child of libertine Paris. At forty-six, she was a marked woman, and she was exhausted.

When Marie was arrested, a sheaf of papers had been discovered in her room – a written confession. Like her lover, Marie had been desperate to unburden her conscience. In the document, she indicts herself of "bizarre and monstrous crimes": killing her father, murdering her brothers, letting La Chausée be broken on the wheel because of her crimes, attempting to poison one of her children, thinking about killing herself, burning down a barn, plotting to kill her sister, and trying to poison her husband. In fact, she more or less recants her whole life. "I accuse myself of having created general scandal," she writes. "I accuse myself that I did not honor my father, and that I did not render to him the respect I owed him." She confesses to having two children with Sainte-Croix and a third child with a cousin, to losing her virginity at age seven to a brother, and to committing incest "three times a week, perhaps three hundred times in all." She also declares that, in giving herself to Sainte-Croix, she caused her own ruin.

Of course, in one fell swoop, Marie distracts us all from murder with her extreme claims of incest, which at least one historian has speculated could be code for childhood abuse. At the time, they merely fueled her reputation as a voraciously lustful woman. But upon reading her confession today, we're confronted with a portrait of a desperate, desolate woman, saturated with regret and exhaustive in her self-immolation: she moves from not honoring her father to killing him, from killing her brothers to sleeping with them, from creating "general scandal" to causing the torture and death of an unfortunate petty criminal. In court, she denied the whole thing, claiming she was out of her mind when she wrote it: feverish, confused, alone in a foreign country.

Since she was a woman of high social standing, the court needed substantial evidence to prove her guilt – and the incriminating "confession" wasn't enough. Many witnesses took the stand against her, and one theme that emerged was that La Brinvilliers had been *obsessed* with poison. One woman testified that Marie had gotten drunk at a dinner party and flaunted Sainte-Croix's box of poisons, laughing, "Here is vengeance on one's enemies; this box is small, but is full of inheritances!" Another man heard that Marie told Briancourt (ah, the Parisian gossip machine!) that there were "ways to make away with people that displeased her." Still, none of these testimonies were quite enough to convict her, until the court brought in the one person who knew all about her crimes: Briancourt himself.

Marie listened to her former lover testify against her for a total of eighteen hours. He told the court everything: how she and Sainte-Croix killed her father and brothers, how she asked him for help with the murder of her sister and sister-in-law, how she plotted to murder him with Sainte-Croix in the closet. Marie listened with frightening hauteur, responding that Briancourt was a drunkard and a liar. When Briancourt began to weep on the witness stand, saying, "I warned you many a time, madam, about your disorders and your cruelty, and that your crimes would ruin you," Marie called him a coward. The court was stunned by her eerie, unfeeling composure, but Briancourt's testimony was exactly what they needed to convict her.

Marie really was a vision in the courtroom: calm, cold, proud. She denied everything, over and over, even as her life was "remorselessly dissected" in front of her. The horrible nature of her crimes made everyone else highly emotional – at one point, even the judges were crying – but Marie "kept her head proudly erect, and preserved undimmed the stony clearness of her blue eyes."

On July 16, 1676, the judges declared her guilty, and sentenced her to the ordinary and extraordinary questions, hoping she'd spill the names of any accomplices during the torture. After the questions, she would be beheaded. In a way, this sentence was merciful. They could have had her burned alive.

De Profundis

Marie was given a confessor, a Jesuit priest named Edmé Pirot, who was every bit as sensitive and empathetic as Marie was proud and cold. Pirot was such a delicate soul, in fact, that he claimed to faint at the sight of blood. The sight of Marie – who was by that point very thin, and of course very doomed – immediately tugged at his heart.

Like Briancourt before him, Pirot desperately wanted Marie to repent, and miraculously, Marie was now willing to do so. After spending some time with him, she declared that she was ready to make a full confession to the court. There, in front of everyone, she finally admitted that she'd killed her father and brothers. Perhaps she was hoping to avoid torture.

Unfortunately, she didn't tell the court anything they didn't already know; they were hoping for accomplices, dark secrets, important names. Poisoning paranoia had begun to creep through the city, and authorities were already panicking about the terrifying subtlety of these sorts of crimes. They feared that after Marie's death, her poisons would somehow kill again. After all, in her written confession, she mentioned selling poison to another woman who wanted to kill her husband. Who knew where this web of feminine evil would spread next?

So the torture began. Marie was stripped naked and bent

backward over a wooden trestle, with her ankles tied to the floor and her hands tied to the wall behind her. The torturer began to funnel water down her throat, and after she came up from each dose, coughing and gasping, she was questioned.

"My God! You are killing me!" she wept. "And I only spoke the truth." More water was funneled down her throat. "You are killing me!" she cried again. The trestle was raised, her body stretched even farther, and the extraordinary question began. "O God, you tear me to pieces!" she screamed. "Lord, pardon me! Lord, have mercy upon me!" Her ankles and wrists began to bleed, and the water kept pouring down her throat, but still La Brinvilliers refused to confess any more than she already had, groaning that she would not tell a lie "that would destroy her soul."

After four and a half hours of torture, the men realized that if Marie carried any dark secrets with her, she was taking them to the grave. So they told her to prepare herself for death, and sent her back to her confessor.

Apparently the indignity and horror of the torture had awoken some of Marie's old fire. She'd been humble and penitent in front of Pirot the night before, but now she was incensed at the humiliation she'd endured as well as the humiliation she was about to endure. She would have to do public penance on her way to the scaffold and then, after her death, her ashes would be scattered to the winds – an unthinkable ending for the haughty marquise. Pirot tried so hard to bring her back to a repentant state that he began to weep. Finally, after an hour of his pleading and tears, Marie began crying, too.

The execution of the scandalous La Brinvilliers was quite the happening event, and many Parisian nobles turned out to see her inglorious processional. A tiny, dirty tumbril arrived to carry her to the scaffold. On her way to the cart, Marie had to walk past a group of nobles who'd weaseled their way into the jail to catch a glimpse of the infamous woman, curious if she was still the same girl that they'd danced with, gambled with, and toasted with iced champagne. Now she was barefoot, wearing a coarse white shift with a noose slung symbolically around her neck.

The ride through Paris – with even more nobles gaping at her and everyone yelling that she deserved to die – was an incredibly demeaning ordeal for a woman of status. Pirot, watching her closely, saw her literally convulse with rage and humiliation: "Her face contracted, her brows were knitted, her eyes flashed, her mouth was distorted, and her whole aspect was embittered." A sketch of this awful moment, immortalized by Charles Le Brun, hangs in the Louvre today. It's a grim portrait of cyclical human brokenness – the killer on her way to be slaughtered.

The procession edged toward Notre Dame, where Marie was forced to get out of the cart to perform a public penance. She knelt, holding a lit torch, and proclaimed, "I confess that, wickedly and for revenge, I poisoned my father and my brothers, and attempted to poison my sister, to obtain possession of their goods, and I ask pardon of God, of the king, and of my country's laws." Later, Pirot wrote, "Some people say that she hesitated in saying her father's name – but I noticed nothing of the sort."

On the scaffold, the executioner shaved Marie's hair and ripped open her shirt to expose her neck and shoulders. Pirot whispered prayers in her ear to calm her, while the snarls of the crowd rose and fell around them like waves. The executioner covered her eyes, and she began to obediently repeat a prayer after Pirot, when a long sword flashed through the air. Marie fell silent.

Suddenly nauseated, Pirot assumed that the executioner had missed her head entirely, because though Marie was no longer speaking, she still knelt upright, with her head on her shoulders. Moments later, though, her head slid off her neck and her body fell forward. The executioner asked Pirot, "Was that not a good stroke?" and immediately drank a mouthful of wine. As Marie had requested, Pirot began to recite a de profundis, the Catholic prayer for the dead, over her bleeding body: *Out of the depths I cry to You, O Lord.*

"We Shall Breathe Her"

La Brinvilliers was dead, and Paris was terrified, scandalized, thrilled. "The affair of Mme de Brinvilliers is frightful, and it has been a long time since one heard talk of a woman as evil as she," wrote one Parisian gossip to another. "The source of all her crimes was love." Since Marie had made no secret of her sexual appetite, flaunting her affair with Sainte-Croix all around Paris, the narrative of the beautiful marquise poisoning for love was a natural one for her peers to latch onto.

Love and its close cousins, lust and obsession, have been identified as the "source" of female crimes since the beginning of time, in a host of archetypal ways: the jealous mistress, the spurned lover, the mad Ophelia, the brainwashed Manson girl. Love makes for a story that's not just romantic, but *pleasant*. It's a clean-burning fire, after all; love may destroy things, but at its core, love is supposed to be true and noble, kind of like how at their core, French nobles were assumed to be good. If the source of Marie's crimes was love, it would seem to negate the worst part of her wickedness, or at least make it more socially acceptable. A good noblewoman was allowed to go a little bit crazy when it came to love, especially a noblewoman in love with a man like Sainte-Croix, who swaggered around boasting about his pseudosciences and attempting to transform base matter into gold.

Today, we can see that love wasn't what drove the marquise to kill, despite what the gossips insisted. She loved, and was loved, and perhaps love led to her downfall, but she was also furious, vengeful, and fixated on her box of "inheritances." ("One should never annoy anybody!") But money was prosaic, and revenge was distasteful in a noblewoman, so the narrative of love was the one that stuck.

Even with its romantic allure, her story left Paris traumatized – and paranoid about the use of poison. If a lovely, wealthy woman could poison the men closest to her, then who *wouldn't* poison? If nobility could turn evil, then who was safe?

"Well, it's all over and done with, Brinvilliers is in the air," wrote Madame de Sévigné to a friend. "Her poor little body was thrown after the execution into a very big fire and the ashes to the winds, so that we shall breathe her, and through the communication of the subtle spirits we shall develop some poisoning urge which will astonish us all . . . Never has such a crowd been seen, nor Paris so excited and attentive."

In fact, some of Paris was so attentive that they watched the burning of Marie's body till the very end. They wanted to see where her ashes would land. The people who stood closest to the scaffold reported that her face was illuminated by a halo just before the beheading. Death had made her a saint, they said, and went searching through the cinders for bits of bone.

Conclusion

Horror

The half-life of murder is forever. The pull of a detective story is strong. And so there are about a million things to wonder about serial killers, a million angles to examine, a million stones to turn over. This in and of itself is kind of a freaky fact. Why is it possible to theorize so extensively about these people? Shouldn't we just wash our hands and be done with 'em? Why are we so *obsessed*? Why did that one friend scoot her chair away from me when I told her I "empathized but didn't sympathize" with every woman in this book?

People typically have one of two reactions when I mention that I'm writing about female serial killers: a frenetic, "That's hilarious!" or an aghast, "That's horrible." (Secret option number three: a nervous chuckle, accompanied by a tiny step backward.) I understand all of these approaches, but taken alone, each one is a fallacy. I believe we have to laugh *and* shudder in order to understand our own human history, which is partially an inheritance of death.

Recoiling from crime is natural, but recoil too far and it becomes a delusion. Psychologists have theorized that we love separating ourselves from "evil" because it makes us feel good about ourselves:

"Locating evil within selected individuals or groups carries with it the 'social virtue' of taking society 'off the hook' as blameworthy." And being blameless certainly sounds lovely. But as Aleksandr Solženicyn wrote after undergoing a series of terrible experiences (prison, forced-labor camp, exile), "If only there were evil people somewhere insidiously committing evil deeds, and it were necessary only to separate them from the rest of us and destroy them. But the line dividing good and evil cuts through the heart of every human being. And who is willing to destroy a piece of his own heart?" I also love the way Joyce Carol Oates puts it: "To examine the mind of the serial killer is to examine the human mind in extremis, and should anything 'human' be alien to us? Where the 'human' crosses over into the 'monstrous' is after all a matter of law, theology, or aesthetic taste."

Ladies

Female serial killers often go undetected for a long time, yes. But just for the record, a lot of the rhetoric about how "nobody even realizes that there *are* female serial killers" can quickly veer into the realm of the ridiculous. Lady killers exist, but underestimating that reality does not mean we are literally putting our own lives at risk every time we talk to a woman. One otherwise-great book on the subject includes a line implying that the "cute girl behind the deli counter slicing our bread" could actually be a heartless murderess. Dude, just order the sandwich, you're going to be *fine*.

Still, female serial killers haven't been studied very extensively, and when they are, the studies are far from exhaustive: they often focus solely on killers in the United States, or killers over the past hundred years, etc. Because of this, I haven't included very many stats in this book; they frequently seem either limited or unreliable.

Here's a stat you may enjoy, though: in the United States, the chances that you will be murdered by a female serial killer could be as low as one in ninety million.

The odds that you will be murdered by a woman in this book, of course, are zero. The choice to keep these lady killers fairly "vintage" (Nannie Doss is the most recent killer, and she hung around in the 1950s) was largely an aesthetic one; with victims and perpetrators long dead, the stories hopefully err on the side of spooky and mesmerizing rather than simply . . . depressing. Today's serial killers are certainly worthy of study, but there's a heaviness and a sadness to modern crimes that history tends to erase, for better or for worse. Anyway, today is not the era of the serial killer. Those sorts of murderers are a rare breed now, an endangered species, unlike during the 1970s and 80s when they roamed the streets in seemingly unstoppable numbers. If crimes reflect the anxieties of our time, then today is the era of the mass murderer, the terrorist. Our violent delights still lead to violent ends, but the ends change as the decades ebb and flow.

One stat that does get confirmed again and again in various studies is that the majority of serial killers, both male and female, are white. (Are we surprised?) Of course, stats come with their own sets of biases. I would say the majority of serial killers who are *written* about in the media, who *appear* in the historical record, are white. When it comes to the "pre-1950s female serial killer of color" category, the information is slim, inaccessible, or else was seemingly never documented at all. Plus, there's a lot of misinformation; if you manage to find a list of historical female serial killers broken down by race, you'll notice many of the women of color who are listed as early "serial killers" are actually mythical figures, bandits, or evil queens. My own research, of course, can't help but be flawed and incomplete, but I'll tell you who I was hoping to include: Clementine Barnabet, a young black girl from New Orleans, and Miyuki Ishikawa, a Japanese midwife. Unfortunately, little has been preserved about them beyond the facts of the crimes themselves, even (for Miyuki) in Japanese, and I was unable to find the degree of detail required to make them fully come alive.

In general, I wonder if female serial killers haven't been studied extensively because at the end of the day, in our heart of hearts, we don't consider them worthy antagonists. Let them slice the bread; let them glare at us from behind the deli counter. We are simply *not afraid of them*.

Heartache

Being a lady killer is quite lonely, it turns out. Not a single woman in this book appears to have had any close friends. Tillie had her cousin Nellie, Raya had Sakina, Anna and Alice had their beloved sons. That was about it. Marriage and children weren't sources of comfort for most of these women, for obvious reasons. And as far as I can tell, the only people who really reached out to them or tried to understand them were pastors, journalists, and the occasional doctor or defense lawyer – in other words, people who were sent to them *after* they'd been locked up, when it was too late to save them from themselves.

Speaking of loneliness, the term "mise en abyme," which literally means "placed into abyss," has started to remind me of these women. The phrase evokes the feeling of a hall of mirrors: an image of an image, something multiplying into infinity. I hear it and I see Erzsébet Báthory standing in her cavernous halls, jangling in the abyss, no one there to reflect anything back at her other than her own twisted reality. I see Mary Ann Cotton, doomed to repeat herself over and over again, forever playing out a dark parody of marriage and motherhood. I see the peasants of Nagyrév, with each of their murders like the play within a play of *Hamlet*, a tiny story reflecting back on the larger one, contributing to the idea that what had happened and what was about to happen was all totally inescapable.

Somehow it doesn't stress me out that we're all obsessed with serial killers. Maybe it should. (Mark Seltzer, a professor at UCLA who's written extensively about violence, calls this obsession "wound culture" – our tendency to gather around trauma, unable to avert our eyes.) I don't think our obsession stems from the fact that we are all secretly violent, using the serial killer to enact our darkest fantasies. I think it comes from our enduring love of stories. That being said, I have been haunted time and again while writing this book with a nagging sense of moral responsibility. I don't want to accidentally make murder sound trivial or hilarious. I don't want to make female serial killers sound like the ultimate feminists. I don't want to be part of the long tradition of glamorizing serial killers, though I'm sure I've slipped up from time to time. But I believe in the healing and illuminating power of narrative, and I think there's something to be gleaned from looking at evil, trying to understand it, wondering if perhaps we are all a little bit responsible. *Should anything human be alien to us?* That question is terrifying, and beautiful.

I cried twice while working on this book, both times over the same moment: the part where Anna Marie Hahn completely loses it on her way to the electric chair. Anna's murders are some of the most coldhearted in the book – but, when faced with her own death, Anna couldn't take it. I think that's so poignant, so sad. It shows how desperately the human body wants to live, no matter how evil or reckless the soul within it has become. Even the most psychopathic woman can realize, when staring death in the eyes, that what she valued, in the end, was *life* all along.

Acknowledgments

Thank you to Emma Carmichael for giving the "Lady Killers" column a home, first at *The Hairpin* and then *Jezebel*. Thank you to the people who actually read the column, especially to the reader who said it paired well with red wine. I like your vibe.

Thank you to the squad of super cool, morbidly hilarious women who worked on the book: to my amazing agent Erin Hosier, for loving psychopaths and immediately getting the feel of the book; to Dame Darcy, cult illustrator extraordinaire, for the gorgeous goth illustrations (some of which were done purely via the strength of her imagination, as there were no paintings or photographs available for a number of these women); and a million thanks to my editor Jillian Verrillo, for the beautiful editing, the encouragement, the answering of my paranoid emails, and all the care you took with the manuscript in general. The book is *so* much stronger because of you. Thank you so much to my editor Stephanie Hitchcock for fearlessly guiding the book to completion, to Sarah Bibel at Harper Perennial for fulfilling my dreams of a pink cover, and to everyone else at Harper Perennial for bringing this book to life.

ACKNOWLEDGMENTS

For their researching, fact-checking, and mad bilingual skills: thank you to Hiba Krisht for help with Moulay and Raya/Sakina; thank you to Taka Okubo for delving into Miyuki Ishikawa (even though we didn't find enough on her to ultimately include her), and to Hungarian Google, which informed me I was totally wrong about Erzsébet Báthory's diary being housed in the national archives in Budapest. (Don't worry, I had other reasons to be in Budapest.) I cannot thank my Russian translators, Rostislav and Alyona Tkachenko, enough – without you, there would be no Darya chapter, period. Thank you to Nefertiti Takla for generously directing me to your brilliant work on Raya and Sakina. Béla Bodó, Diana Britt Franklin, David Wilson, and Kimberly L. Craft – you don't know me, but your meticulously researched books were invaluable to me. And a special shout-out to all the hard-working old-school journalists of the past for all the great headlines, impertinent pull quotes, and wildly inaccurate but colorful anecdotes. Nellie Bly, Genevieve Forbes – your bravery and empathetic spirit live on today in journalists around the globe.

Thank you to my siblings, always. John (my earliest partner in crime/writing) and Jenny: thank you for letting me tell you the news over IHOP and for being my rocks in Los Angeles. Sammy, you are so enthusiastic and unconditionally supportive about *everything*. Anna, my best pal/evil genius/advice-giver, what would I do without you? Hope I didn't accidentally turn you malevolent! Extra love to Sammy and my cousin Aaron for reading the chapter on Alice Kyteler while you were scrambling around South America.

Thank you to my parents, Charles and Rhonda Telfer, for teaching me to love both history's redemptive narratives and odd, forgotten corners. Thank you to all four of my amazing grandparents and my super-cool in-laws Chris and Lori for all the love and support.

And most of all, thank you to Charlie Kirchen – my soulmate

and one true love and someone I am, like, creepily obsessed with – for being there every step of the way (and long before, too). Thank you for letting me regale you with tales of death, for all the perfectly brewed coffee, for being the Clyde to my Bonnie (symbolically, not literally!!), for letting me filch that Nietzsche quote, for encouraging both my writing *and* catering, for inspiring me with your own hard work, and for giving me the type of love that makes it seem like anything is possible. I can't wait for you to read this!

Notes

The Elusive Population

xi   **The Elusive Population:** Farrell, A. L., Keppel, R. D., and Titterington, V. B., "Lethal Ladies: Revisiting What We Know about Female Serial Murderers," *Homicide Studies* 15, no. 3 (2011): 228–52.

xi   **Less than ten percent:** According to stats gathered from the Radford University/FGCU Serial Killer Database and information presented in Hickey, Eric W., *Serial Murderers and Their Victims* (Belmont, CA: Wadsworth Pub., 1997).

xi   **140 known female serial killers:** Vronsky, Peter, *Female Serial Killers: How and Why Women Become Monsters* (New York: Berkley Books, 2007), 3.

xi   **A blog for the Men's Rights movement:** See the index listed on unknownmisandry.blogspot.com.

xi   **Increased in the US since the 1970s:** Schurman-Kauflin, Deborah, *The New Predator – Women Who Kill: Profiles of Female Serial Killers* (New York: Algora Pub., 2000), 12.

xi   **Collective amnesia:** A concept explored in Pearson, Patricia, *When She Was Bad: How and Why Women Get Away with Murder* (New York: Penguin Books, 1998).

xii **Reactive homicide . . . instrumental homicide:** Perri, Frank S. and Lichtenwald, Terrance G., "The Last Frontier: Myths and the Female Psychopathic Killer," *Forensic Examiner* (Summer 2010): 50–67.

xii **Above-average attractiveness:** Harrison, Marissa A., Erin A. Murphy, Lavina Y. Ho, Thomas G. Bowers, and Claire V. Flaherty, "Female Serial Killers in the United States: Means, Motives, and Makings," *Journal of Forensic Psychiatry and Psychology* 26, no. 3 (2015): 383–406.

xiii **The vantage-ground of SEX:** Harland, Marion, "The Truth about Female Criminals," *North American Review* 150, no. 398 (January 1890): 138–40.

xiii **That side of her, however, is rarely invoked:** Perri and Lichtenwald, "The Last Frontier."

xiii **Myth of female passivity:** Ibid.

xiv **One must not suppose them like others:** *Questions sur les empoisonneurs*, BA, MS 2664, fol. 45 trans. in Mollenauer, Lynn Wood, *Strange Revelations: Magic, Poison, and Sacrilege in Louis XIV's France* (University Park, PA: Pennsylvania State University Press, 2007), 63, 159.

xiv **Hot Female Murderers:** This list can be found, as of November 6, 2016, at the revered site holytaco.com/female-murderers -casey-anthony.

xv **Man will desire *oblivion*:** Nietzsche, Friedrich Wilhelm, *On the Geneology of Morals* (New York: Vintage Books, 1989).

Chapter 1: The Blood Countess

1 **The Blood Countess:** This nickname is a common one for Erzsébet, appearing in many of the below publications.

2   **She spoke not only Hungarian and Slovak:** Thorne, Tony, *Countess Dracula: The Life and Times of the Blood Countess, Elisabeth Báthory* (London: Bloomsbury, 1997), 84. McNally, Raymond T., *Dracula Was a Woman: In Search of the Blood Countess of Transylvania* (New York: McGraw-Hill, 1983), 19. Penrose, Valentine, *The Bloody Countess* (London: Calder and Boyars, 1970), 15. Craft, Kimberly L., *Infamous Lady: The True Story of Countess Erzsébet Báthory* (Lexington, KY: Kimberly L. Craft, 2009), 14.

2   **Epileptic seizures:** McNally, *Dracula Was a Woman*, 19. Craft, *Infamous Lady*, 13.

2   **Her parents happened to be cousins:** McNally, *Dracula Was a Woman*, 16, 18–19. Penrose, *The Bloody Countess*, 15.

2   **Horse's body:** McNally, *Dracula Was a Woman*, 21.

3   **Occasional public execution:** Craft, *Infamous Lady*, 13.

3   **Run her in-laws' massive estates:** Thorne, *Countess Dracula*, 89.

3   **Erzsébet, at fourteen:** McNally, *Dracula Was a Woman*, 30. Thorne, *Countess Dracula*, 92.

4   **Occasional flash of the strong-willed personality:** Craft, *Infamous Lady*, 41.

4   **Catch with their severed heads:** Ibid., 63.

4   **Loaning money to the Hapsburgs:** McNally, *Dracula Was a Woman*, 60.

5   **Star kicking:** Ibid., 127.

5   **Clawed glove . . . stung by insects:** Craft, *Infamous Lady*, 64.

5   **Wild beast in female form:** Ibid., 62.

5   **The Lady became more cruel:** Testimony of Ficzkó, trans. in the appendices of Craft, *Infamous Lady*.

6   **Reduced the rights of peasants and serfs:** Bledsaw, Rachael L., "No Blood in the Water: The Legal and Gender Conspiracies Against Countess Elizabeth Bathory in Historical Context" (master's thesis, Illinois State University, 2014), 30.

6   **Practically unpayable debt:** Craft, *Infamous Lady*, 67.

6   **Unknown and mysterious causes:** Ibid., 58, 116.

6   **Three dead bodies:** Ibid., 57.

6   **Your Grace should not have so acted:** Report of Mózes Cziráky, October 27, 1610, Craft, *Infamous Lady* appendices.

7   **She refused to participate in the torture:** Craft, *Infamous Lady*, 104.

8   **Cut off their fingers:** Testimony of Dorka, Craft, *Infamous Lady* appendices.

8   **Until their bodies burst:** Testimony of Ficzkó, Craft, *Infamous Lady* appendices.

8   **No butcher under heaven was, in my opinion, more cruel:** Letter from János Ponikenusz, priest of the church at Csejthe, to the theologian Élias Lanyí, January 1, 1611, Craft, *Infamous Lady* appendices.

8   **Erzsébet liked it all:** All descriptions of torture taken from trial documents and testimonies of Dorka, Ficzkó, Ilona Jó's, and Katalin, Ibid.

8   **Anywhere she went:** Testimony of Ilona Jó, Ibid.

8   **Their mistress could neither eat nor drink:** From András of Keresztúr's report to Mátyás II, July 28, 1611, Ibid.

9   **Written by a Jesuit scholar:** His name was László Turóczi.

10   **Change her shirt:** Testimony of Ilona Jó, Craft, *Infamous Lady* appendices.

10   **Disturbed by dogs:** Craft, *Infamous Lady*, 126, 127, 155.

10   **Forest witch:** Ibid., 99.

11   **Anxious energy:** Ibid., 90.

11   **Erzsébet's bizarre excuse:** Ibid., 107–8, 113.

12   **Knife still quivering in her foot:** Ibid., 110.

13   **Public punishment would shame us all:** Zrínyi's letter to Thurzó, February 12, 1611, Craft, *Infamous Lady* appendices.

13   **Convinced she was trying to poison them:** Craft, *Infamous Lady*, 127–8.

13   **The cats were instructed to destroy:** Letter from Ponikenusz to Élias Lanyí, January 1, 1611, Craft, *Infamous Lady* appendices.

14   **Hidden away where this damned woman:** Letter from Thurzó to his wife, December 30, 1610, ibid.

14   **Dungeons that had held her victims' bodies:** Craft, *Infamous Lady*, 133.

15   **175 to 200 girls:** Ibid., 160.

15   **650 girls:** Testimony of Szuzanna, Craft, *Infamous Lady* appendices.

15   **Serious, ongoing atrocities:** Ibid., 244.

15   **Even if they tortured her with fire:** Testimony of Nicolaus Barosius, pastor of the town of Verbo, ibid.

15   **As the shadows envelop you:** Ibid., 171.

16   **Certain cultural and historical factors:** For an in-depth discussion on the use of torture, the question of framing, and the Common Inquest, see Bledsaw, "No Blood in the Water," 30.

17   **The Countess was put under house arrest:** Thorne, *Countess Dracula*, 167. Penrose, *The Bloody Countess*, 168.

17   **Name would no longer be spoken in society:** Craft, *Infamous Lady*, 180.

19   **Sing, beautifully:** Stanislas Thurzó's letter to György Thurzó, August 25, 1614, Craft, *Infamous Lady* appendices.

19   **No trace of Erzsébet:** Craft, *Infamous Lady*, 184.

Chapter 2: The Giggling Grandma

21 **The Giggling Grandma:** This was one of the more popular nicknames the press bestowed on Nannie during her glory days.

21 **Sick, aged aunt:** *Corsicana Daily Sun*, "Possible Poison Victims Now 14," December 7, 1954.

22 **I'm sure mighty proud:** *Pampa Daily News*, "Nannie Doss Hams It Up for Newsmen," December 8, 1954.

22 **Thinking crooked:** *Lawton Constitution*, "Nannie Doss Enjoyed Good, Clean Romance," June 3, 1965.

23 **Church woman:** *Kansas City Times*, "Doss Tales as False," November 30, 1954.

23 **No more Christian:** *Lima News*, "Jovial Mrs. Doss Never Lost Smile Throughout Four Poison Confessions," December 19, 1954.

23 **Turned black so quick:** Ibid.

23 **I'd get down on my knees:** *Kansas City Times*, "Full Story Not Told," December 1, 1954.

24 **Some men were good:** Ibid.

24 **She talks a lot:** *Great Bend Tribune*, "Reticent Widow Investigated in Arsenic Deaths," November 27, 1954.

24 **Smiling, talkative widow:** *Miami Daily News-Record*, "Nannie Doss Admits Poison Deaths of 4," November 29, 1954.

25 **If you don't come to bed . . . I decided I'll teach him:** *Bridgeport Telegram*, "Affable Grandmother Confesses Poisoning 4 or 5 Husbands," November 29, 1954.

25 **Out of bed:** *Logansport Pharos-Tribune*, "Tulsa Widow Confesses Killing Five Husbands," November 29, 1954.

26 **Will you please take our names off your list:** *Brownwood Bulletin*, "Endorsement of Widow Written by Poison Victim," November 30, 1954.

26 **I lost my head:** *Bridgeport Telegram*, "Affable Grandmother."

27 **He got on my nerves:** *Pampa Daily News*, "Defense Wants to 'Shut Up' Nannie Doss," December 1, 1954.

27 **He sure did like prunes:** *Bridgeport Telegram*, "Affable Grandmother."

27 **Kill someone else:** *Miami Daily News-Record*, "Suspect Gave Autopsy Okay," November 29, 1954.

28 **You can dig up all the graves:** *Logansport Pharos-Tribune*, "Tulsa Widow."

28 **I'll be next:** *Anniston Star*, "Nannie's Conscience Clear," June 3, 1965.

29 **All that happened was that the police:** *Kansas City Times*, "Doss Tales," November 30, 1954.

29 **Simple, open:** Ibid.

29 **Shrewd, very shrewd:** Ibid.

30 **Ain't that the dying truth:** *Pampa Daily News*, "Nannie Doss Hams It Up for Newsmen," December 8, 1954.

31 **Talking to you for a week:** *Moberly Monitor-Index*, "Slayer of Four Husbands Will 'Quit Talking,'" November 30, 1954.

32 **I was a normal person:** Bundy's final interview with James Dobson is available on video at https://vimeo.com/49018764 as of February 5, 2017, and the transcript is widely available around the web.

32 **Epitaphs:** *Brownwood Bulletin*, "Widow Liked to Write Epitaphs for Tombstones of Her Poison Victims," December 5, 1954.

33 **Now maybe I will get some rest:** *Neosho Daily News*,

"Doctors Begin Sanity Tests on Nanny Doss," December 16, 1954.

33 **Maybe those docs at the hospital:** *Lubbock Morning Avalanche*, "Confessed Slayer to Mental Hospital," December 17, 1954.

33 **If you had small children:** *McKinney Daily Courier-Gazette*, "Grandma Doss Described as 'Ideal Patient,'" March 9, 1955.

33 **Mentally defective:** *El Paso Herald-Post*, "Slayer of Four Husbands Held Insane by Examiners," March 14, 1955.

33 **The hearing shapes up:** Greenwood, S.C., *Index-Journal*, "Jury to Decide if Granny Doss Is Legally Sane," May 2, 1955.

34 **I like people:** *Long Beach Independent*, "Killer of Four Husbands Gets New Proposal," March 26, 1955.

34 **Enough husbands:** Ibid.

34 **Mrs. Doss is a mentally defective:** Harlingen, TX, *Valley Morning Star*, "Psychologist Holds Nannie Doss Insane," May 3, 1955.

34 **She is a shrewd, clever:** *Palm Beach Post*, "Woman Termed Shrew Who Slew Four Husbands," May 4, 1955.

34 **Extensively at nothing:** *Pampa Daily News*, "Nannie Doss Called Shrew by Prosecutor," May 4, 1955.

34 **Cleverest criminal:** *Albuquerque Journal*, "Nannie Might Kill Again, Sanity Hearing Jury Told," May 4, 1955.

34 **I've never felt more sane in my whole life:** *Anniston Star*, "Chuckling Mrs. Doss Agrees She's Sane Enough to Face Trial," May 5, 1955.

35 **Wore an attractive blue party dress:** Salem, OR, *Daily Capital Journal*, "Grandma Doss Gets Life Term," June 2, 1955.

35 **This court has never heard of a woman:** *Brownsville Herald*, "Arsenic Slayer Gets Life Term," June 2, 1955.

35 **I have no hard feelings:** *Sedalia Democrat*, "Nannie Doss Gets Life Term for Killing Husband," June 2, 1955.

35 **I thought I was just out of the headlines:** *Miami Daily News-Record*, "Nannie Grants an Interview," September 7, 1955.

35 **From a magazine story:** *Moberly Monitor-Index*, "Accused Poisoner Sent to Hospital for Mental Tests," December 16, 1954.

36 **Sounds sort of crazy:** *Miami Daily News-Record*, "Nannie Grants," September 7, 1955.

36 **Strictly for the fifty women prisoners:** *Miami Daily News-Record*, "'Like Being at Home,' Nannie Says of Her Stay in State Penitentiary," December 1, 1955.

36 **Just like a mother:** Ibid.

36 **Just like being at home:** Ibid.

37 **Numerous studies:** Brower, M. C., "Advances in Neuropsychiatry: Neuropsychiatry of Frontal Lobe Dysfunction in Violent and Criminal Behaviour: A Critical Review," *Journal of Neurology, Neurosurgery and Psychiatry* 71, no. 6 (2001): 720–6.

37 **Grandma, you rat!:** *Gastonia Gazette*, "Grandma, You Rat!" November 30, 1954.

38 **Melissa Ann Shepard:** Quotes taken from the *Guardian*, "Canada's Black Widow," March 25, 2016, and the *Daily Mail*, "The Many Faces of Canada's 'Internet Black Widow,'" March 19, 2016.

38 **When they get short in the kitchen:** This quote was reported widely; the press loved it. The *Edwardsville Intelligencer*, "News Quotes," May 13, 1957.

39 **Maybe they would give me the electric chair:** *Panama City News-Herald*, "Widow Rejects Life in Prison," May 13, 1957.

Chapter 3: The Worst Woman on Earth

41   **The Worst Woman on Earth:** *New York Times*, "LIZZIE HALLIDAY DEAD; Guilty of Five Murders and Described as 'Worst Woman on Earth,'" June 29, 1918.

42   **Peculiar influence:** *Harrisburg Daily Independent*, "Murder Is a Mania with Her," September 11, 1893.

42   **Perfectly sane:** *Algona Upper Des Moines*, "Young Yet a Fiend," July 15, 1891.

43   **She was inclined so much to quarreling:** Blumer, G. Alder, "The Halliday Case," *Brooklyn Medical Journal* 9: 169.

43   **Repulsive face:** *New York Times*, "Distrusted Mrs. Halliday," September 12, 1893.

43   **Naturally ugly:** Blumer, "The Halliday Case," 167.

44   **I am afraid of her:** Ibid., 168.

44   **What's the use of living:** Ibid., 166.

44   **Pounded his first wife to death:** New York, NY, *The World*, "A Woman without a Heart," November 5, 1893.

45   **My boy is now about twelve years old:** Ibid.

45   **Goodbye, if I shouldn't see you again:** *New York Times*, "The Halliday Murder Case," September 7, 1893.

46   **Cut his heart's blood out:** Plainfield, N.J., *The Daily Press*, "Mrs. Halliday's Trial," June 20, 1894.

46   **Sneak look:** *Middletown Daily Argus,* "Lizzie Halliday's Trial," June 20, 1894.

47   **Badly decomposed:** *Lebanon Daily News*, "Watching Her Closely," September 8, 1893.

47   **Deafening shriek:** *New York Times*, "Mrs. Halliday in Jail," September 9, 1893.

48   **Moodily and lost in thought:** *New York Times*, "Mrs. Halliday Not Insane," September 12, 1893.

48   **Widespread abuse of the insanity plea:** *Chicago Tribune*, "To Stop the Insanity Dodge," April 21, 1898.

48   **Public delusion:** *Transactions of the Medical Society of the State of New York*, 1895, 241.

49   **Successful Woman Adventuresses:** Nellie Bly's interviews with Lizzie can be read in "A Woman Without a Heart," *The World*, November 5, 1893, and "Lizzie Borgia," *St. Louis Post-Dispatch*, November 5, 1893.

51   **I thought I would cut myself to see if I would bleed:** *Sun and the Erie County Independent*, "Cut Her Throat This Time," December 15, 1893.

51   **Did not take the usual precautions:** *Middletown Daily Argus*, "Trial."

52   **Wild as a hawk:** New York, NY, *Evening World*, "A Wierd Murderess [*sic*]," June 20, 1894.

52   **Nineteen skunks/she is shamming:** New York, NY, *Evening World*, "Was Like a Tigress," June 21, 1894.

52   **Wild beast or a monster:** New York, NY, *Sun*, "Mrs. Halliday Convicted," June 22, 1894.

52   **Exterminating the prisoner:** *Middletown Daily Argus*, "Trial."

52   **Deserved no friends:** New York, NY, *Sun*, "Convicted."

53   **Cussedness:** *Middletown Times-Press*, "More Mystery," September 11, 1893.

53   **Excessive menstrual flow:** Observations on Lizzie's state appear in Ransom, J. B., "Shall Insane Criminals Be Imprisoned or Put to Death?" *Transactions of the Medical Society of the State of New York*, 1895, 233.

54   **He broke a spine of my ribs:** Blumer, "The Halliday Case," 163.

54   **Demand of an excited and clamorous public:** Ransom, "Insane Criminals," 235.

54 **Power to choose:** Blumer, "The Halliday Case," 173.

55 **Quiet, industrious, and contented:** *Middletown Daily Argus*, "Lizzie Halliday Getting Better," August 21, 1895.

55 **Become sane:** *Washington Bee*, "Mrs. Halliday Tries Again," September 7, 1895.

56 **Thrilling war drama:** York, PA, *Gazette*, "Exciting War Play," November 6, 1898.

58 **She tried to leave me:** *French Broad Hustler*, "Mad Murderess Kills Girl Nurse," October 4, 1906.

59 **Wild mental condition:** *Middletown Times-Press*, "More Mystery," September 11, 1893.

59 **Young and comely member:** *Leavenworth Times*, "The Gipsy Fiend," October 1, 1893.

59 **Do they think I am an elephant?:** *Middletown Times-Press*, "More about Mrs. Halliday," December 4, 1893.

Chapter 4: Devil in the Shape of a Saint

63 **Devil in the Shape of a Saint:** "A True Relation of Four Most Barbarous and Cruel Murders Committed in Leicester-shire by Elizabeth Ridgway" (London: George Croom, 1684).

64 **I have cause for ever to praise God:** Josselin, Ralph, and Ernest Hockliffe, *The Diary of the Rev. Ralph Josselin, 1616– 1683* (London: Offices of the Society, 1908).

64 **Religious Maid:** Croom, "A True Relation."

64 **Indifferently inclined:** Newton, John, *A True Relation of the Fact, Trial, Carriage and Death of Ridgeway* (London: Richard Chiswell, 1684).

65 **Thomas Ridgeway:** The George Croom pamphlet gives his name as William, but since Newton talked to Elizabeth in person, I'm more inclined to believe his account.

65   **Dogged, sullen Humour:** Croom, "A True Relation."

65   **White mercury:** Newton says it was white arsenic. Newton, "Fact, Trial, Carriage."

65   **So free:** Croom, "A True Relation."

66   **Season him some Draught:** Ibid.

66   **Seeming mutual Love:** Newton, "Fact, Trial, Carriage."

66   **Frustrated of her expectations:** Ibid.

67   **Converted her despair:** Ibid.

68   **Great Torment:** Ibid.

68   **Gentleman of great Judgment and Prudence:** Ibid.

69   **Burst out at Nose and Mouth:** Croom, "A True Relation."

69   **Tender people:** Newton, "Fact, Trial, Carriage."

69   **Newton visited Elizabeth in jail:** Ibid. All subsequent quotes from Elizabeth to Newton, or from Newton about Elizabeth, were taken from Newton's recounting of the experience.

73   **Centuries later, researchers would divide female psychopaths into two broad categories:** Perri, Frank S. and Lichtenwald, Terrance G., "The Last Frontier: Myths and the Female Psychopathic Killer," *Forensic Examiner* (Summer 2010): 50–67.

74   **She must die:** Croom, "A True Relation."

74   **In contemplation of approaching Death and Judgment:** Newton, "Fact, Trial, Carriage."

75   **Familiar Spirit:** Croom, "A True Relation."

75   **Read and Pray:** Ibid.

76   **Barbarous Example:** Ibid.

Chapter 5: Vipers

79   **Vipers:** This was one of the many bestial nicknames the sisters received from the press. Lopez, Shaun T., "Madams, Murders,

and the Media," in *Re-Envisioning Egypt 1919–1952* (Cairo: American University in Cairo Press, 2005), 384.

80   **Where are the police?:** Abaza's quote was originally published in *al-Ahram Weekly*, November 25, 1920, and appeared again in Yunan Labib Rizk's "The Women Killers," *al-Ahram Weekly, June 17–23, 1999.*

81   **Raya would join her:** The best source on the sisters' early lives is found in Issa, Salah, *Rijal Raya wa Sekina: Sira Ijtima'yyahwa Siyasiyyah* (Cairo: Dar al-Ahmadi, 2002).

81   **Ten to fifteen glasses of wine:** Takla, Nefertiti, "Murder in Alexandria: The Gender, Sexual and Class Politics of Criminality in Egypt, 1914–1921," PhD diss. UCLA, 146.

82   **Feeble-minded, lustful, hot-tempered, and vengeful:** Ibid., 26.

83   **She always had money in her pocket:** Issa, *Rijal Raya wa Sekina*, 468.

83   **Sakina made extra cash:** Ibid., 168.

83   **That trauma:** Ibid., 111–2.

84   **Underground brothels:** Takla, Nefertiti, "Murder in Alexandria: The Gender, Sexual and Class Politics of Criminality in Egypt, 1914–1921," UCLA Center for Study of Women, March 21, 2016, accessed April 1, 2016, csw.ucla .edu/2016/03/21/murder-alexandria-gender-sexual-class -politics-criminality-egypt-1914–1921/.

84   **Very value of said bodies:** Takla, PhD diss., 79.

85   **Manual labor:** Ibid., 103.

86   **Paralyzing the entire country's economy:** Botman, Selma, *Egypt from Independence to Revolution: 1919–1952* (Syracuse, NY: Syracuse University Press, 1991), 100.

87   **Where was the police:** al-Lataif al-Musawara, November 29, 1920, via "The Centenary of Raya and Sakina," Community

Times, February 11, 2015, accessed February 5, 2017, communitytimes.me/the-centenary-of-raya-and-sakina/. I was unable to locate the title of the original article.

88   **Raya, who may have been the decision maker of the group:** This is what Issa postulates. Issa, *Rijal Raya wa Sekina*, 468.

89   **Killing system:** *Al-Ahram Weekly,* "The Women Killers," June 17–23, 1999.

90   **By and within the lower class:** Lopez, "Madams, Murders, and the Media," 373.

90   **Ever published photos of criminals:** *Al-Ahram Weekly,* "The Women Killers," June 17–23, 1999.

90   **Newspaper boys on every street:** *Al-Haqa'iq,* November 21, 1920, via Lopez, "Madams, Murders, and the Media," 389. I was unable to locate the title of the original article.

91   **What is the force that compelled these women:** Editorial in *Al-Umma,* November 21, 1920, via Lopez, "Madams, Murders, and the Media," 385.

91   **Weak souls: Editorial in** *Al-Haqa'iq,* December 20, 1920, via Lopez, "Madams, Murders, and the Media," 385.

91   **Blackened the forehead:** Abaza, *al-Ahram Weekly.*

91   **Greed and pursuit of pleasure:** Lopez, "Madams, Murders, and the Media," 384.

92   **Lured in on sightseeing trips:** Appleton, WI, *Post-Crescent,* "50 Murder Mysteries Cleared by Confession," February 19, 1921.

92   **Vipers, tigers, snakes, and wolves:** Lopez, "Madams, Murders, and the Media," 384.

92   **There is no escape for you:** From a cartoon published in *al-Rashid,* December 9, 1920.

92   **Raya, you are not human:** Editorial in *al-Rashid,* printed in Lopez, "Madams, Murders, and the Media," 384.

92   **People dashed over:** *Al-Ahram Weekly*, "The Women Killers,"
        June 17–23, 1999.

92   **There is not one person asking for a drop of mercy:**
        Al-Muqattam, "The Trial of Raya and Sakina and Their
        Accomplices," May 11, 1921.

93   **Firstly, women's crimes generally demand:** *Al-Ahram
        Weekly*, "The Women Killers," June 17–23, 1999.

94   **When I asked Sakina about it:** Ibid.

94   **Sever these two corrupt members from the nation:** *Al-Baṣīr*,
        "Qadayyat Raya wi Sakina,"May 11, 1921, via Takla, PhD diss., 182.

94   **Fifteen minutes of sheer pandemonium:** *Al-Ahram Weekly*,
        "The Women Killers," June 17–23, 1999.

95   **Toughen up . . . stand at the scaffold:** The newspaper quotes
        from and about Sakina's final monologue are all found in
        Takla, PhD diss., 191–192.

95   **Rage of women:** Boyle, Stephanie, "Gender and Calamity in
        the British Empire," in *Gender and the Representation of Evil*,
        ed. Lynne Fallwell and Keira V. Williams (New York, NY:
        Routledge, 2017), 94.

96   **Where were the police?:** Ibid., 90.

96   **Insensitivity, by its very nature:** *Al-Ahram Weekly*, "The
        Women Killers," June 17–23, 1999.

96   **Tourists trudge around al-Labbān:** A blog post on the site
        Community Times has a few quotes from current residents of
        the neighborhood, some of whom express "shame" about this
        infamy. See "The Centenary of Raya and Sakina," Community
        Times, February 11, 2015, accessed February 5, 2017,
        communitytimes.me/the-centenary-of-raya-and-sakina/.

97   **Raya and Sakina will find her:** *Haaretz*, "Sisters without
        Mercy: Behind Egypt's Most Infamous Murder Case,"
        December 27, 2014.

Chapter 6: The Wretched Woman

99   **Wretched Woman:** *Leeds Mercury,* "Execution of Mary Ann Cotton," March 25, 1873.

99   **At least nine were convicted:** Crosby, Sara Lynn, *Poisonous Muse: The Female Poisoner and the Framing of Popular Authorship in Jacksonian America* (Iowa City: University of Iowa Press, 2016), 11.

100   **Fine dark eyes:** Appleton, Arthur, *Mary Ann Cotton: Her Story and Trial* (London: Michael Joseph, 1973), 48.

100   **Days of joy:** From Mary Ann Cotton's correspondence in jail. These letters appear in both Appleton, *Her Story and Trial*, and Wilson, David, *Mary Ann Cotton: Britain's First Female Serial Killer* (Hampshire, UK: Waterside Press, 2012).

102   **Snapped:** Whitehead, Tony, *Mary Ann Cotton, Dead, but Not Forgotten* (London: T. Whitehead, 2000). This is a theory set forward by Tony Whitehead, who was perhaps overly sympathetic to Mary Ann.

102   **Used the terms "typhus" and "typhoid" interchangeably:** Wilson, *Britain's First,* 64.

103   **Well proportioned and muscular:** Appleton, *Her Story and Trial,* 56. This is Appleton citing an uncited original source.

103   **Some biographers wonder:** Mary Ann's voracious sexual appetite was a recurring theme of Appleton's. She definitely used sex to achieve what she wanted, but speculating about her sex drive feels voyeuristic.

103   **This sort of speculation:** See Chapter 13 of this book on the Angel Makers of Nagyrév.

104   **Three of the children were rolling about in bed:** Appleton, *Her Story and Trial,* 60.

105   **At the time, he would not let his mind dwell:** Ibid., 61.

105 **No home for me:** From Mary Ann Cotton's correspondence in jail. These letters appear in both Appleton, *Her Story and Trial*, and Wilson, *Britain's First*.

106 **Lusty sailor:** Appleton, *Her Story and Trial*, 63.

108 **Weak-stomached:** Ibid., 76.

108 **Who shall I fetch?:** Ibid., 41.

109 **It is no fever I have:** Wilson, *Britain's First*, 91.

111 **Delicate and prepossessing beauty:** Appleton, *Her Story and Trial*, 32.

112 **Making its limbs writhe:** Wilson, *Britain's First*, 128.

112 **Thare to defende mee:** Flanders, Judith, *The Invention of Murder: How the Victorians Revelled in Death and Detection and Created Modern Crime* (London: HarperPress, 2011), 390.

113 **Lyies that has been told:** From Mary Ann Cotton's correspondence in jail. These letters appear in both Appleton, *Her Story and Trial*, and Wilson, *Britain's First*.

113 **Rubbing its gums with soap:** *Berwick Advertiser*, "Execution of Mary Ann Cotton," March 28, 1873.

114 **Doomed wretch:** Wilson, *Britain's First*, 151, citing the *Newcastle Courant*.

114 **The announcement of her execution:** *Burnley Advertiser*, "Execution of Mary Ann Cotton," March 29, 1873.

Chapter 7: The Tormentor

117 **The Tormentor:** This phrase was hung around Darya's neck during her public punishment in 1768. NOTE: Unless indicated, all subsequent material is taken from G. I. Studenkin, "Saltychikha" (Rus. «Салтычиха»), *Russian Antiquity Journal* 10 (1874), trans. Rostislav and Alyona Tkachenko (2016).

118 **She never learned how to read:** Studenkin notes that various papers concerning the sale of serfs and land are signed by her priest or her son, not by Darya herself.

120 **Russia was approaching:** Montefiore, Simon Sebag, *Prince of Princes: The Life of Potemkin* (New York: Thomas Dunne Books, 2001), 20.

120 **The proprietors sell their peasants:** Imperial ukáz of April 15, 1721.

120 **Weren't allowed to actually kill the serfs:** Montefiore, *Prince of Princes*, 21.

120 **Iron collars, chains:** Catherine II and Anthony, Katharine Susan, *Memoirs of Catherine the Great* (New York: Alfred A. Knopf, 1927).

121 **Insubordination:** Wallace, Sir Donald Mackenzie, *Russia, Volume 1* (London, New York: Cassell and Company, 1912), 263.

121 **Mines of Nerchinsk for life:** Imperial ukáz from Catherine II on August 22, 1767.

127 **Exhaustive and logical theory of the lunatic:** Chesterton, G. K., *Orthodoxy* (New York: Lohn Lane, 1909), 42, 32.

130 **All punishments by which the human body:** Massie, Robert K., *Catherine the Great: Portrait of a Woman* (New York: Random House, 2011), 347.

131 **Not of this world:** This phrase appears in a couple of rather sketchy online accounts of Darya, but I haven't been able to locate it in any primary or secondary sources. My guess is that the report comes from one of the many old Russian-language documents about the case that are, frustratingly, forever out of my grasp until someone translates them.

132 **Virtually ignored the existence of serfdom:** Freeze, Gregory L., "The Orthodox Church and Serfdom in Prereform Russia," *Slavic Review* 48, no. 3 (1989): 361–87.

132 **No branch of Christianity:** Pipes, Richard, *Russia under the Old Regime* (London: Weidenfeld and Nicholson, 1974), 245.

133 **Saltychikha:** My translator, Rostislav Tkachenko, notes, "'Saltychikha' does not sound like an aristocrat's name – it's more rude, 'village-like,' vulgar. When a woman is called 'dya-chikha' or 'Salty-chikha,' it conveys an image of a simple, crude woman – not beautiful, not smart, and not aristocratic. Just a 'normal' person, like other people. So, for Saltykova and her friends, the name would sound derogatory, something that did not correspond to their status as landlords."

133 **Completely godless soul:** These epithets appeared in Catherine's imperial verdict of October 2, 1768.

Chapter 8: Iceberg Anna

135 **Iceberg Anna:** This was the nickname given to Anna Hahn by Karin Walsh, a reporter for the *Chicago Daily Times*.

136 **One of the greatest doctors in the world:** Franklin, Diana Britt, *The Good-bye Door: The Incredible True Story of the First Female Serial Killer to Die in the Chair* (Kent, Ohio: Kent State University Press, 2006), 189.

136 **It was the kind of love:** These quotes are taken from Anna's twenty-page confession, which appeared in newspapers starting on December 19, 1938. Her confession appears in full in Franklin, *The Good-bye Door*, 213–24.

137 **I could no longer stand those things:** *Cincinnati Enquirer,* "Anna Hahn's Death Cell Confession! Four Cincinnati Murders Are Laid Bare," December 19, 1938.

137 **The little pleasure that I have gotten:** Ibid.

137 **Pretty blonde:** *Cincinnati Enquirer,* "Blonde Is Linked with Another Poisoning; Indicted on Charges of Murdering Two," August 17, 1937.

138 **More than able to take care of her own financial needs:** Ibid.

138 **He was nice to me:** *Cincinnati Enquirer,* "Death Cell Confession!"

139 **Hunter . . . gatherer:** Harrison, Marissa A., Erin A. Murphy, Lavina Y. Ho, Thomas G. Bowers, and Claire V. Flaherty, "Female Serial Killers in the United States: Means, Motives, and Makings," *Journal of Forensic Psychiatry and Psychology* 26, no. 3 (2015): 383–406.

140 **My girl:** Franklin, *The Good-bye Door,* 18.

141 **My Dear Sweet Daddy:** *Cincinnati Enquirer,* "With 'Love and Kisses!'" August 19, 1937.

142 **Any old men lived here:** Franklin, *The Good-bye Door,* 25.

142 **I have a new girl:** Ibid., 26.

143 **Just loved to make old people comfy:** *Pittsburgh Press,* "Ohio Widow Held as Police Probe Alleged Poison Plot," August 12, 1937.

143 **Semi-conscious . . . *Ich könnte ein Fass voll Wasser trinken!*:** Franklin, *The Good-bye Door,* 30.

143 **I hereby make my last will and testament:** *Cincinnati Enquirer,* "Woman Found Poisons in Wagner's Dwelling, Hahn Trial Testimony," October 19, 1937.

144 **You wouldn't marry me:** Franklin, *The Good-bye Door,* 36.

147 **Mean little kid:** Ibid., 13–14.

149 **Here I am, boys:** *Des Moines Register,* "Charged with Pouring Death from Bottle," August 14, 1937.

149 **Uninterested:** *Cincinnati Enquirer,* "Aged Mother Unaware," August 22, 1937.

149 **It would be a comfort to me:** Franklin, *The Good-bye Door*, 76.

150 **Telegram . . . hymn:** *Cincinnati Enquirer*, "Thoughts Are of Mother," August 23, 1937.

150 **Killed so many men:** Franklin, *The Good-bye Door*, 88.

151 **A job nobody can handle:** Ibid., 133.

151 **Phlegmatic enigma:** Ibid., 187.

151 **I suppose the death of anyone past sixty:** Ibid., 70.

152 **Living witness:** *Cincinnati Enquirer*, "Wagner's Physician Testifies in Hahn Case," October 16, 1937.

152 **Anna Hahn is the only one in God's world:** Franklin, *The Good-bye Door*, 161–2.

153 **In the four corners of this courtroom:** Ibid., 165–6.

153 **She is the bravest woman I ever saw:** Ibid., 179.

154 **I was sitting there hearing a story:** *Cincinnati Enquirer*, "Death Cell Confession!"

154 **Tried as a hunted animal:** Franklin, *The Good-bye Door*, 183.

154 **Oh my God!:** Ibid., 196.

155 **My God! What about Oscar?:** Ibid., 199.

155 **In her last twenty-four hours:** *Columbus Dispatch*, "True Anna Hahn Seen as Last Day Slipped by, Matron Says," December 8, 1938.

155 **Don't take him from me:** *The Cincinnati Enquirer*, "Anna Hahn Falls and is Carried to Chair; Dies After She Cries Appeal to Spectators," December 8, 1938.

156 **Please don't. Oh, my boy:** Ibid.

156 **Like a Fourth of July sparkler:** *New Castle News*, "Mrs. Hahn Dies in Electric Chair at Columbus, O.," December 8, 1938.

157 **I am surprised she broke:** Franklin, *The Good-bye Door*, 209.

Chapter 9: The Nightingale

159   **The Nightingale:** *Mirror* (Perth, Australia), "'Female Landru' of Morocco – Beautiful Dancer Denies Throttling Dancing Girl," December 17, 1938.

159   **White and dazzling:** Pückler-Muskau, Hermann Fürst von, Semilasso in Africa: Adventures in Algiers, and Other Parts of Africa (London: R. Bentley, 1837), 302.

159   **The most beautiful cabaret girl:** *Daily News* (Perth, Australia), "Glamor Girls' Grim Fate in Morocco," December 21, 1938.

160   **Savage friendship:** Colette, *Looking Backwards* (Bloomington, IN: Indiana University Press, 1975), 35.

160   **Uncertain and miserable number:** Ibid., 34

160   **Fine firm Berber women:** Ibid., 35.

161   **Spread to the streets:** Gershovich, Moshe, *French Military Rule in Morocco: Colonialism and Its Consequences* (London: F. Cass, 2000), 57.

161   **Dancing girls:** *American Weekly* (San Antonio Light), "Wicked Madame Moulay Hassen," September 12, 1937.

162   **She is rich, she is loved, she is adulated:** *Paris-Soir* trial coverage, November 15, 1938. Translation my own.

162   **Because it permitted respectable women:** *American Weekly,* "Wicked Madame."

163   **One thousand Frenchmen:** Ibid.

163   **Sordid, fetid:** Colette, *Looking Backwards*, 37.

164   **The men she receives are demanding:** *Paris-Soir* trial coverage, November 16, 1938. Translation my own.

164   **Fat of middle age:** *Lincoln Evening Journal,* "Former Dancer Sentenced," October 17, 1938.

164 **Feet, hands, a head and its hair:** Colette, *Looking Backwards*, 34.

164 **Boarders:** *Paris-Soir* trial coverage, November 16, 1938. Translation my own.

165 **Mohammed is a fool:** *Goulburn Evening Penny Post* (Australia), "A Landru of Morocco," July 23, 1937.

165 **Four of us:** *American Weekly*, "Wicked Madame." Later accounts insist there were actually five children behind the wall: four girls and one boy.

165 **Snatched from the throat:** Ibid.

166 **Very dark green-brown eyes . . . flat, ungracious:** Colette, *Looking Backwards*, 36.

166 **Scalps rather than almonds:** Ibid., 37.

166 **Chamber of horrors:** *Nevada State Journal*, "World-Famous Courtesan Faces Torture Charges," November 15, 1938.

166 **Of 14 girls known to have been inmates:** Statement of M. Julin, reprinted in the *Mirror*, "Female Landru," and *Paris-Soir*'s coverage of the case.

167 **Lost her health and looks:** *American Weekly*, "Wicked Madame."

167 **Hot Tea Dance:** Ibid.

169 **Moroccan press:** Tayebi, Hamza, "Print Journalism in Morocco: From the Pre-colonial Period to the Present Day," *Mediterranean Journal of Social Sciences* 4, no. 6 (July 2013): 497–506.

169 **Boiled the remains for twenty-four hours:** *Paris-Soir* trial coverage, November 16, 1938. Translation my own.

170 **Utterly loathsome:** Colette, *Looking Backwards*, 38.

170 **Victim? Certainly:** Ibid., 39.

170 **What words or images can we use:** Ibid., 36.

171 **A touch of torture, starvation:** Ibid., 37.

171 **The colonial view of prostitution:** Lazreg, Marnia, *The Eloquence of Silence: Algerian Women in Question* (New York: Routledge, 1994), 58.

171 **Article in a French-language Moroccan press:** Found in Baker, Alison, *Voices of Resistance: Oral Histories of Moroccan Women* (Albany: State University of New York Press, 1998), 20–21.

172 **Once-glamorous:** *Nevada State Journal,* "World-Famous Courtesan."

172 **After she lost her beauty:** *Oshkosh Daily Northwestern,* "Escapes the Guillotine, Gets 15-Year Sentence," November 16, 1938.

173 **The number of victims attributed to her:** Wilmington, DE, *Sunday Morning Star,* "Mass Murderess Once Won the Legion of Honor," October 3, 1937.

173 **Seen to dabble his eyes:** Ibid.

174 **Shrouded figures and forgotten passages:** *New York Times,* "The Soul of Morocco," April 8, 2007.

174 **Political dynamite:** *American Weekly,* "Wicked Madame."

Chapter 10: High Priestess of the Bluebeard Clique

177 **High Priestess of the Bluebeard Clique:** *Chicago Daily Tribune,* "Klimek Poison List Is Twenty; Arrest 1 More," November 29, 1922.

177 **Lumpy figure:** *Chicago Daily Tribune,* "'Guilty' Is Klimek Verdict," March 14, 1923.

178 **Air of peasants:** *Chicago Daily Tribune,* "Arsenic Cousins Go on Trial with Air of Peasants," March 7, 1923.

178 **Four-hundred percent:** Perry, Douglas, *The Girls of Murder City: Fame, Lust, and the Beautiful Killers Who Inspired Chicago* (New York: Viking, 2010), 17.

180 **Two inches to live:** *Chicago Daily Tribune*, "How Mrs. Klimek Jested of Death of Husband Told," March 9, 1923.

180 **You devil:** Ibid.

180 **Woman appeared omniscient:** Ione Quinby, a reporter who covered Tillie's trial a few years later, wrote that "hundreds believed she was possessed of supernatural powers." *Milwaukee Journal*, October 16, 1940.

181 **She had my picture over the mantel:** Genevieve Forbes's interview with Joseph Klimek, *Chicago Daily Tribune*, "Study of Klimek," November 16, 1922.

181 **Some other way:** *Chicago Daily Tribune*, "Poison Evidence Robs Mrs. Klimek of Indifference," March 11, 1923.

182 **You made all my trouble:** Ibid.

182 **I don't know. Don't bother me anymore:** *Chicago Daily Tribune*, "Grave Digger Tells of Goings On at Klimeks,'" March 10, 1923.

183 **Poison mystery trails:** *Chicago Daily Tribune*, "Poison Deaths May Total 12; Babes Victims?" November 12, 1922.

183 **Manner of living:** Ibid.

184 **Victim count:** For a numbered list of victims, see *Chicago Daily Tribune*, "'Mrs. Bluebeards' of Klimek case and 20 Alleged Victims," November 19, 1922.

184 **Voiced objections:** *Chicago Daily Tribune*, "Klimek Poison List."

184 **Poison belt:** *Chicago Daily Tribune*, "Police to Delve Anew for Clews [sic] to Poisoners," November 16, 1922.

184 **High priestess:** *Chicago Daily Tribune*, "Klimek Poison List."

184 **Big men:** *Chicago Daily Tribune*, "Judge Dismisses Koulik Jury," April 14, 1923.

184 **Automaton:** *Chicago Daily Tribune*, "Death Called Mere Routine in Poison Home," November 15, 1922.

185 **I didn't rob nobody:** *Chicago Daily Tribune*, "Klimek Poison Charges Ready for Grand Jury," November 18, 1922.

185 **Most astounding:** *Chicago Daily Tribune*, "'Mrs. Bluebeards' of Klimek case and 20 Alleged Victims," November 19, 1922.

185 **Poison parties:** *Belvidere Daily Republican*, "Ask Hanging for Two Women Charged with Murder Orgy," March 6, 1923.

185 **Fat, squat:** *Chicago Daily Tribune*, "Killing Ladies," February 27, 1927.

186 **Spectator at her own drama:** *Chicago Daily Tribune*, "Death Called Mere Routine."

186 **Locate the nest:** *Chicago Daily Tribune*, "Indict 2 Women in Poison Cases; Below Normal," November 21, 1922.

186 **She has brains:** *Chicago Daily Tribune*, "Death Called Mere Routine."

186 **This is not a theater:** *Chicago Daily Tribune*, "Grave Digger."

186 **Lady undertaker:** Ibid.

187 **I couldn't see in:** Ibid.

187 **I could no help it:** *Chicago Daily Tribune*, "Tillie Klimek Is Strong Witness in Own Defense," March 13, 1923.

187 **Gentlemen, the death penalty has never been inflicted upon a woman:** *Chicago Daily Tribune*, "'Guilty' Is Klimek Verdict."

188 **Dashing . . . no beauty:** Ibid.

189 **Blond curls or dark eyes:** *Des Moines Register*, "Declares the Double Standard of Murder Is Still Invincible," June 25, 1923.

189 **Beauty parlor:** *Chicago Daily Tribune*, "Killing Ladies," February 27, 1927.

190 **Whiff of spousal abuse:** For example, see Cora Orthwein's trial. *Los Angeles Times,* "Sensation is Sprung in Orthwein Trial," June 22, 1921.

Chapter 11: Sorceress of Kilkenny

193 **Sorceress of Kilkenny:** Seymour, St. John D., *Irish Witchcraft and Demonology* (Dublin: Hodges Figgis, 1913), chap. 2.

193 **Europe's first real witch trial:** Thurston, Robert, *Witch, Wicce, Mother Goose: The Rise and Fall of the Witch Hunts in Europe and North America* (Harlow, England: Longman, 2001), 73.

194 **There is nothing more intolerable:** Juvenal, *The Satires of Juvenal*, trans. G. G. Ramsay (New York: G. P. Putman's Sons, 1918).

194 **Flemish merchants:** Neary, Anne, "The Origins and Character of the Kilkenny Witchcraft Case of 1324," *Proceedings of the Royal Irish Academy,* 83C (1983): 343.

195 **Half of that:** Callan, Maeve Brigid, *The Templars, the Witch, and the Wild Irish: Vengeance and Heresy in Medieval Ireland* (Ithaca, NY: Cornell University Press, 2014), 155.

196 **Threw them in jail:** Wright, Thomas, *Narratives of Sorcery and Magic from the Most Authentic Sources* (London: R. Bentley, 1851), 24.

196 **Canceling all of the young man's debts:** Neary, "The Origins and Character," 344.

197 **Straight to court:** Ibid., 344

197 **Pattern:** Ó Domhnaill, Rónán Gearóid, *Fadó Fadó: More Tales of Lesser-known Irish History* (Leicester: Troubadour, 2015), 27.

198 **Score the bishopric:** Neary, "The Origins and Character," 338.

199 **Dark, sorcerous means:** Seymour, *Irish Witchcraft and Demonology*, 44.

199 **What was to come:** Wright, *Narratives of Sorcery and Magic*, 25.

199 **Armed with a religious zeal:** Neary, "The Origins and Character," 340.

200 **Totally lacking in any practical diplomatic sense:** Ibid. This paragraph: 340–1.

200 **Lavish palace:** Callan, *The Templars, the Witch, and the Wild Irish*, 144.

200 **All sorts of grievances:** *Calendar of entries in Papal Registers: Papal Letters,* ed. W. H. Bliss and J. A. Twemlow (London, 1893–1960), 1305–42, 206–7.

200 **Diabolical nest:** Neary, "The Origins and Character," 345.

201 **Clean up:** Callan, *The Templars, the Witch, and the Wild Irish*, 136.

202 **Female inheritance:** For a detailed discussion of this, see Callan's chapter on "Gender and the Colony of Ireland," *The Templars, the Witch, and the Wild Irish.*

203 **To show that Lady Alice:** Cohn, Norman, *Europe's Inner Demons: An Enquiry Inspired by the Great Witch-hunt.* (Chicago: University of Chicago Press, 2001), 138.

203 **Above the forms of the law of the land:** Wright, *Narratives of Sorcery and Magic*, 27.

204 **Bowing to men:** Ibid.

204 **Alien from England:** Neary, "The Origins and Character," 346.

204 **Not technically allowed: See** Code of Canon Law/1917, cc. 2186–2187, in *Codex Iuris Canonici Pii X Pontificis Maximi Iussu Digestus, Benedicti Papae XV Auctoritate Promulgatus,* edited by Pietro Gasparri (New York, NY: P. J. Kenedy & Sons, 1918).

204 **Grievous crimes:** Wright, *Narratives of Sorcery and Magic*, 28.

204 **Pontifical robes:** Ibid.

205 **Vile, rustic, interloping monk:** Seymour, *Irish Witchcraft and Demonology*, 33.

205 **Christ had never been treated so:** Wright, *Narratives of Sorcery and Magic*, 29.

205 **Uncited, unadmonished:** Seymour, *Irish Witchcraft and Demonology*, 34.

206 **Mother and mistress:** Ibid., 35.

206 **First time anyone was given this sentence for heresy:** Ibid., 39.

206 **Pestilential society:** Anonymous, *A Contemporary Narrative of the Proceedings Against Dame Alice Kyteler* (London: Printed by J. B. Nichols and Son, 1843).

206 **Armed to the teeth:** Wright, *Narratives of Sorcery and Magic*, 30.

207 **Ledrede was now convinced . . . cathedral's bell tower collapsed:** Neary, "The Origins and Character," 349–50.

207 **Serial murder:** Granted, I'm not the first to speculate she was a serial killer. Ó Domhnaill and Thorne both wonder it, too.

207 **FBI's website:** That would be right here: www.fbi.gov/stats -services/publications/serial-murder.

208 **Human nails:** Seymour, *Irish Witchcraft and Demonology*, 37.

208 **Insolent fiend:** Yeats, W. B., "Nineteen Hundred and Nineteen." *The Tower* (London: Macmillan, 1928).

Chapter 12: Beautiful Throat Cutter

211 **Beautiful Throat Cutter:** *Jacksonville Journal Courier*, "Was Kate – The Killer – Ever Here?" June 30, 1974.

211 **Both men were named:** Hardy, Allison, *Kate Bender, the Kansas Murderess: The Horrible History of an Arch Killer* (Girard, KS: Haldeman-Julius, 1944), 3.

212 **Dark Stranger:** Ibid., 2.

212 **Neighborliness:** James, John T., *The Benders of Kansas* (Washington, DC: Photoduplication Service, Library of Congress, 1913), 19.

212 **Miniature store and dining area:** Case, Nelson, *History of Labette County, Kansas from the First Settlement to the Close of 1892* (Topeka, KS: Crane, 1893), 86.

213 **Never looked a feller in the eye:** Hardy, *Kate Bender, the Kansas Murderess*, 3.

213 **Lady Macbeth:** Triplett, Frank, *History, Romance and Philosophy of Great American Crimes and Criminals* (New York: N. D. Thompson, 1884), 560.

214 **Like a young eagle:** Hardy, *Kate Bender, the Kansas Murderess*, 3.

214 **Well-formed, voluptuous mold . . . animal attraction:** James, *The Benders of Kansas*, 13.

214 **A beautiful wild beast:** Triplett, *History, Romance and Philosophy*, 557.

214 **Red-faced, unprepossessing:** *New York Times*, "The Kansas Murders," May 13, 1873.

215 **A perfect devil:** *Wichita City Eagle*, "The Cherryvale Murders," May 15, 1873.

219 **"Hell hotel"/"inn of no return":** I took these particular terms from the endlessly fascinating site tvtropes.org, but the concept of these tropes is pretty universal.

219 **Charles Ingalls:** O'Brien, Liam, "Laura Ingalls Wilder and the Bloody Benders: Truth or Fiction?" in Melville House Books, January 29, 2015, accessed April 21, 2016, mhpbooks .com/laura-ingalls-wilder-and-the-bloody-benders-truth-or -fiction/.

221 **I'll find your brother:** Scott, Robert F., "What Happened to the Benders?" *Western Folklore* 9, no. 4 (1950): 326.

222 **Spite-dolls:** Hardy, *Kate Bender, the Kansas Murderess*, 15.

223 **I see graves:** Ibid.

223 **Human hair:** Triplett, *History, Romance and Philosophy*, 569.

223 **$50,000:** Hardy, *Kate Bender, the Kansas Murderess*, 19.

224 **Human Hyenas:** Ibid., 16.

224 **They said that she'd married:** *Camden News*, "Story of Iron-Fisted Kate," September 22, 1971.

224 **They claimed that she started cross-dressing:** *Parsons Daily Sun*, "Another 'Kate Bender,'" March 9, 1904.

224 **Handsome profit:** Kinsley, KS, *Valley Republican*, "Crime," August 21, 1880.

226 **The Night was dark:** *New York Times*, "Dying Man Clears the Bender Mystery," July 12, 1908.

227 **Frederick Jackson Turner:** His quotes are taken from his famous 1893 paper "The Significance of the Frontier in American History," available in a number of forms online.

228 **Shoot and be damned:** Scott, "What Happened to the Benders?": 334.

228 **I tell you, man, she was a bad one:** New York, NY, *Sun*, "The Fate of the Benders," January 9, 1887.

Chapter 13: The Angel Makers of Nagyrév

231 **Angel Makers:** "Angel maker" is a nickname used on many a female serial killer – for example, Amelia Dyer. "The Angel Makers of Nagyrév" is a common (English-language) way to refer to the Nagyrév women en masse.

231 **The authorities are doing nothing:** The letter was reprinted in the *New York Times*, "Murder by Wholesale: A Tale from Hungary," March 16, 1930.

232 **Ringed round:** Ibid.

232 **Nagyrév felt the strain:** For an in-depth look into the sociocultural climate of Nagyrév at the time of the murders, see Bodó, Béla, *Tiszazug: A Social History of a Murder Epidemic* (New York: Columbia University Press, 2002), chap. 4.

232 **Brutish:** *New York Times*, "Murder by Wholesale."

233 **Divorce:** Parascandola, John, *King of Poisons: A History of Arsenic* (Lincoln, NE: Potomac Books, 2012), 37.

233 ***Facsiga:*** Bodó, *Tiszazug*, 190.

233 **The ways to kill an infant:** Ibid., 193.

233 **Suicide rates:** Moksony, Ferenc, "Victims of Change or Victims of Backwardness? Suicide in Rural Hungary," in Lengyel, Gy. and Rostoványi, Zs., eds., *The Small Transformation: Society, Economy and Politics in Hungary and the New European Architecture* (Budapest: Akadémiai Kiadó, 2001), 366–76.

233 **The more marginalized a community:** Bodó, *Tiszazug*, 179.

235 **Alcoholic beast:** Ibid., 209.

235 **You do not have to torture yourself:** Bodó, Béla, "The Poisoning Women of Tiszazug," *Journal of Family History* 27, no. 1 (January 2002): 49.

236 **Sing, my boy:** *New York Times*, "Murder by Wholesale."

236 **Had to be dragged to the city hall:** From novelist Zsigmond Móricz's colorful coverage of the trial. Móricz, Zsigmond, *Riportok, 1930–1935* (Budapest: Szépirodalmi Könyvkiadó, 1958). Reprinted in the appendices of Bodó, *Tiszazug*.

237 **They killed me, they sent me into my grave, they whom I loved most:** Bodó, *Tiszazug*, 16, citing one of the dramatic editorials about the poisonings published in Hungarian newspapers.

237 **My husband was a very bad man:** Bodó, *Tiszazug*, 211.

238 **There are many:** Ibid., 235.

238 **Frenzy:** Bodó, "The Poisoning Women," 40.

239 **Slight greenish coloration:** Bodó, *Tiszazug*, 90.

240 **Fatuous Eastern deity:** Parascandola, *King of Poisons*, 39.

241 **Hurled insults:** *Kis Újság,* August 9, 1929.

242 **With medieval methods:** Bodó, *Tiszazug,* 13.

242 **Rural mystery:** Ibid., 86.

243 **We are not murderesses:** *New York Times,* "Murder by Wholesale."

243 **Almost one-third of all peasant children in Hungary died:** Bodó, *Tiszazug,* 193.

243 **Strange combination of causes:** from *Pesti Napló,* a widely read "liberal-Jewish" paper, December 14, 1929.

243 **Strength and persistence of their passions:** *New York Times,* "Murder by Wholesale."

245 **Fairy tales:** Bodó, *Tiszazug,* 118–9.

245 **Above her station:** Ibid., 101.

246 **We, the women of Nagyrév:** Ibid., 115.

246 **Rope:** Ibid.

246 *Jaj, Jaj, Istenem, Istenem:* Ibid., 123.

247 **They caused the greatest disappointment:** *Szolnoki Újság,* December 15, 1929.

Chapter 14: Queen of Poisoners

249 **Queen of Poisoners:** *The Terrible Book of Poisons, Or the Life and Plots of the Marchioness of Brinvilliers* (London: C. Elliot, 1860).

250 **They are monsters:** *Questions sur les empoisonneurs,* BA, MS 2664, fol. 45 trans. in Mollenauer, Lynn Wood, *Strange Revelations: Magic, Poison, and Sacrilege in Louis XIV's France* (University Park, PA: Pennsylvania State University Press, 2007), 63, 159.

250 **Iced champagne:** Stokes, Hugh, *Madame De Brinvilliers and*

Her Times 1630–1676 (London: Bodley Head, 1912), 71.

250 **Not tall, but** exceedingly well formed: Stokes, *Madame De Brinvilliers*, 65.

250 **Remarkable – bold, firm:** Funck-Brentano, Frantz, and George Charles Maidment, *Princes and Poisoners: Studies of the Court of Louis XIV* (London: Duckworth and Co., 1901).

251 **Utter heartlessness:** Stokes, *Madame De Brinvilliers*, VI.

251 **That was simply unthinkable:** Mollenauer, *Strange Revelations*, 12.

252 **Possessed superabundant vitality:** Stokes, *Madame De Brinvilliers*, 66.

252 **Wax eloquent on anything:** Ibid., 75.

252 **Demon who brought about the storm:** Ibid., 76.

253 **Raged with the blind fury:** Ibid., 80.

253 **One should never annoy anybody:** Saint-Germain, Jacques, *Madame De Brinvilliers: La Marquise Aux Poisons* (Paris: Hachette, 1971), 123, 78.

253 **The surest and most common aid:** Somerset, Anne, *The Affair of the Poisons: Murder, Infanticide, and Satanism at the Court of Louis XIV* (New York: St. Martin's Press, 2004), 10.

253 **The skull of a man:** Ibid., 12.

254 **Experimenting with poisons:** Ibid., 40–41.

254 **Who would have dreamt:** Funck-Brentano, *Princes and Poisoners*, 12–13.

255 **In such extreme peril:** Stokes, *Madame De Brinvilliers*, 139.

255 **Gout:** Somerset, *The Affair of the Poisons*, 46.

256 **Poisonous waters:** L'Estrange, Roger, "A Narrative of the Process Against Madam Brinvilliers; and of Her Condemnation and Execution, for Having Poisoned Her Father and Two Brothers, Translated Out of French," London: Printed for Jonathan Edwyn at the Sign of the Three Roses in

Ludgate-Street, July 17, 1676.

256 **Stinking and infected:** Somerset, *The Affair of the Poisons*, 47.

256 **Violent Passions:** L'Estrange, "A Narrative of the Process."

257 **[Marie] wished to marry Sainte-Croix:** Stokes, *Madame De Brinvilliers*, 148.

257 **She'd bought from him at such a high price:** Funck-Brentano, *Princes and Poisoners*, 22.

258 **Marie was trying to poison the girl:** Stokes, *Madame De Brinvilliers*, 224.

258 **Ah, villain:** Funck-Brentano, *Princes and Poisoners*, 30–31.

259 **My Confession:** Somerset, *The Affair of the Poisons*, 50.

259 **Mysterious vials and powders:** *Memoire Du Proces Extraordinaire Contre Madame D Brinvilliers...* (Amsterdam: Boom, 1676).

259 **All that it contains:** Stokes, *Madame De Brinvilliers*, 166.

259 **Sundry Curious Secrets:** Dumas, Alexandre, *Celebrated Crimes* (New York: P. F. Collier and Son, 1910), vol. 8.

260 **Very eager and extraordinary manner of demanding it:** L'Estrange, "A Narrative of the Process."

260 **Selection of animals:** Somerset, *The Affair of the Poisons*, 52.

260 **Conjectures and strong presumptions:** François Ravaission, *Archives de la Bastille, VI,* 396.

261 **Turkish fashion:** Somerset, *The Affair of the Poisons*, 24.

262 **I accuse myself:** The confession appears in full in Saint-Germain, *La Marquise Aux Poisons*, 131–2.

262 **Childhood abuse:** Somerset, *The Affair of the Poisons*, 57.

263 **Full of inheritances:** Ibid., 25.

263 **Ways to make away with people that displeased her**: L'Estrange, "A Narrative of the Process."

263 **I warned you many a time:** Funck-Brentano, *Princes and*

Poisoners, 68–69.

263 **Remorselessly dissected:** Ibid., 74.

264 **Kept her head proudly erect:** Pirot, Edme, and G. Roullier, *La Marquise De Brinvilliers: Récit De Ses Derniers Moments* (Paris: A. Lemerre, 1883).

264 **Could have burned her alive:** Somerset, *The Affair of the Poisons*, 62–63.

265 **O God, you tear me to pieces:** Dumas, *Celebrated Crimes*.

266 **Her face contracted:** Pirot, *Récit De Ses Derniers Moments*.

266 **I confess that, wickedly and for revenge:** Dumas, *Celebrated Crimes*.

266 **Some people say that she hesitated:** Pirot, *Récit De Ses Derniers Moments*.

267 **The affair of Mme de Brinvilliers is frightful:** Bussy, Roger De Rabutin, and Ludovic Lalanne, *Correspondance De Roger De Rabutin, Comte Bussy Avec Sa Famille Et Ses Amis (1666–1693)* (Westmead, Farnborough, Hants., England: Gregg International, 1972).

268 **Well, it's all over and done with:** Somerset, *The Affair of the Poisons*, 32.

Conclusion

270 **Locating evil within selected individuals:** Zimbardo, Philip G., "A Situationist Perspective on the Psychology of Evil," in Miller, Arthur G., ed., *The Social Psychology of Good and Evil* (New York: Guilford Press, 2004).

270 **If only there were evil people:** Solženicyn, Aleksandr, and Thomas P. Whitney, *The Gulag Archipelago* (New York:

Harper and Row, 1975).

270 **To examine the mind of the serial killer:** Oates, Joyce Carol, "I Had No Other Thrill or Happiness," *New York Review of Books*, March 24, 1994.

271 **One in 90 million:** Mallicoat, Stacy L. and Ireland, Connie Estrada, *Women and Crime: The Essentials* (Thousand Oaks, CA: Sage, 2013), 236.

271 **Unlike the 1970s and 80s:** Beam, Christopher, "Blood Loss: The Decline of the Serial Killer," *Slate*, January 5, 2011, accessed February 6, 2017, slate.com/articles/news_and_politics/crime/2011/01/blood_loss.html.

271 **Are white:** For example, see the stats gathered from the ongoing Radford University/FGCU Serial Killer Database.

About the Author

TORI TELFER is a full-time freelance writer and editor whose work has appeared in *Salon*, *Vice*, *Jezebel*, *The Awl*, *The Hairpin*, *Good Magazine*, and elsewhere. She has worked as a children's magazine editor, an academic proofreader, a corporate semi-ghostwriter, a writing teacher, and a pro bono copywriter; she has also carried appetizers around the room at plenty of glittery catered affairs. She has written, directed, and produced independent plays in both Chicago and Los Angeles. She majored in creative writing at Northwestern University. *Lady Killers* is her first book.

Usborne GROWING UP for BOYS

Alex Frith and Felicity Brook

Illustrated by Kate Sutton

Expert advice from:

Dr Matthew Evans BSc DClinPsy

chartered clinical psychologist

Dr Kristina Routh BSc MD FFPH

Department of Public Health, University of Birmingham

Dr Ellie Hothersall MBChB, MPH, FFPH

University of Dundee

Designed by Hanri van Wyk

First published in 2013 by Usborne Publishing Ltd, Usborne House, 83-85 Saffron Hill, London, EC1N 8RT.
Copyright © 2013 Usborne Publishing Ltd. The name Usborne and the devices are Trade Marks of Usborne
Publishing Ltd. All rights reserved. No part of this publication may be reproduced, stored in a retrieval system or
transmitted in any form or by any means, electronic, mechanical, photocopying, recording, or otherwise, without
the prior permission of the publisher. UKE. Printed in Reading, Berkshire, UK.

Introduction

This book is all about the changes and experiences of puberty, which is the time when you turn from a child into an adult.

A lot of what happens during puberty affects your body, and if you don't know what to expect, these changes can be pretty surprising. Your brain goes through some big changes, too, affecting the way you think, what you think about, and how you react to the world.

This book is full of tips on how to deal with the worries and anxieties that come hand in hand with teenage life, whether it's coping with family life, or dealing with exam stress. There's also lots of information about grown-up stuff, from sex and drugs to money and relationships.

Contents

1.   A new you

Puberty is a big deal. It takes years, and by the end, you'll be a different person. Your face will look a little different, your body will have a different shape, and your mind will think in a slightly different way.

Just like being on a roller coaster, puberty is something you have no control over, so it can be exciting and scary at the same time.

Going through puberty is not just about your body. Chances are, you'll pick up some new friends, and new interests along the way, as well as greater independence and new responsibilities.

What happens?

As you grow up, there are all sorts of things going on outside and inside your body. Here is a list showing the order that these things most often happen. But bear in mind that everyone is different and these stages often overlap each other.

(Don't worry if you don't understand what some of the words mean. There's lots more explaining each stage in the rest of the book.)

- You start to get bigger and taller.
- Your testicles and penis grow bigger.
- You grow pubic hair and underarm hair.
- Your start to get erections a lot and start to produce semen. (These are related.)
- You become moodier.
- Your voice gets deeper.
- Your face and body get hairier.

Puberty can start when you're as young as 10 or 11, but most boys don't really notice a change in themselves until they're 13, 14 or even 15. Most of the major changes brought on by puberty finish by the time you're 18, but some take longer. And although the intense changes of puberty do come to an end, you never stop changing. Most men find they get hairier as they get older, for example.

Have I already started?

If you've already noticed any of the changes in the list on page 8, then yes, you have started puberty! Congratulations.

Believe it or not, the most important change is one that happens in your head. Try the quiz on the next page, to find out if your *mind*, as well as your body, is already in puberty mode . . .

Quick quiz

- Do some activities, outings and games you enjoyed when you were younger now seem babyish or boring?

- Do you find yourself suddenly losing it over little things and getting into silly arguments with your family and friends?

- Do you sometimes feel angry, stressed or a bit miserable for no special reason?

- Do your parents or carers drive you crazy (even when they are doing their best to be helpful and understanding)?

- Do you feel self-conscious about your body?

Answers

- Mostly 'YES' answers?
  You are right in the middle of puberty and everything you feel now is quite normal. There are some 'Think tips' boxes to help you cope with your feelings scattered throughout the book.

- Mostly 'NO' answers?
  You may not have started full-blown puberty yet, but it won't be long. Keep reading to find out more about all the big changes on the way.

- Some 'YES' and some 'NO' answers?
  You have just hit puberty. Exciting times lie ahead!

What's what?

It's impossible to talk about puberty without discussing parts of the body people don't usually bring up in polite conversation. But precisely because people don't talk about them, it's easy to grow up without knowing what to call these bits.

There are countless nicknames for your bits, but they're not always understood by everyone. This diagram shows you the correct names for your private parts — properly known as your 'genitals' or 'sex organs'.

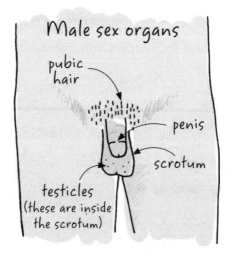

Male sex organs

pubic hair

penis

scrotum

testicles (these are inside the scrotum)

2. Why is this happening to me?

If you're interested in *why* all this starts happening, here's the science.

All the changes that happen during puberty are caused by hormones. These are chemicals produced in glands inside your body and carried around in your blood. They act as signals that tell different parts of your body what to do, often telling your body to start doing something, and when to stop.

Hormones aren't just concerned with puberty. Our bodies can make over 30 hormones and each has a different job. The hormone adrenaline, for example, is released when you are scared and it makes your heart beat faster and speeds up your breathing so you can run away or fight if you need to. You may have heard of a hormone called insulin. This works with another hormone called glucagon to control the amount of sugar in your blood.

The puberty trigger

The hormone which triggers puberty comes from a part of your brain called the hypothalamus. It is only the size of a grape and it is right in the middle of your brain, but it sets your body off on its puberty journey when you are fast asleep.

Once your body is ready, your hypothalamus starts releasing a hormone called gonadotropin releasing hormone, or GnRH. This process always begins at night-time.

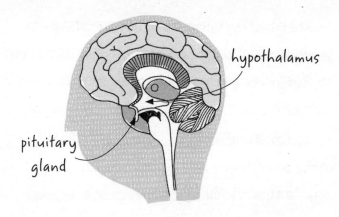

hypothalamus

pituitary
gland

When the levels of GnRH are high enough, they give a signal to another part of your brain, called the pituitary gland, to release two more hormones called follicle stimulating hormone (FSH) and luteinizing hormone (LH).

FSH and LH travel in your bloodstream to your testicles — the two balls that hang behind your penis. Your testicles then start producing high levels of hormones of their own, called sex hormones, and this is when you'll start noticing big changes.

The main sex hormone in boys is called testosterone, though boys also produce low levels of the female sex hormone oestrogen.

Testosterone is responsible for triggering many of the physical changes in your body, not least making your testicles grow bigger, so they can make even more testosterone.

Hormones don't just change your body. They affect your mood and behaviour, too. High levels of testosterone make people more likely to take risks, and can make them more competitive, too.

What triggers the trigger?

Scientists still don't know what causes the hypothalamus to start releasing the hormone that switches on puberty, but they do know this is starting earlier than it used to.

Did you know?

100 years ago, most boys didn't start puberty
until they were 16; now most boys start around 13.
(Although the average varies from place to place.)

Aaaargh! Information OVERLOAD

This is a big book, but don't feel you have to
read all of it at once. You certainly don't need to
know how the hormones work – though it can
help you feel better when you understand
just how much is going on inside your
body at this time.

Turn the page for a simple rundown of puberty
to help you get through teenage life.

- The changes happening to your body are normal.
- Everyone experiences puberty at a different rate: it's normal to start before your friends, and normal to start later, too.
- It's normal to grow hair on your body where you didn't have hair before.
- It's normal for your penis to get stiff, and to play with it a lot.
- It's normal to get upset and angry easily, especially with your family and friends.
- It's normal to get spots, and to think you look odd.
- It's a good idea to start using deodorant.
- Absolutely EVERYONE, even the most self-assured, popular boys and girls you know, is experiencing most of the same worries as you.
- By the time you're about 18, your body will stop changing quite so rapidly, and you'll have time to get used to the new you.

3. Bigger, taller, stronger, faster

One of the first signs that puberty is beginning is that you put on extra weight and start to grow bigger and taller. Growing is one of the best things about puberty, because it means, in time, you'll be much stronger and able to run faster than before. It also means people you meet might think of you as an adult, and may even treat you like one.

Of course, all your classmates grow bigger, too, but not always at the same rate. It can seem unfair at first, but everyone reaches their adult height and body shape eventually.

Some boys go through a few growth jumps from about the age of 11 or even have one big growth spurt. Many boys just grow gradually over several years. Here's how it happens, on average:

- Your hands and feet get bigger first.
- Then your arms, legs and spine grow longer.
- Your face begins to get longer.
- Your shoulders get wider.
- Your muscles get stronger.

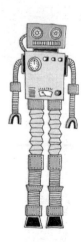

If you have a growth spurt early, you will finish growing earlier too. If you start later, don't worry, you will catch up — and may even overtake — your taller friends.

Waiting to grow can be frustrating, of course! Most boys reach their full adult height between eighteen and twenty.

Growing takes a lot of energy. You'll be hungry more often, and will need to eat more than you used to. You'll need to sleep more, too. Remember that putting on some weight is normal and healthy before and during your teens.

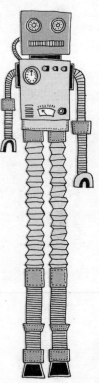

Some boys feel happy with their new size, and are glad they are growing up at last. Others feel a bit self-conscious to start with, and this is natural too. Whatever your shape, it's important to eat healthily and keep exercising when you are growing.

Power and responsibility

Getting bigger and stronger doesn't happen overnight, but it can still come as a surprise when you find that you're able to lift heavier weights than before, unscrew tight jar lids, and maybe even push people around who used to be bigger than you.

When you were an infant, if you had a tantrum, there was only so much damage you could cause. But as you get bigger, you need to start taking responsibility not just for your temper, but for what might happen to things and people around you when you lose it.

4. Getting hairy

One of the first really obvious signs of puberty, and one that you can't help but notice, is pubic hair. It's called 'pubic' hair because it grows on an area known as the 'pubic region' — a patch at the bottom of your stomach above your penis. Curiously, no one really knows why people have pubic hair.

At first, you'll probably only notice a few small hairs growing just above your penis. The hairs usually start out thin, straight and light, but they tend to get thicker and curlier and may well darken as they grow. In time, more hairs will grow, and the patch will spread to the tops of your thighs, and hairs will sprout from your scrotum, too.

Pubic hair doesn't keep on growing like the hair on your head. After about six months of growing each hair falls out and a new one starts to grow in its place. If you shave the hairs or pluck them out, they'll grow back again.

How pubic hair grows

Hair, hair, everywhere

While your pubic hair is getting thicker, you'll also start to grow hair in your armpits, and around your mouth, jaw and neck (your beard). Some boys find many parts of their body get hairy during puberty, although most find new hair grows gradually as they get older, and some never grow much body hair at all. These pictures show some of the places where you might grow hair. Don't worry — it won't all appear overnight!

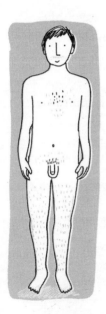

- All around your jaw
- Under your arms
- Around your nipples
- On your chest
- Around your penis
- On your back, especially at the top
- All around your arms and legs
- Around your anus (bottom hole)

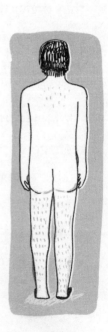

Most men find they keep getting hairier even after they've finished puberty.

Beards and shaving

All that new body hair won't ever grow very long, so you don't need to cut it or shave it (although some people do this for religious reasons, or because they prefer the way they look without hair). If you do shave your body hair, be warned — it'll be stubbly and itchy for a few days while it grows back!

Your beard *will* keep growing, though, and many teenagers prefer to shave their faces regularly to keep it under control. Some shave every day, others less often. Everyone's beard grows at a different rate, and how often you shave, assuming you want to, is entirely up to you.

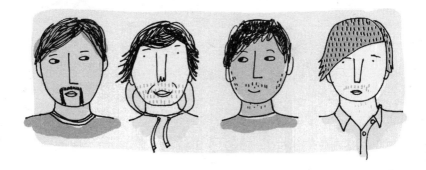

How to shave

Shaving with a razor, often called 'wet shaving', is a skill that takes a bit of practice to get right. Don't be embarrassed if you cut yourself sometimes, or if you find you've missed a patch somewhere. Even grown men cut themselves shaving from time to time.

You can buy razors in most supermarkets or pharmacies. There are many different-looking razors, but they all work in the same way. Basically, it means pulling a sharp blade across your skin to slice off each hair.

Wet shaving

1. Stand in front of a mirror, and wash your face with hot water.

2. Squirt some shaving foam or gel onto one hand, and then rub this over your beard. It doesn't matter if you have a lot or a little.

3. Press the blade firmly onto your skin, and pull it down. Never move the blade sideways.

4. With each stroke, you'll get foam and little hairs in and around the razor. Rinse the blade regularly.

5. You'll probably need to go over some parts of your face a few times. You may want to put on some more foam, but you don't have to.

6 . Shaving your chin, or across moles, can be
   a bit awkward. Go slowly, and try pulling your razor
   in different directions. For example, many boys find
   it more effective to pull their razor up, rather than
   down, when shaving their neck.

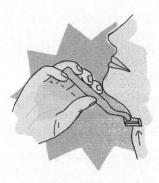

7 . When you've finished, rinse your face in
   cold water, and dry it off. Then take a close
   look in the mirror in case you've missed a bit.

Many men use aftershave gel, lotion, spray or
powder after shaving. Some can sting. Don't use the
same blade for too long, and don't share your razors.

Electric razors

You're much less likely to cut yourself with an electric razor, but they tend not to give as close a shave. They all need charging or plugging in, too.

Body shaving

If you want to shave or trim body hair, you can use electric razors or disposable razors. There are other methods, although they can be painful!

- You can pull hairs out, using wax strips, tweezers, or a device called an epilator.
- Depilatory creams make the hairs breakable so you can scrub them off with a brush.
- Bleaching creams make the hairs lighter, so, if you have light skin, they're harder to see.

5. BOOM squeak BOOM!

Unlike getting hairy, there's one change at puberty that you may well not notice, but other people will. The sound of your own voice will gradually get deeper. People often say your voice 'is breaking', or 'has broken'.

Why does your voice change?

Your whole body grows during puberty, including your insides. One part in particular grows bigger — your larynx. This is a small passageway in your throat that contains vocal cords, which are bands that vibrate when you talk and sing. Having a larger larynx makes your voice sound deeper than it did when you were a child.

A broken voice

To make different noises, you need to relax and contract the muscles in your larynx. Most people can talk without thinking about their vocal cords, but professional singers know it takes a lot of practice to get them to do exactly what you want. It's very common for teenagers to find they squeak out some words from time to time. It doesn't mean your voice is literally breaking!

squeak

The squeaking happens because, from time to time, you instinctively try to move the muscles in your larynx in the way you did as a child. In effect, it means you're trying to speak with a high-pitched voice, but your larynx isn't able to cope with this, so the sounds come out as a squeak.

It can be embarrassing when this happens, especially because it tends to happen when you're excited or nervous. But as embarrassing events go, this is pretty mild. It's also the sort of thing that happens to everyone.

Adam's apple

Most boys find their new larynx gets so big it pushes against the skin on their throat. This creates a small bump on their neck, often known as an Adam's apple.

Adam's apple

thyroid gland

larynx

windpipe

Some people never seem to develop a visible Adam's apple. It doesn't mean your larynx hasn't grown, it just means it's sitting in your throat at a different angle.

Having a prominent Adam's apple doesn't mean a person has an especially deep voice.

Whether your voice develops into a soft tenor or a booming bass, one thing is typical for all boys — people you haven't spoken to since before puberty won't recognize your voice the next time you talk!

6. You and your penis

If there's one part of the body that teenage boys, and indeed adult men, worry about more than any other, it's their penis. A number of new things happen during puberty that all affect the penis, so it's not entirely surprising boys think about it a lot. Here are some things you may have noticed already:

- Your penis is bigger than it used to be.
- Your penis grows and stiffens (called having an erection) a lot.
- Your foreskin (if you have one) gets looser.
- When you touch your penis, and especially when you rub it, it feels good.
- Sometimes – especially after rubbing it a lot – a creamy substance called semen comes out.

Penis parts

Floppy, or flaccid, penis

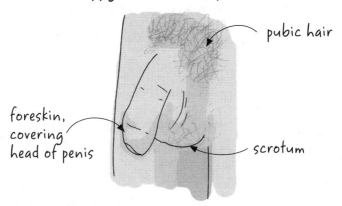

pubic hair

foreskin,
covering
head of penis

scrotum

Stiff, or erect, penis

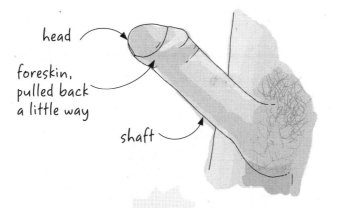

head

foreskin,
pulled back
a little way

shaft

Other boys look different

Chances are, you've seen other boys naked before. At a glance, most penises look largely the same, but there are plenty of variations in the details, as you can see from these pictures:

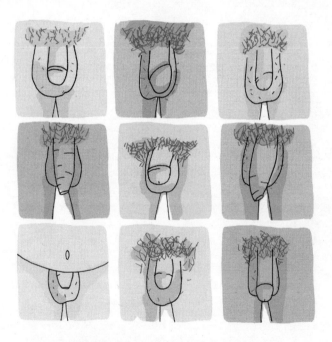

All these penises are normal.

Exposed or enclosed?

Every boy is born with a foreskin — a flap of skin that covers the tip of the penis. But many boys have all or part of their foreskin removed soon after birth in an operation called circumcision, usually for religious reasons.

View looking down
onto your own penis:

View from the
other side:

The head of the
penis is called
the glans.

The hole at the
end is called the
meatus (say
mee-A-tus').

The part that
sticks out is
the corona.

The narrow band that
holds your foreskin to the
tip is called the frenulum.

Your penis will work perfectly well with or without a foreskin. If you don't have one, your glans will probably be less sensitive. If you do have one, there are a few things to be aware of:

- At first, your foreskin may be quite tight.
- As you get older, it begins to come away from the glans, and gets looser.
- When you get an erection, the foreskin is usually pulled back a little, to reveal all, or at least part of, the glans.
- Getting an erection shouldn't be painful, but sometimes, if your foreskin is tight, it can hurt a little if you pull it back. This is normal, but it's also a warning to be careful. Time, and gently stretching the foreskin, will help it loosen.
- By the time you finish puberty, you should be able to roll your foreskin all the way under your glans, even when you have an erection.

Whether you have a foreskin or not, your penis will start to produce an oily gunk called smegma. This helps to lubricate your penis.

Boys with a foreskin find that smegma can build up and turn into little white flakes. These can smell bad, so it's a good idea to wash under your foreskin regularly. Be careful to use mild soap only for this job, as this part of your body is very sensitive!

A matter of size

One of the most common worries boys and men have about their penis is that it isn't big enough. Penises do vary in size, but on average they don't vary by much. Just so you know, the average erect male penis, measured on the top, is between 12.5cm and 15cm (5 and 6 inches) long.

As you will know from your own experience, judging size by looking at your own (or anyone else's) floppy penis is pretty pointless. It changes in length and thickness throughout the day.

Changes happen especially when it is cold. Your testicles need to stay at a certain temperature, so if it's cold, your scrotum shrinks, pulling them up into your body and pulling part of your penis up inside, too.

Boys tend to worry that other people want to date boys who have a large penis. In fact most people are much more keen on finding someone who is kind, funny and interesting.

Think tips

If you're ever in the shower and feeling worried that your penis looks smaller than everyone else's, it may help to think of two things:

1) People who start with a large, flaccid penis find it doesn't get much bigger when they get an erection, whereas people with a small flaccid penis may well find it doubles or triples in length AND width.

2) You will always be looking down to see your own penis. This angle makes it look smaller than it actually is — especially if your stomach sticks out over it.

7. What's it for?

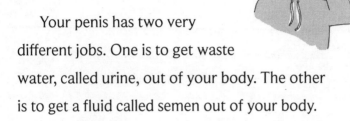

Your penis has two very
different jobs. One is to get waste
water, called urine, out of your body. The other
is to get a fluid called semen out of your body.

Urine and semen both travel through the same
tube and come out of the same hole, but they
physically can't come out at the same time.

Urine is made in your kidneys and stored in
your bladder. Semen is made in glands found in
your reproductive system, usually just before it's
ready to come out. So, what is 'the reproductive
system'? Turn the page to find out . . .

The male reproductive system

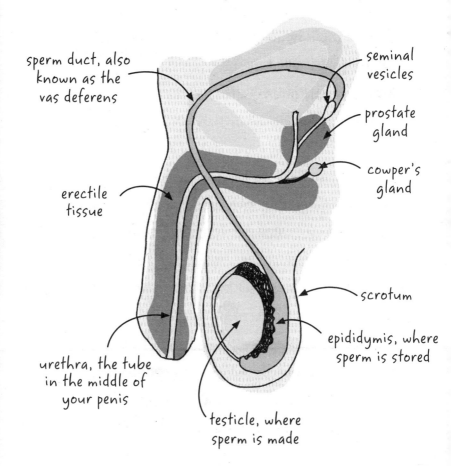

sperm duct, also known as the vas deferens

seminal vesicles

prostate gland

cowper's gland

erectile tissue

scrotum

urethra, the tube in the middle of your penis

epididymis, where sperm is stored

testicle, where sperm is made

What is semen?

Semen is a gloopy liquid
mixture. The most important
parts of this mixture are millions
of tiny things called sperm.
In fact, people often use the word
'sperm' to describe semen as a whole.

Sperm are too small to see without using a
microscope, but they look a bit like tiny tadpoles
with very long tails. Every single one contains a
blueprint of you, holding half the information
needed to make a baby.

Semen is mostly made up not of sperm, but of
a thick gooey liquid that keeps the sperm alive,
and gives it something to swim in. This goo is
made in your seminal vesicles and your glands.

The pain!

Shortly after you reach puberty, your testicles start to make sperm: lots and lots of sperm — several million every day. It's such an important job that your testicles are extremely sensitive. This is why they hurt so much even from a gentle knock, let alone a full-on encounter with a flying football.

Making a mess

The moment when semen comes out of your penis is technically known as ejaculation, but it's very often called 'coming', sometimes spelled as 'cumming'. In turn, semen is often called 'come' or 'cum'. (It has a lot of other nicknames, too.)

Whatever you call it, semen can make a mess. Unlike urine, it's hard to control how it comes out.

Sometimes semen oozes out and dribbles down the side of your penis, but other times it can spurt out and land a little distance away. In either case, it often feels as if there's a lot coming out — but in fact, it's rarely more than a teaspoonful.

One reason why ejaculation is hard to control is because it's almost always accompanied by an incredibly pleasant feeling known as an orgasm. Describing an orgasm is tricky, but you'll know if you've had one. If you haven't, or aren't sure, the chances are you will by the time you're 14 or 15.

Most boys experience their first orgasm, and their first ejaculation, while masturbating. This is the technical term for 'wanking': touching, rubbing or generally playing with your penis. It's an activity that boys and men have made up lots and lots of different words and expressions to describe.

It's also something that virtually all boys do, and indeed have done from time to time since they were little — although most boys start to do it a lot more often, and in a different way, after their first orgasm.

Masturbation is a normal and healthy activity. Unlike lots of things in life, it feels good, it's something you can do entirely on your own terms, and having an orgasm can help relieve stress. Some people do it a few times a day, others a few times a week. But you don't have to do it, and some choose not to.

The 'little death'

Centuries ago, the most popular slang term for an orgasm was 'le petit mort', which is French for 'the little death'. People used to think semen contained vital energies, and that ejaculation brought them closer to death. In fact, your body makes new sperm and semen all the time, and ejaculating does not sap your strength.

Just like going to the toilet, masturbating is something best done in private, and is more effective if you take your time and don't try to rush it. It's also your responsibility to clean up afterwards — semen has a slight smell, and can leave a visible stain on your clothes or sheets. Don't worry, though, it washes out easily.

Wet dreams

Whether you masturbate or not, it's very likely you'll wake up some mornings to find you have ejaculated while you were asleep. This is called a wet dream, or, to be scientific, a 'nocturnal emission'.

Roughly eight out of ten boys have wet dreams from time to time — some more frequently than others — but no one really knows why they happen.

Often, boys wake up at the moment of ejaculation, with a vivid memory of a dream that may or may not be to do with sex. Wet dreams can be as bizarre, or as mundane, as any dream. They don't have any special meaning.

Lies boys tell

When it comes to their penis, boys are as likely to lie as tell the truth. If you ever overhear, or are involved in, a conversation about penises and masturbation, don't believe everything you hear! Here are some common things boys (and men) lie about:

- How big their own penis is
- How small someone else's penis is
- How often they masturbate
- How rarely they masturbate
- How long they can keep an erection for
- How much semen they produce
- That they have masturbated in front of or with other people

8. Coping with erections

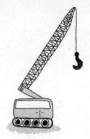

You need to have erections so you can ejaculate, so, when your body starts to produce sperm, it also needs to check that your penis can become erect. What this means is that during puberty, you will probably find you get erections *a lot*. Sometimes, it feels like you're constantly getting erections, and that you have no control over them.

How do they work?

Erections happen when nerve signals make extra blood flow into the penis, so it swells up and stiffens. There's no bone in your penis — the hardness is entirely caused by blood. The erection will go down when the nerve signals stop, and the blood flow in your penis returns to normal.

You're probably familiar with your own erect penis, but it's likely you've never seen anyone else's. Everyone's erection is a bit different.

Some erections stick up almost flat to the chest...

...while others swell up, but hardly point at all.

Some erections point straight ahead...

...and others point to the side.

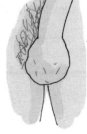

Many erections are a little bit wonky...

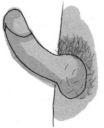

All of these variations are normal.

The shape, angle and direction of your erection is all to do with what's inside your penis, and nothing to do with how you touch it. Bulging veins, a bend to left or right, kinks in the middle are all perfectly normal. You can't give yourself a bend, and you can't smooth one out, either.

When do they happen?

The simple fact is, boys only have limited control over their erections. Most boys find they can give themselves one by rubbing their penis, or by thinking about a person they're attracted to, or even by looking at pictures in a book about puberty. But sometimes you can't get an erection even when you want one, especially if you're stressed.

At the same time, it's very common to get an erection at random, when you're not thinking about sex, your penis, or anything at all. As you get older, you'll find you get random erections less often.

Getting rid of erections

Sometimes it's nice to have an erection — for example, if you want to masturbate. The erection will go away shortly after you ejaculate.

But sometimes having an erection can be annoying, or even a bit painful (if it's pressing against your clothes, for example). Often, it feels as if an unwanted erection will never go down — but in reality, they rarely last for more than a few minutes.

Unfortunately, there really is no way to prevent random erections, or to get them to go down quickly. It can help to think about something really disgusting or boring, such as multiplication tables. But this can be hard to do when you're worried that everyone is looking at the bulge in your pants.

All that's left to do is to be patient, and have something to hand to hide your bulge with, whether it's a book, a bag, or a baggy jumper.

Think tip

If you ever notice that one of your classmates has an erection, think about how embarrassed they probably feel. You could get a cheap laugh by pointing it out to everyone, or you could gain a new friend by keeping quiet – and maybe they'll look out for you in future, too.

Morning glory

Many boys find they wake up with an especially hard erection first thing in the morning. This is often called 'morning glory', or 'morning wood'. It happens because your bladder is full, and it presses against the base of your penis, forcing a valve open that lets extra blood in.

It can help to lie on your side for a bit, but really you need to try to urinate. This requires patience, as you have to wait for your erection to soften a little, and some very careful and gentle angling of your penis so it points into the toilet.

9. Skin care

Many body changes that come with puberty are welcome, and even fun, but there are also some annoying side-effects. Probably the worst, because they're so noticeable, are outbreaks of spots. Spots can appear almost anywhere on your body, but most people get them on their face. The good news is that there's plenty you can do to deal with them.

Whether you call them spots, zits, pimples or acne, outbreaks of these little red lumps are the bane of many teenagers' lives and can make you feel self-conscious.

What causes spots?

Spots are caused by the build-up of a type of oil called sebum. Your body produces sebum throughout your life and it seeps through tiny holes in your skin (called pores or hair follicles) to stop it from drying out. When you reach puberty, changes in your hormone levels can send sebum production into overdrive, and the extra oil sometimes blocks the holes, trapping bacteria and causing spots. This is just a normal part of being a teenager and has nothing to do with being dirty.

Where spots come from

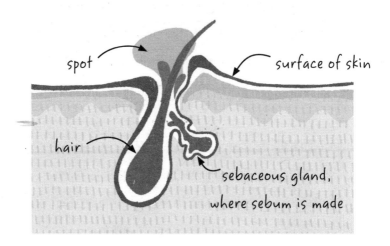

spot

surface of skin

hair

sebaceous gland, where sebum is made

What can I do about spots?

Everyone seems to have their own remedy for spots, but here are some ideas that might help:

- Drink plenty of water and try to eat a healthy diet. (There's no proof that eating lots of chips and chocolate gives you spots, but it probably doesn't help either.)

- Wash your face no more than twice a day with a facial wash or mild antiseptic soap designed for teenage skin. Use warm water and your hands (not a facecloth which can harbour germs).

- Try one of the spot treatments and cleansers you can buy from the chemists. Many people use ones that contain tea tree oil, an antiseptic.

- Keep your hands and nails clean and try to avoid picking, playing with or repeatedly squeezing spots as this can make them worse and may also leave little scars.

- Keep your hair off your face and wash it often. (Lanky hair doesn't really help to hide spots, and it can make them worse.)

- If your spots are bad, visit your GP to ask for advice as there are plenty of treatments available (and they work).

Did you know?

Even the most beautiful people in the world get spots. And most of them spend a lot of their energy worrying about how they look, too.

To squeeze or not to squeeze?

Everyone will tell you not to squeeze your spots, but — in reality — most people can't resist. The reasons not to squeeze are that it can make spots bigger, redder, more painful, more infected and can cause little scars . . . but if you really must squeeze, here's how to do it safely:

- Wash your hands well and use only your fingertips, not your nails, a needle or tweezers.

- Stop if nothing comes out, or if blood comes out.

- Blot the spot with a tissue or cotton pad, then dab an antiseptic such as tea tree oil on the area.

- Wash your hands - and leave your face alone to dry and heal.

Coping with spots

No one likes having spots, but they're so common that people have discovered and invented lots of treatments for them.

In the past, many of these treatments didn't really work, but more recent ones do. If your spots are getting you down, don't suffer in silence. Visit your doctor and get some help.

* * * **Think tip** * * *

Nearly everyone has spots at some point in their lives and most people (at least the ones worth bothering with) will be sympathetic and understanding when you have an outbreak.

Skin and sun

It's easy to think that a sun tan makes you look healthy, but it actually shows that your skin has been damaged by ultraviolet (UV) light from the sun. Sun damage can eventually lead to wrinkles and even skin cancer (the most common cancer in the 15 to 34 age-group) and tanning beds can expose you to even more harmful UV light than the sun does.

It's great to spend time outdoors in the sun, but it's very important to use a sunscreen to keep your skin healthy. Sunscreens are given an SPF (Sun Protection Factor) number, and the one you choose depends on your skin type (lighter skin needs a higher SPF). Visit **www.usborne.com/quicklinks** (see page 287) to find out more about skin types and which SPF you need.

Here is some advice to help you keep your skin healthy in the sun.

- Always use a sunscreen of SPF 15 or higher. Make sure your sunscreen covers both UVA and UVB rays.

- Reapply sunscreen after swimming, sweating and using a towel.

- Avoid spending too much time in the sun between 11 a.m. and 3 p.m. when the sun is strongest.

- Even if it doesn't feel hot, if the sun is shining, it can still burn your skin. On really sunny days, it's better to keep a t-shirt on — however good you think your body looks, it won't look good if it's damaged by the sun.

10. You and your body

There's nothing as off-putting to your friends, and especially to potential boy or girlfriends, as being smelly. The problem is, it's really hard to tell whether you smell good or bad! The best advice is to wash regularly, and not just your face.

This isn't because you are any dirtier than you were as a child, but because you start to sweat more. Sweat doesn't smell when it forms, but it soon comes into contact with the bacteria on your skin, hair and clothes, and before long, it starts to smell bad.

You have sweat glands all over your body, but they are more concentrated in your armpits and around your genitals. For this reason, most teens find they need to shower or take a bath every day (and after exercise) to keep smells at bay. You'll also need to change your underwear every day.

Deodorants

Using a deodorant in your armpits in the morning can stop your sweat from smelling all day. Some are combined with an anti-perspirant which stops you sweating as much. You can use a roll-on or a spray, but remember that using a deodorant is no substitute for washing.

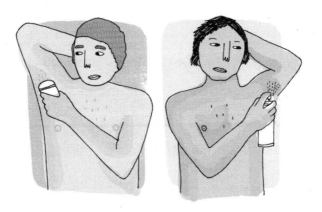

Happy hair

It's not just your body that gets sweaty and greasy — your hair suffers, too. Happily, there's a simple solution to greasy hair — just wash it more often and with a shampoo designed for greasy hair. If your hair is very oily, you may have to wash it every day.

Products such as styling gel or wax don't disguise grease. It's best to apply them after you've just washed your hair, and you might find you'll have to re-wash your hair every morning as some products leave a visible crust after you sleep on them.

Hands and feet

When you were younger, your mum, dad or carer probably trimmed your nails, but now it's your job to do that. It's a good idea to keep your nails trim, and to clean under them regularly for two reasons. Firstly, dirty nails are not a good look! Secondly, getting into good habits now increases your chances of having problem-free nails when you're older.

Teenage teeth

As a child, it can often be fun playing with wobbly teeth and watching as new teeth grow. By the time puberty hits, you'll probably have lost all your milk teeth, and the fun stops . . . If your adult teeth fall out, you won't grow a new set this time. Luckily, this is very unlikely to happen, *as long as you look after your teeth.*

The biggest causes of holes in teeth are thought to be sugary fizzy drinks and sweets, such as toffees, which can stick to teeth.

To keep your teeth healthy, unfortunately the answer is to listen to your dentist and your parents, who probably drone on and on about drinking water or milk instead of fizzy drinks and saving sweets and other sugary things for special treats. This is one example of adult advice that really works.

Here are more tips for healthy teeth and gums:

· Clean your teeth thoroughly using a toothbrush and toothpaste (with fluoride in) for two to three minutes every morning and every night.

· Replace your toothbrush every few months as the bristles start to get worn out.

- Use dental floss or a little interdental brush between your teeth regularly. Flossing covers two vital jobs: it removes bits of food, and it cleans bacteria off the tiny part of your gums between your teeth.

- Visit your dentist every six months for a check-up.

About braces

Many boys and girls find that their adult teeth grow at wonky angles, or crowd together. When this happens, dentists send their patients to see orthodontists, and talk turns to extractions, braces and retainers. These can sound scary or painful —

and indeed braces can be a little painful when they're first fitted — but most people think they're worth it in the long run.

There are two positive sides to braces. Firstly, wearing braces forces you to pay attention to your teeth every day, meaning you'll soon get into the habit of cleaning them regularly. Secondly, after the braces come off, your teeth will be straight and you'll be the proud owner of a winning smile!

Never forget that it's *your* mouth. Listen to advice from your dentist and orthodontist, but don't let them or anyone else pressure you into getting braces unless that's what you really want (or you have to have them for medical reasons).

Piercings and tattoos

There's no legal age restriction on most body piercings in the UK, but you must be 18 or over to have a tattoo. To avoid infection or a botched job (that could scar you and make you very ill), it's vital that any piercing or tattooing is done by an experienced professional who uses sterilized equipment.

A tattoo applied with a needle is permanent (though the colour does fade over time) so, if you're thinking about getting one, ask yourself if it would still look good when you are 30, or 40, or 50 . . . maybe a temporary tattoo is a better idea for now?

11. Food and healthy eating

With all the changes your body has to go through during puberty, it's not surprising you need a good diet to stay healthy. (Your *diet* means the kinds of foods you usually eat, it's not about *going on* a diet.)

Eating the right kinds of food makes you feel more energetic, makes you look healthy and more attractive and it can help you get to and stay at an adult weight that's right for you. Healthy eating really means eating the right mix of food in the right proportions and quantities.

You need to eat different kinds of foods to get all the vitamins, minerals, energy and other things your body needs to stay healthy. Dieticians divide foods into five groups, and you need some of each:

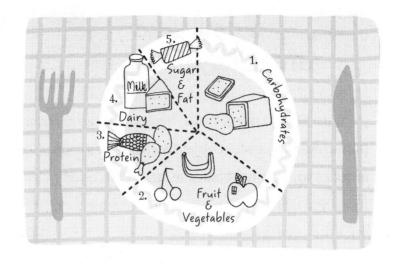

1. Bread, potatoes, rice, pasta, noodles and cereals

These 'starchy carbohydrates' give you energy, so you need plenty. They should make up about a third of the food you eat.

2. Fruit and vegetables

These provide lots of important vitamins and minerals, as well as fibre, which keeps your digestive system healthy. You need at least five portions, each about the size of your fist, every day.

3. Meat, fish, eggs, nuts, beans and lentils

All these foods are high in protein, which is vital for growth and you need two portions a day. A portion is a little smaller than a pack of playing cards (not a huge amount, in other words). This group also includes soya products such as tofu.

4. Milk, cheese, yogurt

These dairy products provide calcium which you need to develop strong bones and teeth, but you only need two portions a day — a portion is a glass of milk, a small piece of hard cheese (about half the size of a pack of cards) or a small pot of yogurt.

5. Foods high in fat and sugar

This group includes cakes, biscuits, crisps, chips, pastry, ice cream and a lot of 'junk' food. It's hard to describe portion sizes for fat and sugar as they are mostly hidden in other foods, but try not to eat too many of these. You need some fat, but not a lot, and it should be mainly 'good' fat such as olive oil, corn oil, nut and seed oil and fish oil, rather than palm and coconut oil or animal fats such as butter and cream.

How much in total?

During puberty, you need to eat as much food as a grown-up because you are growing fast, but the best rule is to eat when you are hungry, give your stomach and brain time to register that you have eaten, and only have more if you are still feeling hungry.

Because food tastes nice, it's very easy to eat more than you need (especially things which are not particularly good for you). Here are some more tips on healthy eating:

Leave yourself time to eat breakfast

After a night's sleep, your body and brain
need fuel to get going. If you skip breakfast,
you're more likely to crave sugary or salty
snacks during the day and be less able to
concentrate on whatever you need to do.

Eat regularly

That's three meals a day and some healthy snacks
in between if you're hungry (fruit, nuts, a small
amount of cheese or some plain popcorn). If you go
too long without food, your blood sugar level drops
and this can make you feel tired and grumpy.

Try to choose wholegrain foods

Such as brown bread, rice and pasta, plain popcorn,
oats and wholegrain cereal. These make you feel fuller
for longer, can stop you from feeling moody, and are
a good source of protein, vitamins and fibre.

Avoid sugary, fizzy drinks

But drink at least six glasses of water a day — carry a bottle with you and refill it regularly.

Try to limit or cut out junk foods

This includes sweets and lollies, crisps, bought biscuits, cakes and chips — these usually contain lots of sugar, fat, or salt. They are fattening and they don't contain many nutrients.

Don't add salt to your food

You should have a maximum of 6g (less than ¼oz) or about a teaspoonful of salt a day, but most people get twice this just in the food they already eat, so you don't need to add more. If you help with shopping, look for low-salt products. Check the ingredients list, or look for a 'food wheel' on packets to tell you how much salt a product contains.

Eat fish

Fish is a good source of protein, vitamins and minerals, and low in fat if you bake or grill it rather than fry it. Oily fish such as salmon, mackerel, sardines and herring contain Omega-3 fatty acids, which are thought to help combat diseases and skin problems. Some scientists say they help your brain to work well.

Eat five portions of fruit and veg a day

This includes fresh, frozen or canned food, and dried fruit such as raisins and apricots. Look out for fruit canned in juice or water with no added sugar. A glass of 100% juice counts as one portion. Baked beans or other canned beans can count as one portion, but potatoes don't count because they are in the carbohydrate food group.

Here are some other things that count
as one portion of fruit or vegetables:

1 apple, 1 banana, 1 pear, 1 orange,
1 nectarine, 2 plums, 2 satsumas, 2 kiwi
fruits, 3 apricots, 6 lychees,
7 strawberries, 14 cherries, half
a grapefruit, 1 big slice of melon, 1 large
slice of pineapple, 4 heaped tablespoons
of spinach, kale or green beans, 3 heaped
tablespoons of carrots, peas or
sweetcorn, 1 fruit smoothie . . .

Visit the Usborne Quicklinks Website
(see page 287) for a full list.

Weight and eating problems

Puberty is a time when many people start to worry about how they look and many think they are putting on too much weight. But it is also the time when you are *meant* to put on weight, especially as your body grows bigger. The keys to staying a healthy weight are to keep moving (there are some ideas on how to make this a habit in chapter 12) and to eat a healthy diet, following the tips in this chapter.

It's easy to compare yourself with friends or with pictures of sports stars and celebrities, but bodies come in all sorts of shapes and sizes all within the normal healthy range. Your weight depends a lot on your build and your genes as well as what you eat. If you are seriously worried about your weight, talk to your school nurse, counsellor or your doctor. And don't ignore your friends and family, either.

Good reasons NOT to 'go on a diet'

1.   A strict diet could eventually make you put on weight – the body's natural response to thinking it is being starved is to store extra fat.

2.   It's dangerous – while you are growing you need a whole variety of healthy foods and diets can mean you don't get all the nutrients you need.

3.   It's boring – you can't really enjoy eating and it means you are thinking about food all the time instead of other things.

4.   It won't make you look like whoever it is you want to look like, because you are not that person.

5.   Severe diets can develop into a fixation with weight, and end up becoming a serious illness called an eating disorder.

Eating disorders

The most common kind of eating disorder is obesity (becoming unhealthily overweight) but many disorders involve not eating enough. If others are worried about your weight loss, listen to them — they are often right even if you don't think they are. Common disorders include:

Anorexia nervosa: when someone cuts down on food until they are actually starving themselves, but they still think they are fat. To others, they often look much too thin.

Bulimia nervosa: when someone gets into a cycle of binge eating (eating far too much) and then feeling guilty and making themselves throw up, or using laxatives (medicines that make you poo) to 'purge' the food from their bodies.

Binge eating and comfort eating: when someone uses food to deal with difficult emotions. They often eat far too much, but don't purge the food and rapidly become dangerously overweight. Binge eaters often do it in private because they feel ashamed both of how much they eat and of feeling out of control.

 ## Help for eating disorders

If you think that you, a friend or family member has or is developing an eating disorder, it's very important to get help. It's easier to recover if treatment starts early. Talk to an adult you trust, such as a parent, carer, teacher, school nurse or counsellor, or your GP. Find out more about eating disorders, and how to get help, on the Usborne Quicklinks website (see page 287).

12. Running and resting

Yes, you've heard it before, but exercise really is very good for you, especially during puberty. This is the time you need to build up your body and get into habits which will help you to stay healthy when you are older.

In case you are not entirely convinced, here's a list of some of the many benefits of regular exercise:

- Exercise reduces body fat and so helps control your weight and makes you look good.

- It makes you feel more energetic, physically and mentally.

- It makes you feel good and can improve your self-confidence.

- Exercise helps you fight worry, anxiety and stress.

- It can lift your mood and helps prevent depression.

- It helps you sleep.

- It reduces the risk of you developing major illnesses such as heart disease, diabetes and some cancers by 50% as you get older.

- It aids co-ordination, balance and flexibility and improves your stamina.

- It helps you build strong bones and muscles, including your heart.

- It can help you develop mental and social skills such as planning strategy, working with others, and thinking ahead.

How much exercise do I need?

To get fit, you need to do some sort of exercise for at least an hour a day to develop stamina, suppleness and strength. This sounds like a lot, but it can be split into chunks and it includes PE at school, bike riding, dancing, or playing games in the park (if you like doing that kind of thing).

If you've been fairly inactive for a while, build up slowly and steadily, setting yourself realistic goals.

The most important thing is to find out what you enjoy and vary your activities so you don't get bored. You don't have to join a gym (although many do welcome younger teenagers) or be the school sports star to enjoy exercise.

Two or three times a week, you need to do some vigorous activity such as sport or fast running that makes you breathe much harder and faster and increases your heart rate (so that you can't say more than a few words without pausing for breath).

If you enjoy team sports and running around with other people, that's great. But there are plenty of ways to get some exercise on your own, without having to worry about how good or bad you are:

- Fast walking (to school or with a dog perhaps)

- Energetic dancing (try one of the interactive screen games that show you the moves)

- Swimming, cycling, trampolining, rollerblading, martial arts, skipping with a rope, running, horse riding, golf, skateboarding, kayaking, yoga, rowing, circuit training . . .

Working out

There are two different types of exercise routines, often described as 'working out', that focus on building up muscles. Both involve doing regular exercise, but neither of them is a substitute for the kind of exercise that gets your heart rate up.

Both forms of working out concentrate on lifting weights — whether using machines in a gym, or doing press-ups, sit-ups and the like — but it's important to know the difference because only *one* of the two is safe for teenagers.

1. Strength training

This simply means doing exercise to make yourself stronger. During early puberty, it will take time for your muscles to get noticeably bigger — but the exercise will reduce your body fat.

2. Body building

This is all about trying to sculpt your entire body to look a certain way. Instead of just building up strength, bodybuilders try to get their muscles to grow in size and shape, and try to make their bodies look symmetrical. They work out in an intense pattern that can be harmful to teenagers while their bones are still growing.

If you want to try strength training, it's very important to talk to your doctor first, to check that it's safe for your body. He or she might tell you to wait a year or two before you start.

It's also important to talk to a trainer or gym instructor, too, so that you can plan a healthy exercise routine. Working out too much can cause serious injuries. Worse still, if you don't get enough sleep or eat the right foods as part of your routine, the training won't work!

Sleep

Sleep is as important as food and exercise, especially for teenage brains and bodies, but most teenagers do not get enough. Not getting enough sleep can limit your ability to learn, concentrate and solve problems; it can make you more prone to spots; make you eat too much and make you feel cranky.

Sleep is especially crucial for teenagers because it's while you're snoozing that your brain reorganizes itself. It's also when your body releases a hormone essential for your growth spurt, so sleep patterns can even affect your height.

How much sleep do I really need?

11 to 15 year olds need just over nine hours of sleep a night, but this can be hard to achieve. The hormones

your brain releases during puberty change your body clock — an internal system that tells your body when it's time to sleep and time to wake up.

Most teenagers find they want to stay up later in the evening, and get up later in the morning. Unfortunately, adults and children aren't affected in the same way, and the world is mostly designed to work for adults. (This may seem unfair, but there are more people aged 20-100 than aged 13-19, after all.)

So even though your body is telling you one thing, you'll have to learn to cope with the demands of the world. It's one of the first examples of taking on an adult responsibility.

If you find it hard to relax and drift off at night, try these bedtime tips:

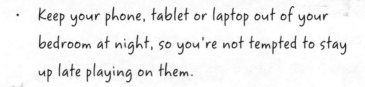

- Keep your phone, tablet or laptop out of your bedroom at night, so you're not tempted to stay up late playing on them.

- If worrying about things you have to do keeps you awake, write them down in a list. Then you can forget about them until the morning.

- Avoid watching television in the hour before it's time to sleep. Try taking a shower or bath, or drawing or reading instead.

- Don't eat, drink or exercise just before bedtime and don't leave homework until the last minute. Your brain and body need time to wind down.

- Tempting as it is, try to avoid long lie-ins at weekends and in the holidays as these can disrupt your sleep patterns.

13. Your brain, moods and feelings

You're bursting with energy and ready to take on any challenge one day, but the next, you find you can't even be bothered to get off the sofa. You feel happy one moment, but miserable the next. You love your parents, but find yourself snapping at them all the time, and tiny things can suddenly make you feel really irritated. Does any of this sound familiar?

If so, you are perfectly normal and you are not alone. Your teenage years are a time of deep emotional changes which can sometimes be uncomfortable as well as exciting. You don't want to feel and act like this; you're not a nasty person and you're not going mad, but when you are going through puberty, mood swings and extreme feelings can be hard to predict, hard to understand, and even harder to control.

Brain changes

Extreme emotions happen because your brain is undergoing massive changes at the same time as your body is surging with hormones.

High risks, high rewards

You use one area of your brain to make carefully thought-out decisions. But it has to compete with another area of your brain that makes you feel good if you try new things — it likes a quick thrill. Even in adults, this feel-good, thrill-seeking area often wins.

For teenagers, the thrill-seeking part of the brain is especially powerful. It means many teens love taking risks, whether it's skateboarding down a steep ramp, trying alcohol for the first time, or maybe just making a point of going out on their own.

Re-wiring your mind

Your brain is made up of millions and millions of cells called neurons. Each neuron is connected to many others, creating huge networks of pathways across your brain. During puberty, your neurons make lots and lots of new connections. They also sever old connections that you don't use much.

New connections are really useful — they help you learn new skills, from karate to guitar to foreign languages. Severing old, unused connections is really useful, too. It means you'll get a lot better at certain specific skills, and that you can do things more quickly, making fewer mistakes.

But all this brain activity has side-effects, too — you may well find you can get bored very easily, and find it hard to concentrate.

All this is guaranteed to set you at odds with your parents, teachers and even your best friends from time to time. Luckily, there are three simple ways to keep on top of your changing brain and unpredictable moods: eat well, exercise every day, and get enough sleep.

Sleep is especially important as it gives your brain a chance to sort through new connections, and pare down old ones. (See chapters 11 and 12 for tips on eating, sleeping and exercising.)

Dealing with difficult feelings

Everyone gets emotional in their life, not just teenagers. But sometimes dealing with your emotions is harder when you're a teenager because you'll find you're experiencing things you haven't had to deal with before.

Young children often feel either happy or sad, and can switch from one to the other quite easily. As you get older, you'll soon learn it's normal to feel lots of emotions at the same time.

Riding on this roller coaster of emotions is often scary and exciting at the same time — it can even leave you feeling sick.

Think tip

If you ever feel overwhelmed by emotions, one way
to help you keep calm is to put a name to them.
For example, ask yourself, do I feel . . .

. . . angry, jealous, frustrated, embarrassed, hurt,
happy, really happy, sad, rejected, excited, nervous,
afraid, let down, disgusted, included, safe, knocked
back, picked on, left out, in control, out of control,
contemptuous, bored, confused, in love?

You can't control your emotional reaction to
events, and you shouldn't feel guilty about what you
feel. But you do have some control over how long
your moods last. Before you think about how best
to cope with your changing moods, here are some
strategies that just **don't** work in the long run:

TICK TOCK

Suppressing or bottling up feelings – locking feelings inside you, trying to bury them, remove them from your thoughts or hold them in makes you feel under greater pressure until you may 'explode'.

Withdrawing – hiding away from everybody, sulking and refusing to speak can make you feel helpless and even depressed.

Dumping feelings – blaming other people for the way you feel and handing responsibility for your feelings over to them will only make you hate them, not help you feel better.

'Acting out' — being taken over by your feelings, so that you start shouting, swearing, hitting out or breaking things, makes other people angry, but won't help you feel better.

101

Here are some tactics you could try instead:

- Let off steam in a safe way – hit your pillow, go for a fast walk or run, sing along to loud music. Cry if you want to.

- Take some deep breaths and give yourself time to acknowledge and think about what you are feeling and why ("I'm feeling really angry because...").

- Talk to someone you trust. It's amazing how just airing and sharing feelings can help you feel better. Listening to someone else's viewpoint, even if you disagree, can help give you ideas on how to improve the situation.

- Write down how you feel in a journal, notebook or diary; write a song or poem or make a piece of art to try to express your feelings.

- Think of what you could do to make things better and make yourself feel better – and think of what has worked before.

- If you need to confront someone about their behaviour or apologize to someone about yours, it's better to do it when you are calmer.

- Try to focus on some good things in your life: What are you looking forward to? What do you like doing? What are you good at? What don't you have to worry about?

- In time, when you have taken notice of your feelings and understood why they're there, you may be able to let them go.

Worries and anxieties

It's normal to feel frightened or worried from time to time. Most people find their worries come and go, and they can handle them fine. But if a person worries about things too much, and this stops them from enjoying life, they may be suffering from anxiety.

All sorts of things can cause anxiety — worrying a lot about what other people think of you; upsetting experiences such as parents being ill, parents arguing a lot or separating; losing someone close to you; a frightening experience happening to you or someone close to you; problems at school; exams looming, or a new experience such as moving home, moving country or changing schools.

Anxiety can cause all kinds of physical symptoms including:

Faster breathing and heartbeat, breathlessness, trembling and sweating, needing to rush to the loo all the time, feeling sick in your stomach, not being able to concentrate on anything, feeling unable to move or talk, disturbed sleep or difficulty sleeping.

Coping with worry and anxiety

Big things that make life difficult and cause worry and anxiety are often out of your control, but there are things that you can do to make them affect you less. If you feel your worries are getting out of hand, here are some things you could try to make yourself feel better:

Talk to someone about how you feel. You will need extra support in difficult times, so you might also need to talk to someone you trust outside your family, such as a school counsellor, a teacher, school nurse, youth worker or a family friend.

Spend more time doing the things you enjoy and that give you a sense of achievement. This may be an after-school or lunchtime activity such as music or drama, swimming, a sport, or a club that you go to.

Think about whether you are really picking up on someone else's worries, rather than the worries being yours. Anxiety often runs in families, so you may be worrying because someone in your family is worried (and that person's worries aren't actually yours).

Try to give yourself more time to get used to changes that happen at home or at school. No one feels instantly comfortable with new experiences and in new situations and you may need longer than other people to get used to them.

Try one of the relaxation techniques on the next two pages. If you enjoy them all, you could try learning meditation, t'ai chi, or yoga.

Breathing relaxation technique

Try this if you're feeling nervous or panicky – or
when stress, shock, anger or anxiety make you
start breathing with quick, shallow breaths and
you can feel your heart beating faster than usual:

1. Find somewhere comfortable to sit down if you can.
2. Put one hand on your stomach to check how fast
    you are breathing.
3. If you're taking a breath every couple of seconds,
    make yourself take a deep breath in and start
    counting in your head.
4. Breathe out slowly through your mouth while
    you count slowly to five.
5. If a worry comes into your head, recognize it,
    and then move your attention back to your body.
6. Take a deep breath in and breathe out again
    counting slowly to five.
7. Carry on doing this until you are breathing in
    and out naturally.

Relaxation routine

You can do this sitting or lying down
somewhere quiet and comfortable.

1. Close your eyes and breathe slowly and deeply.
2. Think about any areas of tension in your body
    and try to relax those muscles.
3. Imagine all the tension leaving your body.
4. Focus on each part of your body in turn, starting
    with your head and neck and working down your
    body. Think of warmth and heaviness as you let
    each part relax completely.
5. After 15 to 20 minutes, take some deep breaths,
    stand up slowly and stretch.

If you have tried these ways of helping
yourself and still don't feel better, you need to
see your doctor who can discuss treatment
and may refer you to a specialist.

Moody or depressed?

Nearly everyone, children and teenagers as well as adults, occasionally feels sad or low for all kinds of reasons. Feeling miserable is a natural reaction to upsetting or stressful experiences. But when these feelings go on and on and begin to take over someone's life, it can become an illness called depression.

Depression affects about five in every 100 teenagers. You are more at risk of becoming depressed if you think you have no one to share worries and problems with and are under a lot of stress. But depression is usually caused by a combination of events and experiences, not by just one thing.

How do I know if I have depression?

If you have most of the symptoms in the list below and have had them for a while, it could mean that you are depressed:

- Feeling miserable and unhappy and 'empty' or 'numb' inside.
- Feeling lonely most of the time.
- Losing interest in and not enjoying things you used to like.
- Becoming withdrawn — avoiding your friends, family and your usual activities.
- Feeling moody and irritable so you are easily upset and often tearful.
- Finding it hard to concentrate and finish things.
- Not taking care of yourself and your appearance.
- Feeling tired and lacking in energy.

- Sleeping too much or too little.
- Feeling bad or guilty; criticizing, blaming and hating yourself.
- Having frequent mild health problems such as headaches or stomach aches.
- Having your appetite change.
- Thinking about death and wanting to die.

Getting help

Depression is a common and treatable illness, but it can be hard to ask for help and talk about how you feel when you are suffering from it. It's vital that you do ask for help though, especially if you are having suicidal thoughts or thinking of harming yourself.

Talking to someone you trust and who you think will be understanding is the first step, but you may

also need professional help from your doctor
or a counsellor to start getting better.

For sources of help and to find out more about
anxiety, depression and other mental health problems
such as bipolar disorder and schizophrenia, go to
www.usborne.com/quicklinks (see page 287).

Did you know?

Four out of ten teenagers say they have felt so
miserable that they have cried and have wanted
to get away from everybody and everything.

One in five teenagers sometimes thinks that
life does not seem worth living.

For the majority of people, depression and
other mental health problems are only
temporary and can be treated.

Anti-misery toolkit

Here are some ideas for ways to cheer yourself up if you're feeling fed-up for whatever reason.

- List in your head five things that you like about yourself. (If you can't, ask someone else to.)
- Look at some photos of times when you felt happy.
- Distract yourself with a film that makes you laugh.
- Listen to music you love, and sing along.
- Go for a walk or a run, or do something else active, such as jumping on a trampoline or dancing.
- Phone a good friend for a chat.
- Write, draw, doodle, play music or cook something.
- Do something you are good at and enjoy.
- Read a book or comic from your childhood.
- Rearrange your room, or reorganize one of your old collections.

14. It's different for girls

One thing that's likely to be on your mind a whole lot is the subject of girls. Young boys often ignore girls, or deliberately exclude them from games, only to find that shortly after they hit puberty, they'll do anything to get a girl to talk to them, never mind join in with a game!

It's also normal not to be interested in girls, and to be confused about why some of your friends seem to make such a fuss about getting a girlfriend.

Even if you've barely spoken to a girl your age, you'll notice that they go through puberty, too. Many things about boys and girls are the same, but puberty is the time when the differences between boys and girls are really highlighted.

What happens to girls?

Here's a simple overview of the changes that affect girls during puberty. You may not know what some of the words mean, but they'll all be explained later on in this chapter.

- They get bigger and taller.
- They grow pubic hair and underarm hair.
- They develop breasts.
- They become moodier.
- Their sex organs develop.
- They start to have periods.
- Their voices get a little deeper.
- Their hair and skin become oilier.
- Their bodies get a little hairier.

Only three things on this list are different from the boys' list on page 8: breasts, sex organs and periods. (Boys have sex organs, too — but they develop in different ways.) To get a better idea of what these things are all about, it's worth knowing more about what girls look like underneath their clothes, and even underneath their skin.

Girls on the outside

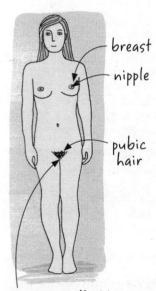

sex organs (hidden beneath the lower part of the pubic hair)

- breast
- nipple
- pubic hair

Girls' sex organs on the inside

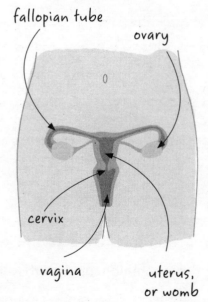

fallopian tube

ovary

cervix

vagina

uterus, or womb

What are breasts for?

Girls have breasts for two reasons. One is to make milk for babies. The other is to make the girl look grown-up and attractive. Virtually all breasts, no matter what size or shape they end up when a girl finishes puberty, can do both things.

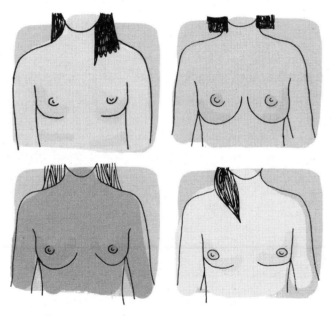

It's common for one breast to be a little bigger than the other, and for nipples to point in different directions.

Cover and support

Once girls start to grow breasts, most soon start wearing a bra. Bras keep breasts under cover, but more importantly they help support the weight, which is especially useful during sports.

Just like breasts, bras come in different shapes and sizes. You might sometimes hear girls or boys talking about a person's bra size using numbers and letters. The numbers describe the measurement around a girl's chest; the letters describe the size of the bra cups (with AA as the smallest, A the next in size, then B, C and so on through the alphabet).

Many girls worry about the size and shape of their breasts, just as boys worry about the size of their penises.

Sex organs and periods

Sex organs are body parts people use for sex.
In this case, 'sex' is short for two different things. One
is 'sexual intercourse', which you can find out more
about in chapter 17. The other is 'sexual reproduction',
which is the scientific term for making babies.

Babies are made when a single sperm from a man
fuses with an egg from a woman, which can happen
after sex (find out how on page 161).

Women have all their egg cells inside them when
they are born. They gradually develop into adult eggs
inside organs called ovaries. While men release millions
of sperm every time they ejaculate, women only
release one egg at time, and they can't control when
each egg is released. It happens automatically, usually
around once every month.

When each egg is released, it is wafted up into the nearest fallopian tube, where it sits for a few days. Meanwhile, the lining of the uterus gets a bit thicker. If, during those few days, a sperm finds and fuses with that egg, the woman may become pregnant.

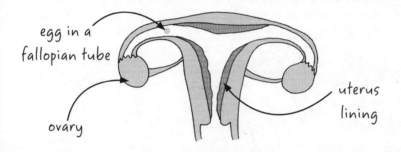

egg in a fallopian tube

ovary

uterus lining

But more often than not, this doesn't happen. The egg, and the thick lining of the uterus, trickle slowly out of the women's vagina, appearing as thick, dark blood. This flow lasts for a few days. Technically, it's described as menstruation, but most people call it 'having a period'.

Periods last for several days each month. Some girls find they are quite painful, but on the whole it doesn't stop anyone from living out their normal daily life. However, girls have to spend money buying things called tampons or sanitary towels that can soak up the blood and stop it from making a mess of their clothes.

And there's more. The cycle of releasing an egg and then having a period is all controlled by a complex mix of hormones. This mix is particularly intense for a few days before a period starts, and it often makes girls feel uncomfortable, irritable and easily upset. This collection of symptoms is known as PMS, which stands for pre-menstrual syndrome.

Girl parts

Most of a girl's sex organs are hidden inside her body. The external parts, known collectively as the vulva, or genitals, are between her legs — but even these are usually hidden behind pubic hair. This picture shows parts of the vulva:

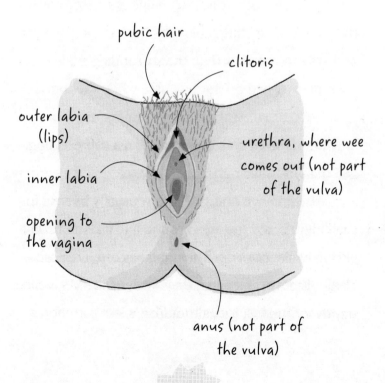

pubic hair

clitoris

outer labia (lips)

urethra, where wee comes out (not part of the vulva)

inner labia

opening to the vagina

anus (not part of the vulva)

Pubic hair grows above the vulva, and on the outer labia. Girls' pubic hair grows gradually, just like boys' pubic hair, and gets thicker during puberty. Some girls choose to trim or even shave their pubic hair once it grows bushy, but many don't.

The most sensitive parts of the vulva are the inner labia, especially a small bulge at the top called the clitoris. The inner labia vary in shape and length, and are often darker than the surronding skin. When a girl gets turned on, for example when she thinks about sex, or when she is masturbating, the labia and clitoris swell up a little, a bit like a soft erection.

Girls can have orgasms, too — usually by rubbing their clitoris and the area around it — but they don't ejaculate like boys do. Their vaginas often release a clear, slippery fluid when they masturbate. Girls can have wet dreams, too, although it's less common.

It's the same for girls

Girls go through many of the same changes as boys. They get bigger, taller and hairier. Their voices get deeper (although they don't change as much as boys' voices do). They are just as likely to get greasy hair as boys, and to get spots, too.

And on the inside, their bodies are flushed with new hormones, and their brains start to make new connections and think in different ways to how they did as children. Just like boys, girls start to think more about sex and relationships, and spend more time worrying about how they look and what other people think of them.

The biggest difference for girls is that they tend to start puberty a year or two earlier than boys. So girls your own age can seem more grown up.

Talking to girls

Girls aren't a different species, so talking to them shouldn't be that hard, right? But it's different when it's a girl you fancy. Whether or not a girl happens to find you physically attractive is mostly a matter of luck — but getting a girl to like you is not impossible. Here are some simple tips:

- Be clean — in your body and your language.
- Look at her face, not at her body or over her shoulder when you are talking to her.
- Don't be afraid to make eye contact.

- Listen to what she's talking about, and show an interest in what she has to say.
- Don't talk about yourself too much.
- If you're nervous, remember that she's likely to be nervous, too.

And another thing – just because you find a girl pretty doesn't mean you'll get on with her. But you might find you really do get on with someone you're not attracted to at first.

15. Who am I?

When things around you are changing, your hormones are working overtime and your brain is being refurbished, it's not surprising that you might start to wonder about your very identity.

Puberty is the time when you can explore the person you *really* are and not the person your parents *think* you are, or — worse — the person you imagine your parents want you to be. It's an exciting period of trying out new things. You can choose what to study, which sports to play, what to wear, what music to listen to, and, most crucially, who to hang out with.

But at the same time, it can be all too easy to lose confidence in yourself and start to feel all sorts of doubts about your abilities, the way you look, your relationships, and even who you are as a person.

Testing, testing

A big part of exploring your identity is testing what you can get away with. This can mean getting to know your body's limitations — how strong or fast you are, how much work you can cram into a short space of time, or how little sleep you need.

It also means finding out how independent you are. Sometimes, you'll be grateful for parents who can look after you and help you make decisions. Often, though, you'll want to choose things for yourself.

Making decisions, big or small, isn't always easy. Many people — without even realizing it — end up making just one decision: what kind of person to be. This informs many other decisions, whether it's little things such as what clothes to wear, to big things such as how kind to be towards other people.

Positive role models

You don't need to read film or football magazines to find people you admire. It's no bad thing to look up to people in your daily life, whether it's a parent, an older sibling, or someone at school.

There's nothing wrong with trying to emulate your heroes, although it might freak them out if you copy someone you know too closely. But it's worth reminding yourself of two things:

- You are not that person, and the way they live their life, and the things they choose to do, may not be right for you.
- Your heroes, whoever they are, are only human. They can mess up as easily as you. And when they do, don't think too badly of them (or yourself, for liking them in the first place).

Unique but similar

What's worse? Feeling like a complete
weirdo who has nothing in common with
anyone you know — or worrying that you're
just another member of a giant flock of
indistinguishable sheep?

The truth is, although everyone is unique,
most people are pretty similar to each other in
lots of ways — especially people from the same
family, neighbourhood or school.

If you're worried that you really don't fit in
with your crowd, one thing to try is spending
time somewhere you've never been before, such
as a different town or even a foreign country.

Meeting people who come from a completely different background can help you appreciate just how varied people can be in their lifestyles and personalities. It may also help you realize you have more in common with your peers than you once thought. Chances are, you're not so terribly weird.

Fitting in

Human beings have an inbuilt instinct to form close-knit groups. It's what kept us from getting killed by wild animals back in the Stone Age.

You'll always belong to your family, but as you get older, you might start to identify yourself more closely with a group of friends. But being part of a group doesn't mean sacrificing your own identity. Ultimately, the trick is simply to be yourself . . .

How to be yourself

Tell yourself you don't have to be good at everything
(nobody is...).

Try to be proud of what you are good at (whatever it is,
no matter how strange) and aim to get even better at it.

Try not to compare yourself with others all the time.
(They don't have your life, your family, your genes,
your talents and they don't share the same passions.)

Don't be too critical of yourself when you make
a mistake – that's how you learn.

Congratulate yourself when you do something well
(even if no one else does).

Tell yourself it doesn't matter if someone doesn't like
you. (Not everyone has to like you and you don't
have to like everyone.)

Confidence

One of the hardest, but most useful, tricks to learn is self-confidence. *Lack* of confidence can make you feel awkward, embarrassed and self-conscious and can lead you to think that you come from the weirdest family on the planet. It can make you unable to resist pressure from other people to try things you really don't want to or don't feel ready to do.

Lack of confidence can make you feel that you just don't fit in and that no one will ever find you attractive. It can convince you that everyone else is cooler, cleverer and more popular than you are.

Being confident doesn't mean you are boastful or that you think you are better than other people. Confident people don't need to criticize, judge or put other people down to feel better about themselves.

(In fact, people who go on about how much better they are than everyone else are often hiding a huge lack of self-confidence).

A strong sign of confidence is that you feel happy being yourself; you value yourself and your talents and abilities, whatever they are, and you don't feel you need to be perfect all the time.

Confidence think tips

Don't spend time with people who mock or say mean things about you (on the internet or in 'real life').

Don't mock or say mean things about other people.

Practise standing up tall and straight, looking people in the eye when you talk, taking a deep breath and saying what you want to say calmly and clearly.

Do spend time with people who make you feel good, who support you and appreciate you for who you are. (Joining a group or club based around a shared interest is a great way to boost confidence).

Develop your own taste and style in EVERYTHING. (You don't have to like the same music, wear the same clothes, eat the same food, watch the same films, or hang out in the same places as everyone else.)

Don't be afraid to try new things — within reason.

Confidence myths

1. Try NOT to believe that drinking will make you more confident. It may make you less inhibited, but then you might make some very bad choices.

2. Just because other people look like they're having fun while drinking or taking drugs doesn't mean they are, or that YOU will, too.

Making room for other people

Sometimes the hardest barrier to being yourself is other people. Either you're comparing yourself to them and worry that you're not good enough, or, worse, you're so caught up in your own world that their problems seem insignificant.

It can be difficult to listen to your friends and family, especially when you're in a bad mood, or feeling competitive. You might find you're so busy thinking up counter-arguments or simply feeling angry, that you forget to listen. It takes a strong person to truly listen to someone else's problems.

Body confidence

Because the media is full of images of seemingly happy and 'perfect' men and women (often all of a similar age, height and body type), it's very easy to get sucked into the idea that your life would be better if only you could change the way you look.

There are some things about the way you look that you simply CAN'T control, such as how tall you will grow, or what your face looks like.

But there are things you CAN control. You can change your hairstyle and your clothes every day if you want to. You can also, to some extent, control the shape of your body. (Read the advice on pages 89 and 90 about working out).

If you're feeling under pressure to change the way you look, try to remember that being good-looking is NOT the same as being happy. In fact psychologists have found that people who are considered conventionally beautiful are just as likely to feel unhappy (or happy) as anyone else.

Self-confidence tip

People who are involved in sport or take regular exercise tend to have more body confidence than those who don't, as they value what their bodies can do, not just what they look like.

16. Relationships

The biggest emotional change
that usually hits you as you go
through puberty is that you start to have exciting
feelings for people that you haven't had before:
perhaps for the first time, you fancy other people.

When you see a person you fancy, you get funny,
warm, fluttery feelings inside. This is because you are
physically attracted to them. You may think about
them all the time, even when they are not there, and
you try to find ways to get them to notice and speak
to you (though, if they do, you may suddenly feel
flustered and do or say something silly that you
didn't mean). All these feelings are normal, but they
can be confusing and a little scary as well as exciting.

Crush or love?

You can fancy or 'have a crush on' someone you don't know, such as a celebrity or actor, or it might be someone you know at school, even a teacher. Your feelings during a crush may be strong and passionate, but they don't usually last longer than a few weeks, especially as it's easy to find you develop a crush on other people fairly easily.

Not all boys find they fancy or have a crush on girls. When you are growing up, it's not unusual to fancy other boys. You might go on to date girls later, or you might find you always prefer boys and men. Some people fancy girls and boys. Finding out who you are attracted to (discovering your sexual orientation) is part of growing up. Find out more about sexuality on page 152 to 156.

Not all crushes are one-sided. It could be that the person you have a crush on fancies you too, and when you find this out, it feels great. If one of you then plucks up the courage to ask the other one out, and you get on well and you like their personality, you might decide to be in a relationship. You may even feel you are in love. But what happens then?

Is it a good relationship?

In ALL your friendships and relationships, it's very important to know if the relationship is a good, or positive one or a bad one. In a positive and caring relationship, two people take time to find out about each other, respect each other and they feel good about themselves and each other (most of the time).

Turn the page for a checklist of the kind of things that good relationships include.

Signs of a good relationship

- Having fun and laughing together
- Having things in common
- Trusting each other
- Being good friends
- Respecting each other's opinions
- Being able to disagree with each other
- Being able to talk about it when you have had an argument
- Making decisions together
- Having time and space to see other friends when you want to
- Having your own interests
- Being able to go at your own pace in the relationship (including sexually)
- Feeling safe
- Feeling confident

Bad relationships

It's normal for a relationship to go through ups and downs. Most partners disagree about things and sometimes argue — just like you do with your family — and may like doing different things from time to time. A healthy relationship can cope with all this.

In a negative or bad relationship, one person dominates and controls the other. They may get angry and jealous if you talk to other people; call you names to make you feel bad; threaten you physically or emotionally; pressurize you to do things you don't want to do or don't feel ready to do, or post unpleasant or revealing things about you on the internet.

If you recognize any of these things in a relationship, it's time to end it (even if you think you are in love). Go to the Usborne Quicklinks Website (see page 287) to find sources of support to help you do this.

Loved-up couple

I can't stop thinking about her.

I hope he asks me to the school dance.

She's so pretty.

He's gorgeous!

She's a really good kisser.

I'm the luckiest girl in school.

On the skids

Do my friends think she's pretty enough to be my girlfriend?

He never listens to me when I'm talking.

I hate that top she's wearing.

He thinks he's so cool.

I wonder what her sister is doing tonight?

Why don't I like him as much as my friends do?

A lasting relationship?

She's a really good listener.

He's really kind, I love that in a man.

How do I tell her she's got bad breath?

I miss going running with the girls.

Hope she likes the new playlist I made her.

Is he ever going to read that book I lent him?

Break-ups and rejections

Sometimes relationships aren't especially negative; they just don't work out. Sometimes two people aren't 'compatible' (they don't fit together and can't get on). It takes two people to make a relationship work, and if one person doesn't want to do that then the relationship needs to end.

If you have been through a break-up, it feels hurtful and sad, but you need to remember that it doesn't mean there is anything wrong with you; it's just that your ex was not the right person for you. Even if the reason for the break-up is that the other person just doesn't fancy you, it's not your fault, and it doesn't mean you are unattractive to other people.

If you are the one being 'dumped' or rejected, try to keep your dignity (though you can cry as much as you like in private) and try not to wallow in self-pity. You could try some of the 'dealing with difficult feelings' tips on pages 99 to 103.

The painful feelings will fade with time, but in the meantime you should be able to fall back on your family and friends and the things you enjoy doing to make yourself feel better. Give yourself a few weeks to get over it and don't feel you have to rush into another relationship just to feel that someone wants you.

Rejecting other people

If someone asks you out and you're not interested, it's best to tell them simply and in as kind and direct a way as you can. It takes courage to ask someone out, and no one deserves to be ridiculed or made to feel bad for doing so.

You could say something along the lines of "Thanks very much for asking, but I am seeing someone else at the moment." Or "That's nice of you, and I'd like to be friends, but I want to stay single at the moment/but I'm afraid I don't feel the same way." Try not to give false hope by suggesting it might happen another time or by agreeing to go on a date when you know you are not interested.

 If you feel you need to tell someone a relationship has to end, try to do it respectfully and be brave enough to do it face-to-face and in private. No one should ever be dumped by text, email, letter, over the internet or with other people around. Explain why you are breaking up, but talk about how you are feeling, rather than blaming the other person.

Don't expect that you will instantly become friends again after a break-up. It takes time to get over feelings of hurt and rejection and to feel comfortable in the same space as someone you have rejected or who has rejected you.

What's wrong with being single?

There's nothing wrong at all with being single. In fact, many people don't have any relationships until after they leave school. Sadly, teenagers often feel under such pressure, they end up going out with the wrong person, because they're so flattered to be asked out; or pretend they have partner, just to fit in.

There's no good reason to go out with anyone, or to kiss someone — let alone sleep with them — unless you really like them, they like and respect you for who you are, and they make you feel good.

151

Sexuality

Like your brain and body, your sexuality develops and may change during your life. When you are finding out about yours, it's important to take your time and to remember that people have the right to express and explore their sexuality in a way that's right for them. Your sexuality is an essential part of who you are, and it's up to you to discover it, not for other people to decide or 'diagnose' it.

You don't choose your sexual orientation (whether you are straight, gay, bisexual, etc.) any more than you choose the size of your feet or height. It is just the way you are and part of what makes you unique. Nobody can 'turn' you gay or straight. Some boys know from quite an early age that they are only attracted to other boys. Others find they fancy both girls and boys and experiment to find out what their preferences are. A lot of people (including adults) are unsure what their sexual orientation is. Just so you know, here are some different terms associated with sexuality and sexual orientation:

Asexual - If someone is asexual, they don't feel sexually attracted or respond sexually to anyone.

Bisexual, or bi - A bisexual person is emotionally and sexually attracted to both men and women, but not necessarily at the same time.

Celibate - A person who is celibate chooses not to have sex.

Heterosexual (straight) - A heterosexual person is emotionally and sexually attracted to the opposite sex (that is a woman to men and a man to women).

Homosexual (gay or lesbian) - A homosexual person is emotionally and sexually attracted to people of the same sex. A gay woman (often known as a lesbian) is attracted to women; a gay man to men.

Transgender - Transgender people have a strong feeling that their gender identity (their sense of being male or female) is not the same as the physical characteristics they are born with. A transgender person can be straight, gay, lesbian or bisexual. Some transgender people want to be another sex and have surgery and take hormones to change their bodies.

Transvestite - A person who (sometimes) likes to wear clothes usually thought of as belonging to the opposite sex. This doesn't necessarily mean they want to become another gender and they can be straight, gay, lesbian or bisexual.

Did you know?

Surveys show that at least five per cent of children grow up to be gay or lesbian.

Many gay people say that they first knew they were gay at primary school.

Coming out

Coming out is when someone
chooses to tell other people that they
are gay, lesbian, bisexual or transgender. This is
a personal decision and should be a positive one.
But many young people fear it will affect the way
their friends and family feel about them and worry
especially what their parents' reaction will be.

Some heterosexual parents may just assume that
their children will also be heterosexual, so it can
come as a shock when they find out their teenager
is gay or bisexual. But many parents find it easy to
accept their child's sexuality and are very
supportive and reassuring.

In reality, people who love you and are real
friends will be supportive and respectful whatever

your sexual orientation is, and if ever you are feeling confused and uncertain about it. If you feel yours aren't, or need support in coming out, there are groups and organizations you can turn to for help. Go to **www.usborne.com/quicklinks** (see page 287) for sources of advice.

Meeting other young people who are going through a similar experience is essential to help you overcome any feelings of isolation and anxiety.

Think tip

If someone reacts badly when they find out that you are not heterosexual, remind yourself that the problem does not lie with you, but with the other person's ignorance and fear of difference.

Homophobic bullying

Hating, abusing or bullying people because they are gay or bisexual, called homophobia, causes huge amounts of misery and suffering. More than half the lesbian, gay and bisexual students in UK schools say they have experienced this.

Homophobic bullying includes pushing, hitting, name-calling, teasing or tormenting someone, or making them feel stupid or uncomfortable (online as well as face-to-face) because of their sexuality.

If you know this is going on, or if you are being bullied, tell someone you trust — a parent or carer, your teacher, your doctor or the police, or call a helpline (see page 287) but don't ignore it. If you are the bully or have got caught up in bullying, you have a serious problem and need to talk to someone about it — urgently.

"That's so gay".

Describing something as 'gay' when you mean it's not very good might seem silly and harmless — but it's not. Even if you are gay yourself and you use the word this way, all you're doing is reinforcing the idea that being gay is somehow less good or less correct than not being gay.

Describing something as 'lame' is similar. The word literally means disabled in the legs and feet, so the implication is that someone who can't walk isn't as good as someone who can — which is rubbish.

Sometimes, an insult doesn't hurt a particular person, but it can massively affect the way people think.

17. All about sex

You start to become a sexual person when your hormone levels change and your sex organs begin to develop, but this usually happens a long time before you are ready to have sex with someone. People have sex or 'make love' mainly because it can feel very good, especially with someone they feel deeply about, are attracted to and are in love with.

People also have sex when they want to have a baby, but you can just as easily get a girl pregnant even if you and she don't want a baby, if you have sex without using contraception (see chapter 18).

If you don't have 'safer sex' (sex using a condom) you also run the risk of getting, or passing on, one of the diseases known as sexually transmitted infections (or STIs – more about all of this in the next chapter).

What is sex?

You probably know all this already, but just in case you weren't paying attention that day. . .

When people talk about a man and a woman 'having sex' they usually mean when a man's penis goes inside a woman's vagina. This is also known (in medical language) as sexual intercourse or (in everyday language) as 'going all the way', 'hooking up', 'doing it', 'going to bed with someone' or 'sleeping with someone' (because most sex happens in a bedroom on a bed).

There are all sorts of other ways people enjoy being sexual with each other. Men can have sex with other men, and women with other women. Almost any example of two people giving each other an orgasm can be described as 'having sex'.

The mechanics of sex

For the baby-making, penis-in-vagina type of sex to happen, a couple kiss, cuddle, and touch each other (called foreplay) until they both become sexually excited. In a good situation, the man gets an erection and the woman's vagina releases some slippery fluid.

The penis fits snugly inside the vagina. Once they're in this position, it's typical for the man and woman to move rhythmically until the man has an orgasm and ejaculates. Some women have an orgasm at the same time, but most don't.

Unless the man is wearing a condom, his sperm can swim up beyond the woman's cervix where one of them may meet an egg and fertilize it. If the fertilized egg then implants itself in the wall of the woman's uterus, a pregnancy begins . . .

Only when you're ready

Even when you know what 'having sex' means, know how to stop babies by using contraception and know how to protect yourself against STIs, it doesn't mean you have to do it or are ready to do it. For sex to be enjoyable and safe, you need to be ready mentally and emotionally as well as physically.

As puberty kicks in, you may find you have sexual thoughts and feelings towards other people. These thoughts can pop into your head at odd times, day or night, and you might find yourself fantasizing about having sex with people you fancy, and masturbating while you fantasize.

These are very normal and safe ways to explore your feelings without hurting yourself or anybody else. Masturbation is a good way to get to know your own body's responses. If you know what makes you feel good, when you do come to have sex with another person, you can let your partner know, too.

A word about pornography

Many boys and men (and girls and women) like to fantasize by using their imaginations. But it's all too easy to get sucked into a habit of turning your brain off and looking at pornography, or porn, instead.

'Pornography' literally means 'stories about prostitutes'. But nowadays it usually means photos and videos of people getting naked, masturbating, and having all kinds of sex. Porn films can be disturbing, and seeing one might fill you with unsettling emotions. You don't have to look at porn, and you're not weird if you don't.

Is it safe?

Accessing porn websites through a phone or computer can put it at risk of getting a computer virus. It's hard to control what you see on some websites, meaning you can easily stumble across really nasty pornographic images that you didn't want to see. Some of them might even be illegal.

People in porn films often look like they're having fun. But in fact many men — and especially young women — are forced into doing it, often because they need money. Looking at porn may give *you* a quick thrill, but it might mean someone else is being exploited.

If pornography is the main way that a person encounters sexuality, it can end up skewing their understanding of real life sex in negative ways.

Things to think about

It's very common for teenagers (and adults) to look at porn, but it can become a habit that affects the way you feel about yourself, about other people, and especially the way you think about sex. Think about your answers to these questions:

- Have you ever seen a pornographic image or video that you really wished you hadn't?
- Do you find that images that you used to think were shocking now seem ordinary?
- Do you find yourself looking for more and more extreme kinds of porn?
- Do you think that sex in real life should be like sex in porn films?
- Do you ever feel that you need to look at porn, rather than just wanting to look at it?

- How would you feel if your little brother or sister saw some of the things that you have seen, either by accident or on purpose?
- How would you feel if you saw your older brother or sister IN one of the videos you were watching?
- Can you imagine asking a real partner to do some of the things you've seen in a porn film?

If you are worried about something you have seen, or that you spend too much time looking at porn, talk to someone about it. The idea of telling anyone that you look at porn may seem mortifying — but it's better than suffering in silence. You could start with your school counsellor, who is likely to have had the same conversation with other students, and will not judge you.

Don't believe your eyes

Just like Hollywood films, porn films do not represent real life. The people who make them use a combination of actors with particular looks, camera angles and sometimes even special effects to show a certain kind of sex — which is almost always unlike sex in a real relationship. Be aware that in real life:

- Most men and women DO NOT have incredibly large penises or breasts.
- Most people do not remove all their pubic hair.
- Most couples cuddle during sex, meaning they can't see the penis going in and out of the vagina.
- Most couples do not stop and get into different positions during sex.
- Most men ejaculate during penetration, and not onto their partner's face or body.
- Most men do not ejaculate lots and lots of semen.

How do I know if I'm ready?

If you are in a good relationship and thinking about having sex with your partner, there are lots of questions you need to ask yourself to find out if you really are ready. So make sure you can honestly answer 'yes' to ALL these questions:

- Do you like, trust and respect your partner?
- Do you really want to have sex? (for you, not because you think you ought to)
- Are you comfortable with all the physical things you have done so far with your partner?
- Do you both know how to take responsibility for safer sex, and especially how to use a condom?
- Are you relaxed enough around your partner that you can tell him or her to stop if you change your mind or you're not enjoying it – and to listen if he or she wants to stop, for any reason?

Some bad reasons to have sex

Because sex happens with another person, it's impossible to do it without it affecting your mind, and especially your relationship with that person. Unlike masturbation, sex can be emotionally harmful if you, or your partner, is not mature enough mentally, even though you might be old enough to want to do it.

Don't have sex just because:

- The other person wants to.
- You want to make someone like you more.
- You're too drunk or too high to stop it from happening.
- Your friends say they've done it.
- You are too scared or too shy to say 'no'.
- You are afraid your partner will break up with you or sleep with someone else if you don't.
- You don't want to be a virgin.

- You just want to find out what it feels like.
- You want to get back at parents who disapprove of your partner.
- You want to rebel against your parents who disapprove of you having sex.
- You want to make someone jealous.
- You like kissing and touching and think this means you have to keep going.
- Someone pressurizes you or threatens you.
- You've done it before so you might as well do it again.

Did you know?

It is against the law for anyone to have sex with a person under the age of 16. This is known as 'the age of consent'. This is the same for men and women and for heterosexual (straight) and homosexual (gay/lesbian) sex.

Everybody else ISN'T doing it

In spite of all the boasting that happens, and all the panic from grown-ups, most young teens are NOT having sex. Surveys show that the average age when people first have sex is about 17, but you're not at all unusual if you want to wait until you're older.

Teenagers often find that changing a relationship into a sexual one is a bigger step than they expected, so don't ever be pushed into doing something you don't want or don't feel ready for.

What counts as 'sex', anyway?

If you are in a happy relationship, there are all kinds of ways to express sexual feelings without 'going all the way', as long as you both feel comfortable. You can hold hands, laugh, flirt, kiss, cuddle, kiss using tongues (French kiss). You can fondle or rub each other's genitals, and gently lick or suck them (called oral sex, or a 'blow job').

Most people believe that, technically speaking, a man remains a virgin until he's had penetrative sex — the kind of sex where his penis penetrates his partner's body. But emotionally, it can be as big a deal to share any experience with another person that means either or both of you have an orgasm.

Whatever kind of sex you and your partner are talking about, make sure you move at a pace that you're both comfortable with. You can even decide not to have ANY kind of sex — there's nothing wrong with not doing it, if you don't want to.

What's it like
for a woman?

The first time

Some women feel a small amount
of pain the first few times they have sex,
and they can even bleed. This usually happens
because a thin membrane of tissue inside the
vagina, called the hymen, gets torn.

It can also hurt a woman if the man puts his penis
in too suddenly, or if she hasn't had enough time to
get aroused and her vagina is dry. (See page 189 to
find out about safe lubricants you could use).

Do women have orgasms during sex?

They may or may not. It doesn't most often
happen just through penetrative (penis-in-vagina
type) sex, as the clitoris doesn't get enough

stimulation – and also because it's common for a man to reach orgasm more quickly than a woman. This doesn't mean women don't enjoy sex. They can show or tell their partners what to do to help them get excited. In fact, unlike men, many women can have more than one orgasm in a short space of time.

Can a girl get pregnant the first time she has sex?

Yes. A girl can get pregnant any time she has penetrative sex, and in any position, even if it's just before or during or just after her period. The only way not to get a girl pregnant is to use a condom, or another form of contraception correctly. (See the next chapter.)

What happens afterwards?

The experience of sex is pretty similar for a man and a woman. But what happens afterwards may not be. It's all too common for teenage boys to brag about having had sex and win adulation and respect (even if they're lying), while a girl who is said to have had sex with someone (even if she didn't) gets branded as a slut. Just because you *think* a girl has had sex with one person, it doesn't mean she is more likely to sleep with another.

No ALWAYS means no

Forcing someone to have any kind of sex with you is a serious crime called rape or sexual assault. Men can be assaulted or raped — by other men or by women — but most cases are about a man attacking a woman, usually someone he knows.

Even if you have had sex with your partner before, you cannot assume he or she wants to have sex with you again. If your partner, or you yourself, decides you want to stop what you're doing — even in the middle of any kind of sex — then STOP!

It's not working!

When it comes down to actually having sex, especially the first time, don't expect everything to go smoothly. Sometimes, a problem can be a sign that you're not really ready. But the real test is how you and your partner react.

If you're ready, and you're with the right person, it won't matter if you have good sex or bad sex. Sex should be something you and your partner can talk about and even laugh about, especially if something goes wrong.

All of the problems listed below can happen to anyone for all sorts of reasons, often to do with stress. None is likely to be permanent, but if you find any of them affects you frequently, you should talk to your doctor. It may be embarrassing to talk about, but remember that these problems are all common, and doctors have heard it all before. Even better, they'll be able to help you overcome them.

Too soft

Sometimes, you just won't get an erection even when you're feeling really turned on. If this happens to a man all the time, it's described as impotence.

Too fast

You might find that you ejaculate almost as soon as you are touched by your partner, or within seconds of penetration. This is known as 'premature ejaculation'.

Too slow

The opposite problem is known as 'delayed ejaculation', and can mean you won't have an orgasm for all the thrusting or rubbing in the world.

It won't go in

You might need your partner's help to guide your penis into her vagina. And it may not go in if she's too dry, or if she is nervous herself. Don't force it.

It hurts

If you have a tight foreskin, you might find that your penis hurts, and can even bleed a little, during penetrative sex. Too much thrusting or rubbing without lubrication can chafe the skin, too.

In all these cases, but especially the last two, it can help to slow things down. Don't forget, penetration is only one kind of sex, and having an orgasm, or giving your partner an orgasm, is not the be all and end all of a relationship.

Sex and lies

Other people, especially teenage boys, tell lies about sex. People lie about sex so easily that even anonymous scientific surveys about sex give very different results. Here are some of the things men may lie about:

- Whether or not they've had sex at all.
- How long it lasted.
- How often they have sex.
- How many people they've slept with.
- How much they enjoyed it.
- How much their partner enjoyed it.
- How many times they had sex in one night.
- How good they are at it.

Lies men tell women

Some men are so desperate to have sex, they try to persuade their partner that it's a medical or moral necessity. You may have heard some of these claims — NONE OF THEM IS TRUE!

- Every time you get an erection, you have to have sex, or at least have an orgasm.
- If you don't have sex every day/week/month, your balls turn blue.
- You need to have sex at least once a day/week/month to stay in good health.
- If your partner doesn't want to sleep with you, it means they don't really love you.
- If a girl makes you think you're going to have sex with her and then changes her mind, you're still allowed to have sex with her — it's not rape. (Make no mistake, this IS rape.)

18. Protecting yourself

If you do decide that you want to, and are ready to have sex, it's vital to protect yourself and your partner both from pregnancy and STIs (sexually transmitted infections) such as HIV and chlamydia.

Contraception (also known as birth control) allows a man and woman to prevent pregnancy when they have sex. All methods of contraception, apart from male condoms, are used by women, which leads some people to assume that contraception is a woman's responsibility. But, in a relationship, it is something you should *both* be responsible for.

In the days before effective methods of contraception were easily available, couples couldn't control when they had a child, and men often didn't care. So women lived in fear of unwanted pregnancy, or resigned themselves to having baby after baby until they were worn out. This may still be the case in places where women don't have access to contraception or can't use it for religious or cultural reasons.

No method of contraception is 100 per cent effective, but, if used correctly, the methods described in this chapter prevent pregnancy 95 to 99 per cent of the time. Don't believe playground myths — a girl or woman CAN get pregnant:

- If it's the first time she has had sex.
- When she is having her period.
- Before she has started having periods.
- Whatever position the couple use for sex.
- Wherever the couple have sex.
- If she does not have an orgasm.
- If it's the first time her partner has had sex.

Quick quiz

Which of these can prevent pregnancy?

- Being drunk
- Having sex standing up
- Having sex with the woman on top
- Having sex in a shower or swimming pool
- Not putting your penis all the way in
- Pulling out before you ejaculate (sometimes called 'the withdrawal method')
- Using cling film or a plastic bag instead of a condom when you have sex
- Squirting water into the vagina after sex
- Crossing your fingers when you have sex

Answer

The answer, of course, is NONE OF THEM.

The only way for a male and female couple to avoid pregnancy is for them not to have the kind of sex where sperm can come into contact with the woman's vagina.

Or for them not to have sex at all.

Or for them to use a reliable contraceptive method when they have sex.

Did you know?

Every year in the UK, over 7,000 girls under the age of 16 become pregnant.

Condoms

Condoms are thin rubber
bags that fit snugly around a
penis. They catch semen and are 99% effective at
preventing pregnancy during sex between a man and
a woman. They also prevent STIs from passing from
one partner to another, which can happen through
most kinds of sex.

Where can I get them?

You can sometimes get condoms for free from a
doctor, nurse, or 'family planning' clinic. But the
easiest way is to buy them. Condoms are usually sold
in small boxes of three, or big boxes of twelve, and
are available in most supermarkets, high street
pharmacies and online, too. There's no age
restriction on buying condoms.

Getting them on and off

When it comes to using a condom, you can get your partner to help, but you can't assume that he or she will know what to do. So it's best to take some time to learn how to handle condoms yourself. It gets easier with practice, so it's better to try it on your own, before you start having sex. Here's what to do:

1. First check the condom packet is not damaged in any way and that it has the BSI or CE 'kite mark' on it. Make sure you're using the condom before the 'use by' date printed on the packet.

2. Open the packet carefully – your fingernails or teeth can accidentally tear the condom inside.

3. Condoms come out of the packet rolled up, like the picture below. You'll find a little teat at the end. Gently squeeze it to get rid of air.

teat

4. Still holding the closed end, place the rolled-up condom over the tip of your penis.

5. With your other hand, roll the condom gently all the way down. (If it won't go down to the base, it may be inside out, so start again with a new one.)

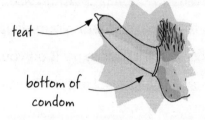

teat

bottom of condom

6. If you have a foreskin, you'll need to experiment to see if you find it more comfortable to roll the foreskin up or down underneath a condom.

7. After ejaculating into a condom, it's best to take it off as soon as possible. Otherwise it'll start to slip off as your erection goes down.

8. Roll the condom back up a little way first, then pull it. Be careful — you might have some hair stuck in the condom and it'll hurt if you yank the condom off too quickly!

Condoms and sex

During sexual play with a partner:

- You need to put the condom on before your penis gets anywhere near her vagina. Even if you haven't had an orgasm, a substance called 'pre-cum' can dribble out of your penis. This can contain sperm, and can pass on some STIs.

- As soon as you come, and while your penis is still hard, hold the condom around the base and pull out carefully.

- Wrap the used condom in a tissue or loo paper and throw it in the bin (NOT down the toilet, as it can block the pipe).

- If you have sex again, use a new condom.

Go to **www.usborne.com/quicklinks**
(see page 287) to see a demonstration.

Bad reasons for not using condoms

If you don't feel comfortable talking to your partner about contraception, you might want to reconsider whether you're ready to have sex. Similarly, if you're putting pressure on your partner to use something other than condoms, this too is a sign that you're in an unhealthy relationship. If you love someone, and you really want to have sex with them, you should be willing to wear a condom.

Don't be the boyfriend who makes
pathetic excuses, like these . . .

"My parents could find out I'm having
sex if we use condoms."
They will *definitely* find out you are having sex if
your partner gets pregnant. Also, having sex
without a condom can get messy, because most
of the semen will dribble out of the vagina — harder
to clean up and hide than a tissue in a bin.

"I'm too embarrassed to buy condoms."
If you're feeling grown-up enough to have
sex, you should be brave enough to cope
with a little embarrassment.

"Stopping to put on a condom could spoil the mood."
Worrying about getting pregnant or contracting
an STI spoils the mood MUCH more.

"It doesn't feel as good with a condom on."
There are lots of varieties of condom designed to enhance sensation for you and your partner. Try them out to see what works best for you both, but always make sure they've got a kite mark.

"I hate condoms."
If you really don't want to wear a condom, then talk to your partner about things you can do together that don't involve penetrative sex.
If you're with a girl, make sure that your semen doesn't go onto or around her vagina.

"I love you and I'll stick by you if you get pregnant, so don't worry."
Are you *really* ready to be a dad? Looking after a baby is incredibly hard work and puts a huge strain on any relationship.

Other contraceptives

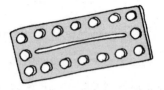

Condoms are the only form of contraception that also prevent both partners from giving each other an STI. But, if your partner is female, and you trust each other (more about what 'trust' means for safer sex on page 198), there are other forms of contraception available:

• Female condom: a soft, thin plastic bag that lines the inside of the vagina and catches semen. Also prevents STIs.

• Diaphragm, or 'cap': a small plastic dome that fits into the back of the vagina and catches semen. It can be washed and re-used.

- Contraceptive pill, often simply called 'the pill': a pill taken daily by the woman that prevents pregnancy. Must be prescribed by a doctor.

- Emergency contraceptive pill, sometimes misleadingly called the 'morning-after pill': a pill that can be taken up to 72 hours (three days) after having sex, that prevents a pregnancy taking hold. Over-16s can buy it from a pharmacy. The sooner it is taken after having sex, the more effective it is.

Think tip

It's really not a good idea to have unprotected sex because you think it's easy to get an emergency contraceptive pill the next day. It's not always easy, and it's just as much your responsibility to ensure that sex doesn't result in a pregnancy.

Sexually transmitted infections

Sexually transmitted infections (STIs) are more common in people aged 16 to 24 than in any other group, so teenagers who have sex without a condom run a high risk of getting an STI or passing one on.

You can't tell that someone has an STI and you can get one any time you have sex, even the very first time. Anybody who has sex — male, female, straight, gay, lesbian, bisexual — can get one and at any age.

STIs can be passed from person to person through their blood or semen. This means you can infect someone else if you have a cut on your penis, as well as through your semen. It also means you can pass on or catch an STI from any kind of sex. But it's far less likely if you wear a condom.

How do I know if I have an STI?

Some common infections *don't* have
obvious symptoms, meaning you could
be infected (and infectious) and not know it.

Symptoms of STIs which do show usually
appear within 14 days, but they can take up to
four weeks to develop.

The most common signs of STIs are . . .

- Any unusual or smelly discharge of liquid
  from your penis.
- Pain or burning when you urinate (pee).
- Pain, itching, rashes, lumps, ulcers, sores
  or blisters on or around your genitals.
- Pain during sex.
- Pain in the lower abdomen, or testicles.

What causes STIs?

There are more than 25 different sexually transmitted infections. Below are some types and what causes them. The first five in this list are the most common:

Chlamydia	– bacteria
Genital warts (Human papilloma virus or HPV)	– virus
NSU (Non-specific urethritis)	– various causes
Herpes	– virus
Gonorrhoea ('clap')	– bacteria
Trichomoniasis (TV, 'trick')	– parasite
Pubic lice ('crabs')	– louse
Scabies ('itch')	– mite
Hepatitis B	– virus
Syphilis ('pox')	– bacteria
HIV (Human immunodeficiency virus)	– virus

Can STIs be treated?

Most STIs can be treated and it is usually best if treatment is started as soon as possible. Some viruses, such as herpes and HIV (the virus that causes AIDS — acquired immune deficiency syndrome) can't yet be completely cured, but there are drugs that can reduce the symptoms and prevent or delay the development of complications. If left untreated, many STIs can be painful and can permanently damage health and fertility. And they can be passed on to someone else.

If you think you could have an STI...

Go to your doctor or a sexual health clinic to get checked. This is free and confidential. There is further information and sources of advice and help at www.usborne.com/quicklinks (see page 287).

A question of trust

A good relationship requires trust. You need to be open with your partner if there's a chance you could have caught an STI from a previous partner, and you need to know you can trust them, too. (Don't forget, you can catch STIs from oral sex and anal sex, too.)

Even if you don't have any symptoms of an STI, you should get checked:

- if you have had unprotected sex with a new partner recently.
- if you and your partner are planning to swap condoms for another form of contraception.
- if you know your partner has had any kind of sex with another person.
- if your partner has an STI.

19. Taking risks, staying safe

As a child, your parents probably didn't
let you do some of the things you really
wanted to do, such as climbing tall trees,
because they were scared you'd get hurt.

As a teenager, you won't be around your parents
all the time, so you won't always have to (or want to!)
ask permission to do things. You need to take
responsibility for your own actions and put some
thought into deciding how risky an activity is (and
whether or not it's a good idea to try it at all).

The fact is, until your brain has finished developing
(when you're in your twenties), you're likely to find it
hard to predict the problems that risky activities could
cause and assess just how harmful things can be.

In fact, a part of you may want to try the very things adults tell you can be dangerous, just to show them how independent you are, or to rebel against them.

Some activities are *so* risky that they're illegal, such as driving without a licence or climbing tall buildings. There are very particular risks associated with drinking alcohol and taking drugs. (You can find out more about these in chapter 20.) But lots of everyday activities, such as sports, can be risky too.

The reality is that you can't avoid all risks. Instead, you need to work out what your own attitude to risk is — but always bear in mind that even though it's your life and health, your family and friends will be affected by anything bad that happens to you.

Going out

The most basic responsibility
you need to take for your own safety starts when
you go out of the house and away from your family.
Here are some simple guidelines for going out:

- Tell a trusted adult where you are going and
  what time you are coming back. Make sure you
  phone them before you set off for home from
  a friend's house.

- Know how you're going to get home after an
  evening out and keep enough money for a taxi or
  bus fare. Only ever use licensed taxi companies.

- Have credit on your phone and make sure it's
  charged when you go out.

- Know your home phone number and your full address and post code.

- Travel with other people whenever possible.

- Never go anywhere with people you do not know, or accept lifts from strangers.

- Avoid potentially dangerous or isolated areas such as quiet pathways, or underpasses.

- Be aware of what is going on around you, especially when crossing roads or on a bike. (Even if this means ignoring your phone or turning your music down for a minute or two.)

- Don't flaunt possessions such as your phone, tablet, music player or money. Make sure they're not hanging out of a pocket or bag, for example.

- If you need to ask someone you don't know for help, try to approach a family group or an official, such as a police officer.

- Keep numbers you can call in an emergency, for example a parent, a carer, or a friend's parent.

- Always wear a helmet for cycling, have reflectors on your bike, and working lights if there's any chance that you may cycle after dark.

- If you're going to do something you know is dangerous, such as a stunt on a bike or board, make sure someone you trust is with you so they can call for help if anything goes wrong.

Staying safe online

You may find it hard to imagine that there was any life before the internet and mobile phones, or to discover that the phrase 'social network' didn't exist until the 21st century.

Interacting with people online can feel very safe. After all, it's incredibly easy to pretend to be someone you're not. (But don't forget that not everyone you interact with will realize you're only pretending). Even online, there are still risks you need to be aware of.

@

Internet tip

Think before you publish anything on your profile. Remember it can be seen by ANYONE (including parents, teachers, future bosses…).

#

Some online threats are greater than others. Read on to find out more about:

- Identity theft
- Grooming
- Sexting
- Online addictions
- Cyberbullying

Protecting your identity

A lot of websites ask you to fill in forms giving out personal information, such as your home address or your bank account details.

There's nothing wrong with this, but unfortunately we live in a world where a small number of people want to steal or use that information. Turn the page for some guidelines to make it harder for them to succeed:

- Make a habit of not sharing personal information. This includes your full name, photos, addresses, school information, telephone numbers and details of places you like to spend time.

- Make sure you have set your privacy settings to restrict access to personal information.

- Never give out a friend's details or secrets.

- Remember that people online may not be who they say they are. Online 'friends' are still strangers even if you've been talking to them for some time.

- If you use chat rooms, forums or instant messenger, always use a nickname instead of your real name.

- To stop people accessing your online accounts, keep passwords secret and change them regularly.

- Block people who send you nasty messages, delete messages from people you don't know and don't open unknown links and attachments.

Grooming

'Grooming' is when someone, usually an adult, tries to make friends with a child or teenager, with the ultimate aim of getting them into a sexual relationship. Grooming itself isn't illegal, but leads to underage sex or underage pornography, both very serious crimes. Here are some guidelines to keep in mind:

- If you see anything that upsets, worries or makes you feel uncomfortable; if you receive any obscene or abusive messages, or if someone you don't know asks to meet you, tell an adult you trust.

- Don't accept gifts from strangers who have contacted you online.

- Never meet someone you've met online without an adult going with you. It could be dangerous.

Sexting risks

Sending and receiving naked or rude photos of yourself and your friends is often called 'sexting'. It can be tempting to think you're in control of a photo you create, but as soon as you've sent it to another person, anything could happen to the image.

Even if you completely trust that person now, can you be absolutely sure they won't lose their phone, or send the image on to someone else one day, maybe in a few years? The risk is yours to weigh up.

> ## Show respect
>
> Don't use the camera on your phone to intrude on the privacy of others. You could be breaking the law by sending or forwarding such an image.

Too much time on the internet?

Knowing how much time to spend online is tricky, because the internet is so useful for doing homework and staying in touch with your friends — as well as being a fun place to explore.

But, it *is* possible to spend too much time online. Your body will suffer if you spend too much time sitting still. It's also important for your mental health to be around people in the real world, and not just interact with them on your phone or on a computer.

Online gambling websites can be especially addictive. It's easy to get sucked into the belief that if you just play one more game, or place one final bet, you'll win enough to be able to pay back anything you've borrowed. If it was that easy, the people who run these sites would go out of business.

 If you're worried that social networking, gaming or anything else starts to take up too much of your time, it may be a sign that you're addicted.

You could try 'deactivating' your online accounts for a few days every so often. This allows you to hide your details as if you've left the site entirely, but you can turn your account back on when you're ready. Try to spend a few days every month without using a computer to help you find a good balance.

Cyberbullying

If you are being bullied on your phone or the internet, often called cyberbullying, don't ignore it. It can be stopped. The first step is to tell someone you trust who can help you take action.

Probably the most reliable way to stop bullying is to do everything you can to ignore the bully and their taunts. This can be incredibly difficult face-to-face, but when it comes to cyberbullying, you could simply try turning off incoming messages or deactivating your accounts for a few days. (Find out more about 'real life' bullying and some coping strategies on page 249-255.)

If the bullying messages continue after you've not reacted to them for weeks, these are some other things you could try:

- You can change your phone number. You'll need to contact your service provider to do this.

- Don't reply to worrying or abusive texts and especially don't send back any abusive texts of your own as this could make matters worse.

- Keep records of bullying messages you receive as evidence. Make a note of when they were received and any details you have about the sender.

- If the messages are threatening or malicious and if they persist, get an adult to report them to the site management or the police and hand in the evidence. This kind of bullying is a crime.

- If someone you know is being nasty to someone else online, tell a parent, carer, or adult you trust.

Staying safe from abuse

If someone is hurting you physically, touching you, or making you do something sexual that makes you feel uncomfortable or unhappy, it is NOT your fault and you DON'T have to keep it a secret. You have a right to be safe, at home, at school and when you are out and about.

Tell someone you trust about what is happening. If you are being hurt at home, tell your doctor or someone at school such as your teacher or school counsellor, or call an anonymous helpline. You can't sort this out by yourself, but there are people who can help make your life safer.

Go to **www.usborne.com/ quicklinks** (see page 287) for advice about staying safe.

20. Drink and drugs

As you grow up there will be all kinds of new experiences available to you. Some will be a little risky, others downright dangerous, and there won't always be adults around to look out for you.

In particular, you may find yourself under pressure to try drugs, from illegal drugs, such as cannabis, to legal — but age restricted — drugs such as cigarettes and alcohol.

Even if your family and friends never take any drugs, your brain is already being bombarded with daily messages urging you to try risky things through adverts, films, TV shows, games, texts, song lyrics, websites, podcasts, tweets, blogs and so on.

Research shows that advertising really *does* work, especially on developing teenage brains. The message your brain gets is: 'Come and try this. It's cool, it's grown-up and fun. Everyone else is doing it . . . so why not you?'

So why not you?

The chances are, you've heard a lot of adults telling you not to take drugs. Unfortunately, it's not that simple — just telling people not to take drugs doesn't stop them from doing it.

Fortunately, teenage brains, while not very good at assessing risks, *are* good at absorbing facts. So it's well worth finding out a bit more about the effects that drink and drugs could have on your body and your brain.

Many people, including some teenagers, take drugs and drink too much. It's likely they do it because they are more concerned with getting a short term high, or are worried about fitting in, than they are with weighing up the facts, and assessing the risks involved with drugs. Reading the facts in this chapter first may help you make your own decisions.

What are drugs?

Drugs are chemicals or substances that change the way the body works. When people take them (usually by swallowing, sniffing, smoking or injecting them) the drugs find their way to the bloodstream and are then carried to different parts of the body, such as the brain. In the brain, drugs alter senses and can make people feel more alert, more relaxed, happier, less anxious, more sleepy or less able to feel pain, for example.

 Medical drugs can cure, treat or prevent many diseases, helping people to live happier and healthier lives. But when people talk about 'taking drugs', they are usually talking about *illegal* drugs, or the misuse of legal, prescribed, medical drugs.

Some drugs are much more common than others. Legal drugs include tobacco and alcohol. Illegal drugs include things such as cannabis, speed, ecstasy, cocaine and heroin. You may have heard of 'legal highs', a general term to describe a range of technically legal, but nevertheless dangerous, drugs including poppers and some kinds of mushrooms.

There are links to websites which explain more about drugs, all the different names for them, and what they do, at the Usborne Quicklinks website. (See page 287.)

Why do people take drugs?

People take drugs because they think this will make them feel good, solve their problems, or help them have a good time. But most people know that drugs are dangerous, and there are other reasons why people choose to take the risk:

- Because they think they will be seen as 'uncool' or won't fit in if they don't.

- Because they hang out with other people who use drugs and don't want to be left out.

- Because they are curious and want to experiment.

- Because they think a drug or drink may make them feel more confident and able to face a difficult situation, or help them to have more fun.

- Because they are unhappy, stressed or lonely and think that taking drugs or drinking will help them forget or solve their problems.

What are the dangers?

Many drugs, both legal and illegal, are addictive. If someone is addicted to a substance such as heroin, it means they feel as if they can't live without it. Very rapidly they find they devote a lot of their time and energy to getting more of it. In particular, they spend almost all their money on that substance. Altogether, this often ends up seriously damaging their health, their finances and their relationships.

Legally prescribed medical drugs such as some painkillers and sleeping pills can be addictive, especially if not used in the way they were prescribed. And *all* drugs have risks and side-effects.

- You cannot know for sure what is in an illegal drug as some people who sell drugs mix them with other things. You may accidentally get a higher dose, which could be harmful or fatal.

- Accidents, arguments and fights are more likely to happen after the use of some drugs.

- Using drugs can lead to health problems, addiction, overdoses and serious mental illness such as psychosis or depression.

- Mixing drugs and alcohol is especially dangerous as each one can increase the effects of the other.

- Mixing ecstasy and alcohol, for example, can lead to dehydration and has been known to cause coma and death.

- Drugs are expensive and people who become addicted may find they face financial problems, cannot afford to buy what they need and so end up finding illegal ways to fund their habit.

- Heavy drug users and people dependent on alcohol often drop out of school, become estranged from their friends and family and may end up having nowhere to live.

Did you know?

Between a third and a half of people sleeping rough have alcohol problems and up to 40 per cent of younger homeless people have drug problems.

Tobacco

One of the drugs which people have most problems with is tobacco. This is the key ingredient in cigarettes, which are legal to buy (if you are 18 or over). Despite all the health warnings, tobacco is used by over a billion people around the world. This is because every person who started smoking believed that they would be able to stay in control and not develop a habit which is extremely harmful, expensive and very hard to break.

Tobacco in cigarettes kills over five million people worldwide every year. It contains the chemical nicotine which is one of the most addictive substances ever discovered and makes people addicted more quickly than any other drug. In addition to nicotine, cigarettes also contain more than 40 cancer-causing chemicals.

In the short term, cigarettes make your hair and clothes smell bad. In the slightly longer term, they make your teeth and fingernails turn yellow.

In the very long term, smoking is a proven cause of lung, mouth and throat cancers and contributes to many other diseases. It damages the skin, gums, teeth and eyes, and it greatly increases the risk of having a stroke or developing heart disease.

Think tips

The best way of not getting addicted to tobacco, or to any other drug, is not to try it in the first place.

If you hang out with people who use a lot of drugs, you are more likely to develop a habit yourself.

Cannabis

Cannabis is the most commonly used illegal drug and many teenagers will come into contact with it at some point. It's often sold in bags of crushed leaves, which can be smoked like a cigarette (often called a joint or a spliff, and often mixed with tobacco), or inhaled through a tube of water known as a bong.

Cannabis is sometimes described as a mild drug — but it's still dangerous. People take it because they want to feel relaxed, but it makes some people feel paranoid and scared, and it is known that cannabis is especially damaging to developing teenage brains.

Regular use of cannabis has been linked to addiction, severe depression, sleep problems, anxiety and panic attacks, hallucinations and serious mental illnesses including schizophrenia and bipolar disorder.

Did you know?

A recent 20-year study of over 1,000 people found that those who started using cannabis below the age of 18 suffered a **significant and irreversible reduction in their IQ** (Intelligence Quotient) and the more people used it, the greater the reduction.

Another study, of 50,000 people worldwide, concluded that drivers who use cannabis up to three hours before driving are twice as likely to cause a car crash resulting in serious injury or death as those not under the influence of drugs or alcohol.

Ecstasy

Ecstasy, usually a small pill, is often taken at clubs and parties because it can intensify music and light effects, boost energy and create feelings of belonging, confidence and happiness.

Ecstasy can also cause a faster heart rate, raised body temperature, shaking, dehydration, dizziness, nausea (feeling sick), anxiety and sweating. In the days after taking it, people may feel cranky, lacking in energy, depressed and unable to concentrate — a feeling known as 'coming down'.

The long-term effects of ecstasy use are not known, but it is associated with memory problems, anxiety and panic attacks. Accidental overdose or mixing it with other drugs or alcohol can cause convulsions, hallucinations, brain damage and heart failure.

Legal highs

All sorts of chemicals, such as solvents used in making glue, can have an intoxicating effect on a person. Some shops deliberately sell these products as 'legal highs'. But it's not a good idea to buy them just because a salesman tells you it'll make you high — you can't be sure what's really in the bottle.

Drugs are only illegal because they're very dangerous. But just because a drug is labelled as 'legal' doesn't mean it's not dangerous. In fact, many legal highs are based on newly discovered or created chemicals and *are* soon classified as illegal.

Saying no

If you're feeling under pressure to take any non-prescribed drug, remember that if you don't use drugs, you're in the majority. Most teenagers (and adults) DON'T take drugs.

It can be helpful to think in advance about how you could respond if someone offered you drugs. If you don't feel confident enough just to say 'no' directly, you could say something like "I've tried it before and don't like it" (even if that's a white lie) or you could just find a reason to leave the situation.

Whatever you say, say it firmly and clearly but don't make a big deal about it. Remember that real friends will respect you if you are clear about what you do and don't want to do. If you're finding it hard to be yourself within a group, take a step back and think about whether it's time to find some new friends . . .

NO

Think tip

Some people lie and exaggerate about taking drugs in the same way they do about sex. Just because someone says they've done loads of drugs, doesn't mean it's true.

Drinking

Like many other drugs, alcohol is addictive and in the long term can cause serious physical and mental health problems. Despite this, in many cultures, drinking with friends is seen as a normal and sociable activity for adults. It is associated with relaxation, celebration when things go well or commiseration when things go badly.

So it's not surprising that many teenagers also think that drinking is an appealing and fun activity and are not fully aware of the risks.

There are some very good reasons why, despite it being a legal 'drug', it is not legal to sell alcohol to younger teenagers, and why starting to drink regularly, getting drunk, or 'binge-drinking', especially under the age of 18 when your brain is still developing, is a very bad idea.

One of the reasons is that alcohol affects a teenager's brain differently to the way it affects an adult's. It can actually damage the parts of the brain responsible for thinking, planning, decision-making, impulse control, learning and memory, and the damage can be long-term.

In addition, recent research has found that people who start drinking during their early teens are more likely to become dependent on alcohol, become dependent faster and have more serious problems than those who wait until they are older.

Did you know?

Alcohol is a depressant, so rather than helping you feel better when you are miserable, it can make things seem a lot worse, especially once its initial effects have worn off.

Many scientists now say that teenagers shouldn't drink any alcohol at all until the age of 18. And to avoid mental health problems, teens should try not to get drunk until their brains have finished developing in their 20s.

Drinking risks

It's not uncommon for people who drink just a little too much to throw up and even pass out. The next day can be spent nursing a feeling of being horribly ill, called a 'hangover'. But being drunk and being around drunk people carries all kinds of other, often more dangerous, risks:

Car accidents – getting in a car with a driver who has been drinking greatly increases your chances of injury or death.

Arguments and break-ups – people often say things they don't mean and fall out with friends and partners after drinking too much.

Violence – the more people drink, the greater the risk of fights breaking out at parties, festivals, on holiday, and so on.

Drowning – many drownings happen when people think it would be fun to go swimming after drinking a lot . . .

Unsafe and unwanted sex – being drunk makes people more likely to agree to do things they wouldn't normally want to do, and make it less likely they will stop to think about things of great importance – such as remembering (or indeed bothering) to put a condom on.

Alcohol poisoning – in the very worst cases, people can drink so much they have to be hospitalized – or die.

Safer partying

If you know you are going to be around alcohol when you go out, try to remember the guidelines on the opposite page so that you stay safe (and don't wake up feeling as if you want to die . . .). And if you can't remember these guidelines, you've definitely had enough.

- Never drink on an empty stomach, and drink plenty of water, especially before you go to sleep.

- Make sure your phone is charged and you have enough credit to phone a trusted adult who will pick you up if necessary.

- Always go out in a group and stick with your friends. Make sure at least one person agrees not to drink so they can look out for you all.

- If you do drink, stick to one kind of drink and always know how much you are drinking. Drink a soft drink, water or a low-alcohol drink in between any alcoholic ones.

- Don't gulp alcoholic drinks or 'down' them in one go. They are meant to be sipped slowly.

- Don't drink 'punches' or cocktails that might have a strange mix of drinks in them.

- Don't accept a drink you didn't ask for from someone you don't know. (Because you can never be sure what they've put in it...)

- Never accept a lift from someone who has been drinking (even if they seem sober and say they are fine to drive).

- Don't leave any of your group behind, even if they are too drunk to walk, and don't hesitate to call an adult if things are getting out of hand.

- In an emergency, such as someone falling unconscious (so that they don't respond when you try to wake them up), call an ambulance.

What if a friend needs help?

It can be difficult to know how to help a friend having a problem with alcohol or drugs. If you see a friend getting drunk or out of control, you could suggest that they should stop drinking or try getting them to a place where there is no alcohol or drugs.

But don't abandon them or try to talk to them seriously while they are drunk or on drugs. It's best to speak to them the next day and you may then suggest that they get some help (see 'Getting help' on page 239). If you have real concerns and they won't listen, you could speak to a member of their family or one of their teachers.

Quick quiz

To find out if you have a problem, read the questions below and try to answer honestly.

Do you think about drugs or alcohol every day?

Is it hard to say 'no' when they are offered?

Would you drink or take drugs
when you are alone?

Does drinking or taking drugs get in
the way of the rest of your life?

If you answer 'YES' to these questions, you may be addicted and need to get help.

Do I have a problem?

The most obvious sign that you have a drug or alcohol problem is when you feel you no longer have a choice. You find yourself having to take the drug or drink more and more often to get the same effect and you find it difficult to cope without it. It has become a habit that you are unable to give up.

Getting help

The first step is to talk to an adult you trust such as a parent, your carer, a family member, a family friend, a school counsellor, school nurse or teacher. You could even speak to your GP who can offer advice or may refer you to specialist help.

Go to **www.usborne.com/quicklinks** (see page 287) for advice about drink and drugs.

21. Life at school

Whether you like it or not, during your teenage years you will spend a lot of your time at school.

As you get older, how you plan and use your time at *home* will have more and more impact on how you get on at *school* — especially as you start to prepare for your exams and do more homework and coursework.

Being prepared

School is always a lot easier to cope with if you are ready for the day ahead. This means knowing in advance what you are going to wear, having homework finished, and leaving yourself enough time to eat a good breakfast and pack your bag with all the things you need. If you're not an early riser, and struggle to get up and out of the door on time, you could try some of these strategies:

- Pack your bag each night with the things you'll need for the next day. Check your timetable or diary to remind you what's going on, and what unusual things you might need. (Science project? Musical instrument? Birthday card for friend?)

- Give any notes, letters and slips from school to your parent or carer as soon as you get them, not as you're rushing out of the door in the morning.

- Lay out the clothes you are going to wear in the evening, so you're not trying to track down a clean shirt, find a missing shoe and stuff toast in your mouth all at the same time.

- Go to bed a little earlier on school nights (see pages 90 to 93 for tips on getting enough sleep).

- If you find it hard to leave on time, set your alarm for a quarter of an hour earlier, so you have more time to get ready in the morning.

- If you need to, work out a bathroom rota with the other members of your family, so you know when it's your turn in the morning.

- Get in the habit of checking your pockets or bag before you leave the house, to make sure you've got the things you always need. (Bus pass? Lunch card? Key? Phone?)

Getting the most out of school

As well as your regular lessons, most schools offer 'extra-curricular activities', such as the chance to join clubs and sports teams, go on trips and outings or take part in extra drama, music, dance, science, art or outdoor activities.

All these are good for making new friends, having fun, getting better at things you enjoy, or getting exercise. It's worth bearing in mind that you're not going to enjoy every session of every activity you do.

Don't give up just because you have a bad day — but don't feel you have to keep on playing an instrument, or a sport, if you almost never get any enjoyment out of it.

The joy of homework...

Homework is one of those things you just have to do, and you'll probably never exactly look forward to doing it. But, there is a point to it, and it's not just to make your teachers happy.

Doing your homework gives you a chance to find out if you actually understand what you've been learning about. If you struggle with homework, it's not your fault. Don't be afraid to ask for help.

Homework also gives you a chance to find out what types of schoolwork you enjoy, whether it's reading and writing, solving problems, learning languages, or learning hard facts. If you find yourself caring about the answer, even on a really difficult piece of homework, it's a sign that the subject is worth pursuing to a higher level.

How, when and where?

The problem some people have with homework is not that they find it too hard, or that it takes too long, but that they forget what they have to do and when they need to get it done by.

To avoid this problem, make good use of your school planner (if you have one), diary or notebook to note down exactly what you need to do and when you need to do it by. It helps to get into a routine of doing homework soon after it has been set, and not leaving it until the last minute.

One simple trick is to set up a permanent space at home with the paper, pens and other bits you need. Simply having a place where you can do your homework makes it easier to knuckle down and get it done.

If you need to, book a regular slot on the family computer, or in the school resources centre, to manage any online homework or printing.

Homework kit

- Pencils
- Pens
- Rubber
- Sharpener
- Crayons
- Felt-tip pens
- Correction fluid
- Ruler
- Maths equipment
  (protractor, compass,
  set square)

- Calculator
- Sticky tape
- Glue stick
- Lined paper
- Plain paper
- Plastic wallets
- Scissors

The other secret to coping with homework is that you don't have to do it all by yourself. You *will* actually have to put some work into it — but it's not cheating to talk to your classmates, your parents, or even your teacher about how to solve a problem.

To pass exams, you will have to learn how to remember facts and how to solve problems all by yourself. But in the real world, many people do their jobs, and find sensible solutions to all sorts of problems, by discussing them with other people.

Homework tip

Try to leave enough time to read through your homework before you hand it in. You may be able to find a way to re-write a sentence to make it clearer, or you'll notice a missing step in a calculation that could change an incorrect answer into a correct one.

Problems, problems, problems

If you are having a problem at school, or with homework, there is always someone who can help you sort it out. The most important thing (as with almost any other problem) is to talk to someone.

If, for example, you feel you are being picked on or are disliked by a certain teacher or you are having problems with a particular subject, talk to another teacher: your class teacher, school counsellor or head of year. It might help to talk to your parents or your carer, too.

One thing many students worry about is bullying at school, whether this is being bullied themselves, knowing what to do if other people are being bullied, or knowing how to stop being a bully if they have become one.

What counts as bullying?

You don't have to be beaten up or physically hurt to be a victim of bullying. Teasing someone, spreading rumours about them, pushing someone, or threatening them are all forms of bullying. Name calling, mocking, somebody, taking or damaging their belongings, excluding someone from groups and writing or drawing offensive messages about them all count as bullying, too.

There are lots of reasons why people are bullied. Some are picked on because of their religion, race or appearance, while others are bullied because of their size, sexual orientation, disability, home circumstances, clothes, or because they're clever — all things that no one should ever be ashamed of.

But it's not always clear why a particular person becomes a victim of bullying — or what turns someone else into a bully. Typically, bullies are most interested in getting their victim to cry, scream, shout or look stupid — and to get a laugh out of their friends by provoking these reactions.

It can be very hard to escape from a cycle of being bullied. Sometimes the best way to start is to try not to react to the bullying at all. On the whole, if a bully stops getting a reaction, even from a really horrible attack, they will, eventually, give up.

It can help to stay calm in the face of a bully's most horrible and personal attacks by telling yourself that they're only trying to get a reaction out of you. It's probably not the case that they actually hate you, think your parents are stupid, or even that they hate your race, religion or sexuality.

For this approach to work, you may have to commit to not reacting to a bully for weeks on end, which is not an easy thing to do. Sadly the bullying will probably get worse at first, as the bully tries harder and harder to provoke a reaction.

How does it feel?

If you are being bullied, you may feel as if you're trapped or alone, or that it's hard to make friends or talk to other people of your age.

Bullying can destroy your confidence and sense of security. It can cause sadness, fear, anxiety and poor concentration. Victims often find that their school work starts to suffer because they're constantly worrying about what might happen at school.

If you're finding it hard to focus on your work and live your life normally, or if you're worried that the bullying is getting violent and you're scared for your safety, you must tell a teacher, your carer or parents.

You may find it difficult to talk at first, especially if your confidence is low, but it's vital you let them know what's happening so they can help you do something about it.

If you're being bullied, you don't have to put up with it. There are many people that can help you do something about it.

Remember that bullying isn't just something that happens when you're face-to-face. It can happen over the phone or on the internet too.

See pages 211-212 for what to do if you are a victim of 'cyberbullying', or page 157 if you're a victim of homophobic bullying.

> ### Think tip
> If you are being bullied, try to remember that it is not your fault and there is nothing wrong with you. It is the bullies who have a problem.

If you see someone being bullied

You may not be affected by bullying yourself, but you may see someone being threatened or teased and want to do something about it.

It's not a good idea to get directly involved with an incident. But don't just ignore it. If you know the person being bullied, encourage them to speak up. If you think it will help, mention it to a teacher or parent in confidence, or write an anonymous note.

Your school may also run anti-bullying schemes that you can get involved in to help get rid of bullying.

Am I a bully?

Sometimes people are egged on by their friends to bully and they do it because they don't want to be left out. Others feel unhappy themselves for some reason, and take it out on someone else. It takes courage to stop being a bully once you're caught up in it. But just because you've been involved in bullying, it doesn't mean you have to continue.

Talk to a teacher, parent or older pupil you get on well with. If there's a teacher who's responsible for stopping bullying, he or she should be able to help you. If you don't want to speak to anyone you know, call an anonymous helpline, but do get help for your problem, one way or another.

Visit the Usborne Quicklinks Website for more details (see page 287).

Friends for life?

Some people are lucky and meet their best friends at school and stay close to them for the rest of their lives. But lots of people don't. Just as you can't choose your family, you usually don't get much choice about where you go to school and you can't choose who is in your class or in your lessons.

Part of the point of school is to learn how to get along with other people, including the ones you don't really like. You probably will make some good friends at school, but if you don't, it's not the end of the world.

One way to find friends is to meet people who share your interests – for example by joining lunchtime or after-school clubs (where you might meet people from different schools). It can help to remember that once you've left school, you're much more likely to meet like-minded people at a college, university or in a job that you have chosen for yourself.

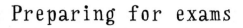

Preparing for exams

School is meant to be a place where you learn things, but all too often it feels as if the only thing you're learning is how to pass exams. Unfortunately, it's almost impossible to avoid taking exams, but until someone invents a fairer way to test learning, exams are going to be a fact of school life.

Almost everyone worries about exams, even if it doesn't come across that way. The keys to being prepared, and avoiding unnecessary stress, are:

1. Knowing what you have to learn
2. Planning your revision
3. Giving yourself enough time to do it

Here are some ideas to help you:

1. Know what you need to do

- If you can, get a copy of the syllabus for each subject. This tells you what you need to know and gives you the topics for revision.

- Find out what form each exam will take, whether written, oral or practical. What sort of questions are there going to be? Essays? Short answers? One-word answers?

- Record the dates and times for each of your exams in your planner or diary.

2. Plan and prepare for revision (about 12 weeks before first exam)

– Make a week-by-week revision timetable chart to display in your work space. Remember to include the topics you need to cover for each subject.

– Remember to block out times when you can't revise because of lessons or after-school activities. Build in time for relaxation, chores, proper meals and exercise, because these will help you revise more efficiently.

3. Start revising

– Start revising early each day, when your mind is fresh. Stick to your timetable and mark off each task as you finish it.

– Build up to working in 45 minute blocks, taking a 15 minute break each hour. Include some longer breaks, and a small reward after a difficult topic.

– Make new notes using any old class notes and revision guides. Highlight key facts, ideas, definitions, theories, etc.

– If there are things you find especially hard to remember, such as vocabulary, write them onto index cards that you can refer to easily.

– Practise questions from past exam papers.

– Study with a friend and test each other.

– If you don't understand something, don't be afraid to ask your teacher.

During your exams

During your exam period you want your brain to work at its very best, so build in relaxation time before bed, avoid late night revision sessions and try to go to bed early so you get enough sleep. If you can, eat regular, healthy meals and healthy snacks and avoid high-caffeine drinks such as coffee, cola and energy drinks.

If panic starts to creep in, try to replace your negative thoughts with more positive ones, such as:

> *'I can only do my best.'*
> *'Relax and concentrate.'*
> *'It's going to be OK.'*

You could write these messages on sticky notes and put them around your revision timetable to encourage yourself if you start to feel anxious.

On exam days, leave plenty of time in the morning to make sure you've got everything you need for the next exam, and for travel, so you don't feel flustered or too stressed.

Think positive

If you find your mind is full of negative messages, such as 'I can't do this', 'I'm useless' or 'I'm going to fail', try visualizing something more positive. Imagine walking into the exam room feeling calm and confident, turning over the exam paper, reading it carefully and then doing your best to answer the questions.

During an actual exam, if you find yourself struggling to answer a question, leave it and move on to the next one — don't spend time tying yourself in mental knots over each question.

Exam tips and techniques

- At the start, read through the whole paper carefully.

- Try not to rush, even if you're nervous. (Try the breathing technique on page 108 if you feel panicky.)

- Check the instructions and underline any key words that show how a question should be answered.

- See how many marks are given to each question and plan how you will use your time. Don't spend too much time on questions that don't give many marks.

- Plan answers carefully, only giving the information you have been asked for.

- Try to answer all the questions that you need to (even if you only have time to make notes for the last one).

- If you can, leave five minutes at the end to check your spelling, grammar and presentation.

Dealing with exam stress

Nearly everyone gets stressed during
exams, even if they have prepared well.
They worry that they will let themselves,
their teachers and their family down or that they
won't do as well as their friends or get the grades
they need to do the course or job they want to do.

A little stress is useful as it can sharpen your mind
and motivate you to do well. But too much stress can
stop you working to the best of your abilities, so it's
important not to let it get out of control.

Did you know?

A recent survey of 1,300 students found that
96 per cent felt anxious about revision and exams.

Learning to relax is vital, both in the run-up to exams and even in the exam room. Try the relaxation routine on page 109 if you find you are getting stressed before exams.

The breathing technique on page 108 is good for helping to calm you down if you begin to feel nervous or panicky before or even during an exam.

Remember you're not alone. Visit the Usborne Quicklinks Website (see page 287) for links to message boards where you can share your worries with others going through the same experience.

22. Life at home

You can learn a lot at school, but some of the most important lessons are best learned at home. After all, it probably won't be too many years before you move into a home of your own — and what happens then?

Well, on the one hand, you'll be able to do pretty much whatever you want, which is brilliant. On the other hand, if you don't do certain things, no one else will do them for you.

What do grown-ups do?

It can sometimes seem as if most grown-ups spend all their free time complaining. This is partly because they have to do all sorts of boring chores, some of them every single day:

- Going to work.
- Choosing and buying food.
- Preparing and cooking food.
- Keeping their home tidy.
- Keeping their home clean.
- Washing dishes.
- Washing clothes.
- Putting clean clothes away.
- Changing bed linen.
- Filling in forms.
- Paying bills.
- Fixing things that break.

You may live with a family that makes everyone take turns to do chores. Sharing the work is part of living together, and if you hope to share a house with friends one day, or even to start your own family, you need to learn how to do your fair share.

There are probably some chores you haven't had to do. Save yourself some future embarrassment by getting someone to show you how to do them.

Do you know:

How to use a washing machine?
How to cook a meal?
How to use a vacuum cleaner?
How to clean a toilet?
How to change a light bulb?

Managing money

No matter how rich they are, most people worry that they don't have enough money. There are just too many things to spend money on, from things everyone needs, such as food and clothes, to things people want, such as chocolate or computer games.

If you're lucky, your parents will spend their money on vital things for you such as shoes, travel to school and your phone bill. This means any money you have you are free to spend on snacks or magazines or sponsoring a friend for charity — anything you like. But it won't always be this way.

Sooner or later, you're going to have to work out how to get enough money to pay for things you need, as well as things you want. Worse, you'll have to learn how to save money so that you can spend it on something you never realized you needed so much until it stops working, such as a computer or a car.

How to get money

- Get pocket money from your parents.
- Earn money by doing odd jobs for people you know, or from a paid job in the real world.
- Borrow money from family and friends. (Be careful to agree a time limit for you to pay the money back.)
- If you're creative, you might be able to make things that you can sell.
- If you can bear to part with them, you could try selling some of your possessions. (Be warned, you're unlikely to get as much money for these things as you think they're worth.)

How to save money

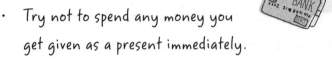

- Try not to spend any money you get given as a present immediately.
- Open a bank account and keep money there, not in your wallet or piggy bank. Some accounts, often called savings accounts, won't let you take your money out for a year or longer.
- If you're responsible for spending your own money on really important things, such as your phone bill or school kit, keep a list of them, and how much they cost, and make sure you put aside enough money to cover them all.
- Keep a box or jar to put money in that you're saving up for a very specific, expensive thing you want to buy, such as a new computer game.
- Every time you spend money on something you don't really need, put aside the same amount of money into a savings jar.

Money in the bank

Real money doesn't exist any more. Coins and notes are worth very little in themselves — they simply represent the *idea* of money. Increasingly, people don't even use cash, they use cards or pay for things using online bank transfers.

If you have a bank account, you'll probably have a *debit card* linked to that account. You can use it to take cash out of your account, or to pay for things in shops. But most banks set a limit on how much money you can take out or spend on a card every day, especially when you're a teenager.

Every time you use the card, your account gets smaller. It's sometimes possible to use your card to spend a bit more money than you have in your account. Banks call the extra money you spend an 'overdraft'. If you end up with an overdraft, your bank will make you pay back the money, *and* may well charge you interest on top of that. If you don't or can't pay the overdraft back, the bank will soon cancel your card and close your account.

Credit cards are more dangerous. Every time you use a credit card, you are, in fact, borrowing money. If you don't pay all the money back each month, the company that runs the credit card will charge you interest. This means paying back the money you spent, *and* paying on top of that for the privilege of borrowing the money in the first place.

Living with your family

There will be times when living with your family can drive you up the wall and make you want to scream. But there are benefits, too. When you really need some help with money, or some comfort after a hard day at school, or when you feel as if no one likes you, it's often your family who can make it all feel better, if only for a while.

On the other hand, it's normal to get into arguments with your parents and your brothers and sisters. Worse, it's very common to say — or, more likely, shout — something really hurtful that you might regret the next day.

These situations are a pretty inevitable consequence of teenage life, with its rush of hormones making it harder for you to think straight. And added to that is the fact that you, quite rightly, are asserting your independence from your parents, who still think they know what's best for you. (To be fair to them, they probably *did* know best when you were little. And they may even be right now, at least some of the time.)

At the same time, the older you get, the more you'll come to realize that other people can be pretty annoying from time to time. At least if you end up shouting at your family, they're much more likely to forgive you, because they are, after all, your family.

Coping with family arguments and stress at home isn't easy. It can help to remember that your parents and siblings have their own problems, and that some of the things that might be causing them stress are nothing to do with you. But even with this in mind, you'll need to find ways that help you let off steam, hopefully without punishing the people you have to live with.

Turn to chapter 13 for tips on dealing with stress, worries and anxieties.

Owning up

If you're in trouble, or if you've done something wrong, or even if you're just really worried about something, it's all too tempting to keep quiet and just hope that everything clears up all by itself. But it's nearly always better to own up to your mistakes, and to talk through your problems.

Owning up is good in the short term because the people you own up to will respect you more for being honest. In the long term, it means they're more likely to trust you, too. At first, you might be scared that your parents (for example) will be angry with you.

But the very act of admitting you've done something wrong makes most people less angry than they might've been. Believe it or not, the bigger a problem is, the more likely you are to find that your parents and friends want to help you, not to punish you.

Think tip

When it comes to talking about your worries, no matter how personal, embarrassing or even petty you might think they are, it can help to remember that the adults you know have probably felt the same worries in their life, too.

Alone time

It's a bit of a cliché that teenagers lock themselves away in their bedrooms for hours — or even days — on end. But if the only space you have to be alone is your bedroom, where else are you going to go?

Spending time away from your family and friends just lying on your bed, thinking, sleeping, reading, listening to music and yes, masturbating, is a perfectly healthy and sensible way to behave, and don't let anyone tell you otherwise.

But it can be tempting to stay in this safe place all the time. The more time you spend entirely on your own, the easier it is to start imagining that your problems are bigger than they really are, and the easier it is to let any resentment against your family and friends build up.

One simple solution to this is to try to spend a little time with your family every day, even if it's only having a short conversation over breakfast.

And if you really want to be on your own in the house — for example if you've invited a group of friends over — talk to your family about it. Instead of resenting them for being around, ask if they'll go out for an evening to give you some space.

How to make home life easier

- Try to be polite.

- Keep yourself clean, and be aware that you might smell bad if you don't wash.

- Eat a meal sitting around the table with your whole family as often as you can manage it. You could even offer to cook for everyone sometimes.

- Watch a TV show or film together — even if it's something you don't think you're going to enjoy.

And finally...

If you've just finished reading this entire book, you'd be forgiven for feeling overwhelmed! Your teenage years may bring lots of ups and downs, but above all else they should be fun. Don't lose sight of the good sides to growing up . . .

As your body and mind grow throughout your teens, you'll gain extra physical strength and mental control that allow you to achieve bigger and better things than you could as a child. On top of these gifts, you'll gain more freedom, to do the things you like and to try all kinds of new experiences.

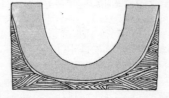

Have fun, and good luck out there!

Index

Getting help

The list below shows pages where you can find basic advice about many teenage concerns. For more detailed information, please visit the Usborne Quicklinks Website (see facing page).

Internet links

The internet is a great source of information about all things to do with growing up, but only if you know where to look and what to believe.

We have selected some useful and fun websites where you can find more information about all the subjects in this book or can access reliable sources of help, support and advice.

For links to these sites go to:
www.usborne.com/quicklinks
and enter the keywords
"growing up for boys"

When using the internet, please follow the internet safety guidelines shown on the Usborne Quicklinks Website. The links at Usborne Quicklinks are regularly reviewed and updated, but Usborne Publishing is not responsible and does not accept liability for the content on any website other than its own. We recommend that all children are supervised while using the internet.

Cover illustration by Katie Lovell

Website research by Jacqui Clark

With thanks to Sarah Jayne Blakemore, Thomas Cannon,
Mark Fifield, James Maclaine, Jonny Melmoth, Sam Taplin,
Fin Woolfson and Minna Lacey for their advice regarding
the contents of the book.

To Little Bookshops everywhere,
and with thanks to David McKee and Tony Ross
for allowing Elmer and the Little Princess
to come out to play.

This paperback edition first published in 2017 by Andersen Press Ltd.

First published in Great Britain in 2015 by Andersen Press Ltd.,

20 Vauxhall Bridge Road, London SW1V 2SA.

Copyright © Michael Foreman, 2015

The rights of Michael Foreman to be identified as the author and illustrator

of this work have been asserted by him in accordance with the

Copyright, Designs and Patents Act, 1988.

All rights reserved.

Colour separated in Switzerland by Photolitho AG, Zürich.

Printed and bound in Malaysia by Tien Wah Press.

10 9 8 7 6 5 4 3 2 1

British Library Cataloguing in Publication Data available.

ISBN 978 1 78344 208 9

THIS BOOK BELONGS TO:

_____

THE LITTLE BOOKSHOP

AND THE

URIGAMI ARMY!

MICHAEL FOREMAN

ANDERSEN PRESS

It was a rainy day.

Joey, the newspaper boy, sheltered in the doorway of The Little Bookshop.

Today, the bookseller wasn't his usual sunny self. He looked as miserable as the weather.

"They are going to close my shop," he said. "Knock it down and build a big superstore."

"They can't do that!" said Joey. "Everyone loves your shop. If we all go to see the Mayor and make a big fuss, I am sure he will stop it."

"It's the Mayor who owns the superstore!" said the bookseller, shaking his head.

"Then we will go to the Prime Minister!"
Joey peeped into his newspaper bag and whispered,
"Origami Girl! Origami Girl, we need your help!"
Newspapers flew out of his bag and transformed into

Origami Girl,   Super Hero!

Joey told her of the threat to The Little Bookshop.

"We need help," Origami Girl said, "and we are in just the right place! Mr Bookseller, which books are the children's favourites?"

The bookseller quickly began pulling books from his shelves.

With a cry of "HAII-YAH!", Origami Girl struck each book with the side of her hand. Pages leapt from the books, transforming into an Origami Army of children's favourite characters.

"To Parliament!" cried Joey, and the Origami Army took to the air. The rain had stopped and a great rainbow of fairytale, myth and legend arched across the city. They descended on Parliament and charged into the Great Hall of Government.

Everyone was asleep, snoring like pigs round a trough. "Wake up! Wake up!" cried Origami Girl. The Prime Minister opened one bleary eye.

"Why?" he said. "It's not time for our holidays yet." Then he closed his eye again.

"These people are useless," Origami Girl said. "Come on, let's go!"

Back across the city they flew to the bookshop. The Mayor, the architects and the planners were already there, measuring and pointing and looking important.

Then, with rattling and roaring bulldozers and diggers, the builders arrived.

"We need reinforcements!" cried Origami Girl, and she flew down the street to the Public Library.

She returned at the head of an even greater Origami Army.

"Destroy them! Destroy them!" yelled the Mayor. "They are only made of paper."

"We are not just made of paper. We are made of IDEAS!" shouted one of the Army.

"And IMAGINATION!" shouted another. "We are made of things you can *never* destroy!"

"We are such stuff as dreams are made on… " said a little bald Origami Warrior, shaking his quill pen like a spear.

"Oh look!" said a builder. "There's Peter Pan. I read Peter Pan to my children last night. They LOVE Peter Pan."

"And there's Alice and the Walrus and the Carpenter!" shouted one of the carpenters.

"And Elmer and the Little Princess! And, look, there's Soggy the Bear! Oh, I wish our children were here to see this," shouted a digger driver to his mates. "They are," called Joey. "Look behind you!"

An army of children had arrived behind the builders. They had seen the Origami Army fly over their schools and had followed them to The Little Bookshop to see their storytime favourites.

The Mayor knew he was beaten.
He ripped up his superstore
plans and tossed them into the air.

Before they left the site, the builders built an extension onto The Little Bookshop and turned the car park behind into a people's park.

The Origami Warriors slipped back into their books,
ready to spring to life each time a page is turned…

… and Origami Girl climbed back into the newspaper bag – ready for the next adventure.